The History of Religious Imagination in Christian Platonism

Also available from Bloomsbury

Debating Christian Religious Epistemology, edited by John M. DePoe and Tyler Dalton McNabb
Four Views on the Axiology of Theism, edited by Kirk Lougheed
Free Will and God's Universal Causality, by W. Matthews Grant
Living Forms of the Imagination, by Douglas Hedley
Sacrifice Imagined, by Douglas Hedley
The Iconic Imagination, by Douglas Hedley

The History of Religious Imagination in Christian Platonism

Exploring the Philosophy of Douglas Hedley

Edited by
Christian Hengstermann

BLOOMSBURY ACADEMIC
LONDON • NEW YORK • OXFORD • NEW DELHI • SYDNEY

BLOOMSBURY ACADEMIC
Bloomsbury Publishing Plc
50 Bedford Square, London, WC1B 3DP, UK
1385 Broadway, New York, NY 10018, USA
29 Earlsfort Terrace, Dublin 2, Ireland

BLOOMSBURY, BLOOMSBURY ACADEMIC and the Diana logo are trademarks
of Bloomsbury Publishing Plc

First published in Great Britain 2021
This paperback edition first published in 2022

Copyright © Christian Hengstermann and Contributors, 2021

Christian Hengstermann has asserted his right under the Copyright, Designs and
Patents Act, 1988, to be identified as Editor of this work.

Cover design by Charlotte Daniels
Cover image: The Morning, Philipp Otto Runge, 1808, Hamburger Kunsthalle Collection.

All rights reserved. No part of this publication may be reproduced or transmitted
in any form or by any means, electronic or mechanical, including photocopying,
recording, or any information storage or retrieval system, without prior
permission in writing from the publishers.

Bloomsbury Publishing Plc does not have any control over, or responsibility for, any
third-party websites referred to or in this book. All internet addresses given in this
book were correct at the time of going to press. The author and publisher regret
any inconvenience caused if addresses have changed or sites have ceased to
exist, but can accept no responsibility for any such changes.

A catalogue record for this book is available from the British Library.

Library of Congress Cataloging-in-Publication Data

Names: Hengstermann, Christian, editor.
Title: The history of religious imagination in Christian Platonism:
exploring the philosophy of Douglas Hedley / edited by Christian Hengstermann.
Description: London; New York: Bloomsbury Academic, 2021. |
Includes bibliographical references and index. |
Identifiers: LCCN 2020049468 (print) | LCCN 2020049469 (ebook) |
ISBN 9781350172968 (hb) | ISBN 9781350172975 (epdf) |
ISBN 9781350172982 (ebook
Subjects: LCSH: Imagination–Religious aspects–Christianity. |
Christian philosophy–History. | Platonists. | Hedley, Douglas.
Classification: LCC BR115.I6 H58 2021 (print) |
LCC BR115.I6 (ebook) | DDC 184–dc23
LC record available at https://lccn.loc.gov/2020049468
LC ebook record available at https://lccn.loc.gov/2020049469

ISBN: HB: 978-1-3501-7296-8
PB: 978-1-3502-1769-0
ePDF: 978-1-3501-7297-5
eBook: 978-1-3501-7298-2

Typeset by Deanta Global Publishing Services, Chennai, India

To find out more about our authors and books visit www.bloomsbury.com and
sign up for our newsletters.

Contents

List of contributors   vii
Preface   ix

Part I   Cambridge Platonism past and present

1. The 'devout contemplation and sublime fancy' of the Cambridge Platonists and their legacy   *Douglas Hedley*   3
2. The chariot, the temple and the city: The imaginative idealism of Douglas Hedley   *Christian Hengstermann*   17
   Response by Douglas Hedley   55

Part II   Spiritual sensation in ancient and early modern Christian Platonism

3. Θεία αἴσθησις: Origen's epistemological concept of spiritual sensation   *Alfons Fürst*   73
   Response by Douglas Hedley   87
4. *Cogitatione attingere*: Divine sensation in René Descartes and the Cambridge Platonists   *Christian Hengstermann*   94
   Response by Douglas Hedley   118
5. *Aids to reflection* and imagining God: Samuel Taylor Coleridge's concept of the imagination   *Friedrich A. Uehlein*   127
   Response by Douglas Hedley   139

Part III   The religious imagination in contemporary philosophy of religion

6. God in the world and ourselves in God: Panentheistic speculation in the early Karl Rahner   *Klaus E. Müller*   145
   Response by Douglas Hedley   160
7. René Girard and Douglas Hedley on violence, sacrifice and imagination   *Per Bjørnar Grande*   163
   Response by Douglas Hedley   171
8. Perceptions of God: Reflections on William P. Alston's theory of religious experience   *Margit Wasmaier-Sailer*   173
   Response by Douglas Hedley   183

9	From Cambridge to Calcutta: The presence of Indian thought in Douglas Hedley's Christian Platonism *Daniel Soars*	186
	Response by Douglas Hedley	203
10	Imagination and religion: Some Shakespearian reflections *Douglas Hedley*	210

Index of names   229

Contributors

Alfons Fürst is Professor of Early Christian Studies and Christian Archaeology and Director of the Origen Research Centre at the University of Münster. His primary research interests are Origen, the Alexandrian tradition and the reception of Origenian freedom metaphysics from late antiquity to modern theology and philosophy. Among his most recent publications are several German translations of Origen's works, the monograph *Origenes: Grieche und Christ in römischer Zeit* (2017) and an edited essay collection entitled *Origen's Philosophy of Freedom in Early Modern Times: Debates about Free Will and Apokatastasis in 17th-Century England and Europe* (2019).

Per Bjørnar Grande is Professor at the Department of Pedagogy, Religion and Social Studies at the Western Norway University of Applied Sciences in Bergen. In his research, he focuses mainly on René Girard, the notion of sacrifice and the religious dimension of literature on which he has published a great number of articles. Among his recent publications is a monograph entitled *Mimesis and Desire: An Analysis of the Religious Nature of Mimesis and Desire in the Work of René Girard* (2009).

Douglas Hedley is Professor of the Philosophy of Religion at Cambridge University and Fellow of Clare College as well as Director of the Cambridge Centre for the Study of Platonism. His research interests focus on contemporary religious philosophy as well as the Neoplatonist and Romantic traditions and Cambridge Platonism. Hedley has published on the history of religious philosophy from antiquity to the present day and the theory of imagination and its role in religious epistemology and ontology. His most recent books are *The Iconic Imagination* (2016) and *Revisioning Cambridge Platonism: Sources and Legacy* (2019), an essay collection co-edited with David Leech.

Christian Hengstermann is an associate lecturer at the Classics Department of Wuppertal University and Fellow of the Cambridge Centre for the Study of Platonism. His research mainly focuses on Origen and the Cambridge Platonists and their relevance to contemporary debates in philosophy and systematic theology. His most recent books are *Origenes und der Ursprung der Freiheitsmetaphysik* (2016) and an edited collection entitled *'That Miracle of the Christian World': Origenism and Christian Platonism in Henry More* (2020).

Klaus E. Müller is Professor of the Philosophical Foundations of Theology and Religious Philosophy at the University of Münster. His chief research interests include pantheist theories of God and panpsychist cosmologies as well as the history of religious philosophy, especially Thomas Aquinas, Baruch de Spinoza, Immanuel Kant and German Idealism. Among his major monographs are a three-volume exposition of the philosophy of religion entitled *Glauben – Fragen – Denken* (2006–10) and *In der Endlosschleife von Vernunft und Glaube: Einmal mehr Athen versus Jerusalem* (2012).

Daniel Soars teaches in the Divinity department at Eton College and is on the editorial board of the *Journal of Hindu-Christian Studies*. He holds a PhD from the University of Cambridge with a dissertation entitled 'Beyond the Dualism of Creature and Creator: A Hindu-Christian Theological Inquiry into the Distinctive Relation between the World and God' (2020). His principal research focus is philosophical theology done from a comparative perspective.

Friedrich A. Uehlein is Professor Emeritus at the University of Freiburg. His principal research interests are Anthony A. Shaftesbury and Samuel T. Coleridge as well as aesthetics, literature, theories of self-consciousness and the philosophy of religion. Uehlein is the author of two monographs on Shaftesbury and Coleridge entitled *Kosmos und Subjektivität. Lord Shaftesburys Philosophical Regimen* (1976) and *Die Manifestation des Selbstbewußtseins im konkreten Ich Bin: Endliches und Unendliches Ich im Denken S. T. Coleridges* (1982).

Margit Wasmaier-Sailer is Professor of Systematic Theology at the University of Lucerne. Her main research interests are contemporary religious philosophy, notably William Alston, the current human rights discussion and Kantian and post-Idealistic philosophy. Her most recent publications include the monograph *Das Verhältnis von Moral und Religion bei Johann Michael Sailer und Immanuel Kant: Zum Profil philosophischer Theologie und theologischer Ethik in der säkularen Welt* (2018) and an essay collection co-edited with Matthias Hoesch entitled *Die Begründung der Menschenrechte: Kontroversen im Spannungsfeld von positivem Recht, Naturrecht und Vernunftrecht* (2017).

Preface

Douglas Hedley's trilogy on the religious imagination is a major work of contemporary philosophy of religion. It propounds a new epistemology of the Divine and a sacramental ontology of a reality suffused by God's ubiquitous creative and salvific work in nature and culture. It also constitutes a revival of the rational theology of the seventeenth-century Cambridge Platonists Ralph Cudworth, Henry More and John Smith, whom the author acknowledged as the greatest of his precursors in his inaugural lecture as Professor of the Philosophy of Religion at the Faculty of Divinity at the University of Cambridge on 7 May 2018. It is under Professor Hedley's leadership that the Cambridge Platonists' major writings have been newly edited and translated on the AHRC-funded project *Cambridge Platonism at the Origins of the Enlightenment*, which ended in the online publication of a major Sourcebook in November 2019.

The chapters collected in this volume are intended to provide an introduction to both Hedley's own thought and the tradition of divine sensation which it seeks to revive and refine. Written by colleagues, friends and pupils, the chapters mostly go back to talks presented at a conference on the trilogy of the *Iconic Imagination* held at the University of Münster from 1 to 2 April 2016. However, they also reflect Hedley's more recent research in the AHRC project and as Professor of the Philosophy of Religion and director of the Cambridge Centre of the Study of Platonism. The additional chapters by Per Bjørnar Grande and Daniel Soars are intended to do justice to René Girard's seminal influence upon Hedley's trilogy and its ecumenical scope and importance to interreligious dialogue. Moreover, an exposition of Hedley's philosophy of religion written by Christian Hengstermann has been added alongside a transcription of the author's inaugural lecture.

It is my great pleasure to express my gratitude to the authors for preparing their chapters for print and to the Bloomsbury editors Colleen Coalter and Becky Holland, and Dhanuja Ravi, the project manager, for their untiring guidance and unfailing support. I am also grateful to the anonymous reviewers for helpful comments. My greatest gratitude is to Professor Hedley himself for a decade of great Platonic dialogue and friendship.

Christian Hengstermann

Part I

Cambridge Platonism past and present

1

The 'devout contemplation and sublime fancy' of the Cambridge Platonists and their legacy

Douglas Hedley

Edward Gibbon, in his *Decline and Fall of the Roman Empire*, while considering the education of Boethius, wrote that he attempted to reconcile the 'strong and subtle sense of Aristotle with the devout contemplation and sublime fancy of Plato'.[1] Most modern commentators seek in the dialogues Plato the dialectician. Yet Plato is also, and perhaps more importantly, a consummate fashioner of philosophical images and scenes in which he invokes a vision of the supreme reality as absolute and fecund goodness. Gibbon is being ironic, of course. Yet in his irony there is much truth about the contemplative power and elevated imagination of the Athenian, and I will endeavour to expand on the reception of that 'devout contemplation and sublime fancy' in the thought of the Cambridge Platonists.

When in 1996 I arrived in Cambridge to give a lecture for my interview in the philosophy of religion, I nervously presented my interest in the Cambridge Platonists. At the end of my presentation, the then Norris-Hulse professor sniffed, and remarked, somewhat disconcertingly, 'Yes, but we in Cambridge are embarrassed about the Cambridge Platonists.' It is very satisfying to reflect that now we have a team in Cambridge and Bristol to research and edit this remarkable group of writers. Even then, these thinkers appealed to me as a paradigm of philosophical activity, a vibrant combination of hermeneutic and speculative interests, open to the great issues of the age while fully cognizant of the rich history of the subject. The Cambridge Platonists are the most important Platonic school between the Renaissance and the Romantic period, and yet never properly edited, though much studied. They exerted an influence upon Leibniz, Locke, Newton, Shaftesbury, Berkeley, Reid, Hume, Coleridge and the German Idealists.[2]

Many of the ideas, arguments and problems of the Cambridge Platonists are currently the focus of attention in philosophy and theology – especially the issues of atheism and religion, nature and the ecological question, tolerance and politics, and the foundation of ethics.[3] Even though they were drawing on a Platonic perspective – many of the problems they are addressing only emerged with the New Science or with other aspects of modern society, such as tolerance and authority, equality and hierarchy.

As an undergraduate in Oxford, I was introduced to the canon of the British Empiricists, reading Locke, Berkeley and Hume. All of those philosophers were influenced by Cudworth, who was rarely mentioned by my tutors. In a sense, Cudworth, Berkeley and Coleridge represent another strand of British thought and one which is critical of Empiricism and appeals generally to Platonism as an alternative.[4] One might claim that this Platonism is a system, but nevertheless an open and flexible structure of thought. And 'Neoplatonism' is used as a term that denotes not so much one school of philosophy, but rather an intellectual paradigm and a way of life, disseminating its influence in myriad forms of thought and culture. It is said, for example, that Hegel is the founder of the Philosophy of Religion. Hegel opened his 1821 Inaugural Lecture on the *Philosophy of Religion* delivered at the University of Berlin with these words: 'The object of these lectures is the Philosophy of Religion, which in general has the same purpose as the earlier type of metaphysical science which was called *theologia naturalis*.'[5] Unbeknownst to many, it is actually Ralph Cudworth who for the first time coined the word 'Philosophy of Religion', and wrote the first treatise that can be called a Philosophy of Religion. George Berkeley, himself openly indebted to 'the learned Dr Cudworth', in his *Siris* (1744) writes:

> Proclus, in his *Commentary on the Theology of Plato* observes there are two sorts of philosophers. The one placed Body first in the order of beings, and made the faculty of thinking depend thereupon, supposing that the principles of all things are corporeal; that Body most really or principally exists, and that all other things in a secondary sense, and by virtue of that.
> Others, making all corporeal things to be dependent upon Soul or Mind, think this to exist in the first place and primary sense, and the being of bodies to be altogether derived from and presuppose that of the Mind.[6]

There are thus for Berkeley two sorts of philosophers. The first placed body first in the order of reality and mind emerges from it. Others, those with whom Berkeley identifies, make corporeal things to be the product of soul or mind. The Cambridge Platonists belong to an Idealistic tradition in Berkeley's sense of 'those who make all corporeal things to be dependent upon Soul or Mind'. They belong, in an important sense, to the tradition that derives from Plato, Plotinus, Origen, Eriugena, Eckhart, Cusa and Ficino. They are Idealists in that they claim the dependency or derivation of the material realm upon or from the spiritual. Hence, their metaphysics attempts to explain the 'lower' (nature) in terms of that which is higher (spirit), whereas the naturalist explains the higher in terms of the lower, the spiritual realm in purely natural terms.

The Idealists follow the 'interior' path. The absolute, or God, is not to be inferred from the facts or the very contingency of the cosmos, but is intuited or apprehended in consciousness or the structure of the spirit. The distinction between the spiritual and material is such that the transcendence of the Divine is not conceived in materialistic terms as remoteness. The refusal to envisage divine transcendence as 'out and up there' and the absolute as the apex of a cosmic pyramid has sometimes been mistakenly interpreted as pantheism when in fact it is the opposite. The enigmatic image of God as a circle whose centre is everywhere and circumference is nowhere is the attempt to dispel materialistic or anthropomorphic conceptions of the first principle:

> A Circle whose circumference no where
> Is circumscrib'd, whose Centre's each where set,
> But the low Cusp's a figure circular,
> Whose compass is ybound, but centre's every where.[7]

And for Ralph Cudworth, in his *Treatise Concerning Eternal and Immutable Morality*, we find the more prosaic explanation:

> Wherefore although some novelists make a contracted idea of God consisting of nothing else but will and power, yet his nature is better expressed by some in this mystical or enigmatical representation of an infinite circle, whose inmost centre is simple goodness, the radii or rays and expanded area (plat) thereof all comprehending and immutable wisdom, the exterior periphery or interminate circumference, omnipotent will or activity by which every thing without God is brought forth into existence.[8]

John Henry Muirhead, pupil of T. H. Green in Balliol, viewed Cudworth and More as the forefathers of British Idealism. According to Muirhead, the following are the main metaphysical points of the Cambridge Platonists:

> (1) Their view of the divine principle in the world as the action not of an arbitrary Will acting on it from without but of an immanent will to good whether conceived of as Beauty, Justice, or Truth; (2) The view of nature which they pressed against the mechanical systems both of other times and of their own; (3) The theory of mind as an active participant in the process of knowledge.[9]

This is almost a paraphrase of Cudworth's words:

> First, for making a Perfect Incorporeal intellect to be the Head of all; and Secondly, for resolving that Nature, as an Instrument of this Intellect, does not merely act according to the Necessity of Material Motions but for Ends and Purposes, though unknown to it self; Thirdly, for maintaining the Naturality of Morality; and Lastly, for asserting the τὸ ἐφ' ἡμῖν, Autexousie, or Liberty from Necessity.[10]

Recently, Dimitri Levitin has questioned the existence of the 'Cambridge Platonists'. I am not quite sure which part of the 'Cambridge Platonists' might be objectionable. Most of them were here! And their enthusiasm for Platonism is hard to question. Yet the central claim has been gathering support and is widely and respectfully cited by historians. One should consider his claims in more detail. He writes:

> One did not have to be a 'Cambridge Platonist', or in any way connected to the supposed group, to be interested in ancient thought. As is shown throughout this

book, there was no such thing as a 'Cambridge Platonist' attitude to the history of philosophy. For a start, apart from Henry More, they were not 'professional philosophers', but – like most senior university fellow – theologians and philologists who used philosophy when it suited them. Second, both their coherence and importance are predicated on the same nineteenth-century whig story that sought to trace a 'rationalist' lineage for 'liberal' Anglicanism. The idea that they represent an anachronistic remnant of 'Renaissance humanism' in an otherwise 'modern' world is based on the old assumptions about 'ancients and moderns' and about traditions of Platonic 'syncretism' we met earlier.[11]

Ralph Cudworth emerges not as an anachronistic 'Platonist' but as a cutting-edge European philologist. Most importantly, a huge number of scholars, natural philosophers and divines were acutely interested in ancient wisdom without having anything to do with the Cambridge group. Levitin's brief is that of a historian rather than a philosopher or theologian and one might excuse a lack of familiarity with some of the salient principles at stake. The mocking tone of Levitin, however, is frankly absurd. The authors known as the 'Cambridge Platonists' were indeed mostly Cambridge figures, and closely knit through friendship and elective affinity; and their adherence to Plato and his school is in marked opposition to the Aristotle of the schools. Unless one is utterly sceptical about tags like 'The Renaissance Platonists' or 'The German Idealists', both of which are more questionable as groups than 'The Cambridge Platonists', it is quite reasonable to use the term helpfully. The existence of figures such as Henry Hallywell (1640–1703) and his teacher George Rust (1628–70), who shared very close beliefs about the soul, enthusiasm and atheism, reveals a wider group of students who paraphrase, develop and repeat the arguments of More and Cudworth.[12] The existence of a school is evinced by contemporary critique in the form of Herbert Thorndike, Joseph Beaumont and especially Samuel Parker's *A Free and Impartial Censure of the Platonick Philosophy* in 1666. And contrary to Levitin's jejune proposition that Cudworth was in reality a theologian and philologist, Cudworth is, in fact, the nearest thing to a professional philosopher in England until T. H. Green in the nineteenth century. In response to Levitin's last point about Cudworth being a philologist rather than a philosopher, we find Cudworth himself asserting:

> We were necessitated by the Matter it self, to run out into Philology and Antiquity; as also in the other Parts of the Book, we do often give an Account of the Doctrine of the Ancients: which however some Over-severe Philosophers, may look upon Fastidiously, or Undervalue and Depreciate; yet, as we conceived it often Necessary, so possibly may the Variety thereof not be Ungratefull to others; *and this Mixture of Philology, throughout the Whole, Sweeten and Allay the Severity of Philosophy to them*: The main thing which the Book pretends to, in the mean time, being the Philosophy of Religion.[13]

It is quite evident from this passage that Cudworth himself views his activity as primarily philosophical, that is, the philosophy of religion. And, later on, Cudworth defines philosophy as not a Matter of Faith, but Reason, Men ought not to affect (as I conceive) to derive its Pedigree from Revelation, and by that very pretence seek to impose it Tyrannically upon the minds of Men, which God hath here purposely left Free to the use of their own Faculties, that so finding out Truth by them, they might enjoy that Pleasure and Satisfaction, which arises from thence.[14]

Cudworth is adducing a theological argument for philosophical autonomy. If we have been endowed with reason by God, then it is legitimate to use it freely. It is quite evident that he sees his own work as proceeding upon this rational basis. Hence the critique of 'latitude' from High Churchman, such as Joseph Beaumont, who was concerned that Cudworth failed to defend the authority of the church.

The philosophical endeavour of Cudworth's magnum opus is clear in the frontispiece of the first edition of 1678. There we find a copperplate engraving by Robert White (1645–1703), after a design by the portrait-painter Jan Baptist Gaspers. Called *The Six Greek Philosophers*, the engraving depicts, in two camps, the 'Theists', on the right (from the book's perspective), and the 'Atheists', on the left: the 'Theists', over whom we find the word 'Victory' in a laurel wreath, are Aristotle, Pythagoras and Socrates. The 'Atheists', who have the word 'Confusion' over their heads in a broken wreath, are Strato of Lampsacus, Epicurus and Anaximander. Spinoza is the new Strato, and Hobbes the new Anaximander. Under the engraving, we find the Greek words of Plato from book 10 of his dialogue on *Laws*, which forms a sort of treatise against atheism: 'Well now, how can one argue for the existence of gods without getting angry? You see, one inevitably gets irritable and annoyed with these people who have put us to the trouble, and continue to put us to the trouble, of composing these explanations.'[15] Book 10 of the *Laws* is perhaps the foundational text of Western natural theology.

Coleridge is perhaps the most significant inheritor of the Cambridge Platonists in the Romantic period. When challenged about his obligations from Schelling, Coleridge replied that he and Schelling shared many similar sources in Platonism and Boehme. However disingenuous Coleridge's response to those legitimate accusations of plagiarism may have been, his claim that the Cambridge Platonists were forerunners of Kant and the post-Kantians was shared by other British philosopher such as Dugald Stewart (in 1815) and later by James Mackintosh (in 1872), two of the most significant early interpreters of Kant in Great Britain.[16] Coleridge writes:

> The greater number were Platonists, so called at least, and such they believed themselves to be, but more truly Plotinists. Thus Cudworth, Dr. Jackson, Henry More, John Smith, and some others. What they all wanted was a pre-inquisition into the mind, as part organ, part constituent, of all knowledge, an examination of the scales, weights and measures themselves abstracted from the objects to be weighed or measured by them; in short, a transcendental aesthetic, logic, and noetic.[17]

Coleridge's criticism of the Cambridge Platonists in this passage amounts to the claim that they did not attain the heights of Kant's transcendental logic!

Coleridge's pupil F. D. Maurice, Knightbridge professor of Casuistry, Moral Theology and Moral Philosophy at the University of Cambridge, following in the footsteps of his mentor, wrote memorably of his seventeenth-century predecessors:

> There were English divines in their time who aimed at this reconciliation in a different spirit – by a different method. Cudworth, More, Whichcote, Worthington, John Smith – those men who have been sometimes called Platonists and sometimes Latitudinarians, who are eulogized by Burnet, whose influence was chiefly exercised in Cambridge, and was felt most there – were not memorable as preachers, and never sought popular reputation of any kind.[18]

Coleridge and Maurice were Platonists themselves, and part of a *living* tradition of Platonic thought. As such, they keenly recognized a kinship, albeit not an uncritical bond, with their intellectual ancestors.[19] Hence the historian John Hunt in his *Religious Thought in England* speaks of the Cambridge Platonists as the 'chief Rationalists of the age' and as critics of Hobbes, Platonists trying to establish 'religion and morality not on anything transient or arbitrary, but on principles immutable and eternal'.[20] Contrary to Levitin, Hunt is not proposing some dubious reification but providing an accurate description of the school, and a classification that draws upon the insights of earlier illustrious writers like Coleridge and Maurice, as well as the reflections of seventeenth-century contemporaries such as Richard Baxter and Gilbert Burnet. Far from being an artificial construction, 'Cambridge Platonists' is a term that denotes a living tradition of thought, and one without which I could not have embarked upon my trilogy.

1 Platonism as a systematic metaphysic and a way of life

The Platonism of the Cambridge Platonists is systematic and yet emphatically a philosophy of life and experience. For Cudworth and More, Plato's philosophy is a system and Plotinus is the greatest of all interpreters of Plato. The Good in Plato as both the sovereign principle of philosophy and beyond Being meant that both ethics and epistemology required a theological foundation. And this meant addressing questions that could not emerge in Plato's age, or that of Plotinus or Ficino. The Cambridge Platonists did just that. They belonged to a post–Galilean-Cartesian universe and they were equipped and ready to make the case for the philosophical truth of Platonism in the age of the New Science.

This stress upon Platonism as a system is linking, in a seemingly paradoxical fashion, with the insistence upon the affective dimension of philosophy. This has its roots in Plato's *Symposium*, but its most striking philosophical expression is in Plotinus's *Enneads*. Our thinkers can be called philosophical contemplatives, and I mean exactly this temper of mind in Plotinus that veers between a strongly contemplative rationalism and an emphasis upon that which resists conceptual analysis: will, life, experience, God. Some make the mistake of seeing 'Platonism' as purely contemplative or rationalist and then argue that the Cambridge Platonists are thus not properly speaking Platonists. In a sense the 'Platonism' of the Cambridge Platonists lies precisely in the tension between 'reflection' and 'experience'. The appeal to 'experience' is characteristic of the Platonic approach in the philosophy of religion.

I have said something about Cudworth's frontispiece. Let me now say something about his title page, on which we find a quote from Origen's *Against Celsus*: Γυμνάσιον [. . .] τῆς ψυχῆς Ἡ ΑΝΘΡΩΠΙΝΗ ΣΟΦΙΑ, ΤΕΛΟΣ ΔΕ Ἡ ΘΕΙΑ.[21] The Cambridge Platonists were great admirers of Origen, 'that Miracle of the Christian world'.[22] This is in part because they associate the Christian and the pagan Origen as a pupil of Ammonius Saccas and schoolmate of Plotinus. Origen is thus integral for the 'Platonism' of the Cambridge Platonists.[23] The Cambridge Platonists are not simply fideists, but they use Origen as the paradigm of the rational theologian rather than Thomas Aquinas or other Schoolmen. Christian theology needs a proper metaphysical structure especially against the modern philosophical criticisms of religious beliefs. This may not be surprising to anyone aware of the significance of Scholasticism in seventeenth-century Europe. Although the Cambridge Platonists are using Scholastic ideas, arguments and themes, their paradigm is not Scholastic, but Patristic, and Alexandrian in particular. This in part explains the particularly strong Platonic strand in their thought. Plotinus, not Aristotle, becomes the 'definite article' philosopher.

The Cambridge Platonists were wary of the powerful justifications of atheism in their own culture. The erosion of teleology or even the very idea of spirit as substance in Hobbes and Spinoza was to these thinkers an index of a new form of atheism. Cudworth and More assert the need for a Christian metaphysics in which the irrational bases of Materialism and Determinism are exposed and confuted. For Henry More, it is essential 'to cut the sinews of the Spinozan and the Hobbesian cause'.[24] And in order to do this, Cudworth deems necessary to construct a metaphysical system by 'joyning *Metaphysicks* or *Theology*, together with *Physiology*, to make up one entire *System of Philosophy*'.[25] Philosophy, however, is not just a system, but also a way of life:

> Were I indeed to define divinity, I should rather call it a divine life, than a divine science; it being something rather to be understood by a spiritual sensation, than by any verbal description, as all things of sense and life are best known by sentient and vital faculties. γνῶσις ἑκάστων δι' ὁμοιότητος γίνεται, as the Greek Philosopher hath well observed: every thing is best known by that which bears a just resemblance and analogy with it. (Plotinus, *Enneads* I 8,1)[26]

For John Smith:

> The true Metaphysical and Contemplative man . . . endeavours the nearest union with the Divine Essence that may be, κέντρον κέντρῳ συνάψας, as Plotinus speaks; knitting his owne centre, if he have any, unto the centre of the Divine Being. . . . This life is nothing else but God's own breath within him, and an Infant-Christ (if I may use the expression) formed in his Soul, who is in a sense . . . the shining forth of the Father's glory.[27]

This 'Metaphysical and Contemplative man' is an image of Plotinus, the 'divine philosopher':

> *Plotinus* aimed at such a kind of *Rapturous* and *Ecstatick Union* with the Τὸ ἕν and Τἀγαθόν, *the First of the Three Highest Gods*, (called *The One* and *The Good*) as by himself is described towards the latter end of this Last Book [*Ennead* VI 9], where he calls it ἐπαφὴν, and παρουσίαν ἐπιστήμης κρείττονα, and τὸ ἑαυτῶν κέντρον τῷ οἷον πάντων κέντρῳ . . . συνάπτειν, *a kind of Tactual Union*, and *a certain Presence better than Knowledge*, and *the joyning of our own Centre, as it were, with the Centre of the Universe.*[28]

One of the inheritors of the Cambridge Platonists in the twentieth century was A. E. Taylor. Taylor was a product of Oxford Idealism (he dedicated his first book to F. H. Bradley) but felt committed to a Neoplatonic variant of theism, in which the conversion of the soul to the Divine source is the pith and kernel of genuine philosophical inquiry. Following in this living tradition, A. E. Taylor writes:

> The first step towards the 'conversion' of the soul from the world to God, as we learn from the Platonic Socrates, is that knowledge of self which is also the knowledge of our own ignorance of true good. How do we pass from the discovery that we are in this miserable and shameful ignorance of the one thing it is incumbent on us to know to apprehension of the scale of true good? How do we get even so far beyond our initial complete ignorance as to be able to say that a good soul is immeasurably better than a good body, and a good body than abundance of possessions? We know how the Augustinian doctrine, which is Christian as well as Platonic, answers the question. It does so by its conception, traceable back to the New Testament, that God Himself is the *lumen intellectus*, a view which has been, in substance, that of all the classical British moral philosophers from Cudworth to Green, and seems, in fact, to be, in principle, the only solution of the difficulty.[29]

The claim is in striking contrast to the interpretations of some of Taylor's brilliant contemporaries such as Cornford and Julius Stenzel. Stenzel, for example, regarded the theory of ideas in Plato as a means that Plato employs to describe the ideal functioning of the polis, and he holds to a view of Plato giving up the theory of forms. Taylor is also quite unlike Cornford in attributing a view to Plato that connects unproblematically, if not without certain modifications, with the views of later Platonists such as Augustine and Cudworth.[30]

2 Contemplating nature, imagination and the sense of the sublime

J. N. Findlay once observed: 'The basic strength of Platonism lies in its appeal to our imagination, our understanding and our sense of values.'[31] The beautiful, the true and the good is at the very mainspring of the Platonic vision in European culture and thought. The link between the axiomatic and the ontological is forged in Plato's *Timaeus*, where the demiurge creates the physical cosmos out of generosity, and the imaginative coupling between beauty, truth and goodness finds expression in Dante or Schiller. The Cartesian or Newtonian universe seemed much less habitable for the radical conjunction of fact and value expressed in the myth of the demiurge of Timaeus. Yet it is precisely this awareness of goodness pervading the cosmos that informs the philosophy of Cudworth. In a passage that is redolent of Rudolf Otto's account of the Holy and the Romantic sublime, Cudworth writes:

> And Nature itself plainly intimates to us, that there is some such absolutely perfect Being, which though not inconceivable, yet is incomprehensible to our finite understandings, by certain passions, which it hath implanted in us, that otherwise would want an object to display themselves upon; namely those of devout veneration, adoration, and admiration, together with a kind of ecstasy and pleasing horror.

This 'pleasing horror' evokes the *mysterium tremendum et fascinans* of Otto, that sense of the holy:

> Which in the silent language of Nature, seems to speak thus much to us, that there is some object in the world, so much bigger and vaster than our mind and thoughts, that it is the very same to them, that the ocean is to narrow vessels; so that when they have taken into themselves as much as they can thereof by contemplation, and filled up all their capacity, there is still an immensity of it left without, which cannot enter in for want of room to receive it, and therefore must be apprehended after some other strange and mysterious manner, *viz.* by their being as it were plunged into it, and swallowed up or lost in it.[32]

Coleridge, in his *The Eolian Harp* (1795), expresses the same feeling:

> And what if all of animated nature
> Be but organic Harps diversely framed,
> That tremble into thought, as o'er them sweeps
> Plastic and vast, one intellectual breeze,
> At once the Soul of each, and God of all.[33]

This 'animated nature', 'Plastic and vast', is a barely veiled reference to Cudworth's plastic nature. What is the relation between spirit and matter? How one goes about answering such a question depends to a very significant degree upon how one imagines nature itself. Thus, from at least the late eighteenth century, the rapid and radical success of the early modern scientific world view appeared to offer an unambiguous answer: there was no relationship between spirit (or the mental) and matter; the mental was either regarded as an epiphenomenon of matter or taken to be explanatorily inert. Of course, this apparent answer has always had its critics. However, contemporary discussions about the relation of 'mind and cosmos' alongside other seemingly intractable difficulties with the problem of consciousness have generated renewed arguments against a narrowly materialistic world view.

René Descartes's philosophy is commonly considered the point of departure for the exorcism of spirit from nature. His strict separation of spirit and matter constituted a methodological revolution with far-reaching ramifications. Descartes interpreted nature as an interaction of mechanical – which is to say, 'spirit-less' – forces. However, a number of brilliant contemporaries of Descartes already argued against his account. Most notably, the Cambridge Platonists insisted that the material and mechanistic world view with its spiritless account of nature left crucial questions unanswered. Drawing especially upon Platonic and Neoplatonic philosophies, they attempted to articulate an account of the ongoing presence of spirit in nature despite emerging Cartesian concerns. Hence, the criticism of a merely mechanistic conceptualization of nature begins with the Cambridge Platonists. Henry More (1614–87), for instance, engaged Descartes's philosophy in a variety of formats, from his comprehensive study *Antidote to Atheism* to his own personal correspondence with Descartes himself. Ralph Cudworth (1617–88) was More's ally in this, especially in his monumental *The True Intellectual System of the Universe*, in which Cudworth develops the notion of 'plastic nature', the idea that nature implies a spiritual but form-giving principle. Although often overlooked today, Cudworth and More's work exerted an enormous influence on thinkers in England and America, but also in both France and Germany.

3 Conclusion

The starting point of the 'philosophy of religion' is not Christian theology but 'religion'. It is the experience of the sacred in human life, together with the sad array of desecration, the sublime and the presence of evil witnessed by the varieties of religious experience in human culture, for example, from the earliest cave paintings to abstract expressionism, from the Vedas to Dostoevsky, from Pythagoras to Gandhi. The Barthian critique of 'religion', together with post-structuralist attacks on 'essentialism', has generated a misplaced hostility to the idea of 'religion'. My own research in Hindu tradition, inspired by Julius Lipner in the faculty, was in the way of those latitudinarians of the seventeenth century who were eager to explore the rites and beliefs of the great cultures, whether that of ancient Babylonia, Egypt, the philosophy of the 'Turks' or the mystical Jewish cabbala. The philosophy of religion of the Cambridge Platonists was more open to non-Christian religion than most proponents in the field in the twentieth century, with notable exceptions such as John Hick and Brian Hebblethwaite. The frequent appeals I have heard within these walls to a deus ex machina in the fideist tradition of Pascal, Kierkegaard and Barth and their Anglo-American epigones have to be rejected, if only because it blocks the exploration of religions outside of Christianity. The philosophy of religion is a *philosophical* activity, not a subsection of Christian apologetics. It may be legitimately used as Christian apologetic, and I have done that myself, but that is not its proper brief.

The bedrock of the strand of Platonic philosophy of religion as a living tradition is a theory of the absolute as the first principle or *arche* and unconditioned principle, which is intelligibility in itself and which furnishes intelligibility for all subordinate beings, and which the Christian Platonists of Alexandria identified with the great I AM of Exod. 3.14. Such an absolute is precisely the kind of limit of explanation that the analytic tradition of philosophy has dismissed or critiqued as straying beyond the bounds of logic and experience. The forgetting of this tradition of ancient Platonic speculation led to the Babylonian captivity of Heidegger's critique of the onto-theological in postmodern theology and phenomenology. Talk of 'theology overcoming metaphysics', so fashionable when I arrived in the faculty, would have been frankly unfathomable to the 'Platonick' divines of this university's greatest era.

Some of the most ancient questions of philosophy remain the stuff of contemporary disputes: How can the mere clutter of phenomena form a harmonious whole? Or does the apparently random concatenation of cause and effect reflect a catena or chain of being? How does the indiscerpible unity of inner experience mirror the unity of a lawlike universe? Do developments in the study of the brain or neurophysiology raise new questions about human freedom, or do the egregious horrors of the English civil war or the tumult and brutality across the world in the last century reignite questions of good and evil? What are the metaphysical implications of postulating or denying values as transcendent verities? These metaphysical obsessions of the Cambridge Platonists remain urgent and pressing questions, and not least because the contemporary legacy of the two powerful models of Hobbes and Spinoza is evident, whether in the form of a neo-Spinozism in which any contingency disappears, or the radical contingency of the purblind Watchmaker of materialistic neo-Darwinian metaphysics. If anything, the sinews of the Hobbesian and Spinozan cause have become all the more powerful in the contemporary period through the post-Darwinian theory of random mutation and natural selection on the one hand and also the deterministic component found in mechanical models of the DNA structure and function on the other. This has been reinforced by widespread and corrosive nominalism, derived more immediately from a heady cocktail of Nietzsche, Marx and Freud, presenting issues of class, race or gender as the final arbiter in questions of intellectual inquiry and the life of the university in particular.

Moving from the principle of the foundational and transcultural sense of the sacred, the insufficiency of piecemeal mechanical explanations, and the capacity of the mind to be an organon of transcendence, all of which I found in S. T. Coleridge and the Cambridge Platonists, I wrote the trilogy on the imagination by a desire to reject any crass dichotomy between rational judgement and imagination, linked to the belief in the capacity of finite images and symbols to unveil the infinite and the eternal. However, even if the religious imagination is endowed with a central role in the philosophy of religion, the logical and moral critic of religious images is equally part of the task of the philosophy of religion.

The religious imagination requires metaphysics in two respects. One positive: our metaphysical reflections can be inspired and shaped by images and symbols – Plato's cave being perhaps one of our most striking. Yet the rational critique of such images is equally necessary. It is chastening to recall in our self-esteem culture, and especially when giving lectures to a tender-minded generation, that false beliefs can be highly inspiring and true beliefs can be profoundly dispiriting. The cool appraisal of consoling phantasies has been a part of philosophy since Xenophanes. If the cosmos is a heap of ultimately meaningless *disjecta membra,* then Nietzsche is right that Platonic–Idealistic metaphysics is the timid refusal to endorse the death of God.

While it was a scholar of literature who coined the phrase 'the anxiety of influence',[34] no one could have more reason for such Oedipal anxiety than students of Plato. Yet Platonism as a live philosophical option has been infinitely fertile in fusing together the legitimate desire for the explanation of value and intelligibility while resisting rationalism of the narrow kind. Long may the endeavour to climb out of the cave and up the divided line continue; long may we contemplate the Good that ultimately overcomes evil and consecrates the finite and the defective; and long may we continue to revere the finite and transitory as a precious icon of the great I AM that alone truly is.

Notes

1 Edward Gibbon, *The Decline and Fall of the Roman Empire*, 6 vols (London: Everyman, 1993), vol. IV, 159.
2 See Douglas Hedley and David Leech (eds), *Revisioning the Cambridge Platonists: Sources and Legacy* (Dort: Springer, 2019).
3 Charles Taliaferro, *Evidence and Faith: Philosophy and Religion since the Seventeenth Century* (Cambridge: Cambridge University Press, 2005).
4 Victor Nuovo, *John Locke: The Philosopher as Christian Virtuoso* (Oxford: Oxford University Press, 2017), 159. I had the good fortune of being taught by Michael Ayers, perhaps the pre-eminent scholar of Locke in recent decades.
5 Hegel, *Lectures on the Philosophy of Religion. Vol. 1: Introduction and the Concept of Religion*, edited by Peter C. Hodgson, translated by R. F. Brown, P. C. Hodgson and J. M. Stuart with the assistance of H. S. Harris (Oxford and New York: Oxfors University Press, 2007), 3.
6 Berkeley, *Siris*, § 263.
7 Henry More, *A Platonick Song of the Soul*. For the full poem, see *A Platonick Song of the Soul*, edited with an Introductory Study by Alexander Jacob (Lewisburg: Bucknell University Press; London: Associated University Presses, 1998), 407.
8 Ralph Cudworth, *A Treatise Concerning Eternal and Immutable Morality With A Treatise of Freewill*, edited by Sarah Hutton (Cambridge: Cambridge University Press, 1996), 27.
9 John Muirhead, *The Platonic Tradition in Anglo-Saxon Philosophy* (London: George Allen & Unwin LTD; New York: The Macmillan Company, 1931), 35.
10 *The True Intellectual System of the Universe* (London: Printed for Richard Royston, 1678), 65.
11 Dmitri Levitin, *Ancient Wisdom in the Age of the New Science* (Cambridge et al.: Cambridge University Press, 2015), 16.
12 See the work of Marilyn Lewis, 'Pastoral Platonism in the Writings of Henry Hallywell (1641–1703)', *The Seventeenth Century* 28 (2013): 441–63. See also her '"Christ's College and the Latitude-Men" Revisited: A Seminary of Heretics?', accepted for publication in *History of Universities* 33 (2020) 17–68.
13 Cudworth, *True Intellectual System*, 'The Preface'.

14 Ibid., 22–3.
15 Plato, *Laws*, X, 887c7–d2: φέρε δή, πῶς ἄν τις μὴ θυμῷ λέγοι περὶ θεῶν ὡς εἰσίν; ἀνάγκη γὰρ δὴ χαλεπῶς φέρειν καὶ μισεῖν ἐκείνους οἳ τούτων ἡμῖν αἴτιοι τῶν λόγων γεγένηνται καὶ γίγνονται.
16 For a more recent argument to this effect, see Ben L. Mijuskovic, *The Achilles of Rationalist Arguments* (Springer: The Hague, 1974).
17 *The Literary Remains of Samuel Taylor Coleridge*, collected and edited by Henry N. Coleridge (London: William Pickering, 1838), 415–16.
18 Frederick D. Maurice, *Moral and Metaphysical Philosophy*, vol. 2: *Fourteenth Century to the French Revolution* with *A Glimpse into the Nineteenth Century* (London: Macmillan and co., 1862), 346.
19 Cf. David Newsome, *Two Classes of Men: Platonism and English Romantic Thought* (London: Murray, 1974).
20 John Hunt, *Religious Thought in England: From the Reformation to the End of Last Century*, vol. 1 (London: Strahan and co., 1870), 410.
21 *Contra Celsum* 6,13: 'Human wisdom is a means of education for the soul, divine wisdom being the ultimate end' (Origen, *Contra Celsum*, translated with an introduction and notes by Henry Chadwick (Cambridge et al.: Cambridge University Press, 1953), 326).
22 Henry More, *The Preface General*, in *A Collection of Several Philosophical Writings* (London, 1662), xxii.
23 On the question of Origen in early modern Cambridge, see Christian Hengstermann, 'Pre-existence and Universal Salvation – The Origenian Renaissance in Early Modern Cambridge', *British Journal for the History of Philosophy* 25 (2017): 971–89, as well as the essay collection by Marialuisa Baldi (ed.), *'Mind Senior to the World': Stoicismo e origenismo nella filosofia platonica del Seicento inglese* (Milan: FrancoAngeli, 1996), and the more recent ones by Alfons Fürst and Christian Hengstermann (eds), *Die Cambridge Origenists. George Rusts Letter of Resolution Concerning Origen and the Chief of His Opinions* (Münster: Aschendorff Verlag, 2013), and *Origenes Cantabrigiensis. Ralph Cudworth, Predigt vor dem Unterhaus und andere Schriften* (Münster: Aschendorff Verlag, 2018).
24 Alexander Jacob, *Henry More's Refutation of Spinoza* (Hildesheim, Zurich and New York: Olms, 1991), 101.
25 Cudworth, *True Intellectual System*, 175.
26 John Smith, *Select Discourses*, 4th edn, corrected and revised by Henry G. Williams (Cambridge: Cambridge University Press, 1859), 1. For John Smith, see Derek Michaud, *Reason Turned into Sense: John Smith on Spiritual Sensation* (Leuven: Peeters, 2017).
27 Ibid., 21.
28 Cudworth, *True Intellectual System*, 549.
29 Alfred E. Taylor, *The Faith of a Moralist: Gifford Lectures Delivered in the University of St. Andrews 1926–1928. Series 1: The Theological Implications of Morality* (London: MacMillan and co., 1930), 238. One might note that the Cambridge Norris-Hulse Professor of Divinity (1960–76) Donald MacKinnon (1913–94) was assistant lecturer in moral philosophy in Edinburgh in 1936–7, and he always referred to this post as 'Assistant to A. E. Taylor'. MacKinnon was less committed to any straightforward Neoplatonism than A. E. Taylor, whose obligations to Cudworth are evident. Nevertheless, Mackinnon shared Taylor's high estimate of Plato and Kant. Mackinnon was a shaping influence in turn upon figures like Iris Murdoch and Rowan Williams.

30 I am thinking in particular of their different views of the *Timaeus*. See Francis M. Cornford, *Plato's Cosmology: The Timaeus of Plato*, translated with a running commentary (London: Routledge, 1937). Alfred E. Taylor, *A Commentary on Plato's Timaeus* (Oxford: Clarendon Press, 1928).
31 John N. Findlay, *Ascent to the Absolute: Metaphysical Papers and Lectures* (London: George Allen & Unwin LTD; New York: Humanities Press, 1970), 252.
32 Cudworth, *True Intellectual System*, 640.
33 Samuel T. Coleridge, 'The Eolian Harp', ll, 44–8. Coleridge, *Poetry and Prose*, edited by Alfred A. Knopf (New York and Toronto: Pocket Books, 1997), 120.
34 Harold Bloom, *The Anxiety of Influence: A Theory of Poetry* (Oxford et al.: Oxford University Press, 1973).

2

The chariot, the temple and the city
The imaginative idealism of Douglas Hedley

Christian Hengstermann

1 Introduction: Idealism reimagined: Symbolic knowledge and the sacrament of the world

Hedley's trilogy of works[1] sets out to provide a first comprehensive philosophical defence of the religious imagination as our primary epistemic power of experiencing and knowing a God ubiquitously present in all of nature and culture. To this end, the author draws upon the idealist tradition of the Cambridge Platonists Ralph Cudworth, Henry More and John Smith and the English Romantics Samuel Taylor Coleridge and William Wordsworth from whom he borrows the conceptual categories for his own draft of a contemporary epistemology and ontology of the Divine. The epistemology of the imagination as a source of symbolic knowledge about God and the ontology of reality as an image of his creative and salvific action provide a via media between the speculative systems of classical idealism and the misguided accounts of man and the world in modern-day naturalism and scepticism.

The chief foil to Hedley's idealism of the imagination delineated and defended in the trilogy is contemporary materialism in its various guises which, the author argues, inevitably falls short of human nature conceived of primarily as a restless striving for the true, the good and the beautiful. Conscious subjectivity, as is evidenced, above all, in the experience of aesthetic beauty, scientific truth and moral goodness, is a stubborn fact, as is its constitutive relationship with its transcendent divine principle revered in occidental and oriental religions. Consciousness, whether human or divine, has so far defied and continues to defy every attempt at reductionistic materialist and psychological naturalization:

> If finite subjectivity were readily explicable, the argument that God is merely the projection of the human agent upon a cosmic landscape might be feasible. But subjectivity, notwithstanding the valiant efforts of eliminative materialism and identity theorists, is far from readily intelligible. Some distinguished philosophers like Nagel think that any progress is very far off; others like McGinn think it a

forlorn hope. If human consciousness is a genuine mystery, the theistic hypothesis of attempting to ground it in the Divine mind seems no less attractive than the agnostic materialism of McGinn or the appeal to the brute givenness of mind in a philosopher like Chalmers.[2]

Beauty, truth and goodness cannot be consistently explained in a naturalistic paradigm of metaphysics, as all three require as the condition of their very possibility man's defining ability to be both in and beyond the world at the same time. Since the subjective experience of an objective world, by its very nature, involves an effort of the imagination on the part of a subject endowed both with self-consciousness and free will, there can be no account of either man or the world without appeal to this distinctly human power: 'It is a paradox of empiricism', Hedley states at the beginning of his three-volume system of imaginative idealism, 'that it cannot deal with experience because our experience is essentially imaginative.'[3]

In response to the prevalent materialism of the modern age which he combats, Hedley, therefore, chooses to view man chiefly as a being of imagery and symbolism that cannot but reach beyond the present world in the three distinct operations of its power of reason in its irreducible experience of the beautiful, the true and the good. The image is the sole means whereby a conscious subject, transcending brute facts, comes to perceive and know the truth of reality in research, whether scientific or philosophical, and, at the same time, feel the appeal of its beauty and obey the imperatives of its goodness. The world encountered by man as a being of the iconic imagination is not one of desiccated naturalism, but one suffused by God's creative and salvific presence. Hence, man, by his very essence, possesses an experiential awareness of God in his imaginative participation in a theophanic cosmos. His capacity for transcendence is, in Samuel Taylor Coleridge's felicitous expression, the 'Sheckinah in the heart', in which man, in the symbolic modes of his theophanic imagination, experiences 'the transcendence of the Eternal through and in the Temporal'.[4]

2 Transcendental epistemology: The theophanic imagination and the realm of the symbolic

Like the earlier great Platonist anthropologies of Plato's own *Alcibiades maior* and Plotinus's *Ennead* I 1: *The Animate and the Man*, to which it is indebted throughout, the transcendental analysis of Hedley's imaginative idealism follows the Delphic imperative of the γνῶθι σαυτόν.[5] At its centre is man's imagination which reveals him to be a being both *in* and *beyond* his environment at the same time: 'The imagination is the basis of the distinctive amphibious capacity of human beings to be both part of a natural environment and to transcend that same environment: we are organisms instinctively adapting to the world and interpreting it as reflective agents with memories and projections.'[6] It is through its own amphibious nature as active and passive, creative and receptive, as well as cognitive and affective that the imagination, the chief power of human subjectivity, also mediates between divine infinity and human finiteness, as it comes to see God in the mirror of humankind's rich symbolism.

At its most fundamental level, the imagination is identical with human subjectivity conceived of as 'the transcendental unity of apperception' in the Kantian vein.[7] Every single act of knowing and acting requires as the condition of its very possibility 'a unified field of perception', in which a subject, distinguishing itself from it and, thereby, constituting itself in its defining activity of the cognitive process, perceives and understands the word as a whole and in its parts. In the tradition of the Greeks' metaphysics of light, or *lux intelligibilis*, in which sight is revered as the highest of our senses, the imagination is likened to sensual vision. As an intellectual analogue, its transcendental unity is not one of *sequentiality* or temporal becoming, but one of *simultaneity* or eternal being:

> Within a field of vision the objects are given 'at once' rather than determined by a succession of times. Because of this, vision enables detachment. Through vision we encounter a simultaneous image and thus are capable of exploring the freedom of the contrast between Being and Becoming. The image of the world at a distance generated by the human imagination is a world that is subject to control. Consciousness can therefore function as an 'inner eye'. For humans, the mind does not depend upon the environment. One can think of dreams. The relationship between this inner world and the outer perceived environment constitutes the distinctively human.[8]

Accordingly, the 'distinctively human' power of the imagination, viewed as the condition of the possibility of all human reasoning, whether theoretical, practical or aesthetical, is defined as an 'amphibious capacity'. It is situated 'on the boundary between sensation and thought', sharing its passive receptivity with the former and its creative activity with the latter. Thus, while *passive and receptive* in its reliance upon the phenomenon presented to it in the world around it, the imagination proves both *active and creative* in the theoretical order which it imposes upon it. It thereby mediates between the *objective and universal* on the one hand and the *subjective and individual* on the other: 'The human imagination possesses a mediating power, or liminal quality. It provides a refuge of irreducible individuality and a part of subjective consciousness and yet draws upon the shapes and forms of physical objects.'[9] As a mediating power, the imagination is characterized by a creative tension informing all of human cognition and action in which its transcendental universal power, paradoxically, brings about a person's irreducible individuality: 'The imagination is uniquely characterized by a tension between the inner and the outer, thought and sense; this tension is unavoidable, and imagination hovers between the manifestation of the inner through the outer and yet the inscrutable private part of consciousness that creatively represents experiences, states of affairs in the theatre of consciousness, remains unmediated.'[10]

In the living history of the concept in British philosophy, Hedley's imagination, therefore, steers a middle path between the infelicitous extremes of Thomas Hobbes's entirely passive and George Berkeley's wholly active power of the same name. Neither is the imagination merely fading sensation, an evanescent remnant of an earlier sensual impression outside a subject's conscious control, nor is it to be identified with the latter's pure sovereign volition by which it evokes images without any prior contact with reality.[11] Instead, Hedley opts for the 'remarkably sane middle way' of S. T. Coleridge,[12] as put forth in the daring system programme of Anglo-Saxon Idealism of chapters XII–XIV of his *Biographia Literaria*.[13] Thus, the author agrees with Hobbes in holding that the imagination is dependent upon prior sense data with which it is furnished by its environment, while concurring with Berkeley in stressing its irreducible transcendental activity in conferring upon them a distinct shape in perception and intellect. The imagination possesses what Coleridge, with a neologism of his own coinage, calls an 'esemplastic' power, that is, the power 'by a sort of *fusion to force many into one*'.[14] To the passive and active dimensions of the imagination in Hobbes and Berkeley correspond the primary and secondary imagination as a 'shaping and modifying power' and fancy as 'an aggregative and associative power'[15] in Coleridge's middle way. In the Romantic philosopher's celebrated definition, the imagination, in its primary form, is no less than 'a repetition in the finite mind of the eternal act of creation in the infinite I AM'.[16] It 'repeats' or participates in the divine *creatio ex nihilo* by turning the many of the empirical phenomenon into the one of a living form of its own making. Its activity is defined as a 'creative *nisus* towards unity'[17] by which the soul, endowing the many with a unitary shape, produces an entirely novel entity. It is the chief error of empiricist concepts of the imagination that they disregard this creative dimension of the human imagination entirely: 'Imagination is more than the mere constitution of items of memory into a new set of relations: it is a fusing power that produces a new unity.'[18] The 'secondary imagination', different from the primary one not in kind, but 'in degree' only, either destroys pre-existing unity in order to bring about new forms of intelligible order 'or where this process is rendered impossible, yet still at all events it struggles to idealize and to unify',[19] thus revealing its defining creativity in both its destructive and constructive work. The third function of the imagination, that is, 'fancy', corresponds to memory and instrumental reasoning by which the soul imposes mechanical order upon present and past sense impressions received and remembered without endowing them with any original form of its own. While lacking the 'esemplastic' work characteristic of the primary and secondary functions of the first power of the human mind, it nevertheless fulfils a vital function of human subjectivity which is key to man's being as an agent both shaping and shaped by his environment in theoretical and practical reasoning: 'As such the term "fancy" is not meant pejoratively; fancy is not bad as such, and can have a perfectly respectable and indeed necessary function. It is hard to see how we could negotiate and adapt to the world without the capacity to use memory in this way.'[20] The 'creative *nisus* towards unity', as the defining work of the imagination in human cognition and action, is displayed in the striving for a unified understanding of the soul's prima facie chaotic manifold environment. It is in Shakespeare's celebrated account of the 'poet's eye', the canonical text of Romantic aesthetics and epistemology, that the *coincidentia oppositorum* wrought by the imagination as the principle of unity in plurality finds a succinct expression. 'Heaven and earth', in Hedley's reading, symbolize the highest and lowest strata of reality to which man, by virtue of his imagination's sublime capacity for divine creativity, gives 'shapes' and 'names':

> The poet's eye, in a fine frenzy rolling,
> Doth glance from heaven to earth, from earth to heaven.

> And as imagination bodies forth
> The forms of things unknown, the poet's pen
> Turns them to shapes, and gives to airy nothing
> A local habitation and a name.
>
> (*A Midsummer Night's Dream* 5.1.12–17)[21]

The work of art, on the principles of Hedley's Romantic Platonism, is a paradigmatic case of the imagination as a paradoxical unity of epistemic activity and passivity working upon a 'many' and turning it into a 'one' as an object of vision and thought. While drawing on a range of pre-existing materials upon which the poet imposes his own unitary artistic vision, the resultant product is entirely new and as such defies any attempt at reduction to the single parts of which it is made up: 'The creation of a work of art as a world *sui generis* cannot be intelligibly reduced to simple mechanisms of addition and comparison.'[22]

Not only is the reality perceived and understood a product of the imagination, but the self as the active source of its intelligible unity is its 'work of art' as well. While it is the pinnacle of man's cognition, sharing in the highest prerogative of God's own primordial creativity, the imagination is also, in a way, the lowest of his manifold powers. As 'the prime agent of all human perception',[23] including those that are subconscious or involuntary, the imagination, for all its divine sublimity, reaches down to the very depths of the soul's lowest vegetative function, thereby again evidencing its distinguishing unitive power in linking the divine and animal parts of man. Quoting the two chief Romantic authorities of his own imaginative idealism, Hedley extols the imagination as the principle of man in the entirety of his amphibious existence:

> Yet it is also 'essentially vital', the primordial and organic 'living Power and prime Agent of all human Perception'. It is a point where human self-consciousness merges with its subconscious roots in the vegetative soul, such that Coleridge can both exclaim 'How much of man lies below his consciousness!' and exalt the point where the human soul can enjoy communion with the Divine, as Wordsworth claims in *The Prelude*:
>> To hold communion with the invisible world
>> Such minds are truly from the Deity.[24]

Man, as an imaginative being of an amphibious nature, is characterized by the tension between the conscious and voluntary and the unconscious and involuntary which are joined in each single act of his defining epistemic power. Dreams are cases in point of the latter part of human nature, its natural 'Plastick Power', shaping the former. Conversely, the poet relies on the sudden inspiration from the unfathomable depths of his psyche to create a work of art in imaginative effort: 'In every work of art', Hedley quotes Coleridge with approval, 'is a reconcilement of the external with the internal; the conscious is so impressed on the unconscious as to appear in it.'[25] Again, the work of art illustrates the imagination's 'creative *nisus* towards unity' in turning the plethora of contradictory aspects constituting an individual human existence, whether subconscious, affective or cognitive and volitional, into a person of recognizable identity over time.

In the terms of the Cambridge Platonists, to whom the Romantic philosopher is indebted throughout, Coleridge's primary imagination corresponds to Henry More's 'active sagacity in the soul',[26] John Smith's '"true Efflux" of divine sagacity'[27] and, most importantly, Ralph Cudworth's '*hegemonikon* or the ruling principle of the soul'.[28] The imaginative power of man is the *hegemonikon* in the theory of personal identity propounded by Cudworth, the greatest philosopher of the early modern Cambridge Enlightenment which Hedley seeks to revive and refine in his own system of imaginative idealism. In contradistinction to the bundle theory of consciousness, as espoused by David Hume and his many contemporary heirs like Simon Blackburn, Hedley follows Cudworth in positing a unitary centre of rational personality and agency by which man, driven by the *a priori* of God's disinterested goodness, imposes order upon his many cogitations, volitions and passions. Neither can the 'hegemonikon', a term which the Cambridge Platonist himself borrows from 'the great Alexandrian Divine Origen',[29] be defined as the final appetite, as in Hobbes's materialistic and hedonistic paradigm of agency, nor as a distinct faculty of the soul, as in John Bramhall's alternative scholastic conception. Instead, it is identical with the agent as an imagined unitary whole as she contemplates her soul and character prior to a decision regarding a possible future course of action. Being wrought by the imagination, the hegemonic unity of the subject in reflection and action is itself deeply imaginative in nature. Human persons, like the greatest of Shakespeare's characters, are 'free artists of themselves',[30] as they seek to confer unity and coherence both upon the tensions of the conflicting parts of their psyche within and the disparate events of their life without. The intense struggles of Augustine's soul narrated to God in the *Confessions*, the archetypal autobiography of Western literature, testify to the conflict between the ideal of imaginative unity and the reality of the Pauline 'divided self', which structures the powerful autobiographical account of the Latin Church Father's conversion.[31] There is a close correspondence between the degree of narrative unity and coherence achieved by a person's imaginative effort and the amount of happiness experienced in their life. The stronger the personality, the stronger the ability to cope with personal setbacks and contingent blows of fate: 'Human happiness must have more continuity and depth. It must be linked to the homogenous functioning of different elements with an overarching element. The stronger the personality, the easier its capacity to endure pain, suffering and misfortune.'[32] However, neither the 'depth and continuity' of human personality nor the 'overarching element' of the autobiographical narrative by which it is brought about can be sought in the realm of finite becoming, but in that of infinite being which is both the principle and ideal informing the process of autobiographical storytelling. Again, it is the creator of the genre of Western autobiography who expresses the intimate link between the finite and infinite 'I am' in the narrative in an existential reading of God's name in Exod. 3.14: 'His Commentary on Psalm 38 dwells upon the soul's ascent to God: "For myself, in my weakness I am so nearly non-existent that God has eluded my memory, God who said, I AM WHO I AM (Ex. 3:14)."'[33]

Both in its knowledge of the world and the self, the imagination is a source of a *sui generis* knowledge about the 'infinite I am' of which it is a 'repetition' in every single finite act of cognition. Man's relationship with the 'infinite I AM' of Coleridge's definition is a paradoxical one of nearness and elusiveness. Neither is the God who, on the Neoplatonic principles of Hedley's imaginative idealism, is both Plato's ἐπέκεινα τῆς οὐσίας and Augustine's *interior intimo meo*[34] beyond any experience whatsoever nor can the contemplation of the Divine be modelled on sense perception. Unlike sense perception, the credibility and certainty of the divine imagination can be grounded neither in the immediacy by which its alleged analogue is defined nor in the doxastic practice of a religious community of which it is part.[35] Instead, the imaginative grasp of the Deity is an overall experience of the whole of being as such in which man comes to feel the infinite ground of all finite subjective and objective reality. Hedley adopts both William James's definition of religious experience as 'a man's total reaction upon life',[36] whether good and life-affirming or bad and pessimistic, as well as its fourfold description as 'ineffable', 'noetic', 'transient' and 'passive'.[37] Thus, while it transcends all discursive language of which its ineffable intuition is the necessary condition, the experience of the primary imagination nevertheless adds to man's knowledge as a reality far greater than himself acts upon him at moments of visionary insight. It applies both to the vision of the self and the world. Thus, it informs the Neoplatonists' introspection into the infinite depths of the soul imagined as a 'shining sphere' stripped of all of its attributes and thereby gradually revealing the irreducible reality of the transcendent One's creative ubiquity.[38] At the same time, it is also the principle of the Romantics' deeply imaginative vision of nature at large as 'a sacrament of the creative divine mind'.[39] As an intuitive grasp of the infinite prior to every finite act of human intellection and volition, the imagination is, by its very nature, anagogic and dynamic. It strives for the infinite fullness intuited in its aesthetical, theoretical and practical contemplation. Quoting a memorable passage from the French novelist Marcel Proust's *Jean Santeuil*, Hedley views the specifically human power of imaginative transcendence over all temporal and spatial bounds as a yearning 'to feed on the eternal' or as the capability of 'wrenching ourselves free from the slavery of the now, letting ourselves be flooded with the feeling of life everlasting',[40] as the soul struggles to assimilate itself to the fullness of divine being. Again, its closeness to the archetypal infinite 'I am', which it seeks to 'repeat' in its acts of narrative self-fashioning, is key to the happiness of the finite 'I am'. The less it manages to embrace the infinite 'I am' or the universal 'field' or 'wave of consciousness' of which it is part in nature and knowledge alike, the more depressed is its overall 'mood'. Conversely, the more the image comes to embrace its infinite archetype, the greater is its overall enjoyment of life in its entirety.[41]

As the 'consciousness of the world as a whole', the primary imagination, therefore, is as much affective as cognitive in character. The mood stirred in the experience of the whole of mind and nature is one of inevitably religious awe, 'a sense of weal or woe',[42] as the finite human 'I am' cannot but encounter the infinite 'I am' of metaphysics and religion:

> It is the participation and imaginative engagement with the whole that generates the specifically religious aspect. This image of the world as a whole is closely linked to our emotional reactions, a sense of weal or woe. The mind can turn around upon itself. Man is self-consciously in the world and thus aware of the world as an arena of free agency: religion and metaphysics are unavoidable.[43]

It is identical with the irreducible sacred intuited in man's most primordial of experiences, the *mysterium fascinans et tremendum* in Rudolf Otto's celebrated expression.[44] The feeling of wonder evoked by its experience in the world and the self alike is one that both exalts and humbles a rational agent, as she contemplates a sublime reality superior to herself. While intimately linked to human rationality whose transcendental ground it is, its primordial 'hidden depth' defies a clear conceptual definition, rather harrowing man with fear and wonder.[45] In the German original of Otto's classic of the philosophy of religion, the author's newly coined *numinose Gemütsgestimmtheit* upon which Hedley comments in great detail hearkens back to the great tradition of the German mysticism of Meister Eckhart and his pupils. It is meant to express the holistic dimension of the finite human soul's infinite divine ground:

> *Gemüt* is almost impossible to translate: in the German Mystical tradition (with which Otto was deeply familiar) it was the personal-affective core of the human agent. Rather than convey just feeling, '*Gemüt*' is the whole thinking-feeling self, even if it later came to be narrowed down to feeling in opposition to thinking. '*Gestimmtheit*' is cognate with '*Stimmung*' or mood or attunement. We might translate/paraphrase '*numinose Gemütsgestimmtheit*' as the 'affective attunement by the experience of the numinous'.[46]

The finite soul's imaginative grasp of the infinite God for whose fullness it strives in every act of theoretical and practical reasoning is thoroughly symbolic in character. Its pre-discursive vision of the infinite or existential 'attunement' to it is one of symbols pointing to an all-embracing natural and intellectual reality: 'Much of this attunement is pre-theoretical. Symbols ignite emotional energies and powers which are not entirely comprehended. Put in another way, the mind is not a *tabula rasa*: it must be attuned and open to truth before it can properly form true beliefs.'[47] The experience of divine infinity is always mediated through imagery and symbolism, which, as a 'medium between the Literal and the Metaphorical',[48] both reveals and conceals the divine reality at once immanent and transcendent to it. Hedley subscribes to Coleridge's theory of the symbol as 'the translucence of the eternal through and in the temporal', also following the Romantic poet philosopher in viewing the relationship between eternity and time along the conceptual lines of Platonic participation: 'It always partakes of the reality which it renders intelligible; and while it enunciates the whole, abides itself as a living part in that unity of which it is the representative.'[49] As such, a symbol, on Coleridge's Platonic theory, is 'tautegorical', that is, whereas an *allegory*, by definition, means something *different* from what it says prima facie, illustrating something abstract by means of a more graphic narrative, a *tautegorical* symbol is *identical* with the meaning it expresses. While an allegory, therefore, can (and indeed is meant to) be translated into conceptual language, symbolic meaning resists any such attempt at translation. Instead, symbols are, in Hans Blumenberg's parlance, 'absolute metaphors', whose irreducible meaning transcends the conceptual.[50] The inexhaustible semantic fullness of a symbol, which sets it further apart from allegory, may itself be viewed as indicative of its close relationship to the Divine of which it is a mirror: 'The symbol is endlessly fertile and suggestive, whereas the meaning of allegory is rapidly exhausted.'[51]

Like the power of the imagination itself, a symbol is both objective and subjective, as the imagination furnishes the finite individual with insight into the infinity of reality, thereby once again revealing its crucial role in a religious epistemology conceived throughout as 'a middle way between a debilitating scepticism and an idolatrous and credulous superstition'.[52] As the means of participating in the divine 'I am' as the condition of the possibility of its every thought and action, it is, hence, the chief mode of human subjectivity: 'Human self-consciousness is a "participation in reality". This means a subjectivity that is constitutive of human existence and an encounter with objective reality. The ensuing vision is not a fanciful construction but an imaginative response to a transcendent mystery.'[53] The transcendental insight into the infinite absolute expressed in the symbol is one of intuitive immediacy, as the soul grasps its meaning prior to any discursive reasoning of which the symbolic imagination, on the principles of Hedley's imaginative idealism, is itself the transcendental prerequisite: 'It is reasonable to appreciate the grasping of ideas as intuitive (although most analytic philosophers deny this). If one views the grasping of ideas as intuitive, then the symbol provides a medium of intuitive vision.'[54] Hence, while the subsequent rational discourse about the matter symbolized is one of the exchange of arguments in time, it throughout relies on an initial vision provided by the timeless symbolism of the imagination. Consequently, contrary to a prevalent paradigm of interpretation, the wealth of symbols that is mythology, whether pagan, Jewish or Christian, cannot possibly be naturalized or translated into the terminology of science without severe loss in meaning. Man's knowledge, on the contrary, is informed by the original myths of his most primordial epistemic power, the imagination: 'The myth does not proceed from the material fact, but shapes how the psyche experiences the biological, historical or material facts. It is not history that determines the mythology of a people, but the mythology which determines the history.'[55] Hence, all sciences and all humanities are narratives themselves, structured throughout by the mythology of the creative imagination: 'Philosophy, history and science are themselves narratives in a strong sense – knowledge is invention (or imagination) rather than discovery.'[56] Since the imagination, moreover, is the 'the prime agent of all human perception', encompassing in itself all the soul's powers as their unifying hegemonic principle, its myths give form and shape not only to the highest of the attainments of human ingenuity but also to the depths of the human psyche. Hence, Hedley follows C. G. Jung in positing imaginative 'archetypes' that inform the deepest layers of the soul's inner life. The unconscious archetype is not part of the dark id of Freudian psychoanalysis, which Jung, drawing upon the rich Romantic legacy from Creuzer to Schelling, subjects to astute criticism, but a person's innermost temple in which she shares communion with the divine principle of her very being: 'Rather than a crude primitive and infantile legacy which should be overcome, this is the holy place or sanctum of the soul, part of the Promethean fire.'[57]

The reality of the beautiful, the true and the good has assumed a plethora of visible forms and shapes in the course of the history of art, whether secular or sacred. Likened to concepts as diverse as Plato's and Plotinus's 'ideas' in the divine intellect, G. Vico's 'imaginative universals' and C. G. Jung's 'archetypes', which shape and inform our every experience,[58] it is, above all, in three deeply ecumenical symbols or poetical-philosophical universals common to humankind's many cultures and religions that man's defining power has found its expression, namely the chariot, the temple and the city of God.

3 The three ecumenical symbols: The ancient theology of the iconic imagination

3.1 Imagery of human triumph: The chariot and the soul's ascent

The first of the three perennial symbols of the religious imagination, the chariot of the soul soaring to the heights of divine contemplation and action, expresses the transcendence of the soul in its striving for scientific truth, moral goodness and the beauty of nature and art. It provides the core of an anthropology of man as a being of imaginative transcendence as well as a rational theology of a God who is identical with the idea of the beautiful, the true and the good beyond and within a cosmos created in his image and likeness.

In Indian, Hebrew and Greek thought, that is, in the *Upanishads*, in Parmenides's *On Nature* and, above all, Plato's Phaedrus, respectively, as well as in the Old and New Testament revelations of the prophets Ezekiel and John of Patmos, the chariot symbolizes the human condition in its yearning for a Divine that is both near and elusive.[59] As a paean of praise of perennial power extolling the 'madness of the Muses',[60] by which man may advance beyond the confines of the visible temporal world, the symbol of the chariot illustrates the Platonic 'conviction that there is a surplus of ultimate meaning that transcends any attempt to express it: the Good is "beyond being". There is an *experiential* if not definitional knowledge.'[61] Its core message is both theological and anthropological, revolving around beauty, truth and goodness as the three objects of the 'experiential knowledge' of the intuitive or imaginative kind in which the soul encounters the Divine in its ascent to the highest realms of reality. Its theology is that of a God who, as the epitome of beauty, truth and goodness, calls on the soul to worship him in art, science and morality in a cosmos created in his own image and likeness. His being is a source of the highest of intuitive insights into the whole of reality. Like mathematical truths which it is called upon to contemplate in preparation for the highest ontological realms of the principles and ideas, the beautiful, the true and the good are such that the soul cannot possibly refrain from giving assent to them when intuiting them. Theirs, therefore, is a sui generis normative quality which, seen by the 'eye of understanding', is the transcendental prerequisite of all subsequent aesthetic, scientific and ethical discourse.[62] The myth's notion of man is that of a restless dynamic as the charioteer or intellect, moved by the beauty of the transient visible world, seeks to steer his vehicle with its obedient horse or courage and the recalcitrant one of desire towards the realm of divine eternity. Human identity is not static, but constantly forged in the approximation to the divine archetype. While 'ratiocentric' in its ideal of the intellect's control over the unruly passions, the soul of the archetypal Phaedrean imagination is also one characterized by the 'responsiveness to the rhythms of the whole self', which the charioteer is at pains to guide towards the heavens alongside its obedient volitional part.[63]

Of the three objects of experiential knowledge by which the finite I am, obeying God's bidding and realizing its vocation, ascends to the latter's infinite subjectivity, the experience of beauty is the first to instil in it the yearning for the Phaedrean Deity. Not surprisingly, the beauty of nature has always been one of the chief sources of religious poetry of which Plato's *Phaedrus* is itself a key example: 'One of the great expressions of Plato's religious imagination is the *Phaedrus*. Beauty can awaken the soul to its true destiny because of its intense experiential power.'[64] The heavenly ideas which the soul seeks to contemplate are the unitary archetypes of the earthly phenomena to which each ectypal image points. As is testified by nature poetry from the Psalms to the Romantics, the beauty of nature is such that it can inspire in the soul 'a transcendental mood which grasps the unity which precedes and transcends the conceptual structures of the world of the primary imagination'.[65] Nature has always had the power of inducing contemplative awe. It is celebrated in the biblical Psalms which, Coleridge averred, 'afford a most complete answer to those who state the Jehovah of the Jews, as a personal and national God and the Jews, as differing from the Greeks only in calling the minor Gods Cherubim and Seraphim and confining the word God to their Jupiter'.[66] Both the Hebrew and the English poets reveal 'a sense of the immanent presence of God in the cosmos, the theophanic dimension'.[67] Nor is it by accident that the great New Testament seer John, like the Old Testament prophet Ezekiel, is granted his vision of a new Jerusalem on 'a great high mountain'.[68] Nature itself is God's own dwelling-place, his icon, by which the human imagination perceives his ubiquitous creative and salvific presence. In cosmic anamnesis, nature itself calls upon man to return to God, its creator. The aesthetic mood stirred by the contemplation of the beauty of nature is not a mere subjective mood alone, but a perception of the original truth of creation as an image of its creator's consummate mind. Reminding man of his divine vocation, beauty, Hedley avers, is neither extraneous to nor merely supervenient upon reality, but, on the contrary, one of its irreducible characteristics. As the first mode of our experience, the beautiful in fact discloses to us 'the ultimate facts of the universe perceived in their intrinsic value'.[69]

In the symbolistic ontology and epistemology of the trilogy, the Phaedrean striving is revealed to be at work in science itself. Only by providing an overall system of which each single piece of information is an essential part do the plethora of facts collected in empirical observation and research become intelligible scientific truth. Far from bearing out the claims of contemporary materialistic metaphysics, modern science itself is, therefore, shown to testify to the necessary truth of the ancient theology of Plato's dialogue. A crude empiricism like eliminative materialism finds itself in a hopeless quandary in the face of the indispensable imaginative dimension of our experience of reality as such. Hedley's anti-materialist argument is that of the ancient academy's time-honoured σώζειν τὰ φαινόμενα, which serves as a yardstick of philosophical systems old and new: 'Strictly the paradox is that of empiricism – that it cannot do justice to experiences, imagination being required in order to "save the appearances".'[70] Among 'the appearances' which, paradoxically enough, materialism, for all its scientific pretensions, fails to 'save' is that of truth itself which defies an explanation in terms of cerebral processes alone, however complex.[71] On Leibniz's definition of the identity of indiscernibles, brain processes and scientific thought should equally share a spatial locality and the predicates of truth and falsity, which clearly they do not. Rather, modern science itself is an extraordinary attainment of the creative imagination, relying as it does throughout upon entities that, on closer inspection, prove to be mental rather than physical in character. Hedley's argument relies on mathematics as the cornerstone of modern physics:

> But if we have reasons for positing mathematic entities, why should the mental not be admitted into the furniture of the universe? After all, the matter that the common-sense, no-nonsense materialist invokes looks increasingly puzzling (and immaterial!) once science gets to the level of electrons, quarks and gluons and the solid objects of the world evaporate into the paradoxical behaviour of quantum components.[72]

Likewise, the powerful imagery in which pioneering scientists like Albert Einstein, August Kekulé and Dmitri Mendeléev expressed their momentous theories[73] points to a 'powerful link between imaginability and intelligibility'[74] which belies any clear opposition between the creative imagination and the scientific intellect. This intimate connection has far-reaching ontological implications. It points to a fundamental isomorphy between the intellectual and the real which we cannot but imagine to be in fundamental agreement with one another. It seems rather counter-intuitive to assume that a mind such as man's with its singular ability to gain a systematic understanding of the cosmos and its laws should emerge from a dysteleological process of natural selection either wholly indifferent or even hostile to it: 'It is difficult for us to imagine a world which radically rebuffs our attempts to find order and meaning in it.'[75] Instead, the remarkable fact of the world's intelligibility, as mirrored in man's iconic intellect, points to a divine agreement between mind and matter:

> But it is much harder to accept that an interest in *abstract* truth emerges through the bleak and harsh sieve of natural selection. Is it not far-fetched to connect the concern with theoretical knowledge characteristic of human science with the kind of adaptive modification evinced in the giraffe's neck? The astonishing capacity of human beings to imagine hidden structures of being, to observe laws and patterns in observable phenomena, suggests that the world is providentially susceptible to systematic intellectual inventions of the finite mind.[76]

In response to the twin spectres of materialism and nominalism, which he rejects as undermining the concept of scientific truth, Hedley, therefore, defends a robust realism in the vein of Plato's doctrine of the first principles of the one and the many and the intelligible realm of the ideas mediating between them and the visible world.[77] Its starting point is the experience of manifold patterns of identity and regularity amidst the diversity and difference of the world around us of which we seek to provide true descriptions in contemporary science. While of Plato's five 'greatest kinds' *difference* appears to be the first category of observable *being* in its prima facie bewildering variety, all scientific research must assume the *identity* of the laws it postulates. Starting with a *uni*verse as an entity that is, by definition, one, rather than many, scientific explanation, in other words, requires a unity *static* and identical to itself and exempt from all *motion* and change whatsoever: 'Science operates with fundamental constants that remain identical throughout time and space (for example, the atomic mass of oxygen). We presuppose uniformity in order to explain the universe, a fact that is puzzling when we assume that the cosmos is a radical plurality.'[78] As well as embracing the two first Platonic principles, the one and the many, and the five 'greatest kinds' of being, identity and difference, rest and motion, Hedley also subscribes to the doctrine of ideas. A scientific epistemology of 'universal predication', viewed as the transcendental sine qua non of all empirical research, is best viewed as being rooted in an ontology of immutable intelligible concepts. Plato's ideas, however, must not be misunderstood as either universals or objects. They are not reified abstractions in a distinct ontological realm. Instead, Hedley, for one thing, follows the Middle Platonic interpretation of Plato's doctrine subsequently adopted by Philo the Jew and the early Alexandrian Church Fathers in placing the ideas in the mind of God. In a middle position between whole-scale dogmatism and universal scepticism, Hedley, thus, distinguishes between an objective divine truth always aspired to, yet never fully reached, in universal scientific predication and our imperfect striving for it: 'With his framework we can combine both realism and scepticism. With regard to the Divine mind, it is clear that we do not have ready access to its "contents"! With regard to universals in the physical world, we can adjudicate the relevant scientific considerations.'[79] An example of the consummate divine intellect's thoughts approximated by the natural sciences is the biological concept of a species. Humanity itself, despite controversies regarding its demarcation, say, from higher apes, is an example of a scientific abstraction which we tend to regard as an objective fact, rather than a mere name of subjective agreement among representatives of one discipline of modern science: 'It is part of the warp and woof of Platonic metaphysics', concludes Hedley, 'to envisage the physical cosmos as exhibiting *patterns* which are exemplified in individuals. Such patterns are repeatable and form the basis of laws, and thus predictions. These law-like regularities are so deeply entrenched that it is implausible to view them in the nominalist mode as conventions.'[80] To the approximation in subjective *knowledge*, significantly, corresponds that in objective *being*. The said biological concept describes a law-guided development as the evolution of a species which, for all its apparent dysteleology consequent upon the Darwinian principle of natural selection, must, on the underlying convictions of Hedley's Platonism, be viewed as both flowing from and aspiring to its respective divine archetypal idea.[81] The whole of the cosmos, therefore, is an image of its divine archetype to which its lawlike patterns, as established in scientific research, bear testimony: 'The physical cosmos is the mirror of the Divine: a theophany. This world is a luminous array of images reflecting (although often enigmatically) the perfect being of the Divine.'[82] Moreover, while the *multiplicity* of the ideas of the divine intellect is the ground of manifold scientific laws governing the processes of life and nature, their essential *simplicity* provides the principle of the cosmos as a single lawlike entity whose truth can be described with an ever-higher degree of objective truth in the plethora of the natural sciences and humanities: 'It is simplicity – the One *in* the many – that forms the precondition of any form of explanation. How can a world that is merely a receptacle of numerically separate and unrelated individuals be an object of scientific inquiry?'[83] Indeed, it is this scientific quest for the one identical law in the many different phenomena both in an individual scientific discipline and in a universal theory of everything that has borne testimony to humankind's Phaedrean striving since its very dawn in prehistoric time. 'Elegance' and 'simplicity' required of a modern theory testify to the intimate link between the beautiful and the true in the scientific imagination of the Homo sapiens sapiens: 'It is through the employment of theories of elegance and simplicity that the turbid, eerie and menacing environment of our hunter-gather ancestors became the intelligible and predictable domain of modern science.'[84] The 'elegance' and 'simplicity' sought for in scientific hypotheses mirrors God as the living archetype of the cosmos, his image, whose truth and beauty are modes whereby he converses with man.

Not only does materialism rule out scientific truth, reducing it, implausibly, to mere brain processes in the subject and accidental patterns in the world around it, but it also undermines both goodness and moral and political duty: 'The normative quality of beliefs about goodness, truth or beauty', Hedley criticizes the prevalent paradigm, 'is very puzzling from a naturalistic perspective. There is a significant asymmetry between the prediction of natural objects and reasoning about persons. How can science describe the process by which one judges an act reasonable or polite? Yet society clearly depends upon the existence of binding norms of behaviour.'[85] To the Phaedrean ascent in beauty and truth, therefore, corresponds that in the good. The archetypal myth of the chariot of the soul can be seen to inform an ethical idealism whose categorical imperative, as is shown with regard to Plato's late antique, early modern and Enlightenment successors Plotinus, Ralph Cudworth and Immanuel Kant, is the gradual realization of the soul's higher part in the ever-growing participation in divine goodness. Not only is the unmeasurable width opened up by the imagination the sine qua non of freedom which cannot be conceived of in terms of stimulus and response alone, but also proof of the human person's divine vocation:

> The creativity and freedom that is definitive for human life points to the ultimate question, which is why is there something rather than nothing: God's own self-diffusive, creative love. Imagination, I argue, is the index of humanity made in the image of God. Better to think human consciousness as inherently creative processing of the environment. Imagination is the mind's freedom from stimulus; this freedom is linked to a vocation for a soul, and the calling of the soul is linked to its image.[86]

In contradistinction to empiricist ethical theories, notably utilitarianism and neo-Aristotelian communitarianism, which Hedley subjects to thorough philosophical criticism,[87] the ethical paradigm of the Phaedrean chariot revolves around a rational 'true self'[88] beyond the restraints of physical causality, including those of biology and economy. Ever since Socrates's celebrated account of his second sea voyage in the *Phaedo*, in which Plato's teacher, on the eve of his execution, insists upon his rational insight into the good and the intelligible, rather than his biological make-up as the cause of his philosophical martyrdom,[89] moral agency has withstood every attempt at naturalization with particular tenacity. While there is no denying man's evolutionary origin in the animal kingdom, any naturalistic account of human virtue and vice in terms of his animal characteristics must inevitably fail to express any moral and judicial notion such as 'murder'. The idea, for instance, that, as has been claimed, 'murder comes naturally to chimpanzees'[90] is exposed as an 'instance of egregious anthropomorphism'.[91] For one thing, there is no correspondence in chimpanzee behaviour to the defining characteristics of the concept of that felony such as the perpetrator's malice and lower motives. For another, the analogy is generally ill-defined in terms of evolutionary biology. Instead, man, as Hedley argues in a strictly metaphysical, rather than functionalist secular or positivistic Christological reading of the biblical creation of humankind 'in the divine image' (Gn. 1.26), is a rational agent capable of moral action beyond the fetters of natural necessity. His supernatural agency is linked to his capability of practical reasoning about means and ends, expressed in discursive language: 'Removed from the normal causal nexus involving all other animals, human beings are language users, free agents and able to contemplate ultimate ends as well as proximate means. We have a traditional language in the West for this – the "image of God".'[92] Following Hans Jonas, Hedley attributes to man 'the freedom of image-making',[93] which, defined as his unique ability to 'represent entities and events through the mind's eye'[94] at will, enables him to transcend the immediate perception of his environment of which, paradoxically, he is and is not a part at the same time and from whose laws, therefore, he is exempt in principle.[95] By virtue of his imagination, which is capable of factual as well as counterfactual 'image-making', man is not slave to either his perceptions or his passions, but literally at liberty to invoke images conducive to laudable actions. Man is, therefore, called upon to foster his capacity for moral 'image-making', thereby gradually climbing the rungs of the ladder of images of divine goodness, which Hedley views as the very core of archetypal human freedom: 'The believer legitimately starts with accessible images like the shepherd or the teacher and gradually evolves towards more spiritual likeness of the transcendent Godhead. What does freedom consist in? It is the seeing, interpreting, and pressing into service of images.'[96] His field of imaginative vision which is the condition of the possibility of man's libertarian action as a rational being is, therefore, not an indifferent power beyond good and evil. On the contrary, it must be likened to or identified with a stance of disinterested universal goodness, according to which we have both the duty and the ability to transcend our petty egotistic and communitarian and tribal motives. For one thing, the imagination is the obvious sine qua non of every altruistic action, as it is imperative that we adopt a fellow human being's stance in moral reasoning and action. Hence, the imagination of Hedley's Platonism, contrary to Descartes's *cogito*, is throughout conceived of as a deeply social faculty of the soul in which empathy is grounded. For another, it is the imagination which provides man with the perspective of universal and objective goodness so crucial to ethics. Translating the rich myth of Plato's *Phaedrus* into ethics, Hedley concurs with Kant and Plato in positing a timeless intelligible subject to which the former's categorical imperative and the latter's ὁμοίοις τῷ θεῷ bear testimony no less impressively than the tragic heroes created by the philosopher poet Shakespeare:

Kant and Plato present an essentially imaginative picture of human vocation. Life is a drama in which each individual has a choice of rising or descending. The ascent may not be as dramatic as the depiction in Plato's *Phaedrus* or the descent as grim as Shakespeare's tragic heroes, yet I cannot see how any approach which does not consider the imaginative dimension of human thought will be very useful in ethics. We possess certain ideals and aspirations which are irreducible to instinct and embedded in an organic history and culture.[97]

According to Hedley, Kant's *homo noumenon*, whom the divine calling of the categorical imperative elevates above nature, is an offspring of Plato's charioteer and Plotinus's undescended 'true self'.[98] Hedley's is a strictly libertarian concept of freedom. By virtue of the imaginative effort of moral reasoning, man is exempt from the constraints of necessary physical laws. While recognizing their causal power, we generally dismiss a naturalistic perspective of an agent's upbringing and environment as necessitating her course of actions of which we approve or disapprove in everyday moral praise and blame. Instead, we cannot choose but adopt the Phaedrean perspective of the soul as a moral agent who *can* transcend nature and nurture alike because she *ought* to. As is clear from the Kantian point of departure of Hedley's libertarianism, the notion of *free* action is essentially that of *moral* action. The infinite 'I am' in which the finite 'I am' participates in the practical reasoning of its theophanic imagination is not morally indifferent, but it is the 'highest good' or 'kingdom of ends' gradually brought about by the combined effort of all rational agents at every place and at every time. In its ethical application, the Phaedrean doctrine of the soul originating in Plato's and Plotinus's concept of the ὁμοίωσις τῷ θεῷ and culminating in Kant's categorical imperative requires a moral agent to disregard her own interests as well as those of her kin and kind in a perspective of disinterested universality:

> The defining component of the human moral agent lies in the capacity of being *more* than the sum of instincts, needs and society – the capacity to act out of reverence for the moral law and not merely in accordance with it. Hence Kant's concept of 'heteronomy' is not so much an absurdly rigoristic dismissal of altruistic behaviour towards friends and family per se but the rejection of ethical naturalism. Kant is attacking the *restriction* of ethical behaviour to those 'nearest and dearest': a restriction which is implied in any theory of ethics (like Hume's) based on sympathy. Autonomy proper means the ability to treat others as ends in themselves without external social pressures or instinctual propensity.[99]

Not only, therefore, does Kant's categorical imperative of the absolute end of universal respect for the humanity in our and every other person disclose to us the moral course of *action*, but, more importantly, our Phaedrean *being* of transcendence.[100] It is by subordinating all of our many personal concerns and prudential considerations to the one moral ideal of the highest good of the kingdom of ends that our finite selves come to acquire a character of moral unity akin to the infinite fullness of archetypal goodness of which they are imperfect images. Kantian ethics is, thus, revealed as another Phaedrean narrative of the self in the ancient theology of man's divine vocation: 'TheZagent who takes a merely prudential interest in his or her own affairs – health and fitness, savings, pensions – is a long way from being a properly moral agent but is acting as if life is a series of merely successive moments rather than a deeper unity.'[101]

However, while being a creature of Phaedrean transcendence and unity, man's experience of the world is one of overwhelming disunity and chaos which cannot but prove a formidable intellectual as well as existential challenge to his iconic imagination. If the whole of being originates in an infinite cause defined as supreme beauty, truth and goodness, why do the many slings and arrows of outrageous fortune to which the human condition is inevitably subject appear to belie the soul's noble origin and destiny in the Divine? It is the second of the three tautegorical symbols, that is, that of the Jerusalem Temple, which mediates between the heavenly ideal of the soul's triumph and ascent and the earthly reality of its tragic descent and fall.

3.2 Symbols of the tragic: The Jerusalem Temple, Christ's death on the Cross and the drama of fall and salvation

The temple, the leitmotif of the second volume entitled *Sacrifice Imagined*,[102] is the archetypal place where the profane, as is evidenced by the etymology of the eponymous term (*sacrum facere*), is 'made holy' in sacrifice, thereby rendering visible the hope for salvation in a fallen world:

> The Jerusalem Temple is the symbolic meeting point of the terrestrial and the spiritual, the material and the heavenly. It is a vision of heaven and image of longing and hope in the midst of suffering and doubt and in a world that seems to exhibit so much cruelty and discord. It is an image of that transcendent beauty that Dostoevsky maintains will save the world.[103]

One of the three foremost imaginative universals, the religious notion of sacrifice is crucial to man as the being of an amphibious imagination that enables him to transcend egotistic subjective necessity in favour of the objective fullness of divine freedom in self-sacrificial theoretical and practical reasoning. Both the symbol itself and the transcendental structure of imaginative subjectivity that it stands for reveal the world to be the stage for the whole of humanity's tragic, yet eventually successful, soul-making overseen and guided by a benign Deity.

Sacred buildings are visible embodiments of the invisible Divine in stone and architecture meant to testify to 'the goodness of existence'.[104] Since the prehistoric origins of humankind, temples have been works of craft and ingenuity that evidence the distinctly human power of the imagination in its defining twofold role expressed by the term itself. Both the English word and its Greek equivalent ποίησις denote necessary drudgery and free creativity as the specific characteristics of the Homo sapiens sapiens. It is the imaginative transformation of its hostile environment in life-sustaining toil which heralds the advent of humankind as a sui generis species in the course of evolution history: 'The shift from the hunter-gatherer society to more advanced civilization has been a poetic activity: a making or shaping of the environment.'[105]

Growing more and more complex, humankind's 'poetic activity' bears testimony to its defining 'creative *nisus* towards unity' in forging more complex meaning: 'The transformation of nature into a habitable world, into towns, agriculture, commerce, etc., is also the conferring of order and meaning. It is derived from a deep need to find meaning and this is connected to the imagination.'[106] Among the first products of the newly born race's poetic imagination is the sacred building of Gobekli Tepe excavated in south-eastern Turkey. It is an awe-inspiring monument of our first forebears' original imaginative inklings of the Divine both around and beyond them: 'One can imagine hunter-gatherers driven by a primordial sense of the sacred, the *mysterium tremendum et fascinans*, and thus seeking and constructing a place of worship. Six millennia older than Stonehenge, Gobekli Tepe is an imposing construction with theriomorphic designs carved into the monumental pillars.'[107] In the midst of the temple, its holy of holies, dwells God himself whom the Old Testament prophet Isaiah, according to R. Otto's seminal interpretation, experiences as the sublime itself, being 'humbled' and 'exalted' at the same time. The purification of his lips stands for the gap between the ordinary human and sublime divine realms of being: 'The prophet is aware of his own unworthiness in the Temple. The idea of purification of the lips of Isaiah is emphasized by Otto in his use of the prophet's encounter with God.'[108]

Countering modern misgivings about the allegedly archaic cruelty which it supposedly extols, Hedley sets out to rehabilitate the much-maligned religious concept of sacrifice. To this end, the author takes issue with the seminal accounts of religious sacrifice by Walter Burkert and René Girard which trace this primordial rite of the temple imagination back to the violence at the advent of human nature and culture, respectively. Burkert's is a naturalistic account of sacrificial killing which is explained as a ritual re-enacting of the early human hunter-gatherers' ambivalent feelings involved in the hunt, that is, the original excitement and the subsequent guilt over the animal's blood spilt and its food consumed. The ritual, therefore, continues closely to mirror the three stages of our first forebears' experience of archaic hunting, that is, 'killing, sharing and penitence'.[109] At the heart of Girard's alternative account of sacrifice, which is literary rather than biological and ethological in origin, are the concepts of 'mimetic desire' and 'mimetic double' whereby human beings, inevitably driven by violence, engage in acts of violence. Only by unleashing their aggression upon a scapegoat victim, rather than upon one another, can the rivals preserve the social bond that unites them in society. Drawing upon literature, both classical and contemporary, Girard seeks to reveal the wanton violence against an innocent object of man's uncontrollable wrath as the thinly veiled core of the religious rite: 'Religion is a complex attempt to obscure the terrible truth of victimization at the root of human culture, sacrificial ritual the inadequate attempt to resolve the problem of violence at the root of all human relations, and myth is a language of concealment.'[110] According to Hedley, neither account does justice to the imaginative depths of the archetypal tautegory of the temple symbol. Drawing upon the 'On Sacrifices in General' by the infamous Roman Catholic counter-Enlightenment thinker Joseph de Maistre, Hedley instead views substitution by which sinful humanity, in pagan, Jewish and Christian ritual, is cleansed of its trespasses and 'made holy' according to the term's etymology as the defining characteristic of sacrifice.[111] Key to the author's own concept of sacrifice imagined is the typological relationship between the pagan rites and the Old Testament temple on the one hand and the New Testament Cross on the other. It is the latter, seen 'in a mirror, darkly' in the former, which discloses the whole meaning of religious sacrifice. The New Testament antitype of the Son's death on the Cross, as disclosed in Philippians and Hebrews, can be seen neither as a re-enacting of the natural urges of prehistoric humanity, as in Burkert, nor as a religious concealment of the mimetic violence at the origins of society, as in Girard. Instead, it is a revelation of self-sacrificial goodness as the principle and purpose of all reality. The Son who acts both as the priest and the lamb is neither worthless prey nor a ritual scapegoat, but the embodiment of the ideal of self-sacrificial love by which the cosmos is redeemed. Hence, sacrifice, reimagined by Hedley in the original terms of Pauline theology, stands not for violence, but 'renunciation' for the sake of the many:

> The key to sacrifice is not the scapegoat but, rather, renunciation. The making holy of sacrifice is expressed in the hymn of *Philippians* 2:7 and the kenotic theology therein. Christ is, as *Hebrews* 9:14 puts it, both priest and victim. The point is not that Christianity perceives reality for the first time from the perspective of the victim, but that Christians have in Christ not merely a substitute (not I but Christ in me) but also a pattern. This pattern of self-sacrificial love is neither reciprocal altruism nor scapegoating. Not the scapegoat but renunciation is the true sacrifice.[112]

'Renunciation' as the core meaning of the archetypal temple symbol informs all acts of human reasoning, notably the aesthetic response to the infinity intuited by the imagination, but also moral volition and action and all theoretical intellection, whether scientific or metaphysical. To the beautiful expressed by the archetypal Phaedrean experience corresponds the sublime both admired and dreaded in the temple experience. In philosophical aesthetics, the experience of the sublime, as defined by Pseudo-Longinus in Late Antiquity and Edmund Burke and Immanuel Kant in the Enlightenment, is one in which the individual is humbled by a phenomenon of extraordinary magnitude: 'The sublime is traditionally an experience of boundless grandeur and immensity of nature, at once conveying danger and inspiring awe or worship: an experience with evidently religious implications.'[113] The concept is applied to man's awe-inspiring capability of transcending the whole universe in his longing for knowledge, an experience which Burke went on to describe in terms of 'terror and pain' and which Kant traced back to our 'humanity' or intelligible self. While inferior to infinite nature in his *phenomenonal* or corporeal reality which the latter can undeniably annihilate in an instant, man is superior to it in his *noumenal* or incorporeal 'personality' which provides the condition of the possibility of the infinite perceived, even proving its better in holding on to its superior moral designs:

> Thus humanity in our person remains unhumiliated, though the individual might have to submit to this dominion. In this way nature is not judged to be sublime in our aesthetical judgements in so far as it excites fear, but because it calls up that power in us (which is not nature) of regarding as small the things of life

about which we are solicitous (goods, health, and life) and of regarding its might (to which we are no doubt subjected in respect of these things) as nevertheless without any dominion over us and our personality to which we must bow where our highest fundamental propositions, and their assertion or abandonment, are concerned.[114]

The awakening of the higher self effected by the experience of the sublime witnesses to the deep elective affinity that links Kant with Plato. It is an imaginative ἀνάμνησις by which man inevitably comes to grasp his higher causality as a supernatural rational agent unbound by the shackles of his corporeal nature in him and around him: 'The sublime represents for Kant transcendence over those sensuous components that constitute mankind as a causally determined part of nature.'[115] The supernatural self and the higher order of things in which it participates is also stirred in man's response to tragedy which likewise is defined by a peculiar ambivalence of pleasure and revulsion. Not only does classical Attic tragedy abound in dramatic depictions of sacrifices such as those of the eponymous heroes of Euripides's *Iphigenia in Aulis* and Aeschylus's *Agamemnon*,[116] but its paradoxical appeal is bound to prove an inexplicable conundrum on the principles of a sombre vitalism of the will like Arthur Schopenhauer's or a modern naturalism of man and world as a mere interaction of matter particles along the lines of Richard Dawkins. Why should our insight into the absurd grimness of a cosmos wholly indifferent or inimical to our concerns, whether it is that of Schopenhauer's *Will and Representation*[117] or that of Dawkins's *Selfish Gene*,[118] be a source of aesthetic pleasure to us? Instead, the metaphysics of Greek tragedy[119] is that of an intelligible reality of elevating and humbling sublimity. The experience of Greek tragedy is deeply religious in character, as its most celebrated protagonists such as Antigone, Orestes and Oedipus are faced with the sublime power of 'the unconditional and normative nature of the ethical'.[120] The duty to bury one's own brother, which must be obeyed even at the cost of one's own life, is an objective reality, as is the guilt of matricide and incest, even if perpetrated for justifiable moral reasons or in ignorance.

It is the aesthetics or the imagination of the sublime that can, therefore, also be seen to inform theoretical and practical reason alike. In science, it is imperative that research be carried out in a spirit of objectivity that requires the sacrifice of one's own subjective biases and interests for the greater good of the progress of knowledge. In ethics, the temple, far from being a religious remnant of a bygone era of archaic violence designed to appease an angry God, stands for the self-sacrifice of the lower empirical self for the sake of the higher intelligible 'humanity' or 'personality' that is the chief end of Kant's categorical imperative. The higher vantage point at which the transient individual 'I am' with all its many private concerns and interests is made to vanish for the sake of the one moral ideal of the eternal and universal 'I am' or its true self is likened to the Platonic notion of philosophy as a 'practice of death' (μελέτη θανάτου) wrought by an agent's moral imagination.[121] Its analogue in both Christianity and Buddhism is the injunction that 'the man must die to an unreal life before he can be born into the real life'.[122] Despite the sacrifice required in giving up all private concerns, man's true life is not that of the body or the *homo phaenomenon*, but that of the immortal soul or the eternal *homo noumenon*, as experienced in the vision of the sublime good in

Plato's and Kant's metaphysics of morals. Only by conforming to the objective value of disinterested universality can the finite subject gain a personality in the strict 'Platonic-Kantian' sense of the supernatural term. In the words of the Cambridge Platonist Ralph Cudworth, who anticipates Kant's notion of a rational agent's autonomy in following the 'internal ought', obedience to the timeless 'true self' is 'true freedom': 'Freedom is defined by Cudworth axiologically. Ultimately, it is moral control of one's self. We are properly "a law unto ourselves". The decisive fact about ethical obligation is its intrinsic nature. To act ethically is to be true to ourselves and to be properly autonomous.'[123] In its commitment to infinite goodness, man's 'true self' ultimately is identical with the divine ground of his soul or, in Cudworth's Origenist critique of Plotinus, the humble Christ in us:

> Origen is preferable for Cudworth because in the term 'hegemonikon' he can insist upon both what is right and wrong with the Plotinian view. Within Christianity Christ is the true 'self'. One of Origen's favourite biblical texts is John 1.26, about the dwelling of Christ among the people. In a piece of exegesis as brilliant as counterintuitive, Origen reads the 'in the midst' announced by John the Baptist to mean in the interior man. For Origen, this is Christ as the hegemonikon of the soul: the ruling principle.[124]

Hence, the 'true self' conceived along the conceptual lines of the temple symbolism which shaped both Cudworth's and Kant's reading of Plato's 'practice of death' is one of sincere humility.[125] Again, the philosophic insight into the nature of the moral agent, as expressed by the symbol of the temple, finds rich confirmation in poetry, notably William Shakespeare's view of man as 'such stuff/As dreams are made on' (*The Tempest* 4.1.156–157) or as 'a poor player/That struts and frets his hour upon the stage, / And then is heard no more' (*Macbeth* 5.5.24–25)[126] and in Friedrich Schiller's Kantian paean to the soul taking upon itself the self-sacrifice of the noumenal ideal:

> But free from the ravages of time,
> ....
> Would'st thou freely soar on her wings on high,
> Throw off earthly dread,
> Flee from narrow, stifling life
> Into the realm of the ideal.[127]

The heavenly 'realm of the ideal' to which the earthly reality of the self is sacrificed is deeply social in character, as the temple is also shown to underlie our social bonds as an indispensable prerequisite. Thus, the temple cleansings represent a 'longing for expiation', which must be viewed as 'a deep and legitimate need' as well as 'a sign of a sophisticated and refined moral sensibility'.[128] Moreover, they express a specifically human capacity irrevocably lost in reductive naturalism: 'The concept of forgiveness also shows the metaphysical inadequacy of naturalism in dealing with ethical questions and the theological frontiers of ethics. Could animals forgive? The answer is clearly no. The capacity to forgive presupposes a uniquely human (or Divine) responsibility and rationality.'[129] Likewise, G. W. F. Hegel's *Phenomenology of Spirit* may be read as a succession of stages of self-sacrifice by which man comes to acquire subjectivity by surrendering (or renouncing) his individuality in universal virtue. Man has to give up his own initial absoluteness both in recognizing others for the confirmation of his own truth claims in interpersonal dialogue and to find self-expression in his work and labour. It is, hence, the other, both personal and impersonal, that at once limits and delimits human self-consciousness to which the self-sacrifice in recognizing it is key. Hence, human subjectivity is, by its very nature, self-sacrificial: 'Self-conscious spirit is the continual sacrifice and restoration of identity through resistance and recognition.'[130] As such, self-sacrificial intersubjectivity is at the core of all political community. The temple is a moral as well as a social and political symbol. Not only does Hobbesian egotism or its more refined Spinozist version of the *conatus* fall short of man's self-sacrificial humanity as his higher self, but both early modern philosophers, contrary to their Cambridge Platonist critics Ralph Cudworth and Henry More, fail to provide a satisfactory foundation for human community.[131] According to Hedley's imaginative idealism, it is not a contract entered into for the purpose of mere self-preservation and self-interest, but the capacity for imaginative self-sacrifice in the self-fashioning of human subjectivity and in disinterested ethical and political reasoning that is key to the flourishing of both state and society, which are both endowed with a providential role in Hedley's symbolistic political philosophy. Since the Son, in Christianity, is both the priest and the victim, his self-sacrifice on the Cross spells the end of all violence as the foundation of human society. Instead of the imperative of self-preservation as the motor of the evolutionary survival of the fittest, it is sacrificial love which literally sanctifies humankind amidst its struggle: 'We are the products of an evolutionary process in which strife and conflict plays a central role. Loss, suffering, and painful toil constitute the stuff and substance of conscious human existence.'[132] In Hedley's imaginative political philosophy, self-sacrifice, therefore, replaces alternative accounts of political obligation such as enlightened self-interest and a contract for a future state's citizens' mutual benefit: 'If the Lamb has been slain from the foundation of the world, one can infer that self-sacrifice is properly the foundation of society.'[133]

Hedley's Christological view of history as salvation history is informed by this archetypal image, that is, the Old Testament type of the temple and its New Testament antitype, the Lamb crucified. Anthropologically, the narrative of the Cross enshrines the depth of human nature which has always defied attempts at a definition in merely biological or physical terms. It is, in Tillich's terms, the 'depth of sacrifice, of suffering, and of the Cross',[134] which discloses the greatness of the human soul as it seeks to embrace the Divine even at the nadirs of abject and tragic failure. Theologically, the Cross is the unshakeable foundation of Hedley's ontology of salvation. Christ, on the principles of his idealism of the symbolic imagination, is the chief metaphor or 'living form' of God. Being, according to the Nicene Creed, 'of one substance with the Father', the Son reveals the most perfect being to be one of self-diffusive love, rather than stern und unforgiving will and omnipotence: 'If that doctrine and life is a mirror into the Divine nature, which Christians wish to maintain with the *homoousios*, then perhaps the teaching and life of the Galilean Rabbi reveals the Divine essence and not the arbitrary will of a cosmic demiurge.'[135] His Cross, interpreted by the four evangelists in the imagery of the Jerusalem Temple, is a symbol of the Father's works of creation and salvation alike. As the apogee of the historical development of humankind's archetypal temple imagery, the Cross symbolizes God's eternal nature as creative goodness that calls into being a plethora of beings created in his own image and likeness:

> For Christians, the sacrifice of the second person of the Trinity, the eternal Logos made flesh, is a death in space and time. But as the death of the God-man, it is the mirroring of that sacrifice which preceded the world, both logically and, as it were, temporally. Salvation should not be understood in the crude forensic terms of a propitiatory sacrifice made by man for God but rather vice versa: as part of an eternal and continual self-abnegation or contraction of the Divine.[136]

It is in order for creative libertarian freedom to flourish in imaginative soul-making that God, in a primordial act symbolized by his Son's kenosis, chooses to 'contract', creating nature and man as 'co-workers' even at the risk of their later apostasy and the consequent arising of both evil and suffering: 'If created beings make themselves, there is a contraction or diminution of the original divine plenitude, but also the surrender of absolute control. In the ushering of co-workers into the created order, God countenances and embraces rebellion.'[137] Moreover, it is not by violence or force, but by sacrificial love that God overcomes the evil springing from man's misguided libertarian choice, not destroying it at once, but patiently transforming it in the course of salvation history[138] by sharing with him the tautegorical symbols of his salvific being in transcendental and historical revelation: '"God makes creatures make themselves". That self-fashioning is through images and myths.'[139] Chief among the symbolic means whereby Christ brings about the restitution of all things is the New Testament antitype of the Old Testament Jerusalem Temple, the Cross. In the symbolism of Hedley's imaginative idealism, it is, in the words of the poet Thomas Traherne, 'the Jacob's ladder by which we ascend into the highest heavens' or 'a tree set on fire with invisible flame, that illumineth all the world'.[140] Hedley's notion of redemption is one that seeks to avoid the equally aporetic 'alternatives of the forensic theory of penal substitution in Calvin and the exemplarist theory of old-style liberalism', which he rejects as overly mythological and overly rationalist, respectively.[141] Neither is Christ's Cross a ransom paid to the devil in a preposterous mythological transaction nor does man save himself by imitating Christ's example in a desiccated practical rationalism: 'The traditional substitutionary theory of atonement seems too crassly forensic, and mere exemplification theory of the cross too insipid. But to attain the just balance between the subjective and the objective dimensions of sacrifice is difficult.'[142] The middle way propounded in the trilogy hinges upon a twofold robustly realistic account of good and evil, both of which are deemed realities in the strong Platonic sense of the word.[143] Since the good is grounded in the archetypal divine mind of which the visible world is an imperfect image, evil must, accordingly, be viewed as an offence perpetrated against the very order of things. Egregious evil, by its very definition as 'motiveless malignity', possesses a 'surd quality' that defies all attempts at rational explanation, whether it is defined as *akrasia* in terms of classical Greek theory of action or explained on political and economic grounds in more modern theories.[144] Nor can the chasm between divine goodness and human wickedness with the concomitant estrangement of humanity from God[145] be ever overcome by the effort of any single individual. However, as an offence against the moral fabric of the world, sin as a trespassing of such cosmic magnitude requires a forgiveness that must be understood neither as pardoning nor as condoning.[146] The temple sacrifice, therefore, satisfies a core longing of the religious soul. It is the key idea expressed by the tautegorical symbol of the temple originating in, yet significantly adding to, the transcendental notion of the self-sacrificial 'practice for death'. The vicarious suffering of the one may expiate the sin of the many: 'We can assume some mysterious principle of unity and transferability or substitution of guilt among human beings, where the sufferings of the innocent atone for the deeds of sinners. One might think of the role of the martyrs in the early Church, or the saints.'[147] As an absolute symbol that is both archetypal and tautegorical in character, the Cross, the supreme self-revelation of the divine nature, symbolizes the ultimate victory of the good over 'surd evil' which the crucified Son, as is symbolized by the instrument of his passion and his posture on it, recapitulates in himself so as to transform and heal it. Whereas the rival accounts of the salvation wrought by Christ's death on the Cross in terms of a ransom paid to the devil or a punishment undergone for our sake are metaphorical at best or anthropomorphic at worst, the Christological tautegory of the Cross with its many layers of meaning is analogical in nature, providing genuine insight into the absolute itself: 'This is "Christus consummator". Some other form of execution – for example, beheading or hanging – would not have served this symbolic purpose. What is unveiled in Christ is neither the arbitrary anthropomorphic deity of much superstitious and subrational folk religion of all ages nor, significantly, the impersonal God of Aristotle or Spinoza.'[148] It is this divine love which enters a world marred by evil and suffering to redeem it in the painful pedagogy of Aeschylus's great πάθει μάθος, which is the foundation of Hedley's theodicy of the sacrificial imagination.

At its heart is what the author calls 'MacKinnon's paradox'. While undermining naturalism in evidencing the existence of genuine value without which evil could not be perceived as evil in the first place, evil also threatens to undermine the classic theism of a benign creator:

> Tragedy reveals an intimation of the depth and meaning in human life, albeit meaning thwarted or truncated by evil, which is at odds with strict naturalism. Yet this very same reality of evil frustrates any attempt to produce a metaphysical theodicy which tries to articulate and explain the inscrutable. Let us call this MacKinnon's paradox. Evil thwarts both strict naturalism and classic theodicy.[149]

In response to the first horn of the dilemma, that is, the incompatibility of the reality of evil with naturalist metaphysics, Hedley, following the Russian novelist Mikhail Bulgakov,[150] provides a formalized proof of God's existence from the reality of evil which, paradoxically, does not refute, but, on the contrary, both proves his existence and discloses his essence as an agent in salvation history. In a first three-part *epistemological* argument, the existence of evil, inexplicable on the principles of reductive naturalism (1), is shown to presuppose a sense of goodness as its transcendental sine qua non (2). In introspection, the objective fact of evil also indicts man as a moral agent chiefly responsible for its occurrence (3). In a two-part *theological* conclusion, the very fact of evil is revealed to prove a panentheistic God both transcendent to a world unlike him in its evil (4) and immanent to it by displaying his love for humankind in a process of the soul-making of responsible rational agents (5).[151] In response to the second horn, that is, the incompatibility of evil with classic theistic theodicy, Hedley rejects the defences of divine goodness and justice along the lines of a theoretical and practical rationalism like G. W. Leibniz's and I. Kant's, respectively. Instead, he opts for the sombre, yet theologically sound, vision of the early modern Catholic counter-Enlightenment thinker Joseph de Maistre, who avoids the twin aporiai of a *theory* of an allegedly higher degree of harmony and order in the cosmos at large which offsets the experience of futile suffering and a Christian *practice* of charity unconcerned with suffering as a theological problem. Hedley's theodicy of sacrificial suffering, put forth in an emphatically Origenistic reading of the much-maligned Maistre, is deeply Christological in character and hinges upon the tautegorical temple imagery. It acknowledges evil in its pervasive and devastating reality. In his interpretation of Maistre's *Soirées de Saint-Petersburg*, which he reveals to be a key work of early modern Origenism in the tradition of the Cambridge Platonists' historic rehabilitation of the Alexandrian Platonist, the author embraces the Savoyard count's grim vision of the world as a gigantic altar upon which the whole of humankind is sacrificed and purged in its return to the Deity: 'The entire earth, perpetually steeped in blood, is nothing but an immense altar on which every living thing must be immolated without end, without restraint, without respite, until the consummation of the world, until the extinction of evil, until the death of death.'[152] In Maistre, the whole of divine and human history is interpreted along the conceptual lines of the second of the three archetypes of the iconic imagination, as man is called upon to share in Christ's suffering. The French theologian refuses to subscribe to the Augustinian *Deus absconditus*, whose counsels spring from inscrutable omnipotence alone, but defends the Origenist God of consummate goodness whose providential work is that of a benign, albeit strict, education of humankind.[153] On such a model, wanton violence and egregious suffering, while retaining all of their horror which the Savoyard count invokes in such graphic detail, are nevertheless rendered intelligible as part of God's design of the salvation of humankind by pedagogical and punitive means after the fall: 'The cosmos is the arena for the painful return to God through submission of the will on the model of Christ's suffering love. War and disease are part of the *via purgativa* to be endured by a sinful humanity.'[154] To this theological end, Maistre provides unsettling examples of violence that, while deeply shocking in themselves, still witness to the divine order in whose image the natural and social world, for all their shortcomings, were created for God's educative purposes. Thus, in his most celebrated example, the executioner, despite his grim task of putting to death delinquents at the behest of the political powers, represents the order of a judicial system even in the despicable spectacle of an execution. Likewise, war, for all its horrors, can be seen to point to the divine order, however obliquely, as soldiers obey certain rules such as the sparing of non-combatants. Though faint, the traces of God's benign providence are felt even at the lowest tier of reality, that is, in the afflictions of fallen humankind, who can feel the pull of divine gravity even amidst the greatest horrors of their immolation on the altar of the earthly temple. The ontological backdrop of the Savoyard count's apparently bleak vision of reality is that of Origen's Christian Platonism. It is a vision of a 'scale of being' in which nothing can possibly fail to point back to its transcendent principle and purpose, albeit 'in a mirror, darkly'. Hence, sacrificial violence, as stated in shocking diction by the Savoyard count, serves as a necessary reminder that humankind is in sinful disunity both with itself and with God:

> Sin is a state of dispersion, of being torn asunder like Isis or Pentheus. And the violence of man's fallen state reflects this dispersion. The visible world is a portion of that transcendent spiritual domain from whence the former is derived. As human beings our vocation is a harmonious communion with this intelligible universe that is the mind of God.[155]

Again, disorder presupposes the *a priori* of an eternal intelligible order, without which, on the principles of Hedley's transcendental analysis of the sacrificial imagination, it could not be perceived as chaotic and evil. In Maistre's sacrificial cosmology of the earth as an altar, on which Christ's sacrifice is time and again re-enacted in the woes of human history, everything is created for the sake of human intelligence. Each of the 'members' of the dissevered Isis or Pentheus to which Maistre likens the pitiful remnants of divine order reminds man of the 'regions of light' originally forfeited in the fall and gradually recovered in the sacrificial πάθει μάθος of human history. Hence, the dissevered members of the pagan types of the archetypal sacrifice of the Cross are protreptic in character, as it were, incessantly calling upon man to follow the Delphic γνωθὶ σαυτόν and rediscover his soul's original *pondus* towards the Divine so as to 'gravitate' back towards Christ the lamb, the antitype of a great many historical and mythological types, whether pagan or Jewish:

> [Man] gravitates [. . .] toward the regions of light. No beaver, no swallow, no bee wants to know more than its predecessors. All beings are calm in the place they occupy. All are degraded, but they do not know it; man alone has a feeling of it, and that feeling is at once the proof of his grandeur and of his misery, of his sublime rights and of his incredible degradation.[156]

Maistre's, therefore, is a 'resolutely providentialist' theodicy.[157] The world's chaos and disorder invoked so powerfully in his descriptions of the human institution of ritualized violence is part of God's punitive pedagogy by which man's yearning for communion with the Divine is once again stirred. Man could not know divine goodness if it were not for the tragic experienced on the world's altar.

As well as proving, rather than disproving, the existence of the God of the sacrificial imagination, the current state of chaotic disorder, on Maistre's Origenst principles, also serves as a powerful symbol of the fundamental Christian truth that salvation is not wrought by the destruction of evil but by its transformation. Embracing Maistre's startling insight that 'Evil is not a hindrance to Divine design and purpose but makes it clear', Hedley invokes the Cross as the key symbol of the divine and human self-sacrifice: 'Let us not forget that Christianity views evil as overcome through transformation rather than separation. The cross is an image of the man-God suffering and transforming evil and violence into peace and harmony. The key to evil is thus not separation but, rather, absorption and change.'[158] In Hedley's imaginative soteriology, the three primordial symbols of God's imagination are shown to fuel Christ's cosmic striving for a *transformation*, rather than *destruction* of evil. Christ, according to the threefold symbolism of the iconic imagination, is the chariot gradually elevating the souls towards the heavenly city in the sacrifice offered in the world's temple from the beginning to the end of all things. The events of Christ's earthly life during as well as before and after his incarnation, that is, his *heavenly Humanity* which constitutes the cosmic chariot in Henry More's reading of Ezekiel,[159] is made up of historical *events* and archetypal *images* explaining one another so as to become genuine *revelations* of the mystery of the infinite God. In his philosophy of revelation[160] which provides a middle position between a strongly metaphysical and merely poetical account of the redemptive process, Hedley concurs with Austin Farrer's quasi-Kantian insight that 'the events without the images would be no revelation at all, and the images without the events would remain shadows on the clouds'.[161] Just as 'concepts without percepts are empty' and 'percepts without concepts are blind', so do the history of Christ and the living forms of the imagination collude to bring about the restitution of a world beset by wanton evil with the latter in particular being seen in the light of the Son's eternal temple sacrifice.

It is the transformation of imperfection and evil in the union with the intelligible realm, the 'infinite I am' as the first principle and final purpose of man's imagination, that is expressed in the last of the three symbols of Hedley's trilogy, that of the heavenly city contemplated by John of Patmos in his sublime visions recorded in the final book of the Holy Writ.

3.3 Emblems of universal salvation: St John's visions of the heavenly city and feast

The vision of the heavenly city promised to the faithful with great imaginative and poetic vigour in the book of Revelation is not one of terror and fear, but one 'of creation restored through Christ'.[162] In the final book of the Holy Writ, John of Patmos describes a messianic feast held in the heavenly city as a symbol of universal salvation. It is the promised end of the temple sacrifice or the painful process of divine punishment and pedagogy for which the second symbol stands. As such, the feast is a deeply symbolic vision of the restitution of all things in the shared vision of God as the beautiful, the true and the good in which each rational agent attains to the universality and unity intuited in the iconic imagination while also retaining her individuality.

Key to the symbolic meaning of the heavenly city in Hedley's trilogy is the notion of the feast at which the eventual consummation of a cosmos united in the imaginative vision of the Divine is celebrated. Deeply influenced by the commentaries of Henry More and Austin Farrer, Hedley's Platonic reading of the final book of Scripture views the apocalyptic feast as a symbol of the union of humankind. As a living form or ideal of the iconic imagination, the one eschatological feast celebrated in the heavenly

Jerusalem is anticipated in many types in human religion and art alike. In the 'Church as paradise provisionally regained',[163] the Eucharist is a sacramental anticipation of the feast in the heavens, its apocalyptic antitype. In his interpretation of the sacrament as a feast, Hedley throughout follows Ralph Cudworth, whose early 1642 works *A Discourse Concerning the True Notion of the Lord's Supper* and *The Union of Christ and the Church in a Shadow* provide a compelling symbolic vision of the Eucharistic communion of God and man. The author concurs with Cudworth's critique of the Roman Catholic interpretation and the notion of the sacrament as festive, rather than sacrificial.[164] Instead, the Eucharist is to be defined as a 'feast upon the True Sacrifice', that is, Christ, thereby revealing the contemplative vision of the divine city as the end of the afflictions of soul-making:

> But now the True Christian Sacrifice being come, and offered up once for all, never to be repeated; we have therefore no more Typical Sacrifices left among us but onely the *Feasts* upon *the* True *Sacrifice* still Symbolically continued, and often repeated, in reference to that ONE GREAT SACRIFICE, which is alwayes as present in Gods sight and efficacious, as if it were but now offered up for us.[165]

While the existence of the many 'Typical Sacrifices' of old evidences God's universal providence by which he cares for all peoples of all times and all places by sharing with them his vision of self-sacrificial love in the temple *a priori*, the Christological 'once for all' expresses the uniqueness of the one historical antitype. This antitype is *Christus consummator* and his Cross by which man, after the woes of soul-making, attains to the weal of the eschatological feast: 'Christ is a way of seeing the invisible world. He is the great High Priest who opens the veil of the Temple and reveals the Divine essence. As the blood-stained Logos, he opens the heavens.'[166] The Eucharistic feast is, thus, a 'Federall Rite between God and us'[167] symbolizing and anticipating the eschatological fullness of communion between God and humanity. Against the backdrop of the Platonic ontology of an archetypal intelligible and an ectypal empirical realm, the feast, hence, marks the final *reditus* of the world to its divine source after its sinful *exitus*. By celebrating the Eucharistic feast amidst the evil and suffering of humankind's immolation on the altar of the present world, the Christian community provides public testimony to the ultimate meaningfulness of all things: 'The capacity for joy invoked by the festival', as will eventually be confirmed in the heavenly city of Jerusalem, 'is incompatible with a belief in the radical contingency or meaninglessness of the cosmos.'[168] Another symbolic expression of the life-affirming festivity, whether earthly or heavenly, is the music played on that joyous occasion. As 'the most immaterial and spiritual of the arts',[169] it likewise is a symbol of the life-giving power of the Divine in creation and salvation. In many ways, it finds its most sublime artistic expression in the Renaissance painter Raphael's *The Ecstasy of St Cecilia*, which depicts the titular patron of church music gazing towards the opened heavens amidst several saints, including John of Patmos, who is holding his visionary book of Revelation in his hands.[170] Its 'Platonic-Pythagorean dimension', already noted by its most ardent Romantic admirers, links the Renaissance painting to the ancient theology of salvation defined as the soul's existential participation in the beautiful, the true and the good as the first cause and final end of all things. Manifold literary analogues to the New Testament seer's profound vision of the heavenly feast are provided by the metaphysical Bard in whose early and late plays alike death and loss are transformed in life-affirming drama. In Shakespeare's early *Romeo and Juliet*, the eponymous 'star-crossed lovers' are united in an imagined feast after the heroine's apparent death:

> Her beauty makes
> This vault a feasting presence full of light.
>
> 5.3.85–86[171]

Likewise, Shakespeare's visionary late masterpieces, his Romances, abound in lost loved ones being restored to life in perplexing turns of dramatic events accompanied by music. Thus, music helps to bring back to life Thaisa and Hermione in *Pericles* and *The Winter's Tale* or allay the devastating storm in *The Tempest*.[172]

The transcendental meaning of the third of the three primordial symbols of the iconic imagination is that of the consummation of all things in humankind's eventual union with the infinite 'I am' which Hedley elucidates in terms of the 'Plotinian vision of the Divine intellect as a "community of living intelligences"'.[173] Not only does man's striving for the fullness of being and beauty find its consummation in the communion expressed by the tautegorical symbol of the city, but his yearning for the highest good of all creation is fulfilled as well, as human and divine freedom coincide in unhampered understanding. Human imagination finds its fulfilment in the infinite width of all rational agents joining in the vision of God's glory: 'The transformation of self-consciousness through the aid of the indwelling Christ is a foretasting of the dwelling in the heavenly city. The heavenly city is an empathic image of transcendence: of that which is "beyond being"'.[174] Both the biblical and Platonic visions are ones of a 'mutual indwelling' in consummate community as free agency epitomized by the chariot, through the struggles symbolized by the temple, finds its consummation in the heavenly city, the chief emblem of universal love:

> Free agents can recognize and avow this often-occluded unity through love. The process of 'union' is through 'free exchange'. The unexclusive life of the City, then, is everywhere vicarious life, up to the level of each capacity. It is as much the instinct of the gentleman as the climax of the saints. The 'bear one another's burdens' runs through all. Unlike commercial exchange, the sharing in the celestial city does not mean loss or diminishing of the goods.[175]

In the Church Father Origen's *Commentary on John*, on which Hedley draws in his Platonic exegesis of Revelation, the 'living precious stones' of which the heavenly city is composed are identified with the rational beings after their purification in the triumphs of the chariot and the afflictions of the temple and the Cross. The alleged violence of the final book of Scripture is not a literal one of strife among agents, either earthly or heavenly, but the spiritual one of humankind's soul-making, as the souls struggle to overcome the sins and vices of their fall. As is shown by the symbol of the feast contemplated in the eschatological vision of the pagan and Christian

Neoplatonists, the individual 'I am' of neither man nor nature is swallowed up into the infinite 'I am' of God at any point. Contrary to Spinoza's naturalist soteriology, salvation, in Hedley's imaginative idealism, is one in which individuality is preserved. Quoting Plotinus with approval, he subscribes to the later Neoplatonic tenet of 'the existence of forms of individuals', which evidences the abiding value of 'personality' and 'individuality' in Platonist soteriology.[176] It is by its individuality that each of the 'living precious stones' of which the heavenly city is made contributes to its splendour.

The reality of the hoped-for restitution of all things is inferred along the argumentative lines of Kant's postulates. Like Kant's threefold postulate of the soul's freedom, its immortality and the eventual correspondence between goodness and happiness, Hedley's hinges upon the chasm between the ideal of the beautiful, the true and the good and the reality of human sin and suffering. Hedley concurs with David Hume that God's goodness cannot be inferred from the state of affairs in the visible world. As in Baruch de Spinoza, whose onslaught on the classical theism of a moral *ens perfectissimum* equals Hume's in its argumentative vigour, the world around us may well be seen as nothing but 'blind nature . . . pouring forth from her lap, without discernment or parental care, her maimed and abortive children'.[177] However, while Hume's critique of religion is one of theoretical reason, arguing from natural evil for a first cause beyond good and evil, Kant's defence of theism is one of practical reason revolving around the notion of the internal ought and its far-reaching implications: 'Hume is inferring from the outward facts to God's existence or absence. Kant is arguing from the interior sense of goodness as revealed in consciousness by conscience as distinct from prudence.'[178] The Phaedrean nature of human existence, that is, man's knowledge of the categorical good and the consequent rational belief in his libertarian freedom, reveals a painful gap between the 'ought' of practical reason and the dire 'is' of the world. It calls for a reconciliation between the ideal and the real at the end of all things:

> But if one does hold to the objectivity of the moral law and to the idea that it cannot be frustrated, this drives one to the acceptance of an eschatological reconciliation between the source of nature and the source of morality in a transcendent, good God. Duty demands that we assume God's existence as a practical postulate, if not as a fact of speculative metaphysics.[179]

The postulate is spelled out in the Origenistic terms of the soul-making theodicy of imaginative idealism. Thus, Hedley follows Origen and his early modern heirs, the Cambridge Platonists and Joseph de Maistre, in subscribing to the postulate of an eventual restitution of all things, rather than Augustine's 'logic of terror' that informs the Latin Church Father's sinister doctrine of the predestination of an irrevocably forlorn *massa damnata*,[180] quoting verbatim the most vocal of the Alexandrian Platonist's early defenders, George Rust. Not only is the earthly vale of tears, according to Rust, an arena for humankind's soul-making, but it also furnishes the most perfect being itself with the 'greater advantage to magnifie [*sic*] his love in our Recovery'.[181] It is by virtue of his own self-sacrificial love that the God of Hedley's panentheism eventually brings about a world in which each and every creature participates in the fullness of divine beauty, truth and goodness. He is the archetype of all unity in creation and salvation alike.

4 Imaginative panentheism: Ontology of the divine 'all in all'

Hedley's rational theology is shaped throughout by the patristic dogma of the ὁμοούσιος and the notion of the Trinitarian God as both infinite reality and personality, as stated with great speculative vigour by the Cambridge Platonist Ralph Cudworth[182] and the Romantic poet philosopher Samuel Taylor Coleridge,[183] respectively. The God of the iconic imagination is a panentheist Deity who is at once a consummate intellect of paradoxical simplicity that transcends the world and the latter's soul that is immanent to it and animates its every part, however minute. Creating all things from the fullness of his own being in the beginning, he is perfect goodness ungrudgingly sharing with nature and man his own vision of the good, the true and the beautiful in the three tautegorical symbols of the iconic imagination and, thereby, gradually guiding the whole of creation towards its restitution in the end.

Of the four primary historical options of the philosophy of religion, that is, Platonism, Spinozism, Deism and German Idealism, Hedley subscribes to the first paradigm, the 'Neoplatonic-theistic view of a hierarchy of being', which posits 'a transcendent unity as perfect being and perhaps personal insofar as this is compatible with the absolute autonomy and self sufficiency of the Principle'.[184] His, therefore, is the God or the *ens perfectissmum* of the rationalist tradition of the ancient theology of Platonism.[185] God's consummate perfection in the tradition of the Christian *philosophia Trinitatis* of which Hedley's own concept is part is that of a 'relational unity' of the two Neoplatonic concepts of divine oneness,[186] namely that of the One 'beyond being' and that of the All-Oneness of Being and Intellect, which are identified with the Father and the Son, respectively. United through the loving bond of the Holy Spirit, they are telescoped into the one θεῖον of the ancient theology, whether philosophical or biblical.[187] As the Father, God is a first primordial unity infinite in its ineffable nature and comprehending in itself all intellectual and natural reality as its 'Origin, Principle or Cause', while being 'beyond it in dignity and power': 'The One is all because everything is through or out of Him. But the One is not "all" in a pantheistic sense; it is the Origin, Principle (ἀρχή) or Cause of all. It is the all-encompassing condition of the many, of difference and division: the ground of precisely all forms of being, but not subject to their conditions.'[188] In the Son, the most perfect being thinks itself as the sum total of the ideas of creation. Whereas the ὁμοούσιος of the First Ecumenical Council of Nicaea in 325 is generally viewed as a rejection of both Arianism and Platonism as related doctrines of the strict subordination of an intellectual second principle to a transcendent first one, Hedley follows Ralph Cudworth in hailing it instead as a distinctly Christian interpretation of the Greek 'metaphysics of intellect'[189] in the vein of Plato's *Sophist* and *Parmenides*. In contradistinction to later apophatic Neoplatonism that denies divine subjectivity as compromising the absolute's perfect simplicity,[190] the first principle of all things is, by its very nature, intellect. Being ὁμοούσιος or 'consubstantial' with the Father, the λόγος of the Gospel of John or the intellectual second unity of Neoplatonism is a 'perfect expression of its source', that is, the first transcendent One, thereby revealing the first principle of all things to be one that is both simplicity and multiplicity in the eternal communion of the three persons of the Trinity:

> The concepts which Augustine and Boethius used to defend the doctrine of the Trinity: 'unity', 'uniqueness', 'simplicity', 'difference', 'identity', 'substance', 'relation', and 'spirit' are, of course, all products of the Platonic-Aristotelian *Geistesmetaphysik*, especially Plato's *Sophist* and *Parmenides*. In a sense, the basic problem of ancient Greek metaphysics was that of the relations of identity and difference and the nature of the ἀρχή. Although many scholars have argued that the Nicaean definition of the relation of the Father to the Son as ὁμοούσιος constituted a rejection of pre-Nicaean Christian Platonism: The role of the doctrine of the Trinity *within* natural theology is profoundly influenced by the tradition emanating from Plato's *Parmenides*; especially the relation of identity to difference. The principle and fount of the Intellectual System is the transcendent ἀρχή which constitutes a relational unity. The realm of ideas do not form an inferior intermediate realm between the causal source of the universe and the physical world but *are* the divine mind.[191]

Hedley's deeply patristic *Geistmetaphysik* is modelled on the Greeks' speculation on a first 'principle' of all things and on the five 'greatest kinds' of Plato's *Sophist*, interpreted against the backdrop of the dialectic of the one and the many in his *Parmenides*. The distinctly Christian metaphysics of the One and the Intellect as a 'relational unity' of two 'consubstantial' expressions of the one divine nature envisages a primordial first mind conceived of as a paradoxical *concidentia oppositorum*. While inevitably *many* in the totality of the ideas which constitute his very essence as an intellectual substance defined as a relationship between the first two hypostases in a third, God is still the *One* beyond all things. In the vein of the theological reading of Plato's μέγιστα γένη in John Scot Eriugena and Nicholas of Cusa, to which Hedley subscribes in his imaginative Trinitarian theism, the absolute is defined as a 'paradoxical unity of intense life and stillness or a paradoxical coincidence of motion and rest as the *motus stabilis* or *status mobilis*'.[192] As such, God is the ground of all determinateness of thought and being whatsoever of which his own simplicity, conceived of as the transcendent fullness of being, is the logical prerequisite.[193] As well as being a perfect intellect, the 'relational unity' of the Father and the Son in the Holy Spirit is also conceived of as personal. To this end, Hedley adopts Coleridge's definition of 'the triune identity of God as ipseity, alterity, and community'.[194] It is by being the Father's 'alterity' that the Son, while being his consummate image and, hence, identical with him in the 'community' effected by the Holy Spirit, nevertheless introduces 'difference' into the θεῖον or the divine nature,[195] which is the sine qua non of personhood defined as an awareness of '*another self*'.[196] In opposition to Spinoza's pantheism, in which the infinite all-oneness as pure 'ipseity' lacks all otherness and, therefore, is of necessity impersonal, the God of Hedley's Christian Platonism is at once infinite being and infinite person, distinguishing himself from another self in his Trinitarian nature which is defined as identity and difference in one all-encompassing community. As such, the God of the iconic imagination is 'a wholly good and omnipotent personal transcendent agent',[197] endowed with freedom and volition. For one thing, he is absolute freedom in that his own will is the sole cause of his being. Hedley's is a rationalism of the first principle that is throughout deeply indebted to Plotinus's speculations on the *Will and Freedom of the One* in his landmark treatise on personal theism and freedom metaphysics: 'The One', he concurs with the greatest of the Neoplatonists, 'is not the product of fate or chance but free will. Plotinus is the first philosopher to identify thought and being with will. The One of Plotinus is distinguished from all "difference". He is what he is absolutely – he is entirely self-constituted (αἴτιον ἑαυτοῦ).'[198] For another, Hedley closely follows Origen and the Cambridge Platonists in viewing God's absolute freedom as one of 'univocal goodness'.[199] In response to Spinoza's substance as the first principle beyond good and evil and exempt from all allegedly anthropomorphist moral categories,[200] Hedley insists upon goodness as the key characteristic of the divine nature. Restating the unshakeable foundation of the Platonic metaphysics of his early modern Cambridge precursors Ralph Cudworth and Henry More, Hedley rejects theological voluntarism *tout court*. Rather than a deity of unrestricted will and omnipotence, as propounded in several books of the Holy Writ, the church fathers and modern thought, the God of the iconic imagination is 'goodness itself, the culmination of being'.[201] Hence, the 'most perfect being' is a 'most moral being' committed to the goodness that constitutes its very essence. A benign agent, the Christian God, as a relational unity of oneness and infinite intellection, cannot but choose to overflow and ungrudgingly share his fullness with a creation distinct from him. Hedley's is a concept of creation revolving around the Neoplatonic notion of emanation or 'undiminished giving' of the divine archetype. God, as the idea of the good or goodness itself, is *diffusivum sui*.[202] To this end, Hedley rejects the 'contrast between the freely chosen gift of creation and the necessary manifestation of an impersonal absolute'[203] generally invoked in classical theology to prove the alleged incompatibility of Christianity and Platonism, insisting instead upon the identity of freedom and necessity in an absolute which is, by its very nature, defined as creative goodness:

> If God's nature is love and it is God's nature to communicate that love, this is a form of necessity. It is a necessity grounded in the divine essence – it is intrinsic to God. Insofar as it is not *extrinsic* to God, we can say that this manifestation of love is an act of self-determination. It reflects God's nature and not any arbitrary will.[204]

On the first principles of Hedley's imaginative theism, to which the notion of the beautiful is key throughout, the relationship of the creator to his creation is neither one of inevitable necessity nor one of arbitrary freedom, but rather one of Hindu *Lila* or 'cosmic play', which the author, in a blend of Western philosophy and Eastern mythology, posits as yet another median category between two competing metaphysical options:

> One may see this concept as attempting to bridge two extremes which also occur in Western theology – extreme voluntarism and necessitarianism: is the world the product of arbitrary and brute will or the mechanical and inexorable emanation of the absolute? Neither alternative is theologically attractive. In the first, the

Divine becomes wilful and anthropomorphic and in the second a sub-personal or impersonal being. The notion of 'play' may be viewed as a median position between these two options. God is not 'constrained' or needful in his activity but neither is this work wanton or groundless.[205]

The whole of reality, proceeding as it does from the divine substance itself, cannot but be spiritual in character itself. Its nature is described as a 'particular density or "thickening" of spirit', body, in the language of Henry More's bold early poetry, being nothing 'but this spirit, fixt, grosse by conspissation'.[206] The relationship of spirit and matter closely corresponds to the identity of symbol and meaning in Hedley's Romantic theory of imaginative tautegory. Being as being, whether material or mental, is a symbolic revelation of the benign divine nature from which it springs. It is life in its manifold variety which discloses the inner essence of all being as 'spirit, fixt, grosse by conspissation' on which God continuously works as its creative form, sharing with it his own beauty, truth and goodness in disinterested love in a process of soul-making.[207] In accordance with the aesthetic first principles of Hedley's imaginative theism, God's action in the world is one of continuous theogonic 'image-making' by which nature and man, from the Big Bang to the eventual restitution of all things, come to participate in the imaginative self-communication of his own relational unity to an ever-fuller degree. Its unfolding is that of the gradual acquisition of more complex unities from the first emergence of the primitive life of one-celled organisms to the advent of sentient beings capable of thought and action in the course of evolution:

> The higher we move in the domain of living creatures, the more complex the unity. The amoeba is close to an arithmetical unity, in that it is one cell possessing one nucleus, and from sponges to more advanced metazoans (like flies or mice) we encounter increased grades of bodily complexity. Observed advances in genomic complexity and morphological diversity, however, have arisen through the interaction of integrated individuals with their environments. [. . .] Consider the increase in complexity but also in integrating *identity* in a fly, a mouse, and a human being. In a human being there is the complex physical structure (body plan) but also the volitional agent, the character over time, the conscious selfhood of the agent, all contributing to personal identity. The first unity, the body plan, is more readily understandable. But perhaps we should be thinking of unity as unity by virtue of its unifying power. The paradigm would be the unification of the heterogenous elements in human personality.[208]

The God of the iconic imagination, like the poet of the Bard's *ars poetica* in the *Midsummer Night's Dream*, 'bodies himself forth'. He is, above all, the poet of the world, who 'as imagination', on the author's Shakespearean model of the titular epistemic power of his trilogy, 'bodies forth/The forms of things unknown' (*A Midsummer Night's Dream* 5.1.14–15)[209] in sacrificial self-communication: 'The cosmos itself is the Divine sacrifice: the metamorphosis of God's identity in difference.'[210] God is immanent to his creation as its inner soul and form. The Son's incarnation is the archetypal symbol of the Father's providence in which he saves each and every being, however vile and insignificant, not acting upon it in occasional interventions *from without*, but perfecting it as the principle of its higher life *from within*: 'Incarnation corresponds with creation and is its fulfilment – a God who acts but is not arbitrary, and whose action is not intervention from without in a mechanical sense, but paradigmatically within the created realm in an organic or plastic sense.'[211] In the vein of the Christian metaphysics of Ws. 11.21: 'Thou hast ordered all things in measure and number and weight', as pioneered, above all, by Augustine, Hedley views God as the principle of the various kinds of identity of which the finite cosmos is composed: 'God is the creative and determining measure or *mensura* of all things. He is also *numerus* as the mathematic harmony of the cosmos.' As such, he is the first cause of the *pondus* or 'teleological gravity' of all things towards their one divine centre: 'Finally, He is also the source of the teleological "gravity" of the universe, as its highest good.'[212]

To the creator's playful self-communication corresponds the creature's own 'creative contemplation' as the 'ontological motor of being',[213] which finds its apogee in the emergence of beings mirroring him in their own imaginative intellection and volition and yielding to the 'teleological "gravity"' implanted in them: 'God', Hedley states the key conviction of his imaginative idealism, as enshrined in the ancient theology of humankind, 'is a transcendent spiritual being and humanity can have communion with him'.[214] The relationship of God's 'infinite I AM' to man's 'finite I am' is that of a dynamic 'realization of the image'[215] in divine and human 'double agency' by which Hedley, again drawing on the 'greatest kinds' of Plato's *Sophist*, seeks to eschew the twin aporiai of Spinozistic identity on the one hand and Gnostic difference on the other. For one thing, the finite creature's participation in its infinite creator who acts as the formal and final cause of its imagination in its every thought and act is that of the image approximating its archetype. Siding with the medieval Platonists Dietrich von Freiberg and Meister Eckhart against Thomas Aquinas, whose primarily functionalist reading he rejects, Hedley provides a densely metaphysical exegesis of the biblical theologumenon of man being created in God's 'image and likeness' (Gn. 1.26), highlighting the ontological *identity* between the ectypal finite and the archetypal infinite I AM, rather than their *difference*. Whereas a physical container is different from its contents, spiritual beings such as God and the soul admit of no such difference.[216] For another, Hedley, following J. Caird and Austin Farrer, subscribes to the notion of 'double agency' in which the finite image and the infinite archetype, by virtue of their shared intellectual nature, act in complete unison whenever multiplicity is turned into complex unity, thereby being endowed with the quality of the beautiful, the true and the good. Again, God addresses man not as an exterior 'thou' from without, as in Martin Buber's dialogical philosophy or Karl Barth's dialectical theology, but works upon him from within, that is, in Spinozist parlance, as the inward principle 'constituting the being of the human mind'.[217]

Since, therefore, the infinite divine 'I am' is not ontologically different from the finite human 'I am', God's creative and salvific action is identical with man's, as Hedley elaborates in a speculative reading of Hamlet's musings on divine providence: 'There's a divinity that shapes our ends, / Rough-hew them how we will' (*Hamlet* 5.2.10–11), which he interprets as a poetic outline of a theory of God's occasionally elusive, yet constant and ubiquitous, providentialist work in the course of nature and history.

Just as the Bard has Fortinbras and Malcolm restore political order to the shattered kingdoms at the end of the two greatest of his tragedies, God is at work wherever man imposes unity upon chaotic multiplicity through his multifaceted imaginative effort, whether in art, in action or in knowledge: 'This is to say that mankind as self-conscious is distinct from the animal kingdom, and that human self-consciousness represents the eternal self-consciousness of God. Shakespeare's Christian providentialist vision is also evident in the suggestion of growth out of chaos. Fortinbras arrives at Elsinore, and Malcolm at Dunsinane, to rebuild from the ruins.'[218] Accordingly, God's first visible providentialist action coincides with the very first artefacts of human ingenuity in prehistoric cave paintings which mark the beginnings of humankind as a species of the religious imagination: 'Humanity has created images of the sacred since prehistoric times. These sublime images and imaginings of the transcendent become an instrument of revelation: the real presence of the eternal in human history and culture.'[219] Hedley imagines the first hominids to have been driven by the newly born species' distinguishing power of the imagination of the infinite. The earliest works of human art such as the paintings of Chauvet or the prehistoric Gobekli Tepi are impressive evidence of religious aesthetics expressing the earliest human beings' 'inchoate *sensus divinitatis*' at the very dawn of humankind.[220] In an audacious 'neo-Schellingian attempt to combine myth with revelation',[221] based on the deeply mythological character of modernity itself,[222] Hedley views the evolution of nature and culture alike as the gradual self-communication of the Deity with the ancient theology of the West and East documenting the 'means by which human consciousness is transformed by, includes and reveals the Divine mind . . . through the imagination'.[223] It is by the imaginative vision of the beautiful, the true and the good which God graciously shares with his kin and offspring that all things, including humankind, will be saved in the end. The historical theism of Hedley's *Iconic Imagination* is not the deflationary one of either Spinoza's *Theological-Political Treatise* or Hume's *Natural History of Religion*, but the vision of world ages in Vico's *New Science* and, above all, of the theogonic history of the human mind in Schelling's *Philosophy of Mythology* in which the various stages of Greek polytheism and Jewish and Christian monotheism trace God's own coming-to-be in the development of the prevalent theological narratives and symbols of humankind. While Coleridge, subscribing to the Platonic variety of theism, rather than its idealist offspring with its postulate of a historical becoming of the Divine, parted ways with Schelling on the question of divine potentiality and change,[224] Hedley allows for passion in the sympathetic God of Christianity as the latter must witness his grand imaginative vision succumb to disorder and evil time and again. While images of God's own struggle for nature's and man's salvation are many and manifold in the pagan types of old, it is in St John and St Paul's notion of the crucified Lord that the process of soul-making is eventually viewed as part of the divine life itself: 'Christianity has a much higher estimate of sympathy than its Stoic or Platonic rivals. It accepts the fact of suffering rather than pleading for detachment. In so doing, it conveys through its Christology and Trinitarian theology an image of the Divine nature that, however enigmatically, integrates sorrow, sympathy and love in the Godhead.'[225] The world and its woe and weal are not extraneous to God, but an essential part of his own being as creative goodness ungrudgingly sharing its riches with nature and man created in its own image and likeness. The Christian Platonist God's vision of the world saved by the beauty of his goodness and his truth is the grand narrative of the world of the Phaedrean chariot, the Old Testament temple and the New Testament heavenly city recounted in the trilogy of the religious imagination.

5 Metaphysics of the image: A new paradigm of religious philosophy

Hedley's imaginative idealism provides a powerful new paradigm of religious philosophy as a middle way between scepticism and dogmatism, which are both rejected as inimical to the cause of rational religion. It, thereby, gives a comprehensive vision of God, man and nature viewed in terms of the three symbols of the rational soul's iconic imagination.

Representing a living tradition of Anglo-Saxon Platonism which originated in seventeenth-century Cambridge Platonism and eighteenth-century Romanticism, Hedley's idealism rests on a compelling analysis of the imagination as the chief power of human subjectivity. Not only does the imagination provide a general field of intellectual vision modelled on the sense of that name, which is the sine qua non of all reflection and action, but its 'esemplastic' power of 'fusing into one' the manifold phenomena of self and world reveals it to be key to human subjectivity as such. It also mediates between the finite and the infinite as the latter is shown to be the condition of the possibility of the former. Hedley's transcendental epistemology, thereby, lays the foundation for a religious philosophy of the Divine intuited in the rich symbolism of all products of the human imagination from the prehistoric origins of humankind to present-day art and literature. The threefold symbolism of the chariot, the temple and the city is meant to provide no less than an exhaustive account of the human imagination and its relationship to the ubiquitous Divine. It reveals man to be a being of Phaedrean striving in aesthetics, physics and metaphysics and ethics. Every act of his imagination is shown to be driven by a longing for an objective truth both aesthetically appealing to and ethically binding upon him. The painful chasm between the triumph of the ideal and the tragic reality of apparently futile evil and suffering is at the core of the religious philosophy of the temple sacrifice which amounts to a highly original soul-making theodicy of self-sacrificial suffering. The heavenly city symbolizes the hope for the fulfilment of man's deep desire for reconciliation. Throughout, human reasoning, based upon the imagination as its chief power, is shown to be informed by all of the three tautegorical symbols.

It is on the basis of his comprehensive transcendental analysis of the original symbolism of the human imagination that Hedley provides an ontology of the Divine. His is a theism in which God is a transcendent agent of infinite goodness, wisdom and power who is also immanent to each and every part of his creation as its soul. He is the *ens perfectissimum* reimagined according to the irreducible transcendental categories of the Phaedrean ascent, the tragic of the temple and the Cross and the hope for reconciliation symbolized by the city. Hence, he is consummate being and unity conceived of as a loving unity of Father, Son and Holy Spirit. As such, he shares with a cosmos created from his own fullness the riches of his being. His sacrifice on the Cross brings about the *reditus* of his prodigal creation as his vision gradually comes to inform the imagination both of man and the world at large. For all its profoundly ecumenical latitude, the grand narrative of the world in its fall and restitution put forward in the idealism of the iconic imagination is profoundly Christian in character.[226]

Hedley's idealism of the imagination is one of the most audacious modern systems of ancient Platonism and modern philosophy of religion whose powerful narrative of God working upon the imagination of his creatures in the history of nature and culture alike is another momentous 'footnote to Plato' as well as a new paradigm of religious philosophy.

Response by Douglas Hedley

Christian Hengstermann has written a wide-ranging synthesis of my 'Romantic Platonism', but one that draws upon the seventeenth-century and various contemporary discussions over a number of years. My approach to philosophy is hermeneutical and deeply shaped by theology. While I have immense respect for the achievements of analytic philosophy in specific areas of philosophical logic such as reference, theory of knowledge and especially philosophy of religion, the tendency of the school is often to foreshorten and obscure the great tradition of the history of philosophy. We are self-understanding creatures, and while that means drawing upon contemporary problems and challenges, we should not ignore those great books which have shaped the very culture we inhabit.

Hengstermann also refers significantly to figures whose import for the project is perhaps more surprising, such as Rudolf Otto or Friedrich Creuzer, and my deep debt to my teacher Werner Beierwaltes. He is correct to see Coleridge as the guiding light of the project. My initial study of Coleridge formed the basis for the systematic endeavour of the trilogy. Yet he also notes the key themes that I wanted to address: imagination as a part of human psychology and the need for stories, while recognizing the danger of the Nietzschean prospect that we can weave the stories and create meaning in a universe inherently without purpose. More than the so-called hard problem of consciousness, it is the mystery of human self-consciousness that is the starting point of any serious attempt to 'save the appearances', and imagination must play a role in that. Stories are one of the primordial features of man's awareness, and I claim that the power of the great stories, as C. S. Lewis and J. R. R. Tolkien averred, lies in their power to summon reality. Many religious stories concern sacrifice and violence: these are features of the world that seem to thwart any facile theodicy or crudely anthropomorphic theology. These are also themes that touch upon psychological, anthropological and literary themes. Tragedy is a genre that relies upon the concept of sacrifice, and it is a topic that divides the great confessions of Christianity and, indeed, the religions of the world. Suffering and guilt are the bedrock of the great religions. Are these atavistic traits in contemporary culture and an embarrassment for the despisers of religion? Or do they, as even atheists such as Sartre or Heidegger admit, offer genuine insight into the human condition? The third volume of my trilogy turns to the idea of the transcendence and immanence of the image. That is one of the most perplexing areas of philosophical theology. If one stresses transcendence too vigorously, only a 'mysterious kind of atheism is left', yet to yoke the Divine too closely to the warp and woof of the cosmos would seem idolatrous or to diminish the glory of the creator. Despite the generous appraisal of Hengstermann, I remain unsure that I achieved the right balance in the trilogy.

Notes

1 The following introduction to Douglas Hedley's idealism of the imagination is based upon its systematic exposition provided in his trilogy of works: *Living Forms of the Imagination* (London and New York: T&T Clark, 2008); *Sacrifice Imagined: Violence,*

Atonement, and the Sacred (New York and London: Continuum, 2011), and *The Iconic Imagination* (New York et al.: Bloomsbury, 2016). His earlier monograph *Coleridge, Philosophy and Religion: Aids to Reflection and the Mirror of the Spirit* (Cambridge: Cambridge University Press, 2000), provides an in-depth account of the eponymous Romantic philosopher's synthesis of Platonism and idealism which is one of the key sources of the author's own im6aginative metaphysics. It also sheds helpful light upon the author's original use of the traditions of Greek Neoplatonism, German Idealism and British Romanticism, which have shaped his own systematic thought. Besides the four monographs mentioned, the author's rich work in historical and systematic religious philosophy has likewise been made use of to provide as nuanced an account of his philosophy of religion as possible. Cf. also my earlier German depiction of Hedley's thought in my 'Kritik der religiösen Vorstellungskraft – Douglas Hedleys Trilogie zur "Imagination" als neues Paradigma der Religionsphilosophie', *Theologische Rundschau* 82 (2017): 174–84.

2 *Sacrifice Imagined*, 37.
3 *Living Forms*, 39.
4 *Sacrifice Imagined*, 48.
5 See the references to the Delphic injunction in *Living Forms*, 171, and the more comprehensive accounts of its original meaning and subsequent legacy in European idealism in *Coleridge, Philosophy and Religion*, 4–5, 109–16 and 169–80, and in 'Forms of Reflection, Imagination, and the Love of Wisdom', *Metaphilosophy* 43 (2012): 112–24, here 115–18.
6 *Living Forms*, 37.
7 Cf. the important reference to Kant's concept of human subjectivity in *Iconic Imagination*, 43.
8 Ibid., 43–4. While the distinction between 'simultaneous unity' and 'sequential unity' is derived from Hans Jonas, 'The Nobility of Sight: A Study in the Phenomenology of the Senses', in *The Phenomenon of Life: Towards a Philosophical Biology* (Evanston: Northwestern, 2001), 135–56, that between being and eternity and becoming and time is Platonic. The *tertium quid* of the analogy is twofold. It consists in the unity of the act of perception and the timelessness of the single moment in contradistinction to the passage of time.
9 *Living Forms*, 59.
10 Ibid.
11 See the concise comparison between these two historically influential notions of the imagination in *Living Forms*, 49–50, notably the perceptive final remarks: 'Hobbes and Berkeley represent two extreme and unsatisfactory accounts of the imagination. Hobbes seems to leave out the evident fact of its spontaneous and creative component. Berkeley, in going to the other extreme, seems to neglect the sub- or semi-conscious aspect of the imagination. The differences between Hobbes and Berkeley on the nature of the imagination resolve into a difference between an excessively active and excessively passive view of mental activity. One might speculate that the theological concerns of both men contribute to the basic difference in their view of the mind.'
12 *Living Forms*, 57. Coleridge is a pivotal figure in Hedley's theological narrative of Greek, German and British idealism. His theory of the imagination is analysed in great detail in the author's 'Platonism, Aesthetics and the Sublime at the Origins of Modernity', in *Platonism at the Origins of Modernity: Studies on Platonism and Early Modern Philosophy*, edited by id. and Sarah Hutton (Dordrecht: Springer, 2008), 269–82, and 'S.T. Coleridge's Contemplative Imagination', in *Coleridge and Contemplation*,

edited by Peter Cheyne (Oxford: Oxford University Press, 2017), 221–36. Besides his early monograph *Coleridge, Philosophy and Religion*, which mainly explores the roots of Coleridge's Romantic philosophy of religion in ancient patristic and early modern Cambridge Platonism as well as its close ties with the German and British idealist tradition of his day, cf. also the author's account of Coleridge's seminal influence upon Anglican theology and British philosophy alike in his important studies of Austin Farrer in 'Austin Farrer's Shaping Spirit of the Imagination', in *The Human Person in God's World: Studies to Commemorate the Austin Farrer Centenary*, edited by id. and Brian Hebblethwaite (London: SCM Press, 2006), 106–31, and 'Imagination Amended: From Coleridge to Collingwood', in *Coleridge's Afterlives*, edited by James Vigus and Jane Wright (Basingstone et al.: Palgrave Macmillan, 2008), 210–23.
13 Samuel Taylor Coleridge, *The Major Works*, edited with an Introduction and Notes by H. J. Jackson (Oxford: Oxford University Press, 1985), 280–320.
14 Coleridge, *Collected Notebooks*, III, 329, *Biographia*, I, 85, quoted in 'Platonism, Aesthetics and the Sublime' (see n. 12), 276. The term is derived from the Greek εἰς ἓν πλάττειν.
15 Ibid., 306.
16 Ibid., quoted and discussed in *Iconic Imagination*, 76–7.
17 This is the apposite description used in *Living Forms*, 52, which is testimony to Hedley's debt to Platonism in its Romantic guise.
18 'Imagination Amended' (see n. 12), 212.
19 Coleridge, *Major Works* (see n. 13), 313.
20 'Imagination Amended' (see n. 12), 212.
21 See, for example, the interpretations of these key verses in *Living Forms*, 20; *Sacrifice Imagined*, 55–6 and 105.
22 'Imagination Amended' (see n. 12), 212.
23 Coleridge, *Major Works* (see n. 13), 313.
24 *Living Forms*, 50.
25 *Biographia Literaria*, II, 258, quoted ibid., 185.
26 More, *Antidote Against Atheism* I, 5, 2, quoted ibid. 48.
27 The concept cited ibid., 145, is borrowed from John Smith, *Select Discourses* (Cambridge, 1660), 2.
28 *Sacrifice Imagined*, 113.
29 Ibid., 111. This sobriquet clearly witnesses to Hedley's own great sympathies for the first major Christian Platonist who, in many ways, may be viewed as a principal authority of his Platonism. On the following brief account of Cudworth's Origenist theory of moral action, see *Sacrifice Imagined*, 113–19, as well as the more comprehensive treatment of this subject in his 'Cudworth on Freedom: Theology, Ethical Obligation and the Limits of Mechanism', in *Die Cambridge Origenists. George Rusts Letter of Resolution Concerning Origen and the Chief of His Opinions*, edited by Alfons Fürst and Christian Hengstermann (Münster: Aschendorff Verlag, 2013), 47–58.
30 A. C. Bradley's Hegelian characterization of the heroes of the Bard's four great tragedies in his brilliant classic *Shakespearean Tragedy: Lectures on Hamlet, Othello, King Lear, Macbeth* (London: Macmillan and Co., Limited, 2nd edn, 1932), 14–16, may well be seen as a particularly apt précis of Hedley's theory of narrative personal identity. See the author's characteristically circumspect caveat ibid., 200, which reveals the author's notion as yet another bold median position between Platonism and Postmodernism: 'Narrative presupposes personal identity and yet personal identity is notoriously elusive. It has long been *de rigueur* in some literary circles

to suggest that narrative *creates* identity. But this is a very strong and somewhat implausible claim. However, it is not entirely without merit.'

31 Cf. *Living Forms*, 199.

32 Ibid., 222. Cf. also *Sacrifice Imagined*, 121, where Hedley highlights the close link between the coherent unity and the morality of a happy life. According to the author, morality provides a degree of unity which is by definition unachievable in hedonism: 'Narrative is used not just in the psychological sense that people do in fact understand themselves in the mode of story or narrative, but the normative sense that narrative is important: a life unified in terms of overarching values is a better life than one that is disoriented and incoherent: the 'ne'er do well' or the indolent searching for distraction from boredom or anxiety or amusement.'

33 *Living Forms*, 203.

34 See, for example, ibid., 90 and 249, respectively.

35 Ibid., 79–113, Hedley rejects the twin errors of radical apophaticism and kataphaticism in a critical close reading of two seminal books on the topic of his trilogy, namely Denys Turner, *The Darkness of God: Negativity in Christian Mysticism* (Cambridge: Cambridge University Press, 1995), and William P. Alston, *Perceiving God* (Ithaca: Cornell University Press, 1995). Both Turner's 'incommensurability thesis', which, following medieval mystics, views the experience of God as transcending all categories, and Alston's 'perception of God', which provides a justification of religious beliefs on the grounds of an alleged analogy between divine and sensual perception and the Wittgensteinian reliability of a lifeform like religion and mysticism, fail to do justice to the dialectics of a Deity at once concealed and revealed in his utter transcendence and all-pervading immanence. It is a key concern of Hedley's trilogy to establish the imagination as a power of an awareness of a transcendent God's paradoxical presence that is perceptive and conceptual as well as cognitive and affective in nature.

36 Ibid., 108, where Hedley quotes William James, *The Varieties of Religious Experience: A Study in Human Nature* (Harmondsworth: Penguin, 1985), 62.

37 Ibid., 82. The reference is to James, ibid., 380–1.

38 See the summary of Plotinus's proto-Cartesian thought experiment in Enn. V 8, 9, 1–2, ibid., 88.

39 Ibid., 80.

40 Proust, *Jean Santeuil*, trans. Gerard Hopkins (London: Weidenfeld; Nicholson, 1955), 409–10, quoted and commented on in detail in *Iconic Imagination*, 61–2.

41 Again, the illuminating quantitative terminology is that of James, *Religious Experience* (see n. 36), 231, which chimes well with the dialectics of infinite and finite subjectivity in Coleridge's notion of the primary imagination adopted by Hedley.

42 *Iconic Imagination*, 45.

43 Ibid., 45–6.

44 Hedley's debt to Otto's seminal masterpiece *Das Heilige* is profound. See, for example, the references to it ibid., 106, and esp. the detailed discussions in *Sacrifice Imagined*, 26–9. Cf. the similar reflections on the 'romantic mood' stirred by the introspection into the infinite horizon of all human subjectivity on the basis of the fictional and non-fictional writings of the novelist metaphysician Charles Williams ibid., 125.

45 Hedley's comment on the work's subtitle in *Sacrifice Imagined*, 30, is revealing. As in Otto himself, the relation of the imagination to reason, for all the emphasis placed on the experiential dimension of man's knowledge of the Divine, is key to Hedley's Romantic Platonism throughout: 'The subtitle of Otto's *The Holy* is *An Inquiry into*

the Non-Rational Factor in the Idea of the Divine and its Relation to the Rational. Otto was not part of the widespread vitalism of the period, largely emanating from Kierkegaard and Nietzsche, and evident in his younger colleague Heidegger. Otto stresses the significance of reason in religion. He means by the "rational" the idea of the Divine as clearly grasped by the powers of understanding and within the domain of customary and recognizable definitions.' However, Otto asserts that 'Beneath this sphere of clarity and lucidity, we go on to maintain, there lies a hidden depth, inaccessible to our conceptual thought which we in so far term "non-rational"'.

46 The careful philological analysis in Hedley's 'Affective Attunement and the Experience of the Numinous: Reflections on Rudolf Otto's *Das Heilige*', *International Journal for the Study of the Christian Church* 17 (2017): 33–45, here 37, testifies to the overall significance of the traditions of German metaphysics to his own idealism of the iconic imagination. The elective affinity with Otto is due not least to the shared debt to Romanticism demonstrated in great historical and philosophical detail in the article cited.
47 *Living Forms*, 113.
48 *Iconic Imagination*, 25.
49 Coleridge, *Statesman's Manual*, 30, quoted in *Iconic Imagination*, 142. See also the succinct line of reasoning for a participationist ontology as a corollary of the very concept of a symbol ibid.: 'The symbol presupposes the metaphysics of participation. The symbol 'partakes' in the reality it conveys.' Coleridge's notion of the symbol is close to Schelling's which, in turn, was deeply influenced by the work of Friedrich Creuzer. As the first German translator of Plotinus, Creuzer, though less well-known today, is a pivotal figure in intellectual history linking Greek Neoplatonism and German Idealism. See the intriguing accounts of Creuzer's seminal role in German and European intellectual history in *Sacrifice Imagined*, 41–4, and *Iconic Imagination*, 203–4.
50 Cf. *Iconic Imagination*, 13–14.
51 *Living Forms*, 135.
52 *Iconic Imagination*, 146.
53 Ibid.
54 Ibid.
55 This is one of the most startling insights of the trilogy expressed in *Living Forms*, 123–4.
56 Ibid., 175.
57 Ibid., 129–30.
58 See the illuminating comment on all three of them in *Sacrifice Imagined*, 42, which applies equally well to Hedley's own concept of the threefold imaginary of humankind: 'One manner of conceiving these imaginative universals, or poetic characters, is as poetic archetypes that lie somewhere between (both conceptually and historically) Plato's ideas and Jung's archetypes.'
59 See the important sketches in *Living Forms*, 14–16 and 171, in which Hedley views the doctrine of the soul's ascent as the shared Platonic and biblical core idea of the Phaedrean myth: 'One need only think of the image of ascent in Diotima's speech in the *Symposium* or the paradigmatic image of ascent in the chariot of the *Phaedrus*. Biblical exegesis of Jacob's ladder, Moses on Mount Sinai and St Paul's experience of the ascent of the mind to God are further instances of this paradigm of ethics as ascent.' It is supplemented by the manifold Eastern sources in the more extensive survey of the principal literary accounts of the seminal mythological narrative of the soul in *Iconic Imagination*, 207–10.
60 Phaedr. 245a.

61 *Living Forms*, 15.
62 See the detailed interpretation of the Phaedrean myth *in Living Forms*, 19, in the light of Plato's doctrine of the first principles and ideas. Based upon a characteristically thorough appreciation of its key terminology, it clearly reveals the myth as a key source of the author's transcendental epistemology of the imagination's intuitive grasp of divine infinity as a sine qua non of all finite knowledge and action: 'The basis for epistemological, ethical and aesthetic judgement, Plato avers, must reside in a transcendent principle, perceived by what he refers to as the "eye of understanding". The idea (ἰδέα) has the primary sense of visible forms and appearances (cf. εἶδος), and is linked to the verb (εἶδον, I saw). Both are cognate with both the Latin *videre* and the German *Wissen*. Many other central epistemological terms in Plato possess this strong visual component, e.g. δόξα and θεωρία. Thus Plato uses the symbol of the eye to convey the power and immediacy of the soul's apprehension of immaterial realities.'
63 Cf. *Living Forms*, 187, where Hedley, referring to and citing the interpretation of the myth by John Cottingham, *Philosophy and the Good Life: Reason and the Passions in Greek, Cartesian and Psychoanalytic Ethics* (Cambridge: Cambridge University Press, 1998), 131, rereads the powerful image of the charioteer in the light of his holistic notion of the self. It is in keeping with the hermeneutics of symbols proposed in the trilogy that a myth of archetypal significance, thanks to its infinite semantic fullness, should contain more meaning than might have been intended by its author in his occasionally more austere rationalism.
64 *Living Forms*, 81. Cf. also the interpretations of the Platonic myth in the later volumes, notably *Iconic Imagination*, 122.
65 Ibid., 81. The mood described is 'transcendental' in that 'unity' and 'infinity' are the defining aspects of the primary imagination as the condition of the possibility of all of the soul's cognitive acts.
66 S. T. Coleridge to William Sotheby, Friday 10 September 1802, quoted ibid., 224.
67 *Iconic Imagination*, 224.
68 Ibid., 225.
69 *Living Forms*, 24.
70 Ibid., 39.
71 Cf. ibid., 63.
72 Ibid., 72.
73 Of the three images mentioned ibid., 67, Einstein's of a 'rider on a beam of light carrying a mirror', may be the most well-known one.
74 Ibid., 71.
75 Ibid.
76 'Reflection, Imagination, Love of Wisdom' (see n. 5), 120, where the wording is particularly precise. Thus, the act of 'imagining hidden structures of being' precedes that of 'observing' them, which is generally taken to be the core of scientific research.
77 See the extraordinarily dense chapter 6 of *Iconic Imagination*, esp. 125–32 and 139–40, which contains the author's theory of scientific knowledge in the language of the Phaedrean symbol of the ascent.
78 'Foreword: The Legacy of the *Parmenides*', in *Plato's Parmenides: Text, Translation & Introductory Essay*, translated by Arnold Hermann in collaboration with Sylvana Chrysakopoulou (Las Vegas, Zurich and Athens: Parmenides Publishing, 2010), vii–xviii, here vii.
79 *Iconic Imagination*, 131. In its claim to truth, Hedley's theory of the science of the iconic imagination of which man's Phaedrean striving for true and objective

knowledge is an integral part is therefore very much in keeping with the general notion of the soul's titular power.
80 Ibid., 143.
81 While undoubtedly controversial, Hedley's espousal of human evolution as necessary ibid., 143 n. 70 is, therefore, a key corollary of the imaginative idealism of his trilogy, which may be extended to all other living beings created by the divine intellect to share in its own fullness.
82 Ibid., 139.
83 Ibid., 136.
84 Not surprisingly, it is aesthetic qualities that Hedley ibid. singles out as key characteristics of science which shows its constitutive link to the transcendental power of the imagination.
85 *Living Forms*, 63.
86 Ibid., 77.
87 See *Living Forms*, 144–51.
88 A key influence on Hedley's notion of the soul's eternal subjectivity in the divine intellect is the exposition of the Neoplatonic philosophy of the true self by his Munich teacher Werner Beierwaltes, *Das wahre Selbst. Studien zu Plotins Begriff des Geistes und des Einen* (Frankfurt: Vittorio Klostermann, 2001).
89 Phaed. 96a–102a.
90 *Iconic Imagination*, 33, quoting an online resource.
91 Ibid., 34.
92 Ibid., 39, where Hedley, significantly, cites Clement and Origen, the great Christian Platonists of Alexandria, in support of his metaphysical–ethical reading of Gn. 1.26. It is, above all, via the Cambridge Platonists or Cambridge Origenists that the latter is a decisive source of the author's imaginative metaphysics of freedom. The libertarian theory of action delineated in the trilogy is one of the work's major philosophical attainments.
93 Ibid., 32. See also ibid., 42, where Hedley expands on this concept on the basis of Hans Jonas, 'Image Making and the Freedom of Man', in *The Phenomenon of Life: Towards a Philosophical Biology* (Evanston: Northwestern, 2001), 157–75.
94 Ibid., 42.
95 In an audacious reading of Jean-Paul Sartre's celebrated doctrine of freedom, Hedley, ibid., 69, follows Roger Scruton, *The Soul of the World* (Princeton: Princeton University Press, 2014), 188–9, in likening the existentialist 'néant' by which man is enabled to transcend the necessity of the real and the present in limitless self-creation to the Neoplatonic ἐπέκεινα τῆς οὐσίας or Eriugena's God as *nihil per excellentiam*. The comparison reveals a striking elective affinity as Hedley's concept of the rational soul as an imaginative being shares with Sartre's notion of nothingness as the specific difference of humanity the key idea of man's practical transcendence as a prerequisite of his libertarian freedom.
96 Ibid., 118.
97 *Living Forms*, 169.
98 The important comparison between Platonist and Kantian metaphysics ibid., 149, reveals the author's own answer to the *Problem of Metaphysics* raised in the chapter to be that of an emphatically practical speculative system: 'If we raise the general question "What is metaphysics?" we may well turn back to Plato: Platonism is the recognition of the world as images and Platonic philosophy is the ascent through duty above nature and constitutes his freedom from the mechanism of nature. Kant's idea of the noumenal character beyond space and time has evident parallels

within the Platonist tradition, e.g. Plotinus's doctrine of the "upper soul". Cf. also the comprehensive historical account of the synthesis of Platonism and Kantianism in early modern British and German philosophy, which informs Hedley's systematic train of the thought in the trilogy on the religious imagination throughout, in his *Coleridge, Philosophy and Religion*, 162–9.
99 *Living Forms*, 151.
100 See ibid., 153, where Hedley, in his Platonic rereading of the great Königsberg philosopher, views the ontology of transcendence as the core of Kant's *Metaphysics of Morals*: 'Ethics is not primarily a matter of action but of *being*.'
101 Ibid., 200.
102 Cf. my review of the second volume of Hedley's trilogy in *Theologische Revue* 109 (2012): 1–2.
103 *Sacrifice Imagined*, 18.
104 *Iconic Imagination*, 230.
105 *Living Forms*, 55.
106 Ibid.
107 *Iconic Imagination*, 226. In *Living Forms*, 43–4, Hedley turns the evolutionary uselessness of the building into a compelling anti-naturalist argument with the chronological priority of sacred edifices pointing to the ontological priority of the divine intellect vis-à-vis matter and nature.
108 *Sacrifice Imagined*, 28.
109 Ibid., 66.
110 Ibid., 85.
111 Cf. the comprehensive discussion of this text ibid., 81–3.
112 This passage ibid., 108, may be read as a succinct summary of Hedley's conception of the titular religious rite which is at the heart both of his transcendental analysis of the sacrificial nature of human reason and his religious philosophy of *Christus consummator* and the salvation of man and the cosmos.
113 Ibid., 28.
114 This key excerpt from Immanuel Kant, *Critique of Judgement*, A104–105/B 106 (Kant's *Critique of Judgement*, translated by J. H. Bernard (New York: Hafner, 2017), 100–1), is cited at length and commented on in detail ibid., 32.
115 Ibid., 33.
116 While the former may be the classic example, the latter is convincingly shown to qualify as a religious act of murder ibid., 92: 'Agamemnon is killed in a bathtub referred to in explicitly sacrificial terms as a λέβης, the sacrificial libation bowl. This usage seems to be a *hapax legomenon*: the sacrificial allusions in Clytemnestra's murder of her husband could hardly be clearer.'
117 Cf. the highly illuminating critique of Schopenhauer's Kantian concept of the sublime, as applied to Greek tragedy ibid., 96–9.
118 Cf. ibid., 102.
119 Ibid., 91, the author is outspoken in pursuing a metaphysical and even theological agenda in his interpretation of the greatest plays of classical antiquity: 'We reject theories of tragedy that revolve around the question of genre and attempt to consider the metaphysical and theological implications of tragedy. Tragedy is a form of *praeparatio evangelii*.'
120 Ibid., 102.
121 *Living Forms*, 157–61, Hedley links Socrates's famous definition in Phaed. 81a with the archetypal Greek philosopher's apparent absent-mindedness before the titular feast in Symp. 175a–b.

122 Ibid., 160, quoting James, *Religious Experience* (see n. 36), 165.
123 *Sacrifice Imagined*, 115, where Hedley endorses the interpretation of Cudworth's theory of action as a variety of Kantian 'internalism' propounded by Stephen Darwall, *The British Moralists and the Internal 'Ought': 1640–1740* (Cambridge: Cambridge University Press, 1995), 109–48.
124 Ibid., 117–18.
125 Cf. also the link between the Platonic metaphysics of the image and the Christian ethics of humility in Hedley's interpretation of Cudworth's notion of deification in terms of Meister Eckhart's mysticism in his 'Image, Idol and Likeness: Ralph Cudworth's *Sermon before the House of Commons 1647*', in *Origenes Cantabrigiensis. Ralph Cudworth, Predigt vor dem Unterhaus und andere Schriften*, edited by Alfons Fürst and Christian Hengstermann (Münster: Aschendorff Verlag, 2018), 51–62, here 61: 'Rather than an "enthusiastic" aggrandizement of the self in the process, it is precisely "self-will" that is the strong "Castle, that we all keep garrison'd against heaven in every one of our hearts, which God continually layeth siege unto". . . . In this, Cudworth is following Eckhart, for whom "all things are accomplished in the truly humble person".'
126 *Living Forms*, 160. In *Sacrifice Imagined*, 162–7, Hedley provides a detailed account of his Platonic reading of Shakespeare's plays, also relating the latter to Florentine Renaissance aesthetics.
127 Ibid., quoting 'Das Ideal und das Leben', in *Sämtliche Werke*, edited by E. V. der Hellen (Stuttgart and Berlin: J. G. Cotta, 1904), I, 192.
128 *Sacrifice Imagined*, 164.
129 Ibid., 167.
130 Ibid., 132.
131 Cf. Hedley's trenchant critique of these two spiritual fathers of modern political philosophy ibid., 114–20.
132 Ibid., 170.
133 Ibid., 171. It is, thus, on the basis of his transcendental image of the temple as self-sacrifice that Hedley subjects contractualist reasoning at large to criticism.
134 Paul Tillich, *Shaking the Foundations* (Harmondworth: Penguin, 1969), 69, quoted and discussed in *Iconic Imagination*, 117–18.
135 *Iconic Imagination*, 143. See also the vigorous defence of the Nicene Creed in *Living Forms*, 220.
136 *Living Forms*, 223.
137 Ibid. Cf. also *Sacrifice Imagined*, 156, where Hedley acknowledges not only the Cabbalistic source of the notion of divine self-contraction, but also its problematic *Nachleben* in German Idealism: God 'is sacrificing himself in the quasi-Cabbalistic sense of a self-contradiction or limitation, for example in German Idealism where God is the infinite who sacrifices himself for the finite and finite beings must sacrifice themselves to reveal the infinite'.
138 In *Sacrifice Imagined*, 109 and 137, Hedley cites A. N. Whitehead's famous distinction which he hails as Plato's original insight in his *Adventures of Ideas* (New York: Collier-Macmillan, 1961), 25: 'In this way, Plato is justified in his saying, The Creation of the world – that is to say, the world of civilized order – is the victory of persuasion over force.'
139 'Analogy or Dialectic? Reflections on the Philosophical Theology of Ingolf Dalferth', *Hermeneutische Blätter* 1 (2008): 95–105, here 102. The article quoted is a key document of Hedley's Christological symbolism which is at the heart of his rational theology.
140 Hedley quotes Thomas Traherne, *Centuries of Meditation* (London: Dobell, 1908) I, §60, 41, at the beginning of chapter 6 of *Sacrifice Imagined*, 161.

141　*Living Forms*, 222.
142　*Sacrifice Imagined*, 163.
143　Hedley's account is not only anti-nominalistic but also anti-Spinozistic, as the philosophy of an unethical first substance propounded by the Dutch rationalist is seen as a decisive break in the Western recognition of the objective reality of moral evil. See his 'Introduction', in *The History of Evil in the Eighteenth and Nineteenth Centuries. 1700–1900*, edited by id., Chad Meister and Charles Taliaferro (Oxon and New York: Routledge, 2018), 1–4, here 1: 'The God of Spinoza's *Ethics*, for example, is emphatically not a moral being. Spinoza was opposed to inherited Western morality in his refusal to recognize evil.'
144　See the powerful description of evil in *Living Forms*, 217, along the conceptual lines of a contemporary reformulation of the Christian Platonist paradox of evil as incomprehensible, yet painfully real, *privatio boni* from which the above concepts have been taken: 'Yet by "explanation" I do not mean a quasi-scientific relation of *explanans* and *explanandum*. Evil has by definition a surd quality. It is precisely the unintelligible nature of evil as "motiveless malignity" and as hatred of goodness that distinguishes it from deplorable selfishness, callousness or greed. Scarcity of resources, conflicts of interests, and limits of sympathy can account for much human malice and cruelty. But such empirical or psychological factors can barely explain the more egregious horrors of human behaviour.'
145　See the rereading of the traditional notion of original sin in terms of a sense of hopeless alienation from the Divine grounded in humankind's structures of sin, whether economic or political, in *Sacrifice Imagined*, 164: 'Original Sin is the doctrine that mankind is at least structurally if not inherently alienated from God.'
146　Cf. the important argument originally advanced by Origen and Anselm of Canterbury ibid., 167.
147　Ibid., 171.
148　This précis of the author's theology of the Cross in *Sacrifice Imagined*, 172, is a highly revealing example of his symbolistic hermeneutics of imaginative rationality applied to the key tenets of Christian faith. While grounded in the transcendental analysis of the role of self-sacrifice in human morality, his Christology nevertheless does justice to the historic importance of Christ incarnate. In so doing, Hedley manages to formulate a notion of divine personhood which is neither a mere metaphor nor a figment of the imagination, as in Spinoza's *Theological-Political Treatise*, but an analogical predicate of the absolute. Cf. also the strong plea for divine personhood in the exegesis of Exod. 3.14 provided ibid., 36–8.
149　*Living Forms*, 147. The whole chapter is devoted to D. MacKinnon, *The Problem of Metaphysics* (London: Cambridge University Press, 1974).
150　Cf. *Sacrifice Imagined*, 138.
151　See the formal account of the argument ibid., 150.
152　In the principal chapter on Maistre's soul-making theodicy, this key text from his *St Petersburg Dialogues Or Conversations on the Temporal Government of Providence*, translated and edited by Richard A. Lebrun (Montreal: McGill-Queen's University Press, 1993), 217, with the leitmotif of the second volume of the trilogy, that is, the altar upon which humanity is sacrificed, is quoted twice, first in its original French ibid., 155, then in an English translation ibid. 157. Cf. also the discussion of this text ibid., 204.
153　See the important remarks on Maistre's commitment to Origenism against the backdrop of the prevalent Augustinianism of Reformation theology ibid., 144: 'Thus

I suspect that the attraction of Origen resided in the latter's resolute attachment to the goodness of God. The espousal of a God of inscrutable will, the Augustine so important for Luther and Calvin as well as Jansenism, is problematic for a thinker like Maistre. Origen is the Church Father who is dedicated to freedom.'

154 Ibid., 153.
155 Ibid.
156 Maistre, *St Petersburg Dialogues* (see n. 152), 43, quoted in its original French ibid. and in an English translation ibid. 158.
157 *Sacrifice Imagined*, 145.
158 Ibid., 156.
159 Cf. ibid., 224–5, where Hedley quotes the early modern Cambridge Platonist's exegesis of the *Divine Dialogues* (London: James Flesher, 1668), 282, 284, 296–7 More's deeply Origenist Christology of the pre-existent Christ whose soul and body are shaped by the Son informs Hedley's cosmic Christology.
160 In *Living Forms*, 225–42, Hedley delineates his concept of historical revelation in a comprehensive defence of Austin Farrer's account in his systematic *Glass of Vision* (London: Dacre Press, 1948), and his exegesis of the book of Revelation in *A Rebirth of Images: The Making of St John's Apocalypse* (London: Dacre Press, 1949). In so doing, Hedley fuses Farrer's notion of 'double agency' with the latter's concept of revelation as an event imagined in terms of the veridic, rather than merely aesthetic metaphors of the iconic imagination.
161 Farrer, *Glass of vision* (see n. 160), 43, quoted in *Living Forms*, 228.
162 *Iconic Imagination*, 218.
163 See the link between Hedley's symbolistic epistemology and rational ecclesiology in his first exposition of the third of the three primordial images in his reading of S. T. Coleridge's 'Kubla Khan', in 'Coleridge's Intellectual Intuition, the Vision of God, and the Walled Gard of "Kubla Khan"', *Journal of the History of Ideas* 59 (1998): 115–34, here 121.
164 The discussion of one of the key sources of the author's account of the second and third ecumenical symbols in *Living Forms*, 231–2, is revealing in terms of his hermeneutic of religious imagery. While agreeing with Cudworth that Christ's sacrifice is an important aspect of the infinite semantic richness of the sacramental symbol, the denominational bone of contention is the question whether the sacrificial or the festive character is to be stressed in the interpretation of the Eucharist, whether in liturgy or in theology. Though Anglican in character, Hedley's philosophy of the sacrament is, hence, deeply ecumenical, as the semantic core of the infinity of meaning expressed by the symbol allows for great liturgical and dogmatic latitude.
165 Ralph Cudworth, *A Discourse Concerning the True Notion of the Lord's Supper* (London, 1642), 15–16, quoted in *Sacrifice Imagined*, 206.
166 *Sacrifice Imagined*, 207.
167 Cudworth, *True Notion* (see n. 165), 54, quoted ibid., 207.
168 *Living Forms*, 230. It is not by chance that the imaginative theodicy of the middle work of the trilogy, true to its Platonic structure of creation, redemption and restitution ends in a comprehensive account of 'joy'. See *Sacrifice Imagined*, 220–4.
169 *Living Forms*, 236.
170 It is not by accident that Raphael's painting is on the front cover of the concluding volume of the trilogy.
171 Quoted in *Living Forms*, 230.

172 Cf. Hedley's penetrating interpretations of Shakespeare's late dramatic work in *Iconic Imagination*, 237–9, which, in many ways, provides the most compelling literary evidence for his own religious vision of salvation.
173 *Iconic Imagination*, 245. Hedley's use of Plotinus's notion of the second hypostasis for the sake of biblical exegesis is a particularly telling example of his Christian Platonist synthesis of biblical and philosophical thought.
174 'Coleridge and "Kubla Khan"' (see n. 163), 131.
175 *Iconic Imagination*, 247.
176 Cf. *Living Forms*, 92–3.
177 David Hume, *Dialogues Concerning Natural Religion*, in *Dialogues and Natural History of Religion*, edited by John Gaskin (Oxford: Oxford University Press, 1993), 113, quoted in *Living Forms*, 167.
178 *Living Forms*, 167.
179 Ibid.
180 As is clear from the graphic terminology, Hedley's rejection of Augustinianism is inspired by the German historian of philosophy Kurt Flasch's formidable philosophical onslaught on the Latin Church Father in his edition of the latter's first comprehensive treatise on divine omnipotence and election as transcending our categories of good and evil: *Logik des Schreckens. Augustinus von Hippo, De diversis quaestionibus ad Simplicianum* I 2, translated by Walter Schäfer, edited and commented on by Kurt Flasch, 3rd edn (Mainz: Dieterich, 2012).
181 *Sacrifice Imagined*, 138–9. However, the quotation is not from the author's celebrated *Letter of Resolution*, published anonymously in London in 1661, which constitutes the first sustained defence of Origenism as a Christian metaphysics, but from the author's sermon on *God is Love*, delivered in Cambridge three years earlier: *The Remains of that Reverend and Learned Prelate Dr George Rust* (London, 1686), 1–20, here 18.
182 See, above all, Hedley's numerous seminal articles on Ralph Cudworth's *True Intellectual System of the Universe*, notably its comprehensive exposition of the ancient theology of pagan and patristic Platonism which the author himself has been instrumental in revealing to be the chief source of the early modern British and European debates on the theology of the Trinity: 'The Platonick Trinity: Philology and Divinity in Cudworth's Philosophy of Religion', in *Philologie und Erkenntnis. Beiträge zu Begriff und Problem frühneuzeitlicher 'Philologie'*, edited by Ralph Häfner (Tübingen: De Gruyter, 2001), 247–63; 'Persons of Substance and the Cambridge Connection: Some Roots and Ramifications of the Trinitarian Controversy in Seventeenth-Century England', in *Socinianism and Arminianism: Antitrinitarians, Calvinists and Cultural Exchange in Seventeenth-Century Europe*, edited by Martin Mulsow and Jan Rohls (Leiden and Bosten: Brill, 2005), 225–40; 'The Cambridge Platonists and the "Miracle of the Christian World"', in *Autonomie und Menschenwürde. Origenes in der Philosophie der Neuzeit*, Alfons Fürst and Christian Hengstermann (Münster: Aschendorff Verlag, 2012), 185–97, esp. 192–6; 'Gods and Giants: Cudworth's Platonic Metaphysics and His Ancient Theology', *British Journal for the History of Philosophy* 25 (2017): 932–53.
183 Cf. the magisterial account of the poet philosopher's seminal role in his reception of Cambridge Platonism and German Idealism after the historic Pantheism Controversy in Enlightenment Germany in: *Coleridge, Philosophy and Religion*, 18–87, succinctly summarized in 'Coleridge as a Theologian', in *The Oxford Handbook of Samuel Taylor Coleridge*, edited by Frederick Burwick (Oxford: Oxford University Press, 2009), 473–

92. Cf. also 'Coleridge's Creative Contemplation', in *Coleridge and Contemplation*, edited by Peter Cheyne (Oxford: Oxford University Press, 2017), 220-36.
184 See the concluding overview in Hedley's concise analysis of Christian theology in his early article 'Pantheism, Trinitarian Theism and the Idea of Unity: Reflections on the Christian Concept of God', *Religious Studies* 32 (1996): 61-77, here 75-7. Deism, the third doctrine, is dismissed out of hand as 'spiritually a rather barren option' (ibid., 76). Hedley's rational theology hinges upon his Platonic concept of the transcendence of the One and the Intellect over the many of material reality, by which it is distinguished from Spinoza's pantheism, which is at once its closest relative and chief foil.
185 Hedley's theology proper can, therefore, be seen as participating in and decisively contributing to the 'revival of Perfect Being Theology' mentioned in *Iconic Imagination*, 127. The author also uses the time-honoured divine name of early modern rationalism without any further comment in 'Forms of Reflection' (see n. 5), 113.
186 See both the stress laid upon the theology of the One in Hedley's 'Legacy of the Parmenides' (see n. 78) and the key concept of 'relational unity' in his work on the Cambridge Platonists in 'Platonick Trinity' (see n. 182), 259-61, and on S. T. Coleridge in *Coleridge, Philosophy and Religion*, 63-4.
187 Hedley's account of the patristic appropriation of the Platonist metaphysics of the One and the Intellect throughout draws upon his teacher Werner Beierwaltes's magisterial exposition of the development of Christian Platonism and idealism from Late Antiquity to the present day in his *Platonismus und Idealismus*, 2nd edn (Frankfurt: Vittorio Klostermann, 2004).
188 'Coleridge and "Kubla Khan"' (see n. 163), 127.
189 Hedley alludes to the classic of German historiography of philosophy by Hans Joachim Krämer, *Der Ursprung der Geistmetaphysik. Untersuchungen zur Geschichte des Platonismus zwischen Platon und Plotin*, 2nd edn (Amsterdam: B. R. Grüner – Publisher, 1967).
190 Hedley concurs with Cudworth in his rejection of this strand of Neoplatonism as 'a certain kind of *Mysterious Atheism*' in 'The Platonick Trinity' (see n. 182), 257, and *Coleridge, Philosophy and Religion*, 61.
191 This is the core of Hedley's compelling interpretation of this decisive part of the history of Christian dogma in 'Platonick Trinity' (see n. 182), 255.
192 *Iconic Imagination*, 219. Cf. also the detailed account of Nicholas of Cusa's celebrated doctrine of God as *coincidentia oppositorum* in 'Coleridge and "Kubla Khan"' (see n. 163), 122-3.
193 Cf. Hedley's line of argument ibid., 136, where he quotes Plotinus's characterization of the One as πρὸ τοῦ τί. God is not a 'thing' in any way, but the principle of 'thingness' itself. He is the principle of determinateness which as such is itself beyond determinate thought and being.
194 'Coleridge as a Theologian' (see n. 183), 482.
195 See the succinct explanation of the Christological concept of 'alterity' in 'Christian Concept of God' (see n. 184), 71, in which Hedley expressly links it to that of the ὁμοούσιος: 'The concept of "alterity" is meant to avoid the strong sense of difference implied by the word "other". The Son, the Word, is not other than the Father but, as the councils said, consubstantial.'
196 See the definition of personhood and the theological aporia of a purely Spinozistic notion of divine infinity in *Coleridge, Philosophy and Religion*, 70: 'Personhood seems intuitively to involve an awareness of otherness and the idealists were convinced

that a minimal requirement of being a person involves distinguishing oneself from another self. Yet this conflicted with the all-oneness tenet of Spinozism. If God is all, he cannot be a person in any remote sense because logically there can be nothing which is "other" to the "all-oneness".

197 'Christian Concept of God' (see n. 184), 62.
198 Enn. VI 8, quoted and interpreted in *Living Forms*, 93. The first treatise on divine freedom, Plotinus's enn. VI 8 is one of the most important Neoplatonic sources of Hedley's own rational theology. See the discussions of this treatise in Hedley's early works such as 'Christian Concept of God' (see n. 184), 70–1, *Coleridge, Philosophy and Religion*, 82, and 'Platonick Trinity' (see n. 182), 257, and his more recent remarks on this text in 'Coleridge as a Theologian' (see n. 183), 486–9, and 'Contemplative Imagination' (see n. 12), 228.
199 See Hedley's explicit affirmation of univocal divine goodness in *Sacrifice Imagined*, 135, and, more recently, in his 'Gods and Giants' (see n. 182), 940.
200 Spinoza is usually mentioned alongside David Hume with the former's *Theological-Political Treatise* and the Appendix to *Ethics* I and the latter's *History of Religion* (1757) and *Natural Dialogues* providing the most trenchant and most formidable critique of religion in the nascent modern age (cf., for example, *Living Forms*, 148, and *Iconic Imagination*, 202). On the anti-Spinozist foundations of Hedley's imaginative idealism, see his critical comments on the Dutch philosopher's *Treatise* and *Ethics* in *Living Forms*, 12–14.
201 In *Iconic Imagination*, 142, Hedley singles out the biblical account of God's arbitrary preference of Jacob over Esau, Augustine's doctrine of predestination and Kierkegaard's admiration for Abraham obeying God in choosing to slaughter Isaac for particular critique. See the more detailed critique of the Danish theologian's 'teleological suspension of the ethical' in matters of religion in *Living Forms*, 154–5.
202 Cf. *Sacrifice Imagined*, 20.
203 *Iconic Imagination*, 140.
204 Ibid., 141.
205 *Iconic Imagination*, 196, where the author goes on to link the Indian theologumenon to the sapiental tradition originating in the Old Testament Wisdom books and culminating in Christ's identification with the Logos in the Gospel of John.
206 Henry More, *A Platonick Song of the Soul*, edited with an Introductory Study by Alexander Jacob (Lewisburg: Bucknell University Press; London: Associated University Press, 1988), 409, quoted in *Living Forms*, 133.
207 Cf. the deeply Platonic meditation on the sun as symbol of the Divine in *Living Forms*, 135: 'For example, the symbol of light conveys the productive bestowing of illumination without exhaustion or depletion of the source, but also joy; awe; insight; warmth; sustenance. There is a continuum between the nature and effects of the symbol (e.g. the sun) and the object symbolized (God).' Sunlight is a telling example of the double agency of God and nature, as the sun participates in divine creativity, bringing about and sustaining life on earth and disclosing to it its archetypal principle for a certain period of its cosmic lifetime. Thus, it is a specific mode of the divine substance within the 'continuum between the nature and effects of the symbol … and the object symbolized'.
208 The dense meditation on different forms of unity ibid., 91, may be seen as providing a key to the cosmology and soteriology of the author's imaginative idealism which is particularly indebted to the first principle of Platonism, the One, as first enunciated in its founder's *Parmenides*.

209 Again, the image, on the principles of Hedley's imaginative idealism, is not a mere metaphor, but possesses a metaphysical *fundamentum in re* in that the finite 'I am', in its imagination, is a 'repetition' of the archetypal infinite 'I am'. Shakespeare's verse, applied to the divine nature, expresses an analogical truth about it. While the 'unknown' cannot refer to the fullness of God's knowledge of the ideas, it may be applied to the creative novelty introduced into the world by the countless myriads of autonomous natural and spiritual agents.

210 *Sacrifice Imagined*, 59, where the author, following the general drift of Scriptural theology, comes close to positing a bipolarity in God as process and reality: 'Scripture provides a vision of God not as pure actuality but relishing the goodness of human beings. There has always been a drive away from the strict aseity of the Divine towards a theogony in which God is involved in the life of the universe and in which human beings play a role in the process of redemption.'

211 *Living Forms*, 238.

212 Hedley's metaphysical reading of Ws. 11.21 in *Iconic Imagination*, 235, is heavily influenced by the seminal article on the Christian Platonist Augustine by his teacher Werner Beierwaltes: 'Augustins Interpretation von *Sapientia* 11,21', *Revue d'études augustiniennes et patristiques* 15 (1969): 51-61. Cf. also the more extensive explanation of the Neoplatonic doctrine in *Living Forms*, 78: 'This is the Neoplatonic tenet that when the soul is liberated from evil it ascends quite naturally to the Good: *omnia in deum tendunt et recurrunt*. This metaphor of the natural place of the soul in God or its gravitation towards the One is employed by Christian theologians of Neoplatonic provenance such as Eriugena and Eckhart.'

213 *Iconic Imagination*, 243. In the grand tradition of the ancient theology of Origen and Plotinus, the fathers of Christian and pagan Neoplatonism, and the Cambridge Platonists and Romantics, their most important early modern heirs, Hedley posits 'creative vision' as the principle of all being as being. The key text, quoted at length and commented on in great detail ibid., 243-4, is Plotinus's philosophy of nature in Ennead III 8. On the seminal role that this treatise, the first to be translated into German by F. Creuzer, played at the early stages of nascent German Idealism, see 'Creative Contemplation' (see n. 183), 228-30. See also the excellent discussion of 'undiminished giving' and 'creative contemplation' as the twin principles of Neoplatonism in: Maria L. Gatti, 'Plotinus: The Platonic Tradition and the Foundation of Neoplatonism', in *The Cambridge Companion to Plotinus*, edited by Lloyd P. Gerson (Cambridge: Cambridge University Press, 1996), 10-37.

214 *Iconic Imagination*, 35.

215 Cf., above all, the chapter of that title in Werner Beierwaltes, *Denken des Einen. Studien zur neuplatonischen Philosophie und ihrer Wirkungsgeschichte* (Frankfurt: Vittorio Klostermann, 1985), 73-113.

216 See the succinct précis of Eckhard's reflections upon the relationship between divine archetype and human image which throughout informs Hedley's account of the intimate link between human knowledge and action and divine creativity in *Iconic Imagination*, 50: 'The image points to that which is beyond itself: it has its essence in its exemplar or archetype (*Urbild*). It is not the relation of accidents to a substance. The specifically Neoplatonic dimension of this metaphysics of the image is particularly clear in Latin Sermon XLIX. In this passage the image is presented as having eight characteristics: it possesses likeness, and secondly is similar in its "nature and species". Thirdly, the perfect image is identical with its source. Fourthly, the image emanates from its source. Fifthly, it excludes any otherness. The image and

its exemplar are not divided things or substances. It is characterized by reflection, by a *reditio completa* (perfect return) of the image to its exemplar. Finally, the image possesses the abundance of its source.'

217 Farrer, *Glass of Vision* (see n. 160), 7–8, quoted and discussed at length in *Living Forms*, 236–8, quotes Spinoza, Eth. 2p13, to whom he attributes his conversion from an exterior to an inward Deity. See also Farrer's further critical explanation of his early 'Spinozism' in hindsight: 'Undoubtedly I misunderstood Spinoza, in somewhat the same fashion as . . . St. Augustine misunderstood Plotinus, turning him to Christian uses. Here, anyhow is what I took from Spinozism. I would no longer attempt, with the psalmist, "to set God before my face". I would see him as the underlying cause of my thinking, especially of those thoughts in which I tried to think of him.' Cf. also the more detailed interpretation of Farrer's theological autobiography in 'Shaping Spirit of the Imagination' (see n. 12), 115–20.

218 *Living Forms*, 166. Not only does this passage from Shakespeare's greatest masterpiece illuminate the principle of double agency, but also the limitations that libertarian human action of necessity imposes upon God's creative vision of the world.

219 *Iconic Imagination*, 57.

220 Cf. ibid., 37–8, where Hedley draws upon the respective excavations to bolster his philosophical argument for the 'precedence of religion over technology', and the more comprehensive discussion of prehistoric art ibid., 54–7.

221 Ibid., 200, where Hedley buttresses his apparently anachronistic philosophical agenda on the basis of his philosophy of the imagination informing all of our thought and language alike: 'Moreover, if language is deeply and necessarily metaphorical, we are always confronting the mythic.' Indeed, if the transcendental analysis of the imaginative idealism of the trilogy is apposite, we cannot but view our history as a theogony in which our Phaedrean striving, despite all the sacrifices symbolized by the temple, will eventually be fulfilled in the divine plenitude of the heavenly city.

222 See the analysis of the narratives of modernity in *Living Forms*, 1–37.

223 *Iconic Imagination*, 202.

224 The debate between Schelling and Coleridge on the relationship between divine and human consciousness, recounted in *Living Forms*, 123–4, is one of considerable systematic interest. Is the cosmic double agency by which nature and man come to participate in a vision of the Divine thegonic in the strict sense of the word? Does it add to the divine life itself, as it communicates itself to the cosmos in triumph and tragedy alike? It is a question explicitly raised at various points in the trilogy. Whereas Schelling views the 'gradual disclosure of truth in myths' of tautegorical power as 'part of a progressive unfolding of the Godhead', Coleridge chooses to see the divine truth as 'essentially timeless'.

225 'Analogy or Dialectic?' (see n. 139), 103.

226 Hedley himself is outspoken in emphasizing the Christological character of the entirety of his narrative *theologia naturalis*, thereby providing a hermeneutical key to the imaginative ontology of his trilogy on the very first page of its first volume, where he invokes the Christological title of *Christus victor*: 'This book is consciously written in a tradition of Christian Platonism, but it emphasizes the eschatological-mythical dimension of Platonism and the apocalyptic-*Christus Victor* gospel of Christian faith. It is a fusion of narrative *and* natural theology' (*Living Forms*, 1). In 'Analogy or Dialectic?' (see n. 139), 102, Hedley provides an explanation of the latter epithet, the *Christus consummator*, expressly linking it to the 'eschatological-mythical dimension of Platonism'.

Part II

Spiritual sensation in ancient and early modern Christian Platonism

3

Θεία αἴσθησις

Origen's epistemological concept of spiritual sensation

Alfons Fürst

1 The concept of spiritual sensation as the 'humble beginnings' of imagination

In his books about religious imagination, Douglas Hedley investigates imagination as the master way to express the inexpressible. Musing about various aspects of this approach to the knowledge of the divine in his book *The Iconic Imagination* of 2016, he refers to the ancient Platonic concept of spiritual sensation coined by Origen and Plotinus.[1] In the previous volume *Living Forms of the Imagination* of 2008, he stated that the ancient philosophers had no concept of imagination, but this need not mean that the phenomenon called imagination did not exist.[2] I would like to propose – and if I do not misunderstand him, this is suggested by Hedley himself in the volume of 2016 – that the concept of spiritual sensation can be seen as an equivalent of the concept of imagination, one of its 'humble beginnings' in Antiquity.[3] Through 'the eye of the soul' or 'of the mind', as Origen and Plotinus said,[4] using a famous phrase of Plato,[5] or through 'the eye of the heart', as Origen said with a synonymous biblical term,[6] finite rational beings can apprehend transcendent forms and ideas.[7] 'Plato uses the symbol of the eye to convey the power and immediacy of the soul's apprehension of immaterial realities.'[8] In the language of spiritual sensation as coined by Origen and Plotinus, this is extended to all five corporeal senses: the eternal God is apprehended via the senses of seeing, hearing, smelling, tasting and touching.

When Hedley uses this tradition to explain 'the living forms of the imagination' and 'iconic imagination', he mostly refers to Plotinus. Origen is mentioned only scarcely, but appropriately in the context of this topic. With regard to the concept of spiritual sensation, we can rightly place Plotinus and Origen next to each other. What Hedley points out about Plotinus and (Neo)Platonism regarding imagination and intellectual perception and knowledge holds true for Origen as well. In support, he can quote one of his own Platonic ancestors at Cambridge: the Cambridge Platonist John Smith (1618–52) 'knew the writings of Plotinus well although the language of the spiritual sensation is taken from Origen'.[9] Smith, who can therefore be deemed an Origenist as well, was not wrong in combining Plotinus and Origen with regard to the topic of spiritual sensation. Both ancient philosophers were Platonists who had the same ideas about the indirect apprehension of the transcendent reality. They shared the same principles of cognition based on the Platonic tenet of participation: the lower, the sensible, the image, is derived from and participates in the higher, the intelligible, the imagined archetype. It is thus not odd at all to put the great pagan Platonist Plotinus besides the great Christian Platonist Origen, and the less so as Hedley's books are 'consciously written in a tradition of Christian Platonism'.[10] The emphasis in the following contribution will thus be put on Origen.

2 A brief history of the research on spiritual sensation

As to the ancient founders of this tradition, Karl Rahner published a seminal article about Origen in 1932,[11] which is his very first academic publication,[12] and two articles in 1933 and 1934 about Bonaventure and the Middle Ages.[13] Hans Urs von Balthasar studied these works of Rahner with great care and devoted a long chapter to the concept of spiritual sensation in his anthology of Origenian texts of 1938 entitled *Spirit and Fire*.[14] By these studies Rahner and von Balthasar set the stage for the subsequent research on this topic up to present times. Both theologians, von Balthasar even more than Rahner, draw a lot on this epistemological concept in their own theological thought – but I am not going to deal with this aspect of Origen's reception, although it was very important for the development of Catholic theology during the twentieth century.[15] In Origen research, however, this topic was well known as a key element of Origen's spiritual theology, although it failed to attract much attention.[16] Only some aspects related to this idea have been treated in a few contributions.[17] As to Plotinus, in 1986 John Dillon published an article in which he discussed Rahner's depiction of Origen's doctrine of spiritual senses and provided a brief outline of Plotinus's concept in *Enneads* VI 7.[18] Dillon's article, especially his interpretation of Origen, was critically reviewed and convincingly confuted by Mark J. McInroy in 2012.[19]

Apart from this small number of scholarly studies of the concept of spiritual senses in Origen (and in Plotinus), the topic as such has attracted wider attention only recently in an essay collection edited by Paul Gavrilyuk and Sarah Coakley in 2012.[20] As to the development of this concept in later epochs, there are some monographs on Byzantine and medieval authors like Simeon the New Theologian,[21] William of Auxerre,[22] Bonaventure,[23] and on the later Middle Ages,[24] but, as noted by Gavrilyuk and Coakley, much more is to be done with regard to other authors in the Syriac, Byzantine and Western medieval tradition and some strands of thought in Early Modern and Modern Times like the Cambridge Platonists, German Pietists, German and English Romantics, French phenomenologists and present-day charismatics.[25]

3 The spiritual senses in Origen and in Scripture

In his pioneering French article of 1932, Karl Rahner takes into account nearly all the passages in Origen's works related to spiritual sensation, except the ones found later in the Tura papyri in 1941 (especially the *Dialogue with Heraclides* and the treatise *On Passover*).[26] Origen alludes to this concept very often, and sometimes he gives a concise description.

The first principal texts are to be found in the early systematic treatise *On First Principles*, written in Alexandria during the late 220s.[27] The *Dialogue with Heraclides* discovered in Tura and thus unknown to Rahner and von Balthasar before its first publication in 1949, which is of uncertain date but almost certainly belongs to the Caesarean period of Origen's life after 233, contains a detailed description of all the five divine senses and extends the concept to the spiritual dimension of other parts of the body like hands, feet, bones, heart, hairs and blood.[28] In a passage in the *Homilies on Isaiah* inspired by Jesus's promise that 'out of his belly shall flow rivers of living water' (Jn 7.38), which is not taken into account by Rahner, Origen explains that we have eyes, ears and feet of the body as well as of the soul or the heart, respectively, and poses the question 'whether we might also have two bellies, a corporeal and a spiritual one'.[29] The most important biblical book in this respect is the Song of Songs, so that in the *Commentary* as well as in the *Homilies on the Song of Songs*, which were most probably written around 240 and 245, respectively, Origen dwells on the concept of spiritual senses, when he explains the 'savour of thy ointments' in Song 1.3-4, and refers to it time and again in his exegesis of the highly metaphorical text of the Song of Songs.[30] Eventually, we find this theory in two late works written between 245 and 249, namely in the *Commentary on the Gospel of Matthew*, where Origen explains the interconnection of the five 'lamps of the senses' (whose principle is Christ as wisdom) as analogous to the interconnection of the virtues (whose content and principle is Christ as well),[31] and in two passages of the apology *Against Celsus*, where he gives a succinct summary of the core of this idea based on the main biblical texts.[32] Apart from these major texts, Origen uses the idea of spiritual sensation as a whole or parts of it throughout his œuvre in order to explain metaphorical and anthropomorphic notions in Scripture and to describe a way how the finite human mind is able to perceive infinite spiritual realities.[33]

For the five senses, Origen has recourse to passages in Scripture where the particular bodily organs are mentioned or used in a metaphorical way: 'the eyes of your understanding' in Eph. 1.18,[34] the 'ears to hear' in Mt 11.15-16; 13.9[35] and the 'unspeakable words heard' by Paul, 'whether in the body or out of the body', in 'the third heaven' in 2 Cor. 12.2-4,[36] the taste according to the commandment in Ps. 33.9 LXX: 'Taste and see that the Lord is good',[37] which is the taste for the 'living bread from heaven, that a man may eat thereof, and not die' but 'live for ever' in Jn 6.32-33 together with 6.50-51,[38] the smell of the 'sweet savour of Christ', 'the savour of death' and 'the savour of life' in 2 Cor. 2.15-16,[39] and the touch 'of the Word of life, that our hands have handled' in 1 Jn 1.1.[40] The most important text is Prov. 2.5, because in his reading it provides a biblical umbrella term for his notion of the spiritual senses: καὶ αἴσθησιν θείαν εὑρήσεις (*sensum divinum invenies* in Latin) – 'thou shalt find a divine sense'.[41] This is not the wording of the Septuagint: καὶ ἐπίγνωσιν θεοῦ εὑρήσεις – 'thou shalt come to the knowledge of God', which is translated in the Vulgate as *et scientiam Dei invenies*. Origen's version is a peculiar one, maybe taken up from Clement of Alexandria who provides the same wording.[42] It need not seem that strange if one notices that in

Clement as well as in Origen αἴσθησις is nearly synonymous with ἐπίγνωσις or γνῶσις in the sense of 'perception'.[43]

4 Spiritual sensation: Mystical psychology, imagery and apologetics

What is 'spiritual sensation'? The concept as such is commonly known in Origenian studies, but it is not easy to explain what we should understand by it. Hedley poses the main question: 'Is the language of sensation merely metaphorical or does it refer to the perception of spiritual realities? Are terms such as "seeing" and "hearing" employed in a figurative manner to denote "understanding", without placing any importance on the sensation?'[44] As we will see in the following, in Origen's concept of spiritual senses sensation does play a real role in the process of perceiving and understanding spiritual realities. 'The image becomes a vehicle of the experience of transcendence,' Hedley states (for Plotinus) with regard to imagination. 'Where conceptual and discursive thought fail, the image becomes an instrument of apprehension of the noetic realm.'[45] This is the core idea of spiritual sensation as well. The senses have a mediatory power: they embody the invisible into forms of corporeal relationship and thus connect heaven and earth.

It is precisely this mediating function of the spiritual senses to which Karl Rahner pointed in the opening statement of his article of 1932:

> If religious, and especially mystical, experience seeks to express the inexpressible despite all the obstacles that lie in the way, then inevitably it must go back to images which come from the realm of sense knowledge. Mystics are happy, therefore, to speak of sight, hearing and taste of a spiritual kind in order to describe their experience of the realities of which they were conscious.[46]

As a contribution to the history of this idea, Rahner analyses the main aspects of Origen's concept of spiritual senses (Rahner himself speaks of a 'doctrine', but this is due to the theological terminology common in those days, it does not match Origen's undogmatic and open-minded style of research). In lack of other evidence of this 'doctrine' before Origen, 'he must have drawn it from no other source than Scripture. Those passages in particular come into question in which religious understanding is expressed in terms which manifest the operations of sense powers.'[47] Although these biblical passages 'simply contain well chosen metaphors',[48] the Origenian concept based on them is not metaphorical.[49] Of course, when Origen explains notions in Scripture like, for instance, seeing and hearing God, he intends to avoid any anthropomorphic understanding. He interprets this metaphorical language as referring not to any material sense knowledge of God, but to the idea of a sense faculty for the divine which is different from corporeal sense perception. In this regard, Origen's concept of a spiritual sense perception is apologetical. Within his system of the ascent of the soul to perfection, however, Origen uses the concept of spiritual senses 'to give a clearer account to the psychology of mystical experience'. Although it is still an open question whether Origen speaks of a mystical experience different from general religious understanding and Platonic enthusiasm, 'it is evident, then, in Origen', Rahner concludes, 'that the spiritual senses can be the organs of mystical knowledge'.[50] In Origen's concept of spiritual sensation, the divine senses are far more than an imagery to explain anthropomorphic metaphors in Scripture. They have a mediating function within the imagination of divine realities. On the one hand, 'divine sensation' is linked to corporeal sense knowledge of material things that are imagined in the language which is used to describe 'divine sensation', and on the other hand it transcends corporeality because 'divine sensation' is not a corporeal, but an incorporeal perception of immaterial, spiritual realities.

In his discussion of 'the most useful article of Karl Rahner', John Dillon, in 1986, made a case for some development in Origen's thought about the spiritual senses.[51] He compares the early Origenian texts on this matter with the late ones and assumes 'that, at the time he wrote the *De principiis*, Origen had not yet fully developed a theory of "spiritual" senses', while 'in the *Dialogue with Heraclides* . . . we find the theory developed noticeably'.[52] In the *Commentary on Matthew* then 'we find the theory fully developed',[53] and in *Contra Celsum* 'Origen propounds a remarkable theory of noetic or spiritual analogues to the five senses'.[54] Dillon argues for a purely metaphorical use of the language of sensation in the early Origen, whereas the late Origen presents the theory of spiritual sensation as a fully developed epistemological concept. As against this interpretation of the evidence, Mark J. McInroy argued convincingly in 2012 'that unexamined aspects of Origen's early writings in fact demonstrate noteworthy continuities between his early and late uses of sensory language'.[55] Whereas Dillon distinguishes a metaphorical use of the language of sensation in the early Origen from an analogical use in his later works, McInroy shows that 'Origen does not cleanly divide his use of sensory language into "analogical" and "metaphorical" moments'.[56] Instead, his use of this language is multivalent, and even in his early works 'Origen uses the language of sensation in a manner that does not seem to be metaphorical'.[57] McInroy corroborates this view on the basis of a number of early texts prior to *De principiis* in which the presence of God to the human senses, namely 'to the eyes of the mind', is described in an unmetaphorical way. The perception of God is rather described in close resemblance to corporeal perception.[58] For instance, Origen speaks of 'a bodiless voice in the depth of the hearts of human beings which they, after recollecting themselves and after entering their chamber and closing the door of their senses, and being wholly outside the body, send up to him who alone can hear such a voice.'[59] 'Instead of an early, metaphorical period that is followed by a late, analogical portion of Origen's career, then', McInroy concludes his study, 'we find in Origen's works an intermingled use of metaphor and analogy throughout his writings, both early and late.'[60]

The result of this small scholarly discussion is that Origen, as has been shown by McInroy, from the outset did not use the language of spiritual sensation only metaphorically. Both aspects, the metaphorical and the analogical ones, are connected to each other. And it was not simply for exegetical-apologetical reasons that Origen coined this concept, as Dillon insinuated from his restricted perspective that was mainly based on Origen's late debate with Celsus.[61] He conceived of the idea of spiritual senses rather as an epistemological theory in order 'to express the inexpressible despite all the obstacles that lie in the way',[62] as Rahner set the task which still remains to be solved.

5 Corporeal and spiritual senses in theory and practice

As shown in Chapter 4, it was not simply reasons of exegetical or apologetical expedience which gave rise to the concept of spiritual senses in Origen's theology, but it was, from the outset, an attempt to deal with a fundamental question of learning and knowing. In the *De principiis*, this question is discussed within a reflection about how corporeal bodies are able to perceive incorporeal things: 'Whence comes it', Origen asks, 'that the power of memory, the contemplation of invisible things, yes, and the perception of incorporeal things reside in a body? How does a bodily nature investigate the teachings of the arts and the meanings and reasons of things? And divine doctrines, which are obviously incorporeal, how can it discern and understand them?'[63] Origen's inference is that mind and soul cannot be corporeal because in this case they would not be able to perceive incorporeal things. The underlying idea is the old Greek hermeneutical principle of knowing 'like by like'. There must thus be something like an incorporeal perception in order to perceive intellectual things: 'There are in us two kinds of senses, the one being mortal, corruptible and human, and the other immortal and intellectual, which here (i.e. in Prov. 2:5) he calls "divine".'[64] This is the core of Origen's concept of 'spiritual sensation'. It is neither a cheap trick to explain anthropomorphic language in the Bible in a more or less allegorical way nor a tool to get rid of anthropomorphic ideas. Instead, the concept of spiritual senses expresses the inextricable connection of mind, soul and body when it comes to the perception of incorporeal things. In Origen's view, the metaphorical language used in Scripture is a sign and an expression of the interconnection of mind and body in the process of perceiving and understanding spiritual realities. It is on the basis of this insight that Origen reads the Bible and tries to explain passages in which the language of sense perception is used to describe intellectual realities.

A further argument for this view is provided at the end of the *De principiis* where Origen finally points to the concept of spiritual senses. He again quotes Prov. 2.5, and he admonishes the reader to take this theory into account when he reads the present book: 'It is with this sense that each of the rational questions which we have dealt with above must be perceived; and with this sense that the words we speak must be listened to and our writings pondered.'[65] The concept of spiritual sensation is here clearly presented as a hermeneutical rule which is of fundamental relevance not only to exegesis but to theological or philosophical perception and knowledge in general. It is a progress, or a passage, *a visibilibus ad invisibilia*:

> A rational mind, by advancing from a knowledge of small to a knowledge of greater things and from things visible to things invisible, may attain to an increasingly perfect understanding. For it has been placed in a body, and of necessity advances from sense-objects which are bodily, to sense-objects[66] which are incorporeal and intellectual. But in case it should appear mistaken to say as we have done

that intellectual things are objects of sense, we will quote as an illustration the saying of Solomon: 'Thou shalt find a divine sense' (Prov. 2:5). By this he shows that intellectual things are to be investigated not by bodily sense but by some other which he calls divine.[67]

Again it becomes clear that for Origen the concept of spiritual sensation is not a tool to explain the metaphorical language of Scripture, but a foundational principle in order to explain how a mind placed in a body can perceive and understand incorporeal objects.

It may be noteworthy, by the way, that Origen here argues in the same way as in the preface to the *De principiis*. At the end of the preface, he presents the hermeneutical and methodological rule of how to deal with theological questions, namely to argue by reason and by Scripture, and for this basic rule he quotes a biblical verse in a special version, in this case the version of the Septuagint: 'Enlighten yourselves with the light of knowledge' (Hos. 10.12). We find the same procedure at the end of the *De principiis*: Origen emphasizes the concept of spiritual sensation as a hermeneutical rule of how to deal with theological questions, that is, questions related to the incorporeal and intellectual but nevertheless accessible to sense perception, and how to read books about these questions. In order to support this idea by Scripture, he quotes Prov. 2.5 (with a special wording). As in the case of Hos. 10.12, this verse is not the initial reason for formulating this concept, but functions as biblical confirmation of a concept coined for philosophical reasons.

In his article about the divine sense in Origen of 2006, Robert Hauck also deals with the question 'whether his understanding of this [i.e. the divine sense] is metaphorical, that is, whether this is a way to illustrate intellectual knowledge of the intelligible world; or whether he thinks there are actually such faculties in the human soul'.[68] In order to answer this question, he places it in the context of ancient Platonic theories of vision and cognition and offers quite interesting insights into how this sense works. According to the Platonic understanding, the eye is a light-emitting organ and its vision is enabled by the light of the sun. Vision occurs when the light from the eye meets the light produced by an object for which the sunlight is the necessary ingredient: 'when the three rays meet, an impression is conveyed to the soul by the eye.'[69] Origen draws on this ancient scientific theory of sensation and knowledge and transfers it to the spiritual senses.

> For Origen, the mind, the perceptive faculty of the soul, operates like the eye by emitting intellectual light that illuminates the soul and coalesces with the divine light from above. [. . .] This coalescence, in which like is known by like, serves as an explanation of the operation of the divine sense. [. . .] Mental vision operates as a coalescence. In this case divine truth is the effluent which meets the intellectual rays of the mind and produces knowledge.[70]

It is in this way that Origen in the *De principiis* describes how the divine sense works:

> Each of the bodily senses is appropriately connected with a material substance towards which the particular sense is directed. For instance, sight is connected with

colour, shape and size; hearing with the voice and sound; smelling with vapours pleasant and unpleasant; taste with flavours; touch with things hot or cold, hard or soft, rough or smooth. But it is clear to all that the sense of mind is far superior to the senses above mentioned. Does it not then appear absurd that these inferior senses should have substances connected with them, as objects towards which their activities are directed, whereas this faculty, the sense of mind, which is superior to them, should have no substance whatever connected with it, and that this faculty of an intellectual nature should be a mere accident arising out of bodies? Those who assert this are undoubtedly speaking in disparaging terms of that substance which is the better part of their own nature; nay more, they do wrong even to God himself in supposing that he can be understood through a bodily nature, since according to them that which can be understood or perceived through a body is itself a body; and they are unwilling to have it understood that there is a certain affinity between the mind and God, of whom the mind is an intellectual image, and that by reason of this fact the mind, especially if it is purified and separated from bodily matter, is able to have some perception of the divine nature.[71]

Origen does not 'simply extend Platonic metaphorical language about the eye of the soul', but 'views the divine sense as a mental organ or a faculty in the soul that has a role in the apprehension of intelligible truth', and in the passage quoted he 'provides insight into his understanding of how it works'.[72] 'As the eye's vision is enabled by the light of the sun, the intellect's knowledge of divine things is illuminated by the light of the Son of God.'[73] Origen thus thinks of the intellect as the perceptive faculty of the soul. Hauck accepts that 'the moral dimension certainly is present', but in his view Origen's 'solution is intellectual'.[74] His reasoning runs as follows: 'For him the moral imperative does not have to do with the health or wholeness of the physical eye, or even the moral disposition in relation to generosity or simplicity, but rather the strength and capacity of the intellectual eye.' 'When our mind is a lover of matter', says Origen, 'then the light in us is darkness.'[75] The enlightening flash of the mind consists of the establishment of the rule of the intellect over the lower parts of the soul. 'For, illumination from the mind is like a gleaming flash, and the light in the body is like a lamp with gleaming rays.'[76,77] Contrary to this claim, I would argue that the strength and capacity of the intellectual eye depends on the moral disposition, as will be seen in the following text, and that the rule of the intellect over the lower parts of the soul is a moral rule. But apart from this evaluation of the moral aspect, Hauck's comments are highly revealing.

It should have become clear by now that Origen, right from the outset, that is, in the *De principiis* and in other early writings, develops the concept of spiritual senses within an epistemological framework. The Scriptural phrases cited may be metaphorical, but their use by Origen is not. He states explicitly that 'all parts of the sensual body are to be found within the inner man'.[78] It is not only a question of how to deal with metaphorical language in Scripture. From Origen's hermeneutical perspective, these passages are verbal expressions about the constitution of the inner man, that is, anthropological statements about the capacity of human beings to grasp the spiritual reality within the framework of their bodily constitution. The perception of mind and soul is not sensible, but nevertheless linked to sensation, as mind and soul are linked to a body. Within this framework the corporeal organs fulfil a specific task during the progress towards spiritual perception and, in the end, to perfection. They have a kind of preparatory function: using the corporeal senses in the right way, that is, according to the commandments of the Gospel, prepares the 'lamps of the senses', that is, the spiritual faculty of sensation, to perceive incorporeal and intellectual objects. 'The ascent from objects perceptible by the senses to those perceptions called divine [. . .] leads to the comprehension of spiritual realities.'[79]

This capacity is acquired and exercised by using the senses properly: the eyes should not see injustice (with Is. 33.15), the ears should not hear idle talk, but the words of Jesus.[80] This is not at all metaphorical or symbolic, but real. As the physical faculties are strengthened by constant practice, so are the spiritual senses.[81] In real practice, the senses get used to the spiritual realities enclosed in corporeal things. This can be called the pedagogical aspect of the concept of spiritual senses: the use of spiritual sensation can and is to be learned. The pedagogical aspect is expressed in the statement of Hebr. 5.14 that 'the perfect by reason of use have their senses exercised to discern both good and evil' – a verse quoted by Origen as biblical evidence for the spiritual senses with regard to the need of exercising them.[82] 'There is no other way to perfection than training in the divine and intellectual senses.'[83] Not everyone possesses these spiritual faculties: 'The utterance of God', Origen writes in the late *Contra Celsum*, 'which is mentioned in Scripture is certainly not vibrated air, or a concussion of air, because it is heard by a superior sense, more divine than physical hearing.' Hence, 'a man who has superior hearing hears God, whereas a man who has become hard of hearing in his soul does not perceive that God is speaking.'[84] In an early text the Alexandrian theologian states quite the same with respect to the eyes:

> Just as with physical light which enables those with healthy eyes to see both the light itself and other sensible objects, so too does God come with a certain power to the mind of each one. As long as those to whom he comes are not all closed off and their ability to see clearly not impeded by their passions, God makes himself known and leads those illumined by him to a knowledge of other spiritual things.[85]

'Only the perfect', Rahner already stated, 'are endowed with these spiritual faculties, which they have brought to a higher level of operation through constant practice.'[86] The dynamic aspect of progression and advancement to cultivate the proper emotional disposition is also expressed in Prov. 2.5 because this verse is a promise: 'Thou *shalt find* a divine sense' – if you do what this promise indicates and suggests, you will find it.[87]

What is to be done then? The means of training the spiritual senses are the respective corporeal senses. The process of learning might be conceived of as a kind of transition: what the soul learns via training the corporeal senses – for example, to hear only the words of Jesus with the corporeal ears – is transferred to the spiritual perception of Jesus, and thus the spiritual sensation is exercised both physically and spiritually. Our bodily behaviour affects our spiritual disposition directly. There is a tight link between the corporeal and the spiritual senses that is far more than only a metaphorical or symbolic relationship and also more than an analogy.[88] On the contrary, the behaviour of the corporeal senses can be regarded as a mirror of the status of the spiritual knowledge. It is therefore not the case 'that the spiritual senses become effective to the extent that the bodily senses are deadened', as Andrew Louth has described the relationship.[89] This is only true if the bodily senses are seen as striving for nothing else but than carnal desires. Taken in this sense, Origen indeed says that the corporeal senses must be mortified, but he makes this aspect clear by calling these senses 'carnal'.[90] Within the hermeneutics of spiritual perception, however, Origen argues that the bodily senses can be tuned towards good actions like hearing the word of God. The spiritual senses thus do not become effective when the bodily senses are deadened, but when the latter are exercised in virtuous behaviour. To this end, the carnal desires of the corporeal senses must be mortified, but not the bodily senses in general. Instead, by deadening the carnal desires of the corporeal senses, the latter are released to evolve the spiritual senses in the soul. For the same reason, the spiritual senses are not 'different figurative expressions for *nous*', but rather 'spiritual counterparts of the bodily senses'.[91]

Consequently, the spiritual senses are connected to each other because if one corporeal sense is abused for bad things, this misbehaviour immediately affects and damages spiritual perception as a whole.[92] All senses, the corporeal as well as the spiritual ones, are focused on Christ as the principle, content and aim of corporeal and spiritual sensation. When used properly, that is, in a virtuous manner, the corporeal senses are tuned towards the spiritual sensation of the virtues, for example, truthfulness and righteousness, and the latter is directed towards Christ as sum and principle of all virtues.[93] In the treatise *On Passover*, Origen can therefore speak of 'the five senses of man' without qualifying them as corporeal or spiritual because both are meant when he says that 'Christ has to come into each of them'.[94] Two aspects of the concept of spiritual sensation are combined in this short note: Christ is coming into the human senses – into the spiritual as well as into the corporeal ones because if the corporeal senses are not used according to the commandments of Christ, he cannot be present in the spiritual dimension of man's senses. And Christ has to come into each of the senses because if he is not present in all senses, he cannot be present in any of them at all, or, as Origen says metaphorically, 'he cannot be sacrificed and consumed'.[95] In an abbreviated way, Origen can thus say that one should exercise one's taste by eating the Lord, smell Christ's savour (with 2 Cor. 2.15 and Song 1.3), touch the 'Word of life' (according to 1 Jn 1.1).[96] A passage like this sounds quite metaphorical, but within the underlying concept it is an abbreviated description of the interconnection of corporeal and spiritual sensation.

Origen, using a neologism, calls this connection 'a not sensible sense'.[97] If the spiritual senses are trained in the way described earlier, that is, by a proper use of the corporeal senses, they will reach a 'divine sense' (θεία αἴσθησις), as he is used to saying in his peculiar version of Prov. 2.5. A 'divine sense' is a sight that sees things superior to corporeal beings like the cherubim or the seraphim. It hears sounds without objective existence in the air, it tastes the living bread from heaven, it smells the sweet savour of Christ and it touches the Word of life. The prophets, Origen says, found this divine sense: they saw in a divine manner, heard in a divine manner, tasted and smelt in a similar way, 'so to speak, with a sense which was not sensible'.[98] This 'superior and incorporeal sense' 'is different from that commonly so called by popular usage'.[99] What Origen means is to be found in the following sentence: 'And they touched the Word by faith.'[100] The interconnection of corporeal and spiritual senses is again made clear in the example of the healing of the leper (cf. Mt 8.3): 'Jesus touched the leper spiritually rather than sensibly, to heal him, as I think, in two ways, delivering him not only, as the multitude take it, from sensible leprosy by sensible touch, but also from another leprosy by his truly divine touch.'[101] Both are meant here, the sensible touch as well as the spiritual, and within the sensible touch and by means of it, the leper is touched in a not sensible way. Through a bodily sense, therefore, he is led to a 'not sensible sensation'. By means of this oxymoron Origen tries to express the inexpressible – as Karl Rahner posed the problem of spiritual perception.

The most compelling account of the spiritual senses as intertwined with the respective bodily senses is to be found in the *Commentary* and *Homilies on the Song of Songs*.[102] Origen interprets the sensuality of the biblical text as a medium to steer the mind from the corporeal sense perception, which is used in a metaphorical sense in the text, to the spiritual perception or, as he says in a Greek fragment, to the 'pneumatic sense' (αἴσθησις πνευματική)[103] and thus to attain the true reality. But the language of corporeal sensuality is even more than a mere medium that can be left behind after having been used. Instead, the corporeal senses are the place where human beings are able to get into contact with intellectual and spiritual reality. Human beings can talk about spiritual sensation only within the confines of their bodily constitution. Origen therefore connects the spiritual senses not only to the mind but also to the soul[104] because the soul is the link of the mind to the body. Human corporeality thus plays an important role in the spiritual relationship to God. Corporeal and spiritual senses are mutually interconnected.

Two examples of Origen's exegesis of the Song of Songs may suffice to demonstrate this connection. The Alexandrian exegete interprets the shared 'bed' of Bride and Bridegroom in Song 1.16 as the human body.[105] He combines this verse with Paul's statement in 1 Cor. 6.15 'that our bodies are the members of Christ' and concludes his explanation with the statement 'that the soul who is able to look at him with spiritual eyes has its body as bed in common with the Word because the divine power extends to the grace of the body'.[106] If the body is shaped according to 'good works and spiritual thoughts',[107] the soul will be able to see the Word in a spiritual sense, and thus the body will be the place where the companionship of soul and Christ is realized. In this sense Origen also explains the 'windows' in Song 2.9: 'Each window is one sense. The Bridegroom looks through this window. Another window is another sense, and through it the Bridegroom looks worried. Since through which senses does the Word of God not look?'[108] The senses here are the corporeal as well as the spiritual ones.[109] They are both the medium of communication between God and the soul. In the concept of spiritual sensation man as a whole, consisting of mind, soul and body, is engaged in the perception of God which, therefore, is described by means of the sensible notions of seeing and hearing, smelling, tasting and touching.

6 Plotinus on spiritual sensation

A brief look at Plotinus's idea of spiritual sensation adds to a better understanding of the specific profile of Origen's reflections on this topic. His concept of spiritual senses is not different from but close to Plotinus's.¹¹⁰ According to Dillon,¹¹¹ Plotinus in *Enneads* VI 7 conceives of spiritual senses in the framework of 'a general principle of his, that the phenomena of this world are just pale reflections of what exists, in a more real way, at a higher level'.¹¹² As this principle works, for instance, for civic virtues and cathartic virtues, time and eternity, or action and contemplation, 'so here, sensibilia are simply dim versions of higher, noetic "sensibilia"'.¹¹³ In this context, Plotinus discusses a passage in Plato's *Timaeus* where the 'Young Gods, under the orders of the Demiurge, are described as fabricating eyes for the soul in the body (and, by implication, other organs of sense), to enable it to function successfully in the sensible world'.¹¹⁴ In order to secure that 'the nature of Man at the level of Form is to be complete', 'we must envisage some form of sense-faculties in the soul before it leaves the intelligible realm'.¹¹⁵ As a solution to this problem, Plotinus thought about an 'analogue or paradigm of sense-perception' at the level of Nous,¹¹⁶ and as Dillon interprets him, he does not simply propose 'forms or paradigms of sensibilia' but rather something like 'noetic correlates of sensibilia'.¹¹⁷ Since 'the sense-world dimly mirror[s] the prior arrangements of the noetic', Plotinus concludes that 'the man in Nous enjoy[s] a full set of faculties answering to sense-faculties and that [he] contemplate[s] or apprehend[s] appropriate objects'.¹¹⁸ Or in Plotinus's own words:

> What we have called the perceptibles of that realm enter into cognizance in a way of their own, since they are incorporeal, while sense-perception here – so distinguished as dealing with corporeal objects – is fainter than the perception belonging to that higher world, but gains a specious clarity because its objects are bodies; the man of this sphere has sense-perception because existing in a less true degree and taking only enfeebled images of things There: perceptions here are dim intellections, and intellections There are vivid perceptions.¹¹⁹

Dillon correctly states 'that we have here, in Plotinus' theory, a far greater degree of "mirroring" of the noetic world by the sense-world than is traditional in Platonism. Everything here is also There, in another, more exalted, mode.'¹²⁰

In contrast to Origen – to come back to him – the spiritual senses in Plotinus's concept are strictly part of the noetic world. Origen, however, conceives of them as belonging to the facilities of man even here on earth, not only in the intelligible world. We find here another aspect of Origen's reassessment of the goodness of the body.¹²¹ In his doctrine of man and of salvation history the body is not only the material expression of punishment for earlier sins but also and even more the necessary form in which man can learn and exercise a virtuous life. Origen's concept of spiritual senses can be seen as a main element of this anthropology. The fallen mind as soul in a body stays connected to the noetic world to which the spiritual senses provide access if they are trained by means of a proper usage of the corporeal senses in this world. In Origen's concept of the spiritual senses, there seems to exist an even closer connection of the noetic and the sense-world than in Plotinus's concept of mirroring. Whereas, according to the Neoplatonic philosopher, sensible perception of corporeal objects in this world is only a faint mirror of sense perception in the intelligible world, for the Christian Platonist the perception provided by the spiritual senses here opens up the way to the noetic world. This claim leads us back to conceive of spiritual sensation as imaginative apprehension.

7 Spiritual sensation as imaginative apprehension

Douglas Hedley's reflections about imagination might help to gain a better understanding of the 'strange' theory of spiritual senses, as Dillon qualified it. This concept expresses the unity of the material and spiritual worlds which is described by Hedley in the following way with regard to 'imagination':

> Imaginative apprehension of the Divine is pre-eminently the awareness of that reality which is pressing and proximate for the soul and yet hard to grasp or articulate in the categories appropriate for the physical domain. For human beings the tension between the material and the spiritual, between inward and outward worlds, is resolved in the imaginative vision of their underlying unity.[122]

Origen's theory of spiritual senses can be regarded as another solution to this problem which works along the same lines. Precisely because spiritual sensation is connected to the sense perception of the bodily organs if the latter are tuned towards a behaviour according to God's commandments, the sensible and the 'not sensible sense' operate together as a vehicle of the perception of the transcendent reality. It may be possible to express this by means of the language of imagination, above all with regard to the Song of Songs: this biblical book is an imaginative text in itself, and by explaining the images of this text, Origen creates new images of sensation for man's perception of and relation to God.

The underlying unity of the material and the spiritual world can be seen in a demanding passage in the preface of Origen's *Commentary on the Song of Songs* where Origen describes the effect of the physical beauty of the world in the following way:

> The soul is moved by heavenly love and longing when, having clearly beheld the beauty and the fairness of the Word of God, it falls deeply in love with his loveliness and receives from the Word Himself a certain dart and wound of love. For this Word is the image and splendour of the invisible God, the Firstborn of all creation, in whom were all things created that are in heaven and on earth, seen and unseen alike (cf. Col. 1:15–16). If, then, a man can so extend his thinking as to ponder and consider the beauty and the grace of all the things that have been created in the Word, the very charm of them will so smite him, the grandeur of their brightness will so pierce him as with a chosen dart – as says the prophet (Is. 49:2) – that he will suffer from the dart Himself a saving wound, and will be kindled with the blessed fire of His love.[123]

The power of physical beauty, the visible beauty of the world, leads the lover (the Bride of the Song) through the experience and presence of the Divine in the world to the truth of spiritual, supersensible beauty. This passage in Origen's commentary is clearly a reflection of Plato's statement in the *Phaedrus*, that aesthetic experience provides compelling images of intelligible reality.[124] Plato and Origen describe 'intellectual love, in which the knowledge of the intelligible is kindled by the sense of visual beauty'.[125] Based on the experiential apprehension of the divine presence in the world, the soul envisages the world as a sacrament of the transcendent God. The beautiful image of the world leads us to imagine the beauty of its creator. Doing this is an act of creativity, not only mimesis. In this activity the senses act as vehicles of awakening the soul to an invisible and untouchable world. They provide a key not only to the relation of the mind to the world but also to the relation of the mind to that which lies beyond this world.

What Hedley writes about Neoplatonism holds true for Origen's world view as well:

> The material realm, for the Neoplatonist, is – though subject to decay – not alien to the soul because it is produced by the non-deliberative intelligence of the World-soul. The apparently inanimate exhibits intelligence. Our planet, and indeed the entire physical universe, is a dynamic and harmonious unity that mirrors the unity of the noetic cosmos. The realm of nature is not simply the sum of its parts. [. . .] Nature is a harmonious unity because it is an image or expression of the divine mind. It is weaker and less valuable than the Intellect, but nevertheless possesses its own derivative goodness – which Plotinus defends vigorously against the Gnostics.[126]

Because the noetic cosmos includes the whole of the sensible cosmos, the language of touch can be used to describe it.[127] This is precisely the point where the doctrine of spiritual senses comes into play. The spiritual or intelligible world can thus be described in terms of sense perception. By virtue of the oxymoron of 'a not sensible sense', Origen tries to express the interaction of the intelligible with the sensible world. By means of the activity of 'a not sensible sense', the whole soul is brought into activity – the whole soul, that is, all its kinds of perception mediated by the corporeal senses. If the soul as a whole, even in its faculties of corporeal senses, is concerned with nothing else than this kind of spiritual perception, 'everything which the rational mind, when purified from all the dregs of its vices and utterly cleared from every cloud of wickedness, can feel or understand or think will be all God, and the mind will no longer be conscious of anything besides or other than God, but will think God and see God and hold God', and God will be 'all in all'.[128] The perfect soul contemplates God not only intellectually but with all his senses of feeling, seeing and touching, that is, as a complete being of mind and body.

Response by Douglas Hedley

Alfons Fürst has provided an illuminating account of spiritual sensation in Origen. Is the language of spiritual sensation merely metaphorical? The reality of spiritual sensation is neither crudely anthropomorphic nor radically apophatic. But the link between the human imagination and spiritual/intellectual realities is grounded in the continuity between the physical and intellectual cosmos, the reflection of the 'yonder' world in the sensible realm. The awakening and recognition of this vision are properly creative and not purely mimetic. I concur with Fürst that the concept of spiritual sensation could be viewed as corresponding to the notion of imagination. Plato was a poet, and he uses myths like his poetic rivals, for his own purposes. The great Platonists of late Antiquity were aware of this dimension of Plato, and the interpretation of myths assumes great significance for them. The key to Platonic metaphysics, the relationship between image and archetype, provides the basis for the doctrine of spiritual sensation. Fürst's contrast and comparison of Plotinus and Origen are most instructive. Yet common to both Christian and pagan Alexandrian Platonists is the acute sense of the presence of the invisible world and the importance of the imaginative and metaphysical reconciliation of the inner and outer worlds. Fürst's analysis of Origen's Song of Songs commentary is particularly helpful in this regard, where the Alexandrian evokes and explains how the love of the intelligible is kindled by sensible beauty.

Notes

1. Douglas Hedley, *The Iconic Imagination* (New York and London: Bloomsbury, 2016), 25–7.
2. Douglas Hedley, *Living Forms of the Imagination* (London and New York: T&T Clark, 2008), 16.
3. Ibid., 3.
4. For example, Origen, *In Exodum homiliae* 10,3; *In Numeros homiliae* 17,3; 20,3; *In Canticum commentaria* II 9,12; *In Isaiam homiliae* 6,3.7; 7,3; *In Hiezechielem homiliae* 2,3; *In Lucam homiliae* 3,2; *De oratione* 9,2.
5. Plato, *Politeia* VII 533c–d; *Sophistes* 254a; *Symposion* 219a.
6. For example, Origen, *De principiis* I 1,9.
7. Cf. Hedley, *Living Forms* (see n. 2), 1 with respect to imagination: 'Through the "inner eye" of imagination, finite beings can apprehend eternal and immutable Forms.'
8. Ibid., 19.
9. Hedley, *Iconic Imagination* (see n. 1), 26.
10. Hedley, *Living Forms* (see n. 2), 1.
11. It was originally published in French: Karl Rahner, 'Le début d'une doctrine des cinq sens spirituels chez Origène', *Revue d'Ascétique et de Mystique* 13 (1932): 113–45. This article contains all of the many references given by the early Rahner to Origenian and other (e.g. Philonian) sources as well as his explanations of textual questions concerning the biblical verses used by Origen. A simplified and abriged German version by Karl H. Neufeld was included in the edition of Rahner's works: 'Die

geistlichen Sinne nach Origenes', in Karl Rahner, *Schriften zur Theologie, vol. XII: Theologie aus Erfahrung des Geistes*, edited by Karl H. Neufeld (Zurich, Einsiedeln and Cologne: Benziger, 1975), 111–36. This German version was translated into Italian as 'I "sensi spirituali" secondo Origene', in Karl Rahner, *Nuovi saggi vol. VI: Teologia dell'esperienza dello Spirito* (Rome: Paoline, 1978), 133–63, and into English as part of the English edition of Rahner's *Schriften*: 'The "Spiritual Senses" according to Origen', in Karl Rahner, *Theological Investigations*, vol. XVI, translated by David Morland (New York: Darton, Longmann and Todd, 1979), 81–103.

12 For the historical circumstances and the spiritual-monastic background, see Andreas R. Batlogg et al., *Der Denkweg Karl Rahners. Quellen – Entwicklungen – Perspektiven* (Mainz: Matthias-Grünewald-Verlag, 2003 (²2004)), 21–35.

13 Karl Rahner, 'La doctrine des "sens spirituels" au Moyen-Âge, en particulier chez saint Bonaventure', *Revue d'Ascétique et de Mystique* 14 (1933): 263–99, and id., 'Der Begriff der Ecstasis bei Bonaventura', *Zeitschrift für Aszese und Mystik* 9 (1934): 1–19. Karl Neufeld combined these two articles and published them in German as 'Die Lehre von den "geistlichen Sinnen" im Mittelalter', in Rahner, *Schriften zur Theologie*, vol. XII (see n. 11), 137–72. This German article was then translated into English as 'The Doctrine of the "Spiritual Senses" in the Middle Ages', in Rahner, *Theological Investigations*, vol. XVI (see n. 11), 104–34.

14 Hans Urs von Balthasar, *Origenes – Geist und Feuer. Ein Aufbau aus seinen Schriften* (Salzburg and Leipzig: Müller, 1938), 319–80. English translation: *Origen – Spirit and Fire: A Thematic Anthology of His Writings*, translated by Robert J. Daly (Washington, DC: The Catholic University of America Press, 1984) (2nd edn 2001), 218–57. Cf. also the chapter on this topic in his *Parole et mystère chez Origène* (Paris: Édition du Cerf, 1957), 65–71 (originally published in two articles in *Recherches de Science Religieuse* 26 (1936): 513–62 and 27 (1937): 38–64), then used for his own theological purposes in *Herrlichkeit. Eine theologische Ästhetik, vol. I: Schau der Gestalt* (Einsiedeln: Johannes-Verlag, 1961), 352–410.

15 Werner Löser, *Im Geiste des Origenes. Hans Urs von Balthasar als Interpret der Theologie der Kirchenväter* (Frankfurt: Knecht, 1976), 83–100; Stephen Fields, 'Balthasar and Rahner on the Spiritual Senses', *Theological Studies* 57 (1996): 224–41; Agnell Rickenmann, 'La dottrina di Origene sui sensi spirituali e la sua ricezione in Hans Urs von Balthasar', *Rivista Teologica di Lugano* 6 (2001): 155–68; Mark J. McInroy, 'Karl Rahner and Hans Urs von Balthasar', in *The Spiritual Senses: Perceiving God in Western Christianity*, edited by Paul L. Gavrilyuk and Sarah Coakley (Cambridge: Cambridge Universtiy Press, 2012), 257–74.

16 It is not by chance that in the entry 'sensi spirituali' in the *Italian dictionary of Origen* no other specific article after Rahner's is noted: Paolo Bettiolo, 'Sensi Spirituali', in *Origene. Dizionario. La cultura, il pensiero, le opere*, edited by Adele Monaci Castagno (Rome: Città Nuova, 2000), 443–4.

17 Marguérite Harl, 'La "bouche" et le "cœur" de l'Apôtre: Deux images bibliques du "sens divin" de l'homme ("Proverbes" 2,5) chez Origène', in *Forma Futuri. Studi in onore del Cardinale Michele Pellegrino* (Turin: Bottega d'Erasmo, 1975), 17–42; Enrico Cattaneo, 'La Dottrina dei "sensi spirituali" in Origene: Nuovi apporti', *Adamantius* 11 (2005): 101–13; Robert J. Hauk, '"Like a Gleaming Flash": Matthew 6:22–23, Luke 11:34–36 and the Divine Sense in Origen', *Anglican Theological Review* 88 (2006): 557–73.

18 John M. Dillon, 'Aisthêsis noêtê: A Doctrine of Spiritual Senses in Origen and in Plotinus', in *Hellenica et Judaica. Hommage à Valentin Nikiprowetzky*, edited by A.

Caquot, M. Hadas-Lebel and J. Riaud (Leuven and Paris: Peeters, 1986), 443–55, again in: John M. Dillon, *The Golden Chain: Studies in the Development of Platonism and Christianity* (Aldershot: Variorum, 1990), nr. XIX.
19 Mark J. McInroy, 'Origen of Alexandria', in Gavrilyuk and Coakley (eds), *The Spiritual Senses* (see n. 15), 20–35.
20 Gavrilyuk and Coakley (eds), *The Spiritual Senses* (see n. 15).
21 Bernard Fraigneau-Julien, *Les sens spirituels et la vision de Dieu selon Syméon le Nouveau Théologien* (Paris: Beauchesne, 1985) (on Origen: 29–43); Rosa Maria Parrinello, 'Da Origene a Simeone il Nuovo Teologo: La dottrina dei sensi spirituali', in *Origeniana Octava: Origen and the Alexandrian Tradition*, edited by Lorenzo Perrone (Leuven: Leuven University Press, 2003), 1123–30.
22 Boyd Taylor Coolman, *Knowing God by Experience: The Spiritual Senses in the Theology of William of Auxerre* (Washington, DC: Catholic University of America Press, 2004).
23 Fabio Massimo Tedoldi, *La dottrina dei cinque sensi spirituali in San Bonaventura* (Rome: Pontificium Athenaeum Antonianum, 1999) (on Origen: 27–32).
24 Gordon Rudy, *Mystical Language of Sensation in the Later Middle Ages* (New York: Routledge, 2002).
25 Paul L. Gavrilyuk and Sarah Coakley, 'Introduction', in id., *The Spiritual Senses* (see n. 15), 1–19, here 19.
26 It is not the aim of the contribution of Cattaneo, 'Dottrina dei "sensi spirituali"' (see n. 17), 102, to deal with this topic in depth, but only to contribute some new texts which he quotes at length.
27 Origen, *De principiis* I 1,7.9; IV 4,9–10.
28 *Dialogus cum Heracleide* 15–24.
29 *In Isaiam homiliae* 7,3.
30 *In Canticum commentaria* prol. 2,9–14; I 4,10–26, II 9,12–14; *In Canticum homiliae* 1,2; 2,4.12. For Song 1.3, see also *Dialogus cum Heracleide* 18; *De pascha* 18; *In Matthaeum commentariorum series* 64, Greek fragment in GCS Orig. 11, 150.
31 *In Matthaeum commentariorum series* 63–64 about Mt 25.1-12.
32 *Contra Celsum* I 48; VII 34. Cf. furthermore ibid. II 72; VII 39; VIII 19.
33 *In Exodum homiliae* 10,3.4; *In Leviticum homiliae* 3,7; *In Psalmum 36 homiliae* 1,4; *Catena Palaestiniana in Psalmum* 118,103; *In Hiezechielem homiliae* 11,1; *In Matthaeum commentaria* XV 33; *In Lucam fragmenta* 186. 192 Rauer^2; *In Iohannem commentaria* X 40,279; XIII 9,51; 24,144; XX 43,405–408; *De pascha* 18.
34 Eph. 1.18: *De principiis* I 1,9. For these eyes, cf. also Ps. 18.9 LXX; 118.18 LXX: *Dialogus cum Heracleide* 16–17. 20; *Contra Celsum* VII 34; *In Canticum commentaria* I 4,25.
35 Mt 11.15-16; 13.9: *Dialogus cum Heracleide* 17 (here together with Is. 42.18 and Ps. 57.4-6 LXX); *De pascha* 18; *Contra Celsum* VII 34; *In Exodum homiliae* 10,3; *In Leviticum homiliae* 3,7; *In Canticum commentaria* I 4,25; *In Lucam fragmenta* 186 Rauer^2.
36 2 Cor. 12.2-4: *Contra Celsum* I 48.
37 Ps. 33.9 LXX: *Dialogus cum Heracleide* 19; *In Leviticum homiliae* 3,7; *Catena Palaestiniana in Psalmum* 118,103; *In Canticum commentaria* I 4,25; *In Iohannem commentaria* XX 43,406.
38 Jn 6.32-33, 50-51: *De principiis* I 1,9; *Contra Celsum* I 48; *In Canticum commentaria* I 4,12–15; II 9,12; *In Lucam fragmenta* 192 Rauer^2; *In Iohannem commentaria* XX 43,406.

39 2 Cor. 2.15-16: *Dialogus cum Heracleide* 18; *De pascha* 18; *In Matthaeum commentariorum series* 64, Greek fragment in GCS Orig. 11, 150; *Contra Celsum* I 48; *In Leviticum homiliae* 3,7; *Catena Palaestiniana in Psalmum* 118,103; *In Canticum commentaria* I 4,25; *In Lucam fragmenta* 192 Rauer^2.

40 1 Jn 1.1 (sometimes together with Jn 1.14): *Dialogus cum Heracleide* 20; *De pascha* 18; *In Matthaeum commentariorum series* 64, Greek fragment in GCS Orig. 11, 151; *Contra Celsum* I 48; VII 34; *In Leviticum homiliae* 3,7; *In Canticum commentaria* I 4,11–12.25; II 9,13; *In Canticum fragmenta* 3 Fürst and Strutwolf; *In Lucam fragmenta* 192 Rauer^2.

41 Prov. 2.5: *De principiis* I 1,9; IV 4,10; *In Canticum commentaria* I 4,16; *In Matthaeum commentariorum series* 63; *Contra Celsum* I 48; VII 34; *In Lucam fragmenta* 186 Rauer^2; *In Iohannem commentaria* XX 43,405; *In Epistulam ad Romanos commentaria* VI 5 p. 210 Scherer.

42 Clement of Alexandria, *Stromateis* I 27,2.

43 See the explanations of the phrase θεία αἴσθησις in Prov. 2.5 by Harl, 'Deux images bibliques' (see n. 17), 26–35.

44 Hedley, *Iconic Imagination* (see n. 1), 26.

45 Ibid.

46 Rahner, '"Spiritual Senses" according to Origen' (see n. 11), 81 (quotes from the English version of 1979).

47 Ibid., 83.

48 Ibid.

49 The latter seems to be the opinion of Jean Daniélou, *Origène* (Paris: La Table Ronde, 1948), 300: 'Il s'agit de métaphores indiquant des expériences spirituelles.'

50 Rahner, '"Spiritual Senses" according to Origen' (see n. 11), 96–7.

51 Dillon, 'Aisthêsis noêtê' (see n. 18), 443–9 (the quote is ibid., 443 n. 1).

52 Ibid., 447.

53 Ibid., 448.

54 Ibid., 443.

55 McInroy, 'Origen of Alexandria' (see n. 19), 20.

56 Ibid., 24–5.

57 Ibid., 31 as a result of McInroy's new assessment of the language of sensation in *De principiis* I 1,9; IV 4,10 and *Contra Celsum* VII 34.

58 *In Lamentationes fragmenta* 116 Klostermann. Cf. *In Iohannem commentaria* I 9,55; 25,161.

59 *Selecta in Psalmos* 4,4. Translation H.U. von Balthasar (R. J. Daly).

60 McInroy, 'Origen of Alexandria' (see n. 19), 34–5.

61 Cf. Dillon, 'Aisthêsis noêtê' (see n. 18), 445, as a result of his interpretation of *Contra Celsum* I 48: 'It is plain that he [i.e. Origen] has here developed a systematic theory of analogical, 'spiritual' senses for the intellect, or *hegemonikon*, apparently to solve a series of problems of exegesis posed by anthropomorphic expressions about the godhead and about spiritual life which abound in both the Old and New Testaments.' This is also the opinion of Henri Crouzel, *Origène et la 'connaissance mystique'* (Brussels and Paris: Desclée de Brouwer, 1961), 262, 505–7.

62 Rahner, '"Spiritual Senses" according to Origen' (see n. 11), 81.

63 Origen, *De principiis* I 1,7. The translations here and in the following quotes from *De principiis*: G. W. Butterworth. Origen then tries to give an answer to these questions ibid., I 1,7–9, where I 1,8 is a digression (to a great extent repeated ibid., II 4,3).

64 Ibid., I 1,9.

65 Ibid., IV 4,10.
66 The translation of Butterworth here and in the following sentence is wrong: he accepts the reading *insensibilia* instead of the correction *sensibilia* and speaks of 'things beyond sense perception *(insensibilia)*, which are incorporeal and intellectual'. But this makes the following explanation senseless because Origen explains there why it is appropriate to say 'that intellectual things are of sense perception', not 'beyond sense perception', as Butterworth translates, because this would need no explanation. The wrong wording is kept and misinterpreted by Harl, 'Deux images bibliques' (see n. 17), 33 n. 22.
67 *De principiis* IV 4,10. Translation Butterworth with the emendations of Dillon, 'Aisthêsis noêtê' (see n. 18), 447, who argues strongly for the correction of *insensibilia* into *sensibilia*, as in the German edition and translation by Herwig Görgemanns and Heinrich Karpp, *Origenes. Vier Bücher von den Prinzipien* (Darmstadt: Wissenschaftliche Buchgesellschaft, 3rd edn, 1992), 821.
68 Hauck, 'Divine Sense in Origen' (see n. 17), 573.
69 Ibid., 563, relying on Plato, *Timaeus* 45b. This passage is also referenced by Plotinus in *Enneads* VI 7, where he puts forward his version of spiritual sensation.
70 Hauck, 'Divine Sense in Origen' (see n. 17), 569–70.
71 Origen, *De principiis* I 1,7. Translation Butterworth, who in a footnote to this text explains correctly that Origen contends that like the corporeal senses mind 'must also have its appropriate "substance" to act on', that is, 'God, truth and the reasons of things. Origen contradicts the view that mind is an *epiphenomenon*, or by-product of matter.'
72 Hauck, 'Divine Sense in Origen' (see n. 17), 566.
73 Ibid., 571.
74 Ibid., 573.
75 Origen, *In Matthaeum fragmenta* 128.
76 *In Lucam fragmenta* 187 Rauer².
77 Hauck, 'Divine Sense in Origen' (see n. 17), 572.
78 Origen, *Dialogus cum Heracleide* 22.
79 *In Iohannem commentaria* X 40,279.
80 *In Matthaeum commentariorum series* 64, Greek fragment in GCS Orig. 11, 150.
81 *In Canticum commentaria* I 4,17–19. Cf. Rahner, '"Spiritual Senses" according to Origen' (see n. 11), 87.
82 *In Canticum commentaria* I 4,13.16–20; II 9,12; *In Hiezechielem homiliae* 11,1; *In Matthaeum commentariorum series* 66; *In Lucam fragmenta* 186 Rauer²; *In Iohannem commentaria* XIII 24,144.
83 *In Lucam fragmenta* 186 Rauer².
84 *Contra Celsum* II 72. Cf. ibid. VIII 19 about 'those who are capable of hearing God's words with a divine power of hearing'. Translation H. Chadwick.
85 *Selecta in Psalmos* 4,7. Translation H.U. von Balthasar (R. J. Daly).
86 Rahner, '"Spiritual Senses" according to Origen' (see n. 11), 84.
87 *In Lucam fragmenta* 186 Rauer², Origen explicitly states that we find the divine sensation in Proverbs in form of a promise.
88 The same link between the practical behaviour of any corporeal sense and its effect on the faculty of spiritual sensation is expressed in a passage in Jerome's *Commentary on Isaiah*, which according to Cattaneo, 'Dottrina dei "sensi spirituali"' (see n. 17), 102–5, is taken from Origen's lost commentary on this prophet: Jerome, *In Esaiam commentaria* VII 16 (on Is. 19.18).

89 Andrew Louth, *The Origins of the Christian Mystical Tradition: From Plato to Denys* (Oxford: Oxford University Press, 1981), 68. Cf. also Daniélou, *Origène* (see n. 49), 301: 'Ils [sc. les sens spirituels] sont liés à la mortification de la vie charnelle. A mesure que l'homme extérieur dépérit, l'homme intérieur se fortifie. Enfin, ils captivent l'âme et l'arrachent à elle-même.'
90 Origen, *In Canticum commentaria* I 4,16.
91 Louth, *Christian Mystical Tradition* (see n. 89), 68, claims the opposite.
92 Origen, *In Matthaeum commentariorum series* 63.
93 *In Canticum commentaria* I 6,14; III 6,4; *In Iohannem commentaria* VI 19,107; XXXII 11,127; *In Matthaeum commentaria* XII 14; XIV 7; *In Matthaeum commentariorum series* 33; *In epistulam ad Romanos commentaria* IX 34; *Contra Celsum* I 57; III 81; V 39; VIII 17. See Christian Hengstermann, 'Leben des Einen. Der Tugendbegriff des Origenes', in *Ethische Normen des frühen Christentums. Gut – Leben – Leib – Tugend*, edited by F. W. Horn, U. Volp and R. Zimmermann (Tübingen: Mohr Siebeck, 2013), 433–53, here 440–51.
94 Origen, *De pascha* 18.
95 Ibid.
96 *In Matthaeum commentariorum series* 64, Greek fragment in GCS Orig. 11, 150–1.
97 *Contra Celsum* I 48; *In Iohannem commentaria* X 40,279.
98 *Contra Celsum* I 48.
99 Ibid. VII 34.
100 *Contra Celsum* I 48.
101 Ibid. Translation H. Chadwick. – The same holds true for the healing of the woman having an issue of blood (cf. Lk. 8.43-48), although Origen does not connect his explanation explicitly with the concept of spiritual senses: *In Canticum commentaria* III 13,48.
102 For a recent interpretation of the relevant passages (noted above in n. 29), see Alfons Fürst, 'Liebe mit allen Sinnen – die Theorie der geistigen Sinne', in *Origenes, Die Homilien und Fragmente zum Hohelied*, translated and edited by Alfons Fürst and Holger Strutwolf (Berlin and Boston: de Gruyter, 2016), 29–35. An older depiction drawing on Rahner's article is to be found in Louth, *Christian Mystical Tradition* (see n. 89), 67–70.
103 Origen, *In Canticum fragmenta* 3 Fürst and Strutwolf.
104 Rahner, '"Spiritual Senses" according to Origen' (see n. 11), 88–9.
105 Origen, *In Canticum homiliae* 2,4.
106 *In Canticum commentaria* III 2,5.8.
107 Ibid. III 2,6.
108 *In Canticum homiliae* 2,12.
109 This is stated explicitly *In Canticum fragmenta* 29 Fürst and Strutwolf.
110 Henri Crouzel, *Origène et Plotin. Comparaisons doctrinales* (Paris: Téqui, 1992), 371–3, understands Origen's concept correctly as not simply metaphorical, but as an epistemological concept of mystical perception and knowledge based on the Greek principle of knowing 'like by like'. However, as regards Plotinus, he only mentions a few passages, mostly ones about the image of touch, like Plotinus, *Enneads* V 1(10),11.12; V 3(49),10.17, but does not describe any concept because, as he wrongly assumes, 'à la difference d'Origène Plotin ne bâtit sur cet usage métaphorique aucune théorie' (ibid., 371). Crouzel does not mention either *Ennead* VI 7 (*Ennead* V 5 is also important) or the article by Dillon.
111 Dillon, 'Aisthêsis noêtê' (see n. 18), 449–53.

112 Ibid., 451.
113 Ibid.
114 Ibid., 449–50, paraphrasing Plato, *Timaeus* 45b.
115 Dillon, 'Aisthêsis noêtê' (see n. 18), 450.
116 Ibid.
117 Ibid., 452.
118 Ibid., 453.
119 Plotinus, *Enneads* VI 7(38),7. Translation Dillon.
120 Dillon, 'Aisthêsis noêtê' (see n. 18), 453.
121 See the fine new article by Jonathan Bieler, 'Origen on the Goodness of the Body', in *Sacrality and Materiality: Locating Intersections*, edited by Rebecca A. Gieselbrecht/Ralph Kunz (Göttingen: Vandenhoeck & Ruprecht, 2016), 85–94. See also Alfons Fürst, 'Matter and Body in Origen's Christian Platonism', in *Origeniana Duodecima: Origen's Legacy in the Holy Land – A Tale of Three Cities: Jerusalem, Caesarea and Bethlehem*, edited by B. Bitton-Ashkelony et al. (Leuven/Paris/Bristol CT: Peeters, 2019), 573–88.
122 Hedley, *Living Forms* (see n. 2), 37.
123 Origen, *In Canticum commentaria* prol. 2,17. Translation R. P. Lawson.
124 Cf. Hedley, *Living Forms* (see n. 2), 20 about Shakespeare and Plato's *Phaedrus*.
125 Ibid., 22.
126 Ibid. We can add that Origen did quite the same against the Gnostics.
127 Ibid., 24.
128 Origen, *De principiis* III 6,3 with 1 Cor. 15.28. Translation Butterworth.

4

Cogitatione attingere

Divine sensation in René Descartes and the Cambridge Platonists

Christian Hengstermann

1 The sovereignty of the good: Platonism and Cartesianism in seventeenth-century Civil War England

In his *Sermon before the House of Commons* of 1647, delivered at the height of the devastating British civil wars, the young preacher Ralph Cudworth provides an intensely topical philosophical reading of 1 Jn 2:3-4: 'And hereby we do know that we know him, if we keep his Commandments. He that saith, I know him, and keepeth not his Commandments, is a liar, and truth is not in him.' At the heart of Cudworth's exegesis is a vision of divine love which he enjoins the members of parliament to imitate by laying aside once and for all their petty disputes about matters of church government and divine grace and election and instead embrace one another in the spirit of Christian charity. Throughout his homily, Cudworth lambasts ill-guided religious zeal as the source of the fierce civil strife afflicting British Christendom. His stated political aim is nothing less than '*a true Reformation*',[1] which he declares to be key to the survival of a Christian body politic time and again. A year before the decapacitation of Charles I, Cudworth impresses upon the members of parliament assembled at St Margaret's Church a deeply ecumenical rational religion based upon God's own disinterested and universal love. Created in God's own image, they are to follow him in humbling themselves and making themselves instruments of his transformative love.[2]

The *Sermon before the House of Commons* delivered by the young *Plato Cantabrigiensis* in Civil War England is the foundational document of the 'Cambridge Enlightenment', whose figureheads are a group of Anglican theologians generally known as the 'Cambridge Platonists' or 'Cambridge Origenists'.[3] Drawing upon the rich resources of the ancient theology of pagan and patristic Platonism, the Cambridge Enlightenment thinkers sought to create a first Protestant rational religion centred upon divine love and human freedom. Cudworth's daring manifesto of the school's irenic ecclesiastical and political latitudinarianism is an enquiry into the right method of the 'philosophy of religion'[4] composed in the vein of the rationalist foundationalism of René Descartes's *Meditations on First Philosophy* and the *Principles of Philosophy*, which Cudworth himself and his fellow Cambridge Platonists, notably his close friend Henry More, were instrumental in introducing at Cambridge University. In the young philosopher preacher's reading, the Johannine verse expounded provides in a nutshell the only 'right way and methode of discovering *our knowledge of Christ*'[5] and our own salvation. In accordance with the overall irenic message which his homily brings home to its listeners, Cudworth's concept of religious knowledge views the soul's purification of its detrimental affects in general and its 'self-will' in particular as the sine qua non of all scientific theology. Hence, the knowledge acquired by the only 'right way and method' of religious philosophy cannot be one of the dead letter of theoretical dogma. Instead, it is one informed by the spirit of the Father's own love and life shared with humankind in the incarnation of the Son in the pious soul:

> Words and syllables which are but dead things, cannot possibly convey the living notions of heavenly truths to us. The secret mysteries of a Divine Life, of a New Nature, of Christ formed in our hearts; they cannot be written or spoken; language and expressions cannot reach them; neither can they ever be truly understood, except the soul it self be kindled from within and awakened into the life of them.[6]

Not only are the 'secret mysteries of a divine life', in which the soul gains insight into God in a life of purity and charity alone, key to salvation, but they also serve as the unshakeable foundation of the Cambridge Platonists' comprehensive religious epistemology. In the momentous seventeenth-century re-enactment of Plato's 'battle of the Gods and Giants', that is, the struggle between the idealists of the Cartesian camp and materialists like Thomas Hobbes or Pierre Gassendi, the Cambridge Platonists developed a first Anglo-Saxon idealism to which the notion of an autonomous subject acquiring knowledge about God, the world and itself not from without, but from within is fundamental.[7] At the heart of their religious foundationalism is the goodness of a transcendent God whom the soul, endowed with freedom in action and thought, knows in pre-discursive intuitive awareness. As in Descartes's celebrated epistemological project, God's goodness and veracity are shown to be the source of the soul's trust in its own epistemic powers and the world around it. The Cambridge Platonists' epistemology of the Divine is one deeply steeped in the Cartesian imagination which views the I of the *Meditations* as literally in 'touch' with divine infinity in every single cognitive act.

2 Transcendent imagination: 'Touching' divine infinity in René Descartes

The 'unshakeable new foundation' of early modern science, laid by Descartes in his *Discourse* and his *Meditations*, is that of simple ideas seen clearly and distinctly by the unprejudiced mind's eye.⁸ In his early *Rules for the Direction of the Mind*, Descartes describes the intellectual intuition of uncompounded truths of which all our later complex science of the extended world of atoms is made up as the means whereby the soul may attain indubitable knowledge. Contrary to its inferior powers of sense and imagination, which cannot but lead it astray, reason, if properly applied, provides the soul with truths which cannot be doubted:

> By 'intuition' I do not mean the fluctuating testimony of the senses or the deceptive judgement of the imagination as it botches things together, but the conception of a clear and attentive mind, which is so easy and distinct that there can be no room for doubt about what we are understanding. Alternatively, and this comes to the same thing, intuition is the indubitable conception of a clear and attentive mind which proceeds solely from the light of reason. Because it is simpler, it is more certain than deduction, though deduction, as we noted above, is not something a man can perform wrongly. Thus everyone can mentally intuit that he exists, that he is thinking, that a triangle is bounded by just three lines, and a sphere by a single surface, and the like.⁹

Besides the attributes of thought and extension which define the two Cartesian substances in their manifold modes, the meditating I, guided by Descartes's rules for the directions of its mind, also intuits God as one of its innate simple ideas. The objective or representational reality of the 'true idea' of God is that of an infinite mind whose manifold perfect modes, joined in consummate 'unity, simplicity and inseparability',¹⁰ admit of no potentiality whatsoever. 'By the word "God"', Descartes defines the soul's inborn idea, 'I understand a substance that is infinite, eternal, immutable, independent, all-knowing and all-powerful, and which created both myself and everything (if anything else there be) that exists.'¹¹ The innate idea of God can neither be a mere negation of the soul's finiteness, which is at odds with the positive infinity of his objective reality, nor a merely potentially infinite augmentation of its own imperfect attributes and modes, which cannot but fall short of his actual infinity. While Descartes admits that as finite minds we can never aspire fully to comprehend God's infinity, he nevertheless insists that we can 'touch it in thought' *(cogitatione attingere)*: God is 'the possessor of all the perfections which, while I cannot grasp them, I can, in some way, touch in my thought'.¹² Our intuitive insight into or immediate touch of God's infinity resembles our view of a vast ocean or a chiliagon. In the *Replies to the First Objections*, raised by Caterus, Descartes expands upon his concept of spiritual sensation in a memorable comparison rich in both visual and tactile metaphor:

> For as regards infinity, even though we understand it to be positive to the highest degree, we nevertheless understand it only in a certain negative fashion, i.e., insofar as we notice in it no limit whatsoever. We understand that which is infinite positively, but not adequately, i.e., we do not understand everything about it that can be understood. Nevertheless, we are said to see the sea when turning our eyes to it, even though we cannot embrace it wholly in our sight or grasp its vast immensity. Seeing it at a distance, thus perceiving it in its entirety at once, as it

were, we see it only confusedly as when we imagine a chiliagon, embracing all of its sides at once. . . . In a similar fashion, God, I concede with all theologians, cannot be grasped by the human mind, nor can he be understood distinctly if we seek to embrace him all at once and view him from afar. . . . . However, if we attempt to focus upon his perfections one at a time, not grasping them, but rather being grasped by them, and devote all the power of our mind to their contemplation, we shall find more copious and more accessible matter for clear and distinct knowledge in them than in any created thing.[13]

However, while there can be no adequate *knowledge* of the fullness of God's objective reality, our *grasp* of its idea surpasses those of finite things both in clearness and in distinctness. Not only is the idea of God superior, but it is also prior to those of finite things, including the *cogito* itself. 'Moreover', Descartes replies to another critic of his *Meditations*, 'it is false that the infinite is understood through the negation of a boundary or limit; on the contrary all limitation implies a negation of the infinite.'[14] Accordingly, the *cogito's* many imperfect modes, revealed in the first and second *Meditations* in the thought experiment of universal metaphysical doubt, presuppose the prior notion of infinite perfection proved only in the third: 'For how could I understand', the meditating I asks, 'that I doubted and desired – that is, lacked something – and that I was not wholly perfect, unless there were in me some idea of a more perfect being which enabled me to recognize my own defects by comparison?'[15] Each single mode of the defining attribute of the thinking substance, therefore, he explains in his *Conversation with Burman*, is nothing but 'a defect and negation of the perfection of God',[16] which, unbeknownst to the Cartesian I at the start of its meditations, turns out to be the necessary condition of its thought throughout its meditative ascent from universal doubt to clear and distinct knowledge about the triad of thinking, extended and divine substances. Hence, while *explicit* knowledge of the *cogito* may indeed be first 'for it', the *implicit* knowledge of God is earlier 'in reality' (*in re ipsa*).[17] The discovery of God as the ground of all thought reveals the protagonist of the *Meditations* as an amphibious creature between the nothingness into which he may, unbeknownst to himself, vanish after each brief moment of conscious introspection, and the fullness of divine infinity: 'I realize that I am, as it were, something intermediate between God and nothingness, or between supreme being and non-being.'[18] Hence, the soul's striving for divine infinity, which it intuits or 'touches in thought' in the intellection of the *Meditations*, finds its chief expression not in intellection itself, but in volition. Of the many modes of cogitation in which its defining attribute expresses itself, the will, even more than reason, proves that the I is 'the image and likeness of God': 'It is only the will, or freedom of choice, which I experience within me to be so great that the idea of any greater faculty is beyond my grasp; so much so that it is above all in virtue of the will that I understand myself to bear in some way the image and likeness of God.'[19]

The metaphorical or analogical touch of the Deity by which the mind, significantly, apprehends the idea of God or nature both clearly and distinctly and partly and imperfectly at the same time plays a crucial role in the meditating I's struggle against scepticism, restoring as it does by conceptual necessity its overall trust in a comprehensive cosmic and epistemic framework. Famously, Descartes, in the first of the two closely intertwined cosmological or causal arguments in the third *Meditation*, appeals to a twofold causal principle which stipulates that nothing can come from nothing and that a cause must have at least as much or more reality than its effect in order to prove that God's 'formal' or actual reality is the sole possible cause of his 'objective' or conceptual reality represented in man's innate idea. So great is the reality of the unique inborn notion of the original infinite substance inscribed in the derivative finite substance that the former cannot possibly originate in the latter. The proofs of God's existence in the third and fifth *Meditations* mark a crucial step in the meditating I's endeavour to lay a new unshakeable foundation for scientific knowledge after its decision to cast into doubt its every earlier belief. After the reliability of its senses and even its once-indubitable mathematical knowledge have been shattered to the core in the thought experiment of an omnipotent malicious demon by which its every cognitive and volitional endeavour might be doomed from the onset, the I regains its trust in its reasoning capacity. Both the cognitive powers which it possesses and the world which it perceives originate in a trustworthy God whose perfect objective reality it sees or 'touches' even before it comes to know its own manifold imperfect modes. Divine infinity, Descartes expresses as the I's 'sure hope' *(spes certa)* in the final sixth *Meditation*, is either the immanent order of nature itself or its transcendent creator: 'Indeed, there is no doubt that everything that I am taught by nature contains some truth. For if nature is considered in its general aspect, then I understand by the term nothing other than God himself, or the ordered system of created things established by God.'[20] The theism of divine goodness which allows the I to trust both its faculties of understanding and the world around it is, hence, essential to Descartes's foundationalism.

It is the divinely guaranteed coherence and trustworthiness of man's thinking and the world's extended substances, perceived in intellectual vision and touch in Cartesianism, that is fleshed out in the ethical epistemology of Cambridge Platonism. Remedying a key shortcoming of the Cartesian synthesis, which lacks an 'understanding of inquiry that is anchored in broader moral precepts',[21] Ralph Cudworth, Henry More, John Smith and George Rust, the most philosophically outstanding representatives of the early modern Cambridge Enlightenment, conceive of the Cartesian *cogitatione attingere* primarily in practical terms.

3 Boniform vision: Divine goodness and the knowledge of the first principle

3.1 Divine sensation: Natural sagacity, the boniform faculty and the superintellectual instinct

The Cambridge Platonists share with Descartes the commitment to the certainty of self-consciousness as the unshakeable foundation of all philosophy.[22] However, in contradistinction to Cartesianism, the first principle of Cambridge Platonism is not subjectivity per se, but rather accountable moral agency. In the school's analogue to

Descartes's *Discourse of Method*,[23] John Smith[24] views the 'good life' as *the true way or method of Attaining divine knowledge*. Practical virtue, to him, is 'the prolepsis and fundamental principle of divine science'.[25] In support of his practical epistemology of the Divine, Smith, as will Samuel Taylor Coleridge and Johann Wolfgang von Goethe a century after him, invokes Plotinus's metaphor of the 'sunlight eye which alone is able to gaze at the sun'.[26] The author goes on to follow the latter's *Enneads* as well as John's Gospel and David's Psalms in positing not only an 'intellectual touch' but several spiritual senses whereby the soul, overcoming its self-love in a long process of active and contemplative self-perfection, gradually comes to grasp the Divine. Whereas speculation in theoretical syllogistic reasoning, which Smith rejects as a 'poor wan light' and 'thin, airy, knowledge', is bound to remain altogether flat and unprofitable, the intuition of the Divine is one that is conceived of as essentially practical and existential.[27] Only through purification and sanctification does the soul acquire an intuitive knowledge of divine goodness that is exempt from any doubt whatsoever. Quoting with approval the Alexandrian Church Father Origen with whom he shares the primacy of practical and experiential participation in the divine first principle vis-à-vis merely theoretical reasoning about it, Smith subscribes to an ethical mode of knowing God. It is at once knowledge and the feeling of awe and fear experienced in the sublime vision of the fullness of God's goodness. Practical knowledge about God, on the general Cartesian principles of Cambridge Platonist epistemology, possesses not only absolute clearness and distinctness but also a higher degree of evidence than mathematics. Like ethical insight, religious knowledge, acquired by spiritual sensation, commands the soul's immediate assent from which the latter, as Smith puts it in the technical neo-stoic vocabulary of the school's theory of religious knowledge, cannot withhold its 'acknowledgement' or assent: 'And these are both available to prescribe out ways of virtue to men's own souls, and to force an acknowledgement of truth from those that oppose, when they are well-guided by skilful hand.'[28] Divine goodness is at once metaphysically 'clear and perspicuous' and ethically binding. As an epistemic power, the spiritual senses by which the soul perceives divine goodness in intuitive immediacy appears to be both distinct from and superior to reason, while also being its highest modus operandi aspired to by the pious soul at the end of its ascent. In a fourfold scheme which traces the Christian soul's spiritual growth, the 'true metaphysical and contemplative man' first overcomes sense and imagination in purification. He, then, identifies solely with his soul and sheds off all of his corporeal passions altogether so as to participate in the fullness of the divine life. In the subsequent union, ordinary discursive reason or διάνοια, which proceeds by arguments and conclusions, gives way to spiritual vision or νοῦς, which grasps its object without any conceptual mediation:

> The priests of Mercury, as Plutarch tells us, in the eating of their holy things, were wont to cry out γλυκὺ ἡ ἀλήθεια – 'sweet is truth'. But how sweet and delicious that truth is, which holy and heaven-born souls feed upon their mysterious converse with the Deity, who can tell but they that taste it? When reason once is raised, by the mighty force of the Divine Spirit, into a converse with God, it is turned into sense: that which before was only faith well built upon sure principles, (for such

our science may be) now becomes vision. We shall then converse with God τῷ νῷ, whereas before we conversed with Him only τῇ διανοίᾳ – with our discursive faculty – as the Platonists were wont to distinguish.²⁹

Spiritual sensation, hence, is paradoxical in nature. It shares the defining characteristics of reason and sense. As supreme rationality, it proceeds from 'sure principles' or the unshakeable practical foundation of theological 'science'. However, as sensuality, it also shares with taste and vision the unmediated presence of its object whose appeal is such that the soul cannot help but savour and enjoy it on experiencing it at the end of a long process of practical purification and sanctification. While being the pinnacle of active discursive reasoning, spiritual sensation is also passive in nature as the soul is 'raised' by 'the mighty force of the Divine Spirit' which works upon it in Smith's ideal of its 'mysterious converse with the Deity'.

While Smith identifies the soul's intuitive knowledge of God and the good with Neoplatonic νόησις, both Henry More and Ralph Cudworth, the two chief philosophical representatives of Cambridge Enlightenment epistemology, choose to view it as a sui generis epistemic power called 'boniform faculty' or 'natural sagacity' and 'superintellectual instinct', respectively.³⁰ Thus, More is wary of identifying the 'pure eye' by which the poor, as Jesus promises them in the beatitudes of the Sermon on the Mount, will 'see God' (Mt. 5.8) with Plato's and Plotinus's concept of νοῦς *tout court*. The Greek concept, he avers, fails to capture the aspect of the mind's immediate assent to the divine object presented to it. Instead, the vision promised is that of a divine sense beyond reason:

> But having regard to our Saviours Discourse in this place, it is plain he intends not so much that which Philosophers call νοῦς, for the Homologous term to that of *the Eye*, as what S. *Paul* stiles φρόνημα; which is not *meer notion* or *perception*, but implies with it *a savour and relish of what is perceived. Get thee behind me Satan* (said Christ to Peter) ὅτι οὐ φρονεῖς τὰ τοῦ Θεοῦ, because thou savourest not the things that be of God. And the Apostle expressly mentions *τὸ φρόνημα τῆς σαρκός*, and *τὸ φρόνημα τοῦ πνεύματος*.³¹

Man's 'Divine Sensations', More elaborates in a letter to John Norris, 'lye deeper than imaginative Reason and Notion',³² of which they are viewed as the necessary condition. The 'boniform faculty' or 'natural sagacity' in which they originate is the power 'to distinguish not only what is simply and absolutely the best, but to relish it, and to have pleasure in that alone'.³³ It instils in man 'a living sense of the Comeliness and Pulchritude of Grace and Vertue',³⁴ which More and Cudworth concur in calling 'intellectual love' (*amor intellectualis*)³⁵ or 'Orphic-Pythagorean love'.³⁶ The soul's love for God's supreme goodness is twofold. It is directed towards him both as the transcendent principle of all of reality and as its immanent form or soul. More draws upon both the vocabulary of the ancient Platonic metaphysics of love and spiritual sensation and that of the early modern Cartesian physics of the world as a 'mass' of atoms engaged in motion to describe the soul's vision in which it 'relishes' and takes 'pleasure' in a God both transcendent to and ubiquitously active in the world:

Hence we are instructed how to set God before our eyes; to love him above all; to adhere to him as the supremest Good; to consider him as the Perfection of all Reason, of all Beauty, of all Love; how all was made by his Power, and that all is upheld by his Providence. Hence also is the Soul taught how to affect and admire the Creation, and all the parts of it; as they share in that Divine Perfection and Beneficence, which is dispersed through the whole Mass: So that if any of these parts appears defective or discomposed, the soul compassionates and brings help, as it is able, to restore every thing to that state of felicity which God and nature intended for it.[37]

In his early metaphysical poetry, More posits as the first principle of all cognition 'all-spreaden love/To the vast Universe' by which the soul, once it has overcome its self-will, is made 'half equall to All-Seeing Jove'. The insight into this first principle is expressed in dense tactile metaphor, as the soul is said to experience all of reality in one comprehensive spiritual touch: 'Then all the works of God with close embrace / I dearly hug in my enlarged arms.'[38] Likewise, Cudworth follows the 'Holy Scripture', which he commends for its general lack of 'Metaphysical Pomp and Obscurity', in viewing '*Love* or *Charity*' as the 'Source, Life and Soul of all Morality', which, as such, cannot itself be 'Better than Reason and Knowledge'. Hence, it must be 'vital and not notional' in nature.[39] The whole intuited in 'vital' sensation, rather than 'notional' reflection, is that of God's own infinity and eternity alike. Cudworth's depiction of the soul's mystical union with God, for one, bears the imprint of the Cambridge Enlightenment's profound debt to Descartes. As well as describing knowledge of the Divine in tactile metaphors along the lines of the Cartesian *cogitatione contingere*, Cudworth invokes the notion of divine infinity as the object of the soul's superintellectual intuition. For another, however, the God touched is not infinity per se, but 'boundless love'. Savouring God's 'boundless sweetness' in superintellectual vision, man transcends all spatial and temporal boundaries whatsoever. Instead, 'he enclasps the whole world within his outstretched arms' with his soul, in this process, becoming 'as wide as the whole universe, as big as yesterday, today and forever':

> No man is truly free, but he that hath his *will* enlarged to the extent of God's own will, by loving whatever God loves, and nothing else. Such a one does not fondly hug this and that particular created good thing, and enslave himself to it; but he loves everything that is lovely, beginning at God, and descending down to all his creatures, according to the several degrees of perfection in them. He enjoys a boundless liberty and boundless sweetness, according to his boundless love. He enclasps the whole world within his outstretched arms; his soul is as wide as the whole universe, as big as yesterday, today, and forever. (Heb 13.8)[40]

However, while the intuitive vision and 'intellectual' or 'Orphic-Platonic love' of divine goodness is above reason, of which it is the principle, it is not contrary to it. The assent given to it is 'vital' or above reason. It denotes the soul's existential commitment to absolute moral value. The insight into goodness itself, however, is 'notional' and reasonable. Thus, More is careful to distinguish between the two defining aspects of the soul's foremost epistemic power: 'Also that all Moral Good, properly so called, is *Intellectual* and *Divine*.' He then goes on to explain its contents in terms of the school's Platonist realism of the forms among which the moral ones, notably that of the good identified with the divine first principle itself, take pride of place:

> *Intellectual*, as the Truth and Essence of it is defined and comprehended by the Intellect: and *Divine*, as the Savour and Complacency thereof, is most effectually tasted through that high Faculty, by which we are lifted up and cleave unto God, (that Almighty One, who is the most pure and absolute Good, and who never wills any thing but what is transcendently the Best.)[41]

In contradistinction to the sectarian enthusiasm of the Interregnum era, Cambridge Platonist mysticism is one of practical reason. In his critique of the irrational enthusiasm of his day, More espouses the vision of a transformative practical vision of God whom the soul imitates in its own love for all of his creation:

> But I say that a free divine universalized spirit is worth all. How lovely, how magnificent a state is the soul of man in, when the life of God inactuating her, shoots her along with himself through Heaven and Earth, make her unite with, and after a sort feel herself animate the whole world, as if she had become God and all things? This the precious clothing and rich ornament of the mind, farre above reason or any other experiment.[42]

The mystical vision of true rational religion revolves around a life of practical universal love. It is expressed by More in the technical vocabulary of Plotinus and Dionysius the Areopagite, those 'mystical divines' who, as he confides in his reader in what his biographer Richard Ward terms the 'Dr's little narrative of himself',[43] helped him overcome his early adulthood 'aporia' of purely theoretical-theological dogma in favour of the 'euporia' of practical purgation and illumination.[44] The experience of God in immediate touch and vision is not enthusiastic fancy, but practical insight into the 'superessential causes' of the soul's virtues exercised in a moral life:

> This is to become Deiform, to be thus suspended (not by imagination, but by union of life, Κέντρον κέντρῳ συνάψαντα, joyning centres with God) and by a sensible touch to be held up from the clotty dark Personality of this compacted body. Here is love, here is freedome, here is justice and equity in the superessentiall causes of them. He that is here, looks upon all things as one, and on himself, if he can then mind himself, as a part of the whole. And so hath no self-interest, no unjust malicious plot, no more then [sic] the hand hath against the foot, or the ear against the eye. This is to be godded with God, and Christed with Christ, if you be in love with such affected language.[45]

The boundlessness of God's creative goodness in space and time, intuited and embraced in the soul's original vision, provides the 'open Champain' or the 'Plain of Truth' (πέδιον τῆς ἀληθείας) of Plato's *Phaedrus*[46] upon which the soul exercises its reasoning powers, both theoretical and practical. In theoretical speculation, the rational belief in 'creation' as a meaningful whole provides 'the first Rise of successful Reason', as it sets out to understand all of reality as one comprehensive and coherent image of archetypal divine perfection from which it proceeds and to which it returns. In the Cambridge Platonists' experiential rationalism, Plato's archetypal 'plain of truth' is identified with Christ who, grasped as the 'spirit of Illumination' or 'Principle of the *purest reason*' in original boniform intuition, guides the soul towards a coherent vision of all reality in discursive reasoning. He is 'the Eternal λόγος, the all-comprehending Wisdom and Reason of God, wherein he sees through the Natures and Ideas of all things, with all their respects of Dependency and Independency, Congruity and Incongruity, or whatever Habitude they have one to another, with one continued glance at once'.[47] The boniform faculty provides the soul with a first original intuition of the comprehensive unity of all reality in God's love. It goes on to serve as the 'measure'[48] or yardstick of all subsequent cognition: 'Therefore, I say, this most simple and Divine Sense and feeling in the boniform faculty of the soul is that rule or boundary whereby reason is examined and approves itself'.[49] In practical reasoning, the boniform faculty is the source of the first general imperative 'to restore every thing to the state of Felicity, which God and Nature intended for it', thereby enabling it to share in the fullness of divine perfection envisaged in the faculty's original vision: 'In short, it turns all its Faculties to make good Men happy; and all its Care and Discipline is to make bad Men good.'[50]

As the 'rule or boundary' of theoretical and practical reason alike, the boniform faculty is situated on the threshold between God and the soul. They act in unison in theoretical intellection and moral action as the all-encompassing vision of divine goodness and love informs human reasoning not from without, but from within. God, as More expounds the etymology of his newly coined neologism of the 'boniform faculty', is 'the form of the good' that 'moves' or 'inactuates' the soul. It is he himself who becomes 'the precious clothing and rich ornament of the mind', that is, the formative principle of all the latter's agency in cognition and action alike. Still, although it is God who moves the soul as its both formal and final cause, the latter's boniform vision is throughout qualified as 'freedome', since the soul acts in accordance with the formative principle of its own essence. Paradoxically, its vision is at once active intellection and passive perception as the soul, while engaged in the highest form of active reasoning, finds its every cognitive act to be passively informed by the principle of God's universal goodness: 'It is very true', More concedes, 'that we may as to this point (with Descartes) allow that all intellection has so much of passion, as it is the perception of something imprinted from without'. Despite that, however, the author is adamant that this does not take away from the soul's own activity in any way. On the contrary, it is the soul itself which rouses itself to reasoning in contemplating and embracing the divine principle of universal goodness in the autonomy of 'intellectual love': 'However, as this perception, which is made by intellection, is not from the body, but rather from the soul exerting and exciting herself into such action, so neither is this love from the body, but either from the soul itself or else from God above who calls and quickens the soul to such a divine effort.'[51] The intellectual love aroused by the boniform faculty is equally divine and human with the one universal love and the many passions corresponding to God himself and the soul, respectively. Drawing upon the key distinctions of his rationalist metaphysics, More likens love to light and colour as one basic substance differentiated in a range of modes or visual impressions and specific shades and hues. Although the love for the good intuited and embraced in the original boniform vision takes on many different modes in man, including 'Hope, Fear, Joy, Anger, Sorrow' or even 'Hatred itself', all of them can be reduced to their first principle or 'general ground-work', thereby revealing divine love and goodness as the very principle and substance of the soul. This love is described in terms of the Phaedrean wings by which the soul ascends to the heavens in pious enthusiasm:

> That Love which I have defined to you, is one simple and uniform thing, like the visible Light. And this is a perpetual well-liking of, or benign affection to the Divine Beauty communicable to man; which is as one still sun-shine day; or (if you will) as the Sun shining in silence and solitude, there being no Earth, or any opake part of the World to reflect and variegate his Rays. Such is the mind of him that is possest with this Divine Love, as it is freely and uncurb'dly working in it self. But lighting upon several objects is after several manners modified and transfigured into several shapes.[52]

There is, hence, but one single love informing the soul's many passions. Its every passion, however vile, reveals the soul to be the image of God by whom it finds itself 'inactatued' in the various degrees of its own freedom: 'Thus we see Divine Love ceases not by other Passions, but remains still the same, though in several postures: And that it is the several operations of one simple Nature about one and the same Object, that is the Image of God or Divine Accomplishments communicable to man.'[53] Universal love is the 'divine life' itself which becomes the soul's own in a triad of virtues. Overcoming the petty passions of its lower 'middle' and 'animal lives' in 'purity', it accepts God or love itself as the source and principle of all its agency in 'humility'.[54] Once the particularity of human passion has been overcome, the universality of divine love or 'charity' is bound to take its place instead, revealing the God of the soul's boniform vision as its 'Primogeneal, or Original Fire' fuelling its every act and motion:

> Surely the purging of it from this foul dross and dregs, must needs wing it, free it, universalize it, and make it as generally benign to all men, as the Sun is universally courteous to all the World, in lending Light and Heat to all. For by how much the Soul doth purge her self, by so much nearer she approaches to that Primogeneal, or Original Fire, which is God himself, that lets his sun rise on the evil and good, and sendeth rain on the just and on the unjust. (Mt. 5.45)[55]

Not only, therefore, do 'our minds', once they are 'inactuated' and informed by his goodness, ascend to God, 'but descend also in very full and free streams of dearest affection to our fellow creatures, rejoicing in their good as if it were our own and compassionating their misery as if it were our selves did suffer and according our best judgement and power ever endeavouring to promote the one and to remove the other'.[56] The agency of universal love and charity is both divine and human as God gradually becomes the form of the soul's many cognitions, volitions and passions. Its jarring discord is thereby reduced to the one harmony of God's own vision of the world at large which he shares with the soul and all his creatures. Once he has adopted the triad of the virtues of the 'divine life', man is, as it were, 'laid fast hold on by the Spirit of God, who guides this faithful and well-fitted Instrument, not according to the ignorant or vicious modes of the World, but his motions keep time to that Musick which is truly Holy, Seraphical and Divine, I mean, to the measures of sound reason and pure Intellect'.[57]

Cudworth agrees with More in identifying divine grace and human freedom. When sharing in God's own being in 'enclasping the world in his outstretched arms' and being 'as big as yesterday, today and tomorrow' in his original superintellectual vision, man is viewed by Cudworth at once as being 'truly free'[58] and having achieved a state of 'Evangelicall liberty'[59] or 'true freedom'[60] and as being subject to 'necessity'. In his two homilies and his many treatises on human agency,[61] of which only one was published a century after its author's death, Cudworth, like More, draws upon the technical vocabulary of early modern physics and ancient metaphysics in viewing God or divine goodness as the 'elater or spring'[62] and 'τὸ πρώτως κινοῦν'[63] of the human soul. Like More's principle of universal divine love which is the moving power as well as the general substance of the soul's many individual passions, Cudworth's 'first mover', grasped by the soul's superintellectual instinct in 'μάντευμά τι, a certain vaticination, presage, scent, and odour of one *summum bonum*',[64] is at once the principle and the sum total of all the soul's living powers. In a stunning comparison, Cudworth expounds the vision of the divine life driving all of man's thoughts and actions in the Cartesian terms of the conservation of motion imparted to the atoms in the beginning:

> Now this love and desire of good, as good in general, and of happiness, traversing the soul continually, and actuating and provoking it continually, is not a mere passion or *horme*; but a settled resolved principle, and the very source, and fountain, and centre of life. It is necessary and nature in us which is immutable, and always continues the same, in equal quantity. As Cartesius supposed the same quantity of motion to be perpetually conserved in the universe, but not alike in all the same bodies, but being transferred, and passing from one to other, and so, more or less, here and there. So is there the same stock of love and desire of good always alive, working in the soul by necessity of nature, and agitating it, though by men's will and choice, it may be diversely dispensed out, and placed upon different objects, more and less.[65]

'Will and choice', however, do not denote a distinct faculty of the soul, but its ἡγεμονικόν[66] or unified centre of agency by which the 'the soul as comprehending itself, all its concerns and interests, its abilities and capacities, and holding itself, as it were in its own had, as it were redoubled upon itself',[67] chooses to yield to or resist the pull of divine goodness which suffuses and impels it in its original multiplicity of passion, thought and will and its subsequent hegemonic unity of 'intellectual volition' and 'volitional intellection' alike.[68] Cudworth's *reductio* arguments both for the human ἡγεμονικόν or the 'redoubled self' as the cause of moral action and the divine πρώτως κινοῦν or the intuition of universal goodness as its first driving force are strictly analogous. The twofold argument proves the necessary reality of the human and divine principles of accountable agency as transcendental prerequisites of moral praise and blame and judicial reward and punishment in politics and religion. Just as the ἡγεμονικόν, by its will and choice, resolves upon a course of action, unifying all the aforementioned aspects of the soul's life recapitulated in itself in the process, so does the πρώτως κινοῦν move the ἡγεμονικόν, endowing it with the unity of the superintellectual vision of God's all-encompassing goodness. God and soul again work in unison as the first mover is not extraneous to, but the very principle and substance of the soul whose every cognition and volition it shapes as its formal and final cause. 'No', Cudworth exclaims in the first of his two homilies, 'then, are we acted by God himself, and the whole divinity flows in upon us; and when we cashiered this self-will of ours, which shackled and confined our souls, our wills shall then become truly free, being widened and enlarged to the extent of God's own will'.[69] In the second, he expressly defines God's action upon human cognition and action as 'the soul's acting from an inward spring and principle of its own intellectual nature, not by a mere outward impulse, like a boat, that is tugged on by oars, or driven by a strong blast of wind'.[70] In one of his unpublished treatises on free will, Cudworth follows the logic of the 'realization of the image'[71] in identifying the ἡγεμον ικόν's divine moving power with its 'inward self', arguing 'that to find God and return to him by grace is nothing but to find ourselves and to return to that divine principle in the bottom of our beings'.[72] Since God is the soul's archetypal principle or 'true self',[73] the motion caused by his universal goodness is both theonomous and autonomous. In its autonomy, it is up to the soul either to give its assent to or withhold it from God's benign moving power. Elaborating upon the nautical metaphor with its Cartesian pedigree, Cudworth likens the soul's autonomy to that of a sailor's who, while inevitably being pushed forward by the wind, may influence his ship's direction:

> I may compare the human soul to a ship under sail moving upon the waters and necessarily carried along with the winds and tide in which the chief pilot himself is carried as well as the other mariners, as being passive to its motion, and yet, notwithstanding, he, sitting at the helm, has also some power of determining the motion of that ship in which he is carried on, can direct its course to some port rather than another.[74]

Hence, even though the soul's motion is caused by God as first 'spring and elater', it is not imposed upon it from without, but stirred in it from within, as the ectypal hegemonic self is linked closely, if not indeed identified to its divine archetype. Inevitably driven forward by divine love which is the principle and substance of his passions, volitions and cognitions, it is up to man's soul either to allow or to not allow himself to be carried forward by the wind of divine goodness. Trespassing and sin, paradoxically, but consistently, are called 'the voluntary non-exercise of free-will'.[75] The soul itself is a 'vital life and energy', either engaging or failing to engage in the 'Self-exertive conation'[76] imparted to it in the superintellectual vision of divine goodness which it 'touches' and 'enclasps' in its first quasi-instinctual *conatus*:

> To conclude therefore, *Liberum Arbitrium* is not Indifferency but Self-power, a Power which the Soul as redoubled and Self-active hath of exerting a Vigorous

Conatus towards the Higher Principle of Honesty and Reason, or of not exerting the same, of Determining it Selfe towards the better or the worse, of exerting it Selfe more ore lesse together with full Command over the Famulative Powers, the Understanding as to Exercise and Object and the locomotive.[77]

It is the chief fulfilment of the human soul's *conatus* as God's image to participate in the archetypal divine motion of disinterested self-communication which the Cambridge Platonists view in terms of the Deity's kenotic goodness.

3.2 Kenotic goodness: Images of living sacrifice

At the heart of Cambridge Platonism is the notion of God or kenotic goodness ungrudgingly sharing with all of reality the fullness of his own being in creation and salvation. Throughout the extant sermons of the Cambridge Platonists, the insight into God and goodness, achieved in purification of self-love and the imitation of his creative and salvific self-communication, possesses a sacrificial dimension.

More's and Cudworth's pupil George Rust shares with his two teachers the Neoplatonist notion of creation and salvation as God's disinterested self-communication. Drawing on the Neoplatonic dialectic of one and many, he defines the perspective adopted in the soul's existential union with God as an utter annulment of all particularity and individuality whatsoever in the undifferentiated universality of divine goodness. Like his two mentors, Rust expounds man's boniform or superintellectual vision of God in the predominantly ethical terms of the school's shared religious philosophy of the first principle as *ens moralissimum*: 'He looks not on himself as a partial and determinate being, but as a part and member of the universe and accordingly serves not his own particular interest, but the good and welfare of the whole.'[78] The ethical point of view adopted by the pious soul discloses to it a God whose goodness is that of kenotic self-sacrifice. Christ's voluntary death on the cross, the nadir of his voluntary descent praised in Paul's celebrated hymn, is a symbol of the kenosis of the first simple principle in creation. The Father, of his own benign volition, 'lays aside this State' so as 'to communicate his Goodness and to take up his Creation into a participation of his own Happiness and Bliss':

> And though it seems becoming the Simplicity and Majesty of God, that he should be alone within himself, retired into the inapproachable recesses of his own Being; yet through the infinite desire of communicating and diffusing his own Love and Goodness, he lays aside this State, and goes forth of himself, and by his tender care and Providence is intimately present with the longest Projection of Being. No Man hateth his own Flesh, (saith the Apostle) but rather cherisheth it; and we are (as I may speak) flesh of his flesh, and bone of his bone, and the whole Creation is but the Expansion and Dilatation of Divine Simplicity and Perfection. And all Creatures do more properly belong to God than Faculties or Actions to their Principles from whence they flow. And God pronounces concerning the Works of his Hands, that they are very good.[79]

So close is God to the soul that the Father is even said to suffer in its moral shortcomings and failures which do violence to his Son born and crucified in each human being's life. Thus, the young metaphysical poet More ponders on the sublimity of the drama of a Divine apparently thwarted in Christ's cruel crucifixion at the hands of sinful humankind: 'Is Gods own life of God himself forlorn? Or was he to continuall pain of God yborn?',[80] More asks in daring verse, questioning the tenability of the orthodox notion of divine impassibility:

> For the life that is in him and should flow into us, is hindred in its vitall operation. But if any man make it a light matter that God himself or the Word himself is not hurt, let him consider that he that can find of his heart to destroy the deleble image of God, would, if it lay in his power, destroy God himself, so that the crime is as high and as much to be lamented.[81]

Cudworth, too, likens the triumphs of virtue and vice in the life of the Christian soul to Christ's birth in the manger and his death on the cross respectively. As infinite goodness and love personified, the Father, he avers, cannot but commiserate with the afflictions of the soul in whom his Son, in the virtuous extirpation of passion and self-love, is born in another incarnation. To the comprehensive view of reality as the one coherent 'plain of truth' in Cambridge Platonist epistemology, therefore, corresponds the categorical imperative of disinterested self-communication in the school's ethics of the Theateatan 'assimilation to God'. Like all of reality, the soul originates in the primordial divine self-sacrifice in which it emerges from the simple goodness of the Father as 'flesh of his flesh, and bone of his bone'.[82] It is, hence, called upon to participate in God's creative and salvific self-giving, ungrudgingly passing on to its fellow creatures the riches of his being that it has received itself. Like God who, as overflowing goodness, shares with his creatures the fullness of his being, the soul is called upon not to keep its own, but humble itself, giving to its fellow creatures the physical and intellectual gifts it has received. Thus, Smith, using the school's hylemorphist language of God as the boniform first mover shaping all of human cognition and action, views the Christian life as one continuous sacrifice in which God, as the 'protoplastic virtue of our being', gradually consumes the soul in the latter's voluntary self-sacrifice: 'Thus we should endeavour to preserve that heavenly fire of the divine love and goodness (which, issuing forth from God, centres itself within us, and is the protoplastic virtue of our being) always alive and burning in the temple of our souls, and to sacrifice ourselves back again to Him.'[83]

Of the Cambridge Platonists' two principal treatises on sacrifice, the first, Cudworth's daring youthful first treatise on *The True Notion of the Lord's Supper*,[84] draws upon a comprehensive survey of Jewish, Greek and Roman religious custom to establish the ritual of feasting on sacrificed animals as the heart of the Christian Eucharist which Roman Catholic theology erroneously interprets as a repetition of Christ's sacrifice on the cross. In his typological exegesis, both the pagan and the Jewish rites are shown to be 'types and shadows of the true Christian sacrifice' anticipated in the prophetic ancient theology of pre-Christian time:

> Now having thus shewn, that both amongst the Jews under the law, and the Gentiles in their Pagan worship (for Paganism is nothing but Judaism degenerate), it was ever a solemn rite to join feasting with sacrifice, and to eat of those things which

had been offered up; the very concinnity and harmony of the thing itself leads me to conceive, that that Christian feast under the gospel, called the Lord's supper, is the very same thing, and bears the same notion, in respect of the true Christian sacrifice of Christ upon the cross, that those did to the Jewish and Heathenish sacrifices; and so is *epulum sacrificiale*, a sacrificial feast – I mean, a feast upon sacrifice; or, *epulum ex oblatis*, a feast upon things offered up to God.[85]

To feast upon Christ's body 'is to be made partaker of his sacrifice offered up to God for us'.[86] In accordance with ancient custom, the festive sharing of food and drink is 'a federal rite between God and those that offered them'[87] or 'a symbol of love and friendship'[88] meant to serve as visible confirmation of the 'sacred covenant, and inviolable league of friendship with him'.[89] At the heart of Cudworth's typology of religious sacrifice in Judaism, paganism and Christianity is Christ. His sacrifice discloses to humankind the goodness of a God who shares with them his archetypal fullness in the many images of the types and shadows of sacrificial ritual in human religion.[90]

The second major treatise on the notion of sacrifice expounds the 'federal rite' between God and man in terms of the Cambridge school's practical epistemology of the superintellectual instinct and the boniform faculty. In his sermon on Heb. 13.16: 'To do good and communicate forget not, for with such sacrifices God is well pleased', More views self-sacrifice as the first duty of the soul created in the image of the moral first principle. Human self-sacrifice is shown to take the two forms of a disinterested sharing of the material and spiritual goods received from God's fullness. Enjoining the Christian soul to vie with God in whom 'there is neither envy, want nor niggardness'[91] and be 'but one intire Sacrifice, whom that great High Priest, Christ Jesus, offers to his Father',[92] More assumes the role of the creator himself addressing his creature: 'So surely God will reason with us in this matter too, That which thou hast, I gave it thee; why therefore dost thou not imitate me, and impart somewhat to thy Neighbour of that I gave thee? Freely you have received (saith our Saviour) freely give.'[93] On sacrificing to God its base passions, notably its petty and pernicious self-will, in a 'triumph . . . over the animal life'[94] in purity, the soul acknowledges in humility that it owes everything that it is and that it does to God's own primordial self-sacrifice alone. In accordance with the notion of divine agency as God's 'universal spirit' informing and acting upon the soul in the intuitive immediacy of the vision and touch of the boniform faculty, the soul is, therefore, called upon to allow God alone to perform his creative and salvific work by means of its own 'perfect exinanation' in disinterested charity: 'Which is a perfect exinanition of our selves, that we may be filled with the sense of God, who worketh all in all, and feelingly acknowledge what ever good is in us to be from him, and so be no more elated for it, than if we had none of it, nor were conscious to our selves we had any such thing.'[95] As God's image and likeness, the soul must follow the example of its archetype and give freely, that is, in disinterested and cheerful generosity, to its neighbours both material and spiritual things. It must give to its brethren, as More details in his scriptural ethics of sacrifice, both 'rem & consilium; A supply of outward necessaries, or seasonable and friendly advice'.[96] 'Charity' or 'charitable duties to [our] neighbour'[97] are viewed as 'the true Christian Sacrifice and Holy

Worship of God',[98] in which Christian souls imitate the Son in selflessly coming to the aid of their neighbours whom More expressly calls 'those living Temples of God':

> But to be crucified with Christ, to suffer with him, to undergo the deadly dolorous pangs of mortification, to sweat drops of Blood, and endure the unspeakable agonies of dying to sin, this is a harder way: To give Alms and relieve the needy, to furnish those living Temples of God, the poor Christians Souls with necessaries, this way is more chargeable.[99]

Reviewing a host of relevant passages in the Old and New Testaments, More goes on to refute the charge that moral duty 'is not truly a *Sacrifice*; but Metaphorically, and improperly so called'. On the principles of the Cambridge Platonist theology of the *ens moralissimum*, a Christian soul's disinterested morality is in reality the true archetype of all sacrifice: 'The service of the Old Law and its Ceremonies, are but Types and Shadows of the Righteousness that is required of us Christians under the Gospel.'[100] If God, as is intuited by the soul in boniform vision, is kenotic goodness, then the triad of Christian virtues, that is, the soul's sincere 'purity' and 'humility' and its universal and disinterested 'charity', is the true sacrifice 'seen in a mirror, darkly', by the authors of the sacred writings of the Greek and Hebrew ancient theology. The three primary Old Testament sacrifices, that is, those of animals, of things and of drinks, can hence be shown to be types and images of the univocal archetype of moral self-sacrifice. The animals slaughtered are types of our brutish passions and bestial oblivion of which we need to purify ourselves and our neighbours in the triad of the fundamental sacrificial virtues of purity, humility and charity. Likewise, the sacrifice of drink, quite literally, is offered in beverages shared with the thirsty. The four incenses which God asks Moses to burn on the altar in Exodus symbolize the true sacrifice of the self in its virtuous return to its divine source, as More paraphrases the exegesis of Philo the Jew: 'Philo Judaeus will have these four ingredients to be Emblemes of the four general Principles or Elements of which this World consists; and the evaporation of this fume, to be that acceptable re-ascending of the Creature to God in holy thankfulness, and evacuation of it self into the great ocean.'[101] As well as possessing a spiritual sense of smell by which it perceives and participates in divine goodness and virtue as the source of all its own motion and love, the soul is obliged to transform itself into odorous incense, thereby gradually becoming an 'emblem' or image of God viewed as the loving archetype and source of all things. Its every charitable act, therefore, is a finite expression of the infinite sacrificial love at the origin of all things intelligible and sensible. As 'Goodness it self and allembracing Love', More avers, 'God alone' is the 'beginning and end' of every good deed, even though the neighbour is its recipient. Thus, the priest's or agent's consecration stipulated by the definition of sacrifice occurs in the 'outward mystical ceremony' in which the visible act, whether it is practical benevolence and charity or verbal counsel and consolation, discloses the invisible good or its divine first principle and final purpose:

> But now that this action of doing good, whither by hand or tongue, is not without an outward mystical Ceremony, is hence plain: For whether it be the munificence of our hands, they are but a resemblance of his munificence, that openeth his

hands, and filleth with good every living thing: Or if of tongue, whereby we do beget the holy life in others, or direct in doubt or danger, this is an emblem of the eternal λόγος, the everlasting word, whereby all things were made, and are now governed and directed.[102]

Lastly, recognizing that the goodness which he freely gives to others originates in and is aimed at God alone, every Christian is ordained a 'Lawful Minister', as is required by the Protestant notion of sacrifice.

The first intuitive insight into God as supreme kenotic goodness, gained in a life of self-sacrificial love, provides the unshakeable foundation of the Cambridge Platonists' epistemology of the iconic intellect which gradually gains fuller participation in the fullness of the divine vision of all things in every cognitive act.

4 Iconic intellection: Idea and unity in discursive knowledge

The comprehensive and coherent vision of divine all-oneness intuited or touched by the mind's eye or its distinct power of spiritual sensation informs all of cognition. Every finite cognition is viewed by the Cambridge Platonists as springing from the soul's original boniform or superintellectual vision of God's sacrificial creative goodness.

As in Descartes's *Third Meditation*, the trustworthiness of the finite mind's clear and distinct knowledge originates in the infinity of the all-encompassing archetypal mind, 'touched in thought' or tasted and intuited prior to and in every individual cognitive act. However, whereas in Cartesian theism God's veracity as the sine qua non of the soul's trust in its own epistemic powers is inferred from his perfection, deceit being ruled out as an imperfection incompatible with the innate idea of the *ens perfectissimum*, Cambridge Platonism envisages divine goodness, grasped by the boniform faculty as an indubitable analytic truth *a priori*, as the foundation of all claims to objective truth. In his *Discourse of Truth*, George Rust, anticipating a key argument of the later critique of Cartesianism, exposes what he perceives to be a vicious circle at the heart of Descartes's foundationalist project. If only insight into veracity as a divine perfection can guarantee epistemic certainty, this insight is based upon a number of conceptual inferences, including those that 'Veracity is a perfection' and 'that there be an intrinsecal relation betwixt Veracity and Perfection'.[103] In response to the aporia of Cartesian foundationalism, Rust instead follows 1 Jn 4.16: 'God is Love', which he subjects to in-depth rationalist exegesis, elevating divine goodness into the rank of a first principle 'of whose Truth', he explicitly takes issue with Cartesian epistemology, 'I make no more doubt than I do of my own Existence, which the so much admired Monsieur hath made the first Principle of his Philosophy'.[104] God's goodness, in turn, is the transcendent source of the 'clear intelligibility'[105] of intellect as the sum total of all truths. Descartes's criterion of truth is transformed into an ontological sphere of its own whose every part is defined as an object of clear and distinct knowledge. While 'pure falsehood', on the Cambridge Platonists' privation theory of error and evil, is 'pure nonentity' which, Cudworth avers in his earliest work, 'could not subsist alone by itself',[106] truth is equated to God's own archetypal being. According to the Cambridge

Platonist Trinitarianism of the *ens perfectissimum* as goodness, intellect and will or omnipotence, the middle hypostasis possesses 'clear intelligibility' as its *modus essendi* and *modus cognoscendi*. Proceeding from the first principle, the sum total of truth as the second is superior to the third and, hence, exempt from any change wrought by any arbitrary divine omnipotence:

> I answer therefore, that the criterion of true knowledge is not to be looked for any where abroad without our own minds, neither in the height above, nor in the depth beneath, but only in our knowledge and conceptions themselves. For the entity of all theoretical truth is nothing else but clear intelligibility, and whatever is clearly conceived is an entity and a truth. But that which is false, divine power itself cannot make it to be clearly and distinctly understood because falsehood is a non-entity, and clear conception is an entity. And omnipotence itself cannot make a non-entity to be entity.[107]

It is through its own autonomous discursive activity that the soul gains an ever-growing participation in the one and coherent divine whole of reality of which it acquires a first intuitive grasp by virtue of its boniform faculty or superintellectual instinct. In their sharp critique of nascent contemporary empiricism, as put forth, above all, in their philosophical archfoe Hobbes's *Elements of Philosophy* and *Leviathan*, both More and Cudworth go to great lengths to prove that human perception and intellection must not be understood along the lines of the celebrated empiricist metaphor of a *tabula rasa* gradually filled with external sense impressions beyond the subject's control. Instead, they argue, not even sensation can be understood as entirely passive. It requires an 'active vigour' on the part of an incorporeal soul without which no sense impression can be explained. Cudworth's argument hinges upon the atomistic cosmology of Descartes's *Principles of Philosophy* and the concomitant epistemological distinction between primary and secondary qualities. If body, as has been established beyond doubt by the atomism of the ancient theology and early modern cosmology alike, in reality consists of nothing but the primary qualities of size, shape, place and locomotion, its secondary qualities such as the 'ideas of heat, light and colours and other sensible things', which Cudworth, endorsing the usage of Descartes's *Meditations*, views as 'several modes of cogitation', cannot be accounted for without 'some inward vital energy of the soul itself' giving rise to them:

> Neither is this passion of the soul in sensation a mere naked passion or suffering, because it is a cogitation or perception which hath something of active vigour in it. For those ideas of heat, light, and colours, and other sensible things, being not qualities really existing in the bodies without us, as the atomical philosophy instructs us, and therefore not passively stamped or imprinted upon the soul from without in the same manner that a signature is upon a piece of wax, must needs arise partly from some inward vital energy of the soul itself, being phantasms of the soul, or several modes of cogitation or perception in it. For which cause some of the Platonists would not allow sensations to be passions in the soul, but only active knowledges of the passions of the body.[108]

However, despite the vital active contribution whereby a subject turns the senseless locomotion of atoms into sensual impressions, sense is subject to physical stimuli from without and physiological responses from within and as such predominantly passive. While emerging from the ἡγεμονικόν as the source and principle of intentionality by which a subject may choose to perceive any given object, the process of perception itself occurs in accordance with 'a necessary and fatal connection between certain motions in some parts of the enlivened body and certain affections or sympathies in the soul'[109] beyond the latter's voluntary conscious control. Conceptual reasoning, by contrast, is pure 'active vigour'. It brings to bear upon reality without its own categories and concepts from within. Whereas in sense the rational mind bows to the ineluctable laws governing the physico-biological interaction of the world's void and atoms and the body and its sense organs, in knowledge, the soul, as Cudworth sets out to prove in his in-depth rebuttal of empiricist sensualism, 'conquers' the reality outside itself, subjecting it to its own categories. 'Sense, that suffers from external objects, lies at it were prostrate under them, and is overcome by them: wherefore no sense judges either of its own passion, or of the passion of any other sense, but judgement or knowledge is the active energy of an unpassionate power in the soul.'[110] In response to the empiricist notion of the soul as a passive 'Abrasa Tabula', the Cambridge Platonists instead choose to endow it with 'some innate Notions and Ideas' which it possesses prior to all sense experience.[111] The erroneous empiricist conception of knowledge arising solely from sense impressions from without, rather than conceptual reasoning from within is traced back to its proponents' failure to distinguish 'betwixt extrinsecall Occasions, and the adequate or principal Causes of things'.[112] Opting for the former, rather than the latter epistemological model, Cambridge rationalism reveals human cognition to be the soul's participation in God's own creative activity which it mimics and aspires to in every cognitive act, however minute and insignificant. The object known is not the 'adequate or principal cause' of knowledge, but merely the 'occasion' for the rational soul to exercise the pure 'active vigour' of its own innate *a priori* concepts and categories. According to the two chief Cambridge Platonists' epistemological occasionalism, therefore, the occurrence of a possible object of cognition acts as a catalyst for the soul to make use of its own rich conceptuality to acquire and create knowledge, thereby exercising its highest capacity of participating in God's own creative power. But for its own categorical and conceptual resources, the soul would be as unable even to engage in cognition in the first place as a person would be to identify an unknown person amidst a crowd of people. While rejecting the concomitant dogma of the pre-existence of souls,[113] Cudworth, therefore, subscribes to the time-honoured concept of knowledge and learning as recollection delineated in Plato's *Meno* and the *Phaedo*. Knowledge, on his account, is not imposed upon a passive subject from without, but acquired by the latter's own conscious activity from within. The Cartesian 'adventitious ideas' are likewise revealed to be 'innate' ones instead:

> So when foreign, strange and adventitious forms are exhibited to the mind by sense, the soul cannot otherwise know or understand them, but by something domestic of its own, some active anticipation or prolepsis within itself, that occassionally reviving and meeting with it, makes it know it or take acquaintance with it. And

this is the only true and allowable sense of that old assertion, that knowledge is reminiscence, not that it is the remembrance of something which the soul had some time before actually known in a pre-existent state, but because it is the mind's comprehending of things by some inward anticipations of its own, something native and domestic to it, or something actively exerted from within itself.[114]

The mind's 'inward anticipations of its own' are not ideas of all the things which a soul may come to know in its lifetime. In fact, More ridicules the very idea of a crude innatism which posits 'a certain number of Ideas flaring and shining to the Animadversive Faculty, like so many Torches or Starres in the Firmament to our outward Sight'.[115] Instead, the *a priori* of the soul's 'inward anticipations' by which it knows external objects as 'something native and domestic to it' is strictly formal in character. The 'inward anticipations' upon which the soul, whenever 'occasioned' to do so by sense and perception, draws are several kinds of abstract concepts and categories, notably those that define its own practical and theoretical cogitation and those that constitute an object *qua* object such as 'cause and effect' and 'means and end'.[116] The discursive knowledge emerging from the soul's 'recollection' throughout bears the imprint of its original intuition of the all-oneness of divine goodness as its intellect exercises its 'unitive, active and comprehensive power'[117] upon the manifold contents of sensual perception. Hence, it views each particular object as a structured whole *(totum)* defined by its form and function *(ratio)* to which its every single part is actively judged to be subservient in purposeful cooperation with all the others.[118] In a memorable three-part comparison, Cudworth likens the levels of epistemic ascent and activity to a watch reflected by a mirror, seen by a mindless animal and understood by the rational human mind. Whereas there is no perception or intellection on the part of the mirror, the animal clearly perceives the artefact and its different components. Only in human intellection, however, is the watch understood as a watch, that is, as a functional whole of parts constructed with the purpose of indicating the time of the day. Guided by the boniform faculty as its formal and final cause, the rational mind, therefore, knows an object, whether natural or artificial, as one whole 'formed' or composed of many different parts with a view to fulfilling a 'good' or a purpose. Not only does the abstract nature of the first categories of 'form' and 'good' and the many subsequent related ones, without which there could be neither a subject knowing nor an object known, rule out their origin in perception or imagination, but Cudworth, like Descartes, also cites the analogue of the 'universal and necessary truth'[119] of geometrical theorems to highlight the sui generis quality of the categories shaping human intellection.

The soul's innate power of acquiring knowledge by actively making use of abstract concepts to transform prima facie chaotic multiplicity into unified objects of rational functionality finds its logical upshot in the holistic vision of the cosmos at large. In its most comprehensive of insights, iconic intellection can be seen to approximate the soul's original boniform intuition which throughout acts as its first moving principle, its chief criterion and its final objective. More's definition of 'reason' reveals the close tie between the soul's initial universal boniform vision and its subsequent particular iconic intellection. Drawing upon the formal *a priori* of its concepts and the *a posteriori* of sense perception and secular and religious tradition, the mind acquires knowledge by placing a part into a coherent whole for the sake of rational scientific enquiry into and ethical and political action in the world. The iconic intellect, according to the Cambridge Platonists' distinction between intuitive vision and discursive reasoning, is

> a Power or Facultie of the Soul, whereby either from her Innate Ideas or Common Notions, or else from the assurance of her own Senses, or upon the Relation or Tradition of another, she unravels a further clew of Knowledge, enlarging her sphere of Intellectual light, by laying open to her self the close connexion and cohesion of the conceptions she has of things, whereby inferring one thing from another she is able to deduce multifarious Conclusions as well for the pleasure of Speculation as the Necessity of practice.[120]

Invoking the 'greatest kinds' of Plato's *Sophist*, More views the relationship between discursive human reason and intuitive divine intellect as that of an ever-changing partial understanding to a comprehensive vision at eternal rest: 'And what is this but *Ratio stabilis*, a kind of steady immovable reason, discovering the connection of all things at once? But that in us is *Ratio mobilis*, or reason in evolution, we being able to apprehend things only in successive manner one after another.'[121] Hence, the mind's inner conceptual fecundity displayed on the occasion of each object known as an intelligible structure, whether artificial or natural, testifies to its deeper longing for an absolute ideal of a consummate whole of which each object known forms an integral part. The iconic intellect, as Cudworth puts it with another neologism of Cambridge Platonist epistemology, possesses 'a potential omniformity'. It is 'all things intellectually' or 'in a manner all things', as Plato and Aristotle concur.[122] Man's intellect is a universal icon potentially encompassing in itself the representations or images of the whole of the outer world which it, as it were, gradually paints and recreates upon the canvass provided in its original vision of God's all-encompassing creative goodness. In so doing, it throughout re-enacts God's primordial act of creative and self-diffusive kenotic goodness of which its every cognition and action is an imperfect image: 'The mind being a kind of notional or representative world, as it were a diaphanous and crystalline sphere, in which the ideas and images of all things existing in the real universe may be reflected or represented.' The analogy between the creator's one archetypal and the creatures' many minds is twofold and links the latter to the former both in theoretical vision and creative action. The human soul, for one thing, participates in the divine intellect in all subjectivity and self-knowledge: 'For as the mind of God, which is the archetypal intellect, is that whereby he always actually comprehends himself, and his own fecundity, or the extent of his own infinite goodness and power – that is the possibility of all things – so all created intellects being certain ectypal models, or derivative compendiums of the same.'[123] For another, the soul's metaphysical vision driving its every conscious act is both aesthetic and ethical in character. Its 'idea of God', which it inevitably forms in its reflection upon the principle of its own 'unitive' or 'comprehensive' reasoning power, is that of 'a mind infinitely good and wise' as the active source and principle of the archetypal perfect unity of utmost complexity of which all of its cognition is a faint image:

But the intellect doth not rest here, but upon occasion of those corporeal things thus comprehended in themselves, naturally rises higher to the framing and exciting of certain ideas from within itself, of other things not existing in those sensible objects, but absolutely incorporeal. For being ravished with the contemplation of this admirable mechanism and artificial contrivance of the material universe, forthwith it naturally conceives it to be nothing else but the passive stamp, print, and signature of some living art and wisdom, as the pattern, archetype, and seal of it, and so excites from within itself an idea of that divine art and wisdom. Nay, considering further, how all things in this great mundane machine or animal (as the ancients would have it) are contrived, not only for the beauty of the whole, but also for the good of every part in it, that is endued with life and sense, it exerts another idea, viz. of goodness and benignity from within itself, besides that of art and wisdom, as the queen regent and empress of art, whereby art is employed, regulated, and determined.[124]

Like all ideas, the idea of God is not one inscribed into the soul's mind from the outset, but one freely and creatively, yet necessarily and inevitably, framed in autonomous cognitive activity of which it is shown to be the formal and final cause. God is the transcendent ideal and unity of all of multiplicity, whether artificial or natural, to which the soul ascends as the principle and aim of its own 'unitive, active and comprehensive power'.[125]

5 Living images of God: The contemporary significance of Cambridge Enlightenment epistemology

At the heart of Cambridge Platonist epistemology is the intuition of God as universal goodness. Not only does it furnish a first ground of indubitable certainty to which the soul cannot but assent in intuitive practical insight, but it also serves as the principle of unity informing all of human cognition and action alike. As such, it cannot but surpass all intellection of which it is the principle. The Cambridge Platonists' notion of the soul's intuitive insight into God's love and goodness can be seen as a reimagining of Descartes's notion of a God 'touched in thought' as the transcendental first principle of all the modes of the I's thinking substance and the transcendent first ground of the extended world. Like Descartes, More and Cudworth espouse a theism of divine goodness as the source of the soul's trust in its own cognitive powers and the world around it. In response to what they perceive as shortcomings of Descartes's foundationalist project, however, the Cambridge Platonists view practical ethical insight as the chief means whereby the soul may acquire indubitable knowledge about the first principle of thought and being.

The boniform vision is an intuitive first insight into God's universal and disinterested creative goodness which, as the 'superessential cause', chooses to share with all of reality the riches of its own fullness in sacrificial self-communication. Hence, Cambridge Platonist subjectivity, by its very nature, is not one either of intellectualistic or of solipsistic self-reflection. For one thing, the sui generis epistemic power postulated by More and Cudworth is not a power distinct from the soul's cognition and volition, but, on the contrary, the unifying principle and form of all expressions of the finite mind. Its every cognition, volition and passion are shown to be an imperfect image approximating consummate archetypal divine goodness which the soul intuits and embraces in the intellectual love for creator and creation stirred by the highest of its epistemic powers. For another, the original intuition of God's ungrudging self-communication is deeply practical and universal in character. The soul is called upon to participate in the self-sacrifice of creation and salvation which God undergoes for its sake, not shutting itself off from reality in petty 'self-will', but, on the contrary, converting towards it in universal charity and generosity: 'The spiritual life is one of participation in a reality greater than the self; however it can only be interpreted and appreciated through self-consciousness. The self that rises to the Divine is the product of conversion not replacement.'[126]

Iconic intellection, defined as the knowledge of a phenomenon as a structured unity and whole, is shaped by the soul's original boniform vision which acts as its principle and purpose as well as its truth criterion. The universality of the divine perspective adopted in the original contemplative vision of and concomitant active assent to God's goodness as the beginning and end of all reality defines all of human cognition. While the twin doctrines of sacrificial goodness and divine emanation clearly go back to the ancient theology of pagan and patristic Platonism, as revived by Giordano Bruno and Nicholas of Cusa at the dawn of the early modern age, the Cambridge Platonists' epistemological line of argument is clearly that of the new 'way of ideas' championed by Descartes, Hobbes and Locke. Subjecting human consciousness to in-depth transcendental analysis, More and Cudworth are careful to distinguish between its subjective perception of reality, its many secondary qualities, and the objective characteristics of reality, its primary qualities, in order to arrive at a notion of sensation as inherently active. The Cambridge Platonists' distinct version of the British 'way of ideas' is, hence, that of the ascent of the soul as it engages in autonomous moral and cognitive activity in embracing its original vision of the infinite space of creative divine goodness of which it is an image and likeness. More's and Cudworth's doctrine of the soul's 'boniform' or 'superintellectual' vision of God's creative goodness as the principle and purpose of all of thought and reality continues to be one of the most compelling epistemologies of the Divine.

Response by Douglas Hedley

Christian Hengstermann's beautiful account of the Cambridge Platonist notion of the soul's 'boniform' or 'superintellectual' vision of Divine goodness elaborates the profoundly 'modern' aspect of these thinkers. To read the Cambridge Platonists often seems like an exercise of pursuing the recondite interests and obsessions of erudite but anachronistic scholars. Hengstermann's chapter bolsters the thesis of Charles Taliaferro in his magisterial work *Evidence and Faith: Philosophy and Religion since the Seventeenth Century*, that the Cambridge Platonists constitute the beginning of the Philosophy of Religion in modern thought, especially in their kinship with Descartes. Hengstermann's exposition of the notion of *cogitatione attingere* or touching in thought the Divine infinity as an instance of the proximity between the Cambridge men and the 'Father of Modern Philosophy' is a case in point. Yet he also demonstrates with great power the stress upon the ethical component in the leading lights of the Cambridge school, who conceive of love as a prolepsis of true Divine knowledge, as a practice of 'affectionate' religion. The Cambridge Platonists develop a vision of the subject that combines intellect with feeling and ethical seriousness.

For the Cambridge Platonists, the term 'imagination' is usually employed in a negative way. Henry More uses the word in order to explain the errors of the enthusiasts like Boehme. Such enthusiasts, according to More, confuse the dark materials of finite fancy with intelligible realities and, thus, confuse God and world. Yet I think Hengstermann is correct to see the 'Divine Sensations' in figures like More as instances of a purified and truly contemplative imagination as the soul relishes contact with the presence of the goodness of God in the world. The analysis of the boniform faculty in Henry More deserves particular attention in this context. Yet it is striking that Hengstermann notes the dimension of sacrifice in these figures. These are writers living in a turbulent and brutal age. Notwithstanding their recognition of the goodness of God, they are conscious of costly ethical self-sacrifice as the true archetype of the sacrificial ceremonies. Hengstermann is correct to highlight the contrast between the static Cartesian attribute of Divine perfection and the dynamic self-communication of Goodness in the God of the Cambridge Platonists.

Notes

1 Ralph Cudworth, *A Sermon Preached before the House of Commons*, in *The Cambridge Platonists*, edited by Constantinos A. Patrides (London et al.: Cambridge University Press, 1969), 127.

2 See the most recent interpretation of Cudworth's sermon as a theology of the divine image deeply influenced by Meister Eckhart's mysticism of the birth of Christ in the midst of the faithful heart in Douglas Hedley, 'Image, Idol and Likeness: Ralph Cudworth's *Sermon before the House of Commons 1647*', in *Origenes Cantabrigiensis. Ralph Cudworth, Predigt vor dem Unterhaus und andere Schriften*, edited by Alfons Fürst and Christian Hengstermann (Münster: Aschendorff Verlag, 2018), 51–62.

3 'Cambridge Enlightenment' is the most recent designation of the group of philosophers and theologians commonly known as the 'Cambridge Platonists', as suggested in Sarah Hutton, *British Philosophy in the Seventeenth Century* (Oxford: Oxford University Press, 2015), 136–59. As is shown in the essays collected in Alfons Fürst and Christian Hengstermann (eds), *Die Cambridge Origenists. George Rusts Letter of Resolution Concerning Origen and the Chief of His Opinions* (Münster: Aschendorff Verlag, 2013), 'Cambridge Origenists' may be as fitting a designation as 'Cambridge Platonists' considering the general Christian outlook of their Platonism and their concern with divine goodness and human freedom in a rational theodicy. The original sobriquet was coined by John Tulloch in his classical exposition of their thought in his *Rational Theology and Christian Philosophy in England in the Seventeenth Century*. Vol. 2: *The Cambridge Platonists* (Edinburgh and London: William Blackwood and Sons, 2nd edn, 1874). The identity of the Cambridge Platonists as a distinct group of philosophers and latitudinarians is also established and explored in great detail in the important essay collection by Alan J. Rogers, Jean-Michel Vienne and Yves Ch. Zarka (eds), *The Cambridge Platonists in Philosophical Context: Politics, Metaphysics and Religion* (Dordrecht et al.: Springer, 1997). The existence of a group of Cambridge Enlightenment thinkers or Cambridge Platonists has recently been called into question by Dmitri Levitin, *Ancient Wisdom in the Age of the New Science* (Cambridge et al.: Cambridge University Press, 2015), 126–38. The author's altogether feeble argument rests solely upon the allegedly divergent concepts of the history of philosophy held by the representatives of the group. He fails to take into account the historical constellation around the committed university teacher Ralph Cudworth and, most surprisingly, any of the school's shared deeply held philosophical convictions such as God's goodness and man's freedom. A compelling rebuttal of Levitin's ill-founded claim is provided in Douglas Hedley, 'Gods and Giants: Cudworth's Platonic Metaphysics and his Ancient Theology', *British Journal for the History of Philosophy* 25 (2017): 932–53, esp. 949–50.
4 The term itself is one which the philosopher preacher went on to coin alongside several other philosophical key words in the philosophical vernacular in his monumental, albeit unfinished and fragmentary, principal work of 1678 entitled *The True Intellectual System of the Universe* (London: Printed for Richard Royston, 1678), 'The Preface'.
5 Cudworth, *Sermon Preached before the House of Commons*, 93.
6 Ibid., 92.
7 See Hedley, 'Gods and Giants' (see n. 3), who throughout interprets Cambridge Platonism against the backdrop of the celebrated dichotomy of Plato's *Sophist*.
8 Besides the expositions of the 'theological' third and fifth Meditations in the classical monographs by Bernard Williams, *Descartes: The Project of Pure Enquiry* (New Jersey: Humanities Press, 1978), 130–62, and Margaret D. Wilson, *Descartes* (London and New York: Routledge, 1978), 100–38, and the important article by Jean-Marie Beyssade, 'The Idea of God and the Proofs of His Existence', in *The Cambridge Companion to Descartes*, edited by John Cottingham (Cambridge: Cambridge University Press, 1992), 174–9, the following outline is indebted to the sympathetic rereading of Descartes's theistic foundationalism from the vantage point of religious philosophy offered in the magisterial historical account by Charles Taliaferro, *Evidence and Faith: Philosophy and Religion since the Seventeenth Century* (Cambridge: Cambridge University Press, 2005), 57–109.
9 *Regulae* 4 (AT 10, 368; CSM 1,14).

10 *Meditationes* 3 (AT 7, 50; CSM 1, 34).
11 Ibid. (AT 7, 45; CSM 1, 31).
12 Ibid. (AT 7, 51; CSM 2, 35).
13 *Primae responsiones* (AT 7, 113–14). My translation.
14 *Quintae responsiones* (AT 7, 365; CSM 2, 252).
15 *Meditationes* 3 (AT 7, 48–9; CSM 2, 31).
16 *Descartes's Conversation with Burman*, translated with introduction and commentary by John Cottingham (Oxford: Clarendon Press, 1976), 13.
17 Ibid.
18 *Meditationes* 4 (AT 7, 54, CSM 2, 38).
19 Ibid. (AT 7, 57; CSM 2, 40).
20 Ibid., 6 (AT 7, 81; CSM 2, 56).
21 Cf. this Cambridge Platonist critique levelled at Descartes in Taliaferro, *Evidence and Faith* (see n. 8), 73, on which the following exposition of Cambridge Platonist epistemology builds: 'But there is not in Descartes' extant publications the fuller Cambridge Platonist understanding of inquiry that is anchored in broader moral precepts, a tradition of inquiry that prizes reverent practice.'
22 The Cambridge Platonists' elective affinity with Descartes runs deeps and bears upon nearly every tenet of their philosophy of religion. On their general reception of Cartesianism, its historical background and its philosophical topics, see the survey by Marjorie Nicolson, 'The Early Stage of Cartesianism in England', *Studies in Philology* 26 (1929): 356–74. There are several detailed studies devoted to Descartes's thought in the two major Cambridge Platonists Henry More and Ralph Cudworth. For More, see, above all, the classic article by Alan Gabbey, 'Philosophia Cartesiana Triumphata: Henry More (1646–1671)', in *Problems of Cartesianism*, edited by Thomas M. Lennon, John M. Nicholas and John W. Davis (Kingston and Montreal: McGill-Queen's University Press, 1982), 171–249, and the more recent special issue of *Les Études Philosophiques* 2014/1: *Descartes et More*. For Cudworth, see the book-length study on his relationship to Descartes by Lydia Gysi, *Platonism and Cartesianism in the Philosophy of Ralph Cudworth* (Bern: Herbert Lang, 1962), to which the subsequent exposition is indebted throughout.
23 On Smith's appropriation of Descartes, which differs from that of his fellow Platonists in a number of crucial regards, see J. E. Saveson, 'Descartes' Influence on John Smith, Cambridge Platonist', *Journal of the History of Ideas* 20 (1959): 258–63. Cf. the analysis of Smith's important treatise on the school's practical religious epistemology in Ernst Cassirer, *Die platonische Renaissance in England und die Schule von Cambridge*, *Gesammelte Werke*, edited by Friederike Plaga and Claus Rosenkranz (Darmstadt: Wissenschaftliche Buchgesellschaft, 2002), 242–9, who credits Smith's first discourse with putting forth 'the really pivotal *principle* of their [i.e. the Cambridge Platonists'] doctrine'. See, above all, ibid., 243–4: 'Wie sehr dieser Gedanke von der gesamten Schule von Cambridge als das eigentlich entscheidende *Prinzip* ihrer Lehre empfunden wird: das geht mit besonderer Deutlichkeit daraus hervor, daß sie selbst ihn als *methodischen* Grundsatz vor allen inhaltlichen Sätzen, die die Bestimmung und nähere Ausgestaltung der Religionsphilosophie betreffen, unterscheiden.'
24 Besides Cassirer, Derek Michaud, *Reason Turned into Sense: John Smith on Spiritual Sensation* (Leuven: Peeters, 2017), and Mario Micheletti, *Il Pensiero Religioso di John Smith, Platonico di Cambridge* (Padua: La Grangola, 1976), 207–46, provide the most thorough and most philosophically satisfactory expositions of Smith's

religious epistemology. While the former defends the systematic significance of the Cambridge Platonist's vision, the latter contains a plethora of illuminating historical materials which link the author's notion of God's salvific immanence in the soul to the Puritan teaching and preaching of his day. A convincing systematic reading of Smith's notion of spiritual sensation is offered in Hedley's trilogy on the religious imagination, notably in *Living Forms of the Imagination* (London and New York: T&T Clark, 2008), 81–2, *Sacrifice Imagined: Violence, Atonement, and the Sacred* (New York and London: Continuum, 2011), 14–16. 51–3, and *The Iconic Imagination* (New York et. al.: Bloomsbury, 2016), 46–7, 166.

25 John Smith, *Select Discourses*, 4th edn, corrected and revised by Henry G. Williams (Cambridge: Cambridge University Press, 1859), 2.
26 Ibid.
27 Ibid., 2–3.
28 Ibid., 14.
29 Ibid., 17. Cf. the systematic exploration of the relationship between ethical transformation and metaphysical cognition as well as that between incorporeal and corporeal sensation in Hedley, *Iconic Imagination* (see n. 24), 254, in which the author cites the aforementioned passage in support of his own imaginative epistemology: 'On the view we have been exploring, this is fundamentally because a transformation in the person, as they approach the condition of enlightenment, or as they develop spiritually, will make for a reciprocal transformation in the appearance of the sensory world – and accordingly far from being simply a movement "upwards" or "inwards", enlightenment, or spiritual awakening can also be an opportunity for, and will be partly constituted by, a movement "outwards" and into the realm of the senses. As the Cambridge Platonist John Smith notes: "When reason once is raised by the mighty force of the Divine Spirit into a converse with God, it is turned into sense."'
30 The following depiction of the soul's highest epistemic power builds upon the important research articles by David Leech, 'Does Henry More's Conception of a "Divine Life" Bear Traces of Origen's Influence?', in *'That Miracle of the Christian World': Origenism and Christian Platonism in Henry More*, edited by Christian Hengstermann (Münster: Aschendorff Verlag, 2020), 125–40, and 'Cudworth on Superintellectual Instinct as Inclination to the Good', *British Journal for the History of Philosophy* 25 (2017): 954–70. A first overview of the two major Cambridge Platonists' theories of cognition is provided in the classical monographs by Aharon Lichtenstein, *Henry More: The Rational Theology of a Cambridge Platonist* (Cambridge, MA: Harvard University Press, 1962), 31–95, and J. A. Passmore, *Ralph Cudworth: An Interpretation* (Cambridge: Cambridge University Press, 1951), 29–39. The first principle of More's and Cudworth's ethics and epistemology has sparked off one of the most philosophically fruitful discussions about Cambridge Platonist thought. Cudworth's doctrine of 'love' in particular has been hailed both as a precursor of Kantian internalism and Humean sentimentalism. See the differing accounts of the foremost Cambridge Platonist's system of ethics by Stephen Darwall, *The British Moralists and the Internal 'Ought'* (Cambridge: Cambridge University Press, 1995), 109–49, and Michael B. Gill, *The British Moralists on Human Nature and the Birth of Secular Ethics* (Cambridge: Cambridge University Press, 2006), 38–57. While Leech generally offers a middle path, the following account views both thinkers as deeply original representatives of a practical rationalism based upon the doctrine of eros as put forward in Plato's *Symposium*, Plotinus's *On Beauty* and

Origen's *Commentary on the Song of Songs*. On the profound elective affinity between Plato and Kant, see Hedley, *Living Forms* (see n. 24), 148–51.

31 Henry More, *Discourses on Several Texts of Holy Scripture* (London: Printed by J. R., 1692), 62–3.
32 The correspondence was published as an appendix to John Norris, *The Theory and Regulation of Love: A Moral Essay* (Oxford: Printed at the Theatre for Hen. Clements, 1688), 188.
33 More, *Enchiridion Ethicum* I 2,5 (*Opera Omnia* III /1, 12; *Account of Virtue*, 6). The bibliographical references given are those of the 1679 complete edition of More's Latin works and the early modern English translation by Robert Southwell, *An Account of Virtue or Dr Henry More's Abridgement of Morals*, London: Printed for Benj. Tooke, 1690. More's highly successful *Enchiridion Ethicum* may be the single most important work on the subject. A first helpful, yet overly critical, survey of More's principal ethical concepts of the 'boniform faculty' and 'right reason' is provided by G. N. Dolson, 'The Ethical System of Henry More', *The Philosophical Review* 6 (1897): 593–607, who wrongly judges More's attempt at the said 'system' to be contradictory.
34 More, *Divine Dialogues*, 2nd edn (London: Printed and sold by Joseph Downing, 1713), 170.
35 Id., *Enchiridion Ethicum* II 9,16 (*Opera Omnia* II/1, 61; *Account of Virtue*, 157).
36 Cudworth, *True Intellectual System*, 375.
37 More, *Enchiridion Ethicum* II 9,16 (*Opera Omnia* II/1, 61; *Account of Virtue*, 157–8).
38 More, *Cupid's Conflict*, in *The Complete Poems of Dr Henry More*, collected and edited by Alexander B. Grosart(Printed for private circulation, 1878), 171.
39 Cudworth, *True Intellectual System*, 315.
40 Id., *Sermon before the House of Commons*, 126–7.
41 More, *Enchiridion Ethicum*, I 5,1 (*Opera omnia* II/1, 24; *Account of Virtue*, 28).
42 More, *Second Lash of Alazonomastix* (Cambridge: Printers to the University of Cambridge, 1651), 43.
43 Id., *Praefatio Generalissima* VII (*Opera Omnia* II/1, V–VI) = Richard Ward, *The Life of Henry More*. Parts I and II, edited by Sarah Hutton et al. (Dordrecht, Boston and London: Springer, 2000), 15.
44 See More's two short poems tracing his conversion in his *Complete Poems*, 182.
45 More, *Second Lash*, 43. Daniel Fouke, *The Enthusiastical Concerns of Dr. Henry More. Religious Meaning and the Psychology of Delusion*, Leiden/New York/Cologne: Brill 1997, 124–5, overlooks the emphatically ethical character of More's early vision of the Divine which, despite all verbal resemblances, clearly sets Cambridge Platonist mysticism apart from Vaughan's alchemistic variety of Hermeticism and Platonism: 'More inadvertently displayed the value of ecstasy and extroversive mysticism (or nature-mysticism) as elements of his own spirituality. More's language was suggestive of the very pantheistic tendencies he found in Vaughan.'
46 Id., *The Preface Generall*, in: *A Collection of Several Philosophical Writings*, 4th edition, London: Printed by Joseph Downing, 1712, viii.
47 Id., *Enthusiasmus Triumphatus* (*Collection of Several Philosophical Writings*, 39).
48 See, for example, id., *Enchiridion Ethicum* I 3,11 (*Opera Omnia* II/1, 16–17; *Account of Virtue*, 19) I 3,11: 'Wherefore, if men will abide by the Judgment of *Aristotle* or *Pythagoras*, or others of the most celebrated, they must own that the Measure of *Right Reason* is to imitate the Divine Wisdom, and the Divine Goodness, with all our Might.'
49 Ibid., II 9,16 (*Op. Omn.* II/1, 61; *Account*, 157).

50 Ibid., II 9,15 (*Op. Omn.* II/1, 61; *Account*, 156–157).
51 Ibid. (*Op. omn.* II/1, *Account*, 158). More could in fact have replaced the 'either or' with a 'both and' as the form of the good is both the divine principle beyond and the highest cognitive power in man.
52 More, *Discourses on Several Texts*, 479.
53 Ibid., 483.
54 More provides the most detailed treatment of his trichotomy of lives and virtues in his principal theological work *The Grand Mystery of Godliness* (*The Theological Works of Henry More* (London: Printed and sold by Joseph Downing, 1708), 28–30).
55 More, *Discourses on Several Texts*, 484–5.
56 More, *Grand Mystery of Godliness*, 37.
57 More, *Divine Dialogues*, 131.
58 Cudworth, *Sermon before the House of Commons*, 99.
59 Ibid., 125, where the preacher uses a plethora of synonymous terms to extol the soul's permanent participation in divine love as the archetypal principle of freedom.
60 In his major exposition of his concept of freedom in *A Treatise Concerning Eternal and Immutable Morality With A Treatise of Freewill*, edited by Sarah Hutton (Cambridge: Cambridge University Press, 1996), 196–7, Cudworth expressly excludes contingent choice from the 'true liberty of a man': 'I have now but one thing more to add, and that is to take notice of a common mistake which learned men have been guilty of, confounding this faculty of freewill with liberty as it is a state of pure perfection, for what is more common than in writings both ancient and modern, to find men creaking and boasting of the ἐξουσία τῶν ἀντικειμένων, the liberty of contrariety, *i.e.* to be in an indifferent equilibrious state to do good or evil, which is too like the language of the first tempter, "Thou shalt be a God knowing good and evil" (Gen. 3:5). Whereas the true liberty of a man, as it speaks pure perfection is when by the right use of the faculty of freewill, together with the assistances of Divine grace, he is habitually fixed in moral good, or such a state of mind, as that he doth freely, readily, and easily comply with the law of the Divine life, taking a pleasure in complacence thereunto; and having an aversation to the contrary; or when the law of the spirit of life hath made him free from the law of sin, which is the death of the soul.'
61 While in agreement with More in general intention and argument, Cudworth provides the most philosophically satisfactory doctrine of divine and human double agency.
62 Cudworth, *A Sermon Preached to the Honourable Society of Lincoln's Inn*, in *The True Intellectual System of the Universe*, A new Edition by Thomas Birch (London: Printed by J.F. Dove, 1820), IV, 377.
63 Cudworth, *Treatise of Freewill*, 173.
64 Ibid., 174. The passage in *A Treatise of Freewill* is remarkable for the density of metaphorical expressions ranging from technical Aristotelian language and the vocabulary of spiritual sensation to words and images borrowed from Hellenistic ethics and early modern alchemy: 'But above all these, and such like things, the soul of man hath in it μάντευμά τι, a certain vaticination, presage, scent, and odour of one *summum bonum*, one supreme highest good transcending all others, without which, they will be all ineffectual as to complete happiness and signify nothing, a certain philosopher's stone that can turn all into gold.'
65 Ibid.
66 On Cudworth's doctrine of the ἡγεμονικόν, which amounts to a major early modern theory of human self-consciousness and agency, see Jean-Louis Breteau,

'Un grand espace pour la liberté? Le dilemme du libre arbitre dans la pensée de Ralph Cudworth', *Archives de Philosophie* 58 (1995): 421–41, and 'Origène était-il pour Cudworth le modèle du philosophe chrétien?', in *'Mind Senior to the World': Stoicismo e origenismo nella filosofia platonica del Seicento inglese*, edited by Marialuisa Baldi (Milan: FrancoAngeli, 1996), 127–47, esp. 140–4. See also the most recent depiction by Oscar M. Esquisabel and María Griselda Gaiada, 'Le libre arbitre et "le paradoxe des facultés". Suárez, Hobbes et Leibniz selon le jugement de Cudworth', *Studia Leibnitiana* 47 (2015): 162–85, and Christian Hengstermann, 'Platonismus und Panentheismus bei Ralph Cudworth', in *Persönlich und alles zugleich. Theorien der All-Einheit und christliche Gottrede*, edited by Frank Meier-Hammidi and Klaus Müller (Regensburg: Friedrich Pustet, 2010), 192–211. Hedley provides a historical and systematic reading of Cudworth's momentous Origenist concept of the practical unity of the self in: 'Cudworth on Freedom: Theology, Ethical Obligation and the Limits of Mechanism', in Fürst and Christian (ed.), *Cambridge Origenists* (see n. 3), 47–58, and *Sacrifice Imagined* (see n. 24), 113–19, respectively. See, above all, the précis of Cudworth's Christian Platonist view of hegemonic moral action in the second volume on the religious imagination (113–14), in which the author, using Morean terminology, highlights its connection with the Cambridge Platonist mysticism of the boniform vision of the kenotic Deity: 'Insofar as the finite will is conformed to, contemplates and participates in, its transcendent source, boniform, as it were, right action follows. The goal is not the coordination of will and intellect as "that which is properly we ourselves." Cudworth uses the term "hegemonikon" (τὸ ἡγεμονικόν) to mark his distinctly Christian philosophy. The ruling self is not oblivious to the suffering, misery, and misfortune of the humble and the unlettered like the great Stoic or Platonic sages. Following Origen, Cudworth thinks that love fulfils the Platonic ideal of Goodness.'

67 Cudworth, *Treatise of Freewill*, 178.
68 Ibid., 179. Cudworth does not eschew deliberate paradox in his description of unified hegemonic agency which must possess both intellectual and volitional traits: 'And thus may it well be conceived that one and the same reasonable soul in us may both will understandingly, or knowingly of what it wills; and understand or think of this or that object willingly.'
69 Cudworth, *Sermon before the House of Commons*, 126–7.
70 Cudworth, *Sermon Preached to Lincoln's Inn*, 37.
71 This is the title of the seminal chapter on Neoplatonist anthropology in Werner Beierwaltes, *Denken des Einen. Studien zur neuplatonischen Philosophie und ihrer Wirkungsgeschichte* (Frankfurt: Vittorio Klostermann, 1985), 73–113.
72 Cudworth, British Library, Ms. Add. 4982, 50.
73 'True Life' is the titular concept of the important monograph by Werner Beierwaltes, *Das wahre Selbst. Studien zu Plotins Begriff des Geistes und des Einen* (Frankfurt: Vittorio Klostermann, 2001).
74 British Library Ms Add. 4979, 39.
75 British Library Ms. Add. 4982, 40.
76 British Library Ms. Add. 4980, 83.
77 Ibid., 10.
78 George Rust, 'God Is Love', in *The Remains of that Reverend and Learned Prelate, Dr. George Rust, Late Lord Bishop of Dromore, in the Kingdom of Ireland*, collected and published by Henry Hallywell (London: printed by M. Flesher, 1686), 7.
79 Ibid., 5.

80 More, *Complete Poems*, 36.
81 Ibid., 146.
82 Rust, 'God Is Love', 5.
83 Smith, *Select Discourses*, 159. Cf. the analysis of the Cambridge Platonists' notion of sacrifice in terms of the Neoplatonist dialectic of archetype and image in Hedley, *Sacrifice Imagined* (see n. 24), 16: 'If we are to think of sacrifice as the reigniting of the spark of the soul, then we need to consider this idea of a soul center kindled at the Divine altar, and its return to its source – transformed into the "likeness" of God.'
84 Cf. the in-depth analysis of Cudworth's neglected early work in Hedley, *Sacrifice Imagined* (see n. 24), 203–11.
85 Cudworth, *The True Notion of the Lord's Supper* (*True Intellectual System*, IV, 231).
86 Ibid., 268.
87 Ibid., 271.
88 Ibid.
89 Ibid., 283.
90 See Hedley's speculative Christological interpretation of Cudworth's early treatise in *Sacrifice Imagined* (see n. 24), 207, which revolves around the latter's 'concern to show the legitimacy of the link with the Passover Festival in *Christus Consummator*': 'The Christian sacrifice can symbolize the sacrificial energy that finds expression in much human culture. Anthropology and revelation touch. Christ is a way of seeing the invisible world. He is the great High Priest who opens the veil of the Temple and reveals the Divine essence. As the blood-stained Logos, he opens the Heavens.'
91 More, *Several Texts of Holy Scripture*, 315.
92 Ibid., 316.
93 Ibid., 320.
94 More, *Grand Mystery of Godliness*, 28.
95 Norris, *Theory and Regulation of Love*, 187. Cf. also More, *Divine Dialogues*, 164, where the author puts forth this notion against the backdrop of his soul-making theodicy of adversities as the sine qua non of the providential flourishing of human virtue and humility.
96 More, *Several Texts of Holy Scripture*, 323.
97 Ibid., 342.
98 Ibid., 340–1.
99 Ibid., 340.
100 Ibid., 344.
101 Ibid., 355.
102 Ibid., 351.
103 *Two Choice and Useful Treatises: The One Lux Orientalis; The Other, A Discourse of Truth, By the Late Reverend Dr. Rust Lord Bishop of Dromore in Ireland. With Annotations on them Both* (London: Printed for James Collins, 1682), 179.
104 Rust, 'God Is Love', 14.
105 Cudworth, *Eternal and Immutable Reality* (see n. 60), 141.
106 Cudworth, *Lord's Supper*, 217.
107 Cudworth, *Eternal and Immutable Reality*, 138.
108 Ibid., 51.
109 Ibid., 53.
110 Ibid., 54.
111 See More's succinct juxtaposition of empiricism and rationalism in *An Antidote Against Atheism* (London: printed by Roger Daniel, 1653), 13, which is virtually

identical with Cudworth, *Eternal and Immutable Morality*, 84. On the Cambridge Platonists' innatism, see Robert L. Armstrong, 'Cambridge Platonists and Locke on Innate Ideas', *Journal of the History of Ideas* 30 (1969): 187–202.
112 More, *Antidote*, 13.
113 Although Henry More does subscribe to the dogma of pre-existence, he never makes use of it in the context of his rationalist epistemology. Instead, his is a thoroughly Origenist, rather than Platonist doctrine of the pre-existence of souls, which he posits not on the grounds of *a priori* knowledge, but rational theodicy alone.
114 Cudworth, *Eternal and Immutable Morality*, 74.
115 More, *Antidote*, 13.
116 Contrary to the overly lavish praise bestowed upon the Cambridge Platonists by Arthur O. Lovejoy, 'Kant and the English Platonists', in *Essays Philosophical and Psychological: In Honor of William James by His Colleagues at Columbia University* (New York: Longmans, Green and Co., 1908), 265–302, who credits Cudworth with virtually anticipating all of subsequent German critical thought, the lists of categories provided in the author's *Eternal and Immutable Morality*, 80, 84, lack the systematic coherence of the later Kantian doctrine. However, a distinction between the most fundamental categories of thought as thought and an object as object appears to be at work in the first survey of categories cited earlier.
117 Cudworth, *Eternal and Immutable Reality*, 93. Cf. ibid., 90, where Cudworth attributes to man's intellect 'a logical unitive, comprehensive power and activity as can frame out of them [i.e. relative ideas] one idea of the whole.'
118 Ibid., 92.
119 Ibid., 121.
120 More, *Grand Mystery of Godliness*, 51.
121 More, *Conjectura Cabbalistica or A Conjectural Essay of Interpreting the Mind of Moses in a Threefold Cabbala* (London: Printed by James Flesher, 1653), The Preface to the Reader.
122 Cudworth, *Eternal and Immutable Morality*, 77.
123 Ibid.
124 Ibid., 96.
125 Ibid., 93.
126 Hedley, *Iconic Imagination* (see n. 24), 151.

5

Aids to reflection and imagining God
Samuel Taylor Coleridge's concept of the imagination

Friedrich A. Uehlein

1 Introduction

How can we begin and make sure that 'imagination' does not lose half its meaning and the reality meant? Coleridge's aid to reflection is to fall back on principles. 'Whatever may have been the specific theme of my communications, and whether they related to criticism, politics, or religion, still PRINCIPLES, their subordination, their connection, and their application, in all divisions of our tastes, duties, rules of conduct and schemes of belief, have constituted my chapter of contents' (LS 125–6).[1] According to his aid, the attempt to tackle the investigation of the imagination, what it is and what it does, directly would not lead far. Its foundation in the principle *I am* and the eduction from it has to be undertaken.[2]

The final question touched on in this chapter, which is whether the imagination is able to evoke and transform things of the experiential life, so that they become translucent symbols of an encompassing reality, presupposes this foundation and eduction.

2 Foundation

2.1 The principle *I am*

The thought *I am* manifests 'that which affirms its own existence and whether mediately or immediately that of other beings' (Lects Phil 371). 'In the SUM or I AM', Coleridge writes in the twelfth chapter of the *Biographia Literaria*,

> and in this alone, object and subject, being and knowing, are identical, each involving and supposing the other. In other words, it is a subject which becomes a subject by the act of constructing itself objectively to itself; but which never is an object except for itself, and only so far as by the very same act it becomes a subject. (BL I 272–3)

The I, the subject-object, does not exist apart from this original act. The truth of this act of self-consciousness is original, immediate and independent.[3]

But when *the I* grasps and knows itself as the self-constructing subject-object, does it not remain undetermined and inane? The object determined is the determining subject, the determining subject, however, is to determine itself, since 'by constructing itself objectively to itself [. . .] it becomes a subject'. And yet, this unity (unification and even identity) of subject and object, thought and being, is the principle of knowledge 'of itself and of other beings'. In case there should be other beings, they must be for *the I am*. They cannot be given to *the I* somehow, from somewhere: an unnameable, unknowable no-thing. To become something – objects – the principle of knowledge must produce them for itself. Furthermore, how could there be an outside somewhere, an 'Outness', unless *the I* had not produced for itself such a sphere beyond itself? The principle of knowledge is consummate knowledge.[4] The subject-object cannot rest in the self-evidence of its original act, in which it is and is for itself. In the original act it is and has itself in an open, incomplete and still indefinite form: in the dynamical process of Self-seeking and Self-finding.[5]

I repeat the last step of the argument by means of another quotation from Coleridge's *Notebooks*:

> The I = Self = Spirit is definable as a Subject whose only possible Predicate is itself – Ergo, a Subject which is its own Object, i.e., a Subject-Object. But Object quoad Object is necessarily [. . .] self-capable of no Action but only the Object of the action. The Spirit therefore cannot *be* an Object, [. . .] it is *a being* it – (nicht seyn, sondern werden). It becomes an Object thro' its own act – But whatever is ipso termino and in its essence finite, is essentially an object.[6]

The object under consideration so far, however, has neither been incapable of action nor been essentially finite. The object determined has been the determining subject, the finite has been the defining. For this very reason, the act *I am* does not lead to any definite contents of self-knowledge. And still, it does not lack determination; its determination is to produce and to encompass all finite determinations. To know itself, it must limit itself in finite objectifications and cannot terminate in any:

> Is it then infinite? [. . .] it can neither be infinite without being at the same time finite, nor can it be finite (for itself) without being at the same time infinite. – It is therefore neither the one nor the other, alone, but [. . .] the primary Union of Finity and Infinity – and this is the third characteristic, or form of development. (CN III 4186)

It 'cannot *be* an Object, it is *a being* it' in its self-development[7] through the history of its Self-seeking and Self-finding.

2.2 The self-development of the principle

Coleridge pursues this history in a subtle dialectical chain of arguments. (On the whole he follows Schelling.[8]) I follow him, though not in full details. My aim is to find the position of the imagination within the course of the development of *the I*.

The *I am* is 'the most original union' and 'originally the identity of both', subject and object (BL I 280; CN III 4186). It neither exists before this union – it originates in it – nor does it result from it and is left behind, a dead end. What remains after constructing itself objectively to itself still is the most original union and identity giving origin to further objectifications. 'Most original union' and 'original identity' express the actuality (taken literally) of the *I am*. Subject and object neither part nor neutralize each other. Their opposition does not drive them apart; neither can it be settled nor can it vanish: 'In the existence, in the reconciling, and the recurrence of this contradiction consists the process and mystery of production and life' (BL I 280–1).

'Identity' in Coleridge's philosophy neither means a fact nor depends on a solid thing or a core of stillness; it consists in the process, production and life of the principle.

In the entry of his notebook just quoted, Coleridge interrupts the string of arguments and anticipates a later stage of the development. He speaks about the individual person and her essence: 'In this absolute Co-presence of the Infinite and the Finite lies the essence of an Individual Nature, of the Self (der Ichheit)' (CN III 4186 f33^v). When we think and begin to reflect, we are already single cases of the *Ichheit*. But we do not know it yet. We are essentially *I am* and encompass the stages of development which we have passed through so far unconsciously. The self 'then is no other than this activity and this limitation, both conceived as co-instantaneous' (ibid., f34^v). How can it reconcile its boundless (subjective) activity with the bounds of (a determinate) objectification? It limits itself:

> It is Power self-bounded by retroition on itself, and *is* only for itself –. –But in Self-limitation is implied the co-existence of Activity & Passivity – The Spirit is at once active & passive, and as this is a condition sine quâ non of our Consciousness, this union, this absolute Oneness of the Active & the Passive must be another characteristic of an individual Nature – i.e. a new development of the original Self-predication [*I am*]. (ibid)

'Passivity' does not suggest that *the I* is affected by something unknowable, from the outside. It can only be conceived in the co-existence – or strictly speaking – the 'absolute Oneness' with activity: 'Passivity = negative Action' (ibid). In the union of activity and passive activeness, the spirit limits itself, constructs itself objectively to itself, but does not lose itself in the bounds of objectivity. The 'Power self-bounded' transcends them by re-introition on itself: it beholds itself within its limitations.

The co-existence and wavering between being active and being passive, and the union and absolute oneness of both within the self-bounded power, is termed by Coleridge 'imagination'. Coleridge reads the German equivalent – 'Einbildungskraft' – as 'In-eins-Bildung' and consequently understands the imagination to denote the power of 'shaping into one'. The *I am* at this stage of self-development, unifying (*ineinsbildend*) activity and passivity, and beholding itself (*sich selbst anschauend*) is 'Imagination', 'Einbildungskraft', 'In-eins-Bildung', 'Eisenoplasy'.[9] Imagination, Coleridge adds, is not only actualized in this 'development of the original Self-predication' but in different potencies: 'In philosophical language we must denominate this intermediate faculty in all it degrees and determinations, the IMAGINATION. But in common language, and especially on the subject of poetry, we appropriate the name to a superior degree of this faculty, joined to a superior voluntary control over it' (BL I 124–5). To sum up:

a. Imagination is the 'eisenoplasy' (εἰς+ἕν+πλάσσω), *In-eins-Bildung*, unity and oneness of activity and passivity.
b. It is a certain stage in the self-development of the principle.
c. It is a characteristic of an individual nature.
d. It is realized in different degrees and determinations or potencies. Coleridge resumes this distinction in his famous definition of 'the primary Imagination', that is, the original potency as touched on in a.–c., and 'the secondary Imagination'(BL I 304).

2.3 The systematic position of the imagination

The position of the imagination is determined by its origin in the principle and by the development that arises from it.

In the union of activity and passivity, the spirit limits itself and beholds itself within its limitation. The object or presence beheld is the intuiting spirit. The present beholding and the presence beheld coincide. They are one and indistinct since it is still the original self-production of the *I am* that has developed into this intuition or simple, direct beholding. Therefore the spirit does not rest (and lose itself) in this intuition and the presence beheld. Even in this *immediate vision* it is still the intuiting subject: the *I am*. It transcends the limitation of the direct intuition and the presence beheld by going back to what it has been and is through all moments of its process. Coleridge calls this 'retroition on itself'.[10] The spirit reflects the direct intuition and its presence beheld, so that it becomes *visio visa*: 'Anschauung des Angeschauten [i.e. primary intuition, *visio*] und Anschauung der Anschauung des Angeschauten [i.e. *visio visa*]'.[11] The reflection does not leave the intuition alone, as it were; it does not let it be what it is. By re-introition on itself the *I am* proves to be the very beginning and pervading force of the process – 'the Spirit snatches it self loose from its own self-immersion, and self-actualizing distinguishes itself from its Self-realization' (CN III 4186 f 35 v). The moments of the direct, simple intuition differentiate into the intuited (the limited self), the intuition (the act of limitation and beholding) and the intuiting and reflecting self. *The I* distinguishes itself and feels its own self-realization, feels its own state of being. In order to explain the specific meaning of 'feeling', Coleridge refers repeatedly to its German equivalent: 'the German word for (. . .) feeling is Empfindung, i.e. an *inward finding*' (C&S 180). 'A sensation, a Feeling is what I *find in* me *as* in me – Emp = intra euphonicè for Ent; – finde'[12] (CN III 4443). 'A Sensation = a Feeling referring to some *Thing*, and yet not organized into a definite *Object* nor separated from the sentient Being' (CN II 3605).

No more immersed in its immediate *visio,* but reflecting it by retroition on itself, the *I* finds in itself some 'Thing', neither separated nor organized into a definite object. What is found is not a feeling, but something felt. The *I* grasps its own state of being. In this new objectification, it has developed a new self-consciousness. Feeling itself, it becomes a sentient, percipient consciousness which finds and discerns for itself something different from itself. What is perceived is not a perception, but something perceived: 'In every act of conscious perception, we at once identify our being with that of the world without us, and yet place ourselves in contra-distinction to that world' (Friend I 497). In the union of activity and passivity, that is, the 'primary IMAGINATION', originates the course of objectifications and stages of self-consciousness that will lead eventually to the temporal, individual, embodied person in the common interpersonal world.[13]

3 Finite and infinite *I am*

3.1 *Principium Cognoscendi et Essendi*

'I AM (...) In this and in this alone, object and subject, being and knowing, are identical' (BL I 272-3). The question whether the subject-object *is* does not make sense. The *I am* is in its own act and knows itself to be. The act affirms its existence (BL I 251). Coleridge compares this ἐνέργεια αὐτόνομος (CN III 4265 III) of self-production with the contemplation (θεωρία) of Nature (φύσις), discussed by Plotinus in the third Ennead (III 8,4). The lines which bound the bodies come to be through her contemplation. 'Plotinus (...) speaking of the geometricians and then of Nature as acting geometrically (...) says θεωρουσα θεωρηματα ποιει, her contemplative act is creative and is one with the product of her contemplation' (Logic 74). The analogy seems obvious but needs further discrimination. Nature beholds the boundaries not as already existing. In her act of beholding ὑφίστανται αἱ τῶν σωμάτων γραμμαί, Coleridge translates ὑφίστανται with 'rise up into existence': the act of contemplation makes the things contemplated; in her contemplation the forms of things rise up into existence.[14]

Is the original act of the subject-object such a creative beholding? Does the *I* in its 'realizing intuition' in which it affirms its existence bring itself forth into existence? Nature – dramatized into a person – says that she does not stem from her own realizing intuition. She rises into existence out of the θεωρία of 'greater rational principles, and as they contemplate themselves I come to be' (Enn III 8,4,12). In order to know herself, she has to turn inward upon herself and to return to the higher principles in which she has her ground and from which she came to be. At this point of his theses on transcendental philosophy (BL I 274 scholium; cf. also CN III 4265,I-V; Logic 84-5), Coleridge distinguishes the *I am* and the individual person who, actualizing the absolute act, knows herself to be. In this spontaneous, free act she becomes what she essentially is, a self-conscious being, but does not rise into existence. The principle of knowledge – *principium cognoscendi* – and the principle of being – *principium essendi* – are set into relief:

> If a man be asked how he *knows* that he is? he can only answer, sum quia sum. But if (the absoluteness of his certainty having been admitted) he again be asked, how he, the individual person, came to be, then, in relation to the ground of his *existence*, but not to the ground of his *knowledge* of that existence, he might reply, [...] sum quia in Deo sum. (BL I 274)

The man asked – the individual person, ourselves doing philosophy here and now – is and is self-known. He is (a case of the) *I am*, a transcendental subject, and therefore *principium cognoscendi*, but, nevertheless, does not come to be from his own free act, but from 'another': 'I know that I am because I am and am self-conscious; but that I am and know myself to be, there is but one assignable reason – the Being and Will which we express by the word 'God'' (Logic 84–5).

3.2 The absolute I AM

And yet, the one in which he exists and is a transcendental subject cannot be different from him. It cannot be an object, since objects depend on his objectifying acts. Neither can it be another self equally indigent of being. The ground in which he is and from which he came to be is no other thing or self but the *non aliud*: the absolute self:

> But if we elevate our conception to the absolute self, the great eternal I AM, then the principle of being, and of knowledge, of idea and reality; the ground of existence, and the ground of the knowledge of existence, are absolutely identical, Sum quia sum; I am, because I affirm myself to be; I affirm myself to be because I am.[15]

The individual person elevates her thought to the eternal I AM. The moment of being that cannot be posited by the transcendental subject – I exist and am a self-developing subject-object – manifests the absolute self: 'We begin with the I KNOW MYSELF, in order to end with the absolute I AM. We proceed from the SELF, in order to lose and find all self in GOD.'[16]

The individual person has become conscious and Self-conscious within the process of Self-seeking and self-finding, that is, through the subconscious history and her experiencing, thinking and practical life. She knows herself and still loses herself since she does not exist through the original act *I am*. By a deliberate act of reflection, she snatches herself loose from her still ungrounded existence and elevates herself to the eternal self-finding of the absolute self (CN III 4351). Nothing remains to be objectified and mediated in further steps of self-seeking. And yet, there is no final act and fixed state. The self-finding does not terminate, but wells up in itself in a *processio intercircularis* (CN IV 400). It is the eternal act of the inner-Trinitarian life of the absolute: 'I am, because I affirm myself to be; I affirm myself to be because I am' (BL I 275). The absolute self is grounded in itself and for itself: *causa sui*.[17] *Causa sui* therefore means the 'Antecedent of Being [. . .] the absolute Will, the ground of Being – the Self-affirming Actus purissimus' (CM II 287) and the life of the absolute self. Both aspects express one and the same thing. (What grounds itself cannot be a result, it lives in itself; what lives by and in itself cannot have a cause apart from itself.) Coleridge endeavours to grasp *causa sui* as the intrinsic self-disclosure of 'the One and the Absolute' (LS 32). He conflates the Neoplatonic Ἕν and Νοῦς, the One and the Spirit. Ἕν and Νοῦς, the ὑπερούσιον, that is, the One beyond being, and the Spirit, that is, the principle of reflexive rationality and fullness of being (pleroma), the One beyond any relation and the consummate relationship of all into one, are thought together.[18]

The absolute self is 'the only *One*, the purely and absolutely ONE' (CN I 1680). Before all alterity and anterior to the unity and opposition of subject and object, it has disclosed itself into its inner-trinitarian life. It contains in itself the ground of its own nature, and therein of *all* natures (LS 32), and *can* be the ground of other beings.

3.3 Creation

Pantheism and Spinoza's concept of God have been attacked by Coleridge almost throughout his whole career.[19] How does the *processio intercircularis* of the Trinity include and bring forth the creation of the contingent world? Coleridge's critique pivots on the freedom of 'the abysmal Ground of the Trinity'. It is free, that is, not limited by conditions and alternatives, and is beyond the bounds of decision. He therefore conceives it as the absolute Will: I shall be in that I will to be (CM II 287). The *causa sui* is beyond any relation and therefore not the necessary cause of the world. Causality would relate it to the contingent world and make it dependent on it. It is cause in and for itself and not through the causal interrelation with the world. That the abysmal ground permits contingent beings (including the finite *I am*) to exist and to become what they are in the process of the universe is not necessary to it. But neither can it be a random act, since there is nothing erratic and accidental in the absolute. Creation is the free resolution 'of a self-comprehending Creator. These two words, "self-comprehending", and "Creator" involve the (...) Trinity, and the essential distinction between the (...) eternal *generation* of the Logos [νοῦς, pleroma] and the *creation* of the universe of finite Beings' (CN III 3878).

3.4 Corollary

With his turn to the individual person, Coleridge parts company with pure transcendental philosophy that does not search for an absolute principle of being, but an absolute principle of knowledge. He cannot accept its claim to absoluteness because the finite self, still considered to be the principle of knowledge, is grounded in the absolute self. Transcendental subjectivity as the principle of philosophy is limited and transformed into the philosophy of the finite mind,[20] and at the same time universalized: the principle of knowledge and the principle of being are identical in the One and the Absolute: 'We begin with the I KNOW MYSELF, in order to end with the absolute I AM' (BL I 283). Transcendental philosophy loses its claim to absoluteness, is enclosed, as it were, and sublated in 'a total and undivided philosophy' (ibid. 282). A similar metamorphosis can be observed in Schelling. In his Philosophy of Identity – with the end of the *System* (1800) and onwards – transcendental philosophy proper becomes obsolete. When it reappears later on, for example, in the *Freiheitsschrift*, it has lost its original status. Like Schelling, though not to the same extent and in a different style, Coleridge endeavours to grasp all and everything as an ordered and graduated universe, grounded in the One and Absolute. The elaboration of this total and undivided philosophy raises and provides answers to central questions of metaphysics and the Platonic tradition in particular.

4 Imagination

4.1 Primary imagination

'The primary IMAGINATION I hold to be the living Power and prime Agent of all human Perception, and as a repetition in the finite mind of the eternal act of creation in the infinite I AM' (BL I 202). 'Perception' means the feeling and finding, the act of receiving and taking possession of, the awareness, apprehension and sensation and even comprehension, understanding and notion of something. When Coleridge speaks of 'all human Perception', he implies the whole spectrum. But why can the imagination be called the 'living power and prime Agent of all Perception'? He has conceived of imagination proper as the unification of passivity and activity in the incipient self-development of the *I am*. In the 'eisenplastic' power originate the course of objectifications and the stages of our subconscious, conscious and practical life. All human perceptions arise from it and are activated by it. Thus, the first part of the definition of the imagination goes back to the transcendental structure of the *I*. The second resumes the manifestation of the absolute in the finite person. We need not read and neglect this completion as an excessive assertion. It does not come unheralded. On the contrary, Coleridge has good reasons to speak of the imagination 'as a repetition in the finite mind of the eternal act of creation in the infinite I AM'.

Creation does not originate in the imagination. The One beyond being actualizes the processual universe in a free act out of the fullness of being. Each existent is determined by the ideas, that is, the differentiated and unified 'distinctities' of being.[21] By participation in them it is something, does appear, and can be felt and found, perceived and understood. Through them it is intelligible. The finite mind repeats the eternal act of creation. In the process of Self-seeking and Self-finding, it objectifies a world for itself. The creation and the construction of the objective world show traits of an analogy. The temporal process of self-development is conceived of as an image of the eternal self-finding; the free act in which the universe comes to be is seen as the paradigm of the objective construction. Imagination and its product are 'a dim Analogue of Creation, not all that we can *believe*, but all that we can conceive of creation' (CL II 1034). Being a finite *I am* in the eternal I AM, he repeats the eternal act in the primary imagination and what originates in it, that is, the temporal acts of self-development, in which the common world becomes objective. Without this repetition there could be nothing for us, nothing felt and found, sensed and perceived. The primary imagination repeats the creation insofar as we construct the world objectively to us.

Insofar as we become subjects in the very same process, the analogy breaks. The dissimilarity of the image breaks through. The process of objectification is the counterpart of self-development. None does exist without the other. Between the absolute and the universe, however, there consists no correlation, let alone a development of the absolute I AM. The world rises into existence by the free act of its will. The term 'repetition' captures the similarity and the categorial difference between the infinite and the finite self, the paradigm and the dim analogue.

4.2 Secondary imagination

Not only in the original *In-eins-Bildung* of activity and passivity, but in all its degrees and determinations (BL I 124) the imagination remains a repetition of the eternal act:

> The secondary Imagination I consider as an echo of the former, co-existing with the conscious will, yet still as identical with the primary in the *kind* of its agency, and differing only in *degree*, and in the *mode* of its Operation. It dissolves, diffuses, dissipates, in order to re-create; or where this process is rendered impossible, yet still at all events it struggles to idealize and to unify. (BL I 202)

The secondary imagination differs in two characteristics. It is not the prime agent and it co-exists with the conscious will. It is not the life and agent of all human perception, but presupposes it. It receives its materials from it. But it still echoes the primary imagination insofar as it recreates what it receives. The materials received obviously consist of the perceptions of the subconscious and conscious life of man. The second difference appears to be even more important. How can the conscious will be brought together and mediated with the imagination? The *I am* is and knows itself unconditionally, in a free act. It is not apart from it. It is no thing, nor does it depend on anything. It is in this act that it constructs itself objectively to itself and 'becomes' the self-grounded subject-object:

> the spirit (originally the identity of object and subject) must in some sense dissolve this identity, in order to become conscious of it: fit alter et idem. But this implies an act, and it follows therefore that intelligence or self-consciousness is impossible except by and in a will. The self-conscious spirit therefore is a will; and freedom must be assured as a ground of philosophy and can never be deduced from it. (BL I 279–80)

Transcendental philosophy conceives of the *I am* as the aboriginal will of self-production. This still unconscious will pervades the primary imagination. The objectification of the world, however, remains incomplete as long as it is not realized in the *practical interpersonal* life. In its process the self eventually develops into a conscious and self-conscious individual person within the objectified common world shared with other persons. The aboriginal will becomes conscious, conscious will, moral will and conscience in their practical lives.[22] The materials received from the primary imagination and the later stages originating in it comprise the results of our perceptive and practical life, namely, what we construct subconsciously in passive activity and active passiveness, what we feel, sense and desire, what happens to us, what we experience and live through, what we suffer and do, wish and intend, bring to pass and miss. Commending Cervantes, Coleridge sums up in a deceptively simple statement what the secondary imagination receives and what it does to it: 'his imagination was ever at hand to adapt and modify the world of his experience' (Literary Remains I 131).

How can it be creative? Is it not fettered by the particular items of experience? There exists indeed such a power of spontaneous receptivity which 'has no other counters to play with, but fixities and definites' (BL I 305). Coleridge calls it 'fancy'. Fancy retains the perceptions when the acts of perception and volition and their correspondent objects pass out of their present beholding and presence beheld. Detached from their immediate presence, they are re-presented and reproduced according to the law of association. 'The Fancy is indeed no other than a mode of Memory emancipated from the order of time and space' (ibid.).[23] Without retention, representation and reproduction 'there would be no fixation, consequently, no distinct perception and conception' (CN III 4066). The continuous mental life would disintegrate into an atomic multiplicity. Strictly speaking, it would not even have come to pass at all. The mind could not come back to what it has perceived and conceived. Experience, sustained thought, language and any kind of anticipation would be rendered impossible. In the present context, Coleridge is less interested in the epistemological function of the fancy than in the service it does to the secondary imagination, notwithstanding their difference.[24] The secondary imagination receives its materials mediated through the fixation of fancy. Like the primary one it is *vital*, whereas the products of fancy, the 'objects *(as* objects) are essentially fixed and dead'. They can be remembered and fancy seems to be 'a mode of Memory emancipated from the order of time and space'. Imagination does not remember and associate the fixed items of the empirical life; it recollects them: 'It dissolves, diffuses, dissipates, in order to re-create' (BL I 202). The particulars are released from their fixation. They become disponible. They pass away in the process of recreation and unification into new wholes. When the imagination fails to succeed in this process, when it cannot help keeping close to single occurrences and items of the empirical life, even then – and it could not be expressed more emphatically – it struggles to idealize and unify, at all events. It recreates with regard to an idea, idealizes with a view towards a specific form of being that unifies the many into one. In the last resort it looks to the ideas or 'distinctities' in the fulness of being.

4.3 The symbol

'I adopt with full faith the principle of Aristotle that poetry is essentially *ideal*, that it avoids and excludes accident' (BL II 45–6). The world of experience as presented by fancy and memory is full of accidents and fringes out in loose ends. The poetic imagination recollects what it receives and unifies it into a meaningful whole: the unifying idea shines through the sensible appearance. The poem and the world it creates come to be in the process of re-creation and idealization. The imagination directs the conscious will during the labour of writing and – when it succeeds – embodies the idea 'in Images of the Sense, and (. . .) gives birth to a system of Symbols'. The famous passage reads in full: the imagination 'that reconciling and mediatory power, which incorporating the Reason [i.e. the power of viewing ideas] in Images of Sense, and organizing (as it were) the flux of the Senses by the permanence and self-circling energies of Reason, gives birth to a system of Symbols, harmonious in themselves and consubstantial with the truths, of which they are the conductors'.[25]

However, is the poem and what it creates not undervalued when it is reduced to a system of symbols? Does it mean something different from itself? Is it degraded to a set of arbitrary signs which are noticed, superficially, and can justly be forgotten, when they have done their job? The term 'symbol' does not imply such an anti-climax. On the contrary, it is an abbreviation of the whole argument. The sensual-symbolical world of the poem does not vanish in pointing to something that it is not. It is neither a metaphor nor an allegory, but tautegorical: 'a Symbol ὅ ἔστιν ἄει ταυτεγόρικον' – a symbol is always what it expresses (SM 30). It *embodies* what it means and 'always partakes of the Reality which it renders intelligible' (ibid.), namely, the idea which determines and unifies and appears in it: *Forma formans in formam formatam translucens* (BL II 215).

5 Imagining God

What appears and shines through the symbols of the re-creation of the natural and human world? In the first instance the specific ideas of each poem. All those individual forms of being, however, do not rest in splendid isolation. Each form relates to each other. They are mediated by virtue of their identity and alterity.[26] What shines through are the companionship of human persons, the community with nature and the connectedness in an ordered universe, the 'inbeing of all in each' (LS XXX). Fundamentally, in the last analysis, it is the creation, the fulness of all forms of being (*pleroma*), and the free will of the absolute that shine through the symbolical re-creation. The human world, imagined symbolically, might mirror the inherence of the finite *I am* in the absolute I AM. 'a Symbol (ὅ ἔστιν ἄει ταυτεγόρικον) is characterized by a translucence of the Special in the Individual or of the General in the Especial or the Universal in the General. Above all by the translucence of the Eternal through and in the Temporal' (LS 30). This characterization, formulated in the neutral indicative mood, invites a simplistic reading. 'Translucence of the Eternal through and in the Temporal', however, and the participation of the symbol in the reality symbolized name a dialectical relationship which cannot be flattened to an easy, undistinguished transition from one to the other. The sensuous symbol, by virtue of its ontological relationship to the reality it makes visible, *mediates* in a 'visionary gleam'[27] infinity and finitude.

In the margin to Schelling's *System* (1800) (p. 410), Coleridge notes 'that the I itself in the absolute Synthesis [i.e. the subject-object *I am*] supposes an already perfected Intelligence, as the ground of the possibility of its existence, as it does exist' (CM IV, 460). The *I am* cannot posit its own existence and that it is what it is: a self-developing subject-object. What it is has to be realized. What poetry is and does, what the poet (in ideal perfection) is capable of[28] has to be fulfilled. It may fail. The perfected Intelligence, in contrast, is the absolutely identical ground of existence and the knowledge of existence, of idea and reality.[29] In the elevation to it, the finite person presupposes her own ground in and from whom she exists and is a finite *I am*. She is similar in dissimilitude, finite mind from the perfected intelligence, grounded from and in the groundless (*causa sui*). This contrast, the ontological difference, deeper and yet more indifferent than any other, determines the work of the imagination and the symbol in particular. Imagination, imaging God, at the same time carries with it and even exhibits the sphere of finitude in which it operates: the writer, his/her (sympathetically imaginative) readership, their life, their language and historical situation.[30] Imaging God in the sphere of dissimilitude, therefore, cannot 'Defecate[s] to a pure transparency / That intercepts no light and adds no stain'.[31] Therefore the translucence of the eternal will often be realized only in 'dark fluxion, all unfixable by thought'[32] dark images and almost blind mirrorings. In the darkest poems, poems of loss, the visionary gleam weans into the imageless flight to the Absolute: 'Ignore thyself, and strive to know thy God!'[33]

For Coleridge and his compeers in this respect, like Wordsworth, Schelling, Hegel, Hölderlin, Shelley and others, all specific ideas and their embodiment in sensual-symbolical works are enveloped by the horizon of the absolute. This horizon of the imagination seems to fade in the course of history. Yet there survives the most intense yearning that at least the arts might allow the last metaphysical activity and open up the other state, the moment of fulfilment and an ecstasy transcending the human condition. What then shines in and through the works and actions of art?

Response by Douglas Hedley

Friedrich Uehlein's magisterial chapter on Coleridge's concept of Imagination expounds one of Coleridge's most influential and complex theories. The imagination functions as an isthmus between the finite and the infinite. It furnishes a means of avoiding the Scylla and Charybdis of either a crudely literalistic materialism or a Gnostic escape from the real. Like Uehlein, I see Coleridge as a thinker in the Platonic–Idealistic tradition rather than the eclectic and essentially unsystematic thinker favoured by many commentators, an English Victor Cousin, one might say. The imagination is unintelligible without an explication of the finite 'I AM' and ultimately the great 'I AM' of Exod. 3.14. The philosophical exploration of subjectivity generates theological reflection upon the co-presence of the infinite I AM in self-consciousness, not as *totaliter aliter* but, in the language of Nicholas of Cusa, as *non aliud*. 'We begin with the I Know myself, in order to end with the absolute I am. We proceed from the Self, in order to lose and find all self in God.' Coleridge is pursuing an absolute principle of being, and not simply an absolute principle of knowledge. In this manner, Coleridge moves beyond transcendental philosophy that mirrors Schelling in some respects, and yet is different in others. Coleridge's theory of the Imagination culminates in a theophanic metaphysics in which the translucence of the symbol in nature and art provides the culmination of the work of Imagination, both primary and secondary. The development from the more preliminary questions in *Living Forms of the Imagination* to the metaphysics of the image in *The Iconic Imagination* is certainly inspired and informed by the work of Coleridge.

Notes

1 Coleridge's writings are quoted according to the following abbreviations (taken from Frederick Burwick [ed.], *The Oxford Handbook of Samuel Taylor Coleridge* (Oxford: Oxford University Press, 2009), x–xii): Biographia Literaria (BL), Collected Letters (CL) On the Constitution of the Church and State (CCS) The Notebooks of S.T. Coleridge (CN), Lay Sermons (LS), Lectures 1818-1819: On the History of Philosophy (Lects Phil). In the case of Coleridge's *Notebooks*, the manuscript page of an entry is also occasionally given.
2 An allegedly simpler direct approach in the name of 'phenomenology' forgets that any phenomenological description and investigation leads back to the transcendental Ego and its passive and active life. Notwithstanding their differences, both kinds of philosophy do not undertake an immediate inquiry.
3 Following Coleridge's (and Lord Shaftesbury's) example, I take the liberty of using *the I* for the subject-object, instead of the ambiguous term 'the Ego'. Coleridge's synonyms in various contexts are *Sum, self, spirit, mind, self-consciousness, personeity, das Ich, die Ichheit,* etc.
4 See, for example, CN III 4351: 'Το απειρον νοητον, (πᾶν ἀλλα καὶ ἕν,) intellectual (i.e. *unal*) Infinity.'
5 See, for example, CN III 4351.
6 CN III 4186 and Thesis VII and VIII, BL I 276–9. See Schelling, *System des transcendentalen Idealismus* (1800), in Schelling, *Sämtliche Werke*, edited by K. F. A.

Schelling (Stuttgart et al.: Cotta, 1856–1861), vol. I/3, 380, and his *Abhandlungen zur Erläuterung des Idealismus der Wissenschaftslehre*, in *Sämtliche Werke*, vol. I/1, 366–8.

7   BL I 286; CN III 4265 viii and note. See, for example, Schelling, *System* (1800), 431–2.

8   Coleridge's debt to Schelling and others has been known since the first appearance of BL, since he himself drew the attention to it. Sarah Coleridge provided a selection of her father's borrowings and comments in her edition of *Biographia Literaria*, 2 vols (London: Pickering, 1847), vol. I, 293–323. The literal transcriptions, parallels, variations and free appropriations have been documented by James Engell and W. Jackson Bate in their edition of *Biographia literaria or Biographical Sketches of My Literary Life and Opinions* (London: Routledge and Kegan Paul; Harvard: Harvard University Press, 1983), and in Kathleen Coburn's annotations on Coleridge's *Notebooks*, volume 3, London: Routledge and Kegan Paul, 1973.

9   The imagination, or esemplastic power as 'the living principle [. . .] in the process of our self-consciousness' is treated in BL I, ch. 13 (299–306). Further elucidations of 'esemplastic' in BL I, 168–74 with concise annotations by the editors on Coleridge's appropriation of the German debate pertaining to the imagination. See also CN III 4176, III 4244 f164^v.

It is hardly necessary to mention that the self-development of the *I am* does not depend on the rather bold etymology 'In-eins-Bildung' and 'Eisenoplasy'. On the contrary, the concept of the *I am* reached so far allows the expressive 'etymology'.

10 '"The spirit" is Power self-bounded by retroition on itself and *is* only for itself' (CN III 4186 f34^v). 'Whatever in the strict sense of the word *is*, all that possesses actual Being, *is* only in consequence of the *Direction upon itself*, or act of Introition' (ibid). Equivalent terms are 'self-introition" and 'turn inward upon oneself"'.

11 Notes on Schelling, in Henri Nidecker, 'Notes Marginales de S. T. Coleridge', *Revue de littérature comparée* 7 (1927): 130–46, 336–48, 521–35, 736–46, here 533 (my additions in brackets).

12 Coleridge follows Fichte and reads '*emp*finden' and the rare form of the word '*ent*finden' – which does not please the ear, as he thinks – as an *inward* finding. 'Die abgeleitete Beziehung heißt Empfindung (gleichsam *Insichfindung*. Nur das fremdartige wird *gefunden*; das ursprünglich im Ich gesetzte ist immer da.) . . . Hier zuerst löst sich, dass ich mich so ausdrücke, etwas ab von dem Ich; welches durch weitere Bestimmung sich allmählig in ein Universum mit allen seinen Merkmalen verwandeln wird.' *Grundriss des Eigenthümlichen der Wissenschaftslehre* (*Fichtes Sämmtliche Werke*, edited by Immanuel H. Fichte (Berlin: Mayer & Müller, 1845/1846), vol. I, 339).

13 We have to refrain from the admittedly difficult task of reconstructing this evolutionary process. For a more detailed account see my essay *Die Manifestation des Selbstbewußtseins im konkreten 'Ich bin'. Endliches und Unendliches Ich im Denken S. T. Coleridges* (Hamburg: Meiner, 1982), 33–52. For the rôle of the body in the temporal, embodied person, see my note 'The Medium. S. T. Coleridge's Concept of the Human Person', *Glimpse. Publication of the Society for Phenomenology and Media* 13 (2011): 1–7.

14 See Coleridge's translation of Ennead III 8,4,6–10 in BL I 251–2.

15 BL I 275. Cf. Werner Beierwaltes, 'Deus est esse – Esse est Deus. Die onto-theologische Grundfrage als aristotelisch-neuplatonische Denkstruktur', in *Platonismus und Idealismus* (Frankfurt: Vittorio Klostermann, 2nd edn, 2004), 5–82.

16 BL I 283; cf. also CN III 4265; Logic 85, § 31. The footnotes to these passages show that Coleridge distinguishes 'the empirical "I"' (*das empirische Ich*) and the absolute

"I am"' (...) in whom we live and move and have our being' (Logic 85 § 31 note). The 'followers of Kant' (ibid.), in striking contrast, distinguish the empirical I from the transcendental subject: 'Transcendental philosophy does not talk of an absolute principle of being (...) but of an absolute principle of knowledge' (Schelling (1800), *System* (see n. 6), 354 passim).

17 C&S 182; On the Trinity, SW&F 1510-1512; LS 32; CM IV 400 (a note on Schelling's *Philosophie und Religion*); CM II 287: 'I that shall be in that I will to be – the absolute Will, the ground of Being – the Self-affirming Actus purissimus.'; CN III 4427 (Τὸ ὑπερούσιον – the One beyond being); CN IV 5413 and in many other places. Cf. Douglas Hedley, *Coleridge, Philosophy and Religion. Aids to Reflection and the Mirror of the Spirit*, Cambridge: Cambridge University Press, 2000, 65–87. For a systematic exposition of *causa sui*, see Werner Beierwaltes, *Das wahre Selbst. Studien zu Plotins Begriff des Geistes und des Einen* (Frankfurt: Vittorio Klostermann, 2001), 123–60. For the Trinity and the inner-Trinitarian life, see my essay *Manifestation des Selbstbewußtseins* (see n. 13), 94–131.

18 Cf. Werner Beierwaltes, *Denken des Einen. Studien zur neuplatonischen Philosophie und ihrer Wirkungsgeschichte* (Frankfurt am Main: Vittorio Klostermann, 1985), 65: 'In der christlichen Theologie werden die zwei Aspekte der philosophischen All-Einheits-Lehre: das In- und zugleich Über-Sein des Einen und die Einheit der reflexiven Rationalität – das Prinzip 'Geist' – in der Einheit des Ersten zusammengedacht.' The νοῦς, the 'Prinzip Geist', is the *absolute alterity* of the One beyond being, 'the Supreme being, (...) whose Definition is, the PLEROMA of being, whose essential poles are Unity and Distinctity (...) The Distinctities in the pleroma are the Eternal Ideas, (...) each considered in itself, an Infinite in the form of the Finite; but all considered as one with the Unity, (...) they are the energies of the Finific' (On the Trinity, SW&F 1511–12). The rare word 'finfic' – perhaps Coleridge's own coinage – points forward to the creation of the universe of finite beings. Their definiteness and distinction originate in the eternal ideas. Cf. Uehlein, *Manifestation des Selbstbewusstseins* (see n. 13), 120–31. These all too short and poor allusions to the Trinity and the inner-Trinitarian life are, nevertheless, necessary. Without this perspective, Coleridge's famous definition of the imagination remains incomprehensible.

19 Thomas McFarland, *Coleridge and the Pantheist Tradition* (Oxford: Oxford University Press, 1969). Richard Berkeley, *Coleridge and the Crises of Reason* (London: Macmillan, 2007).

20 Cf. CN V 5581: the twofold finiteness of the human *I am*; CN V 5670: mind in the universal idea and in the individual *I*.

21 On the Trinity, SW&F 1511–1512.

22 I can only hint at the decisive rôle of will and conscience in Coleridge's philosophy. He has not worked it out in the context of the imagination. When it becomes prominent in his later philosophy, it is intimately connected not with the imagination, but with reason.

23 The faculty of fancy has been treated by philosophers and critics under various names and certainly in different contexts. John Locke, for example, speaks of 'the faculty of laying up, and retaining the Ideas' (*Essay* II, x, § 10). It enables us to form complex ideas and consequently all higher forms of human understanding. The *reproductive Einbildungskraft* in Kant's *Critique of Pure Reason* allows us to have representations (*Vorstellungen*) when the object is not present. It combines those representations associatively. James Engell, *The Creative Imagination: Enlightenment to Romanticism*

(Cambridge, MA and London: Harvard University Press, 1981), has written a history of this concept.

24 The distinction of imagination and fancy is his constant theme. As a rule, he devalues fancy and its indispensable achievement. The reason for that is obvious. The blindfold estimation of fancy and its products, the allegedly solid facts of reality, leads to a split between the subject and its objectifications, the subject and object, the *res cogitans* and the *res extensa*, man and nature, and to the mechanical-empirical philosophy he strives to overcome. In a similar way he criticizes literary works, *fanciful* products that do not create something new, but select and combine representations from the stock of fixities and definites. The discussion of imagination and fancy has produced a wealth of literature. Cf., for example, Ivor A. Richards, *Coleridge on Imagination* (London: Routledge and Kegan Paul, 3rd edn, 1962); Owen Barfield, *What Coleridge Thought* (Middletown: Wesleyan University Press, 1971), chs 6 and 7; Günther H. Lenz, *Die Dichtungstheorie Coleridges* (Frankfurt a. M.: Athenäum, 1971), ch. IV and V; James Engell and W. Jackson Bate, 'Introduction', to BL I, LXXXI–CIV. Cf. also Wolfgang Iser, *Das Fiktive und das Imaginäre. Perpektiven literarischer Anthropologie* (Frankfurt a. M.: Suhrkamp, 1991). In particular the chapter 'Die Imagination als Vermögen (Coleridge)'. Professor Iser writes from a strictly anthropological perspective. Central tenets of Coleridge's argument, for example, the absolute I Am, the One beyond being and the one ground of being and thought, the Trinity, the free and eternal act of creation and its similar-dissimilar reiteration in the finite mind, in short, Coleridge's speculative elaboration of transcendental and idealist philosophy and its transition to or at least affinity with metaphysics, are missing. Iser's selective interpretation centres round the groundlessness (Grundlosigkeit) and the play or wavering (Spielbewegung) of the imagination within changing contexts.

25 LS 29. For a short introduction see Nicholas Halmi, 'Coleridge on Allegory and Symbol', in Burwick (ed.), *Samuel Taylor Coleridge* (see n. 1), 345–58. Joel Harter, *Coleridge's Philosophy of Faith: Symbol, Allegory, and Hermeneutics* (Tübingen: Mohr Siebeck, 2011). In particular chs 3–5 and pp. 151–5: 'Symbol, Allegory, and Irony'. See also Douglas Hedley, *Living Forms of the Imagination* (London and New York: T&T Clark, 2008), 115–43, and *The Iconic Imagination* (New York et al.: Bloomsbury, 2016), 105–46.

26 Plato, *Sophist*, 249–59.

27 Wordsworth, *Immortality Ode*, l. 57.

28 See BL I 304 (secondary imagination); BL II 16-18 and CN III 3827 f115, f115^v (table of the primary faculties of man).

29 BL I 275. See above III 1 and 2.

30 'It is the honourable characteristic of Poetry that its materials are to be found in every subject which can interest the human mind' (*Lyrical Ballads* [1798], Advertisement).

31 Cf. the end of Coleridge's *On the Constitution of the Church and State* (C&S 184).

32 See Coleridge's poem *Self-knowledge* (1832), line 7.

33 *Self-knowledge,* last line. John Beer writes in his selection of Coleridge's *Poems* (London: Everyman's Library, 1974, 337): 'the philosopher who had in *Biographia Literaria* written in praise of the Greek maxim "'Know Thyself'", now crosses out those words and writes instead the poem *Self-knowledge*.' I read the poem not as a crossing out but as a repetition of the *Know Thyself* in the sphere of dissimilitude. Only a person – *I am* – can produce such a self-reflexive monologue. It repeats the impossibility of self-production, the failing knowledge and lack of self-possession, and echoes the elevation to the 'great eternal I AM' in the flight to the Absolute. Cf. *Manifestation des Selbstbewußtseins* (see n. 13), 55–6.

Part III

The religious imagination in contemporary philosophy of religion

6

God in the world and ourselves in God

Panentheistic speculation in the early Karl Rahner

Klaus E. Müller

1 Methodological preface

The starting point of the following analysis of Karl Rahner's thought is the striking fact that his two principal works on religious philosophy, that is, *Spirit in the World* and *Hearer of the Word*, were written at about the same time as a plethora of spiritual texts which have only recently been made accessible in their entirety again in the newly completed *Sämtliche Werke* (*Complete Works*).[1] When reading texts of both genres alongside one another, one cannot help but wonder how one and the same author could at the same time write down both such extraordinarily intense speculations in transcendental Thomism (in his *Spirit in the World*) and Maurice Blondel's programme of immanence apologetics with its equally Thomistic grounding (in his *Hearer of the Word*) and such overtly panentheistic thoughts in meditations and prayers of existential spirituality. As we shall point out, Rahner, in fact, never in his life gave up writing texts in the latter genre. If we enquire about the systematic and speculative point of contact between the two which may help account for Rahner's twofold approach to theology, we come across the rather short third part of *Spirit in the World* which is entitled 'The Possibility of Metaphysics on the Basis of the Imagination'.[2] This chapter provides a dense summary of Rahner's comprehensive reading of the few texts of Aquinas's devoted to the question of knowledge. At its heart is the indissoluble link between sensual knowledge and the *Vorgriff* or the 'pre-apprehension' of being as such (i.e. God) which has always already occurred prior to our knowledge of concrete beings of which it is the condition of the possibility:

> For strictly speaking, the first-known, the first thing encountering man, is not the world in its 'spiritless' existence, but the world – itself – as transformed by the light of the spirit, the world in which man sees himself. [The world as known is always the world of man, is essentially a concept complementary to man.] And the last-known, God, shines forth only in the limitless breadth of the pre-apprehension, in the desire for being as such by which every act of man is borne, and which

is at work not only in his ultimate knowledge and in his ultimate decisions, but also in the fact that the free spirit becomes, and must become, sensibility in order to be spirit, and thus exposes itself to the whole destiny of this earth. Thus man encounters himself when he finds himself in the world and when he asks about God; and when he asks about his essence, he always finds himself already in the world and on the way to God. He is both of these at once, and cannot be one without the other.[3]

In a way, the passage quoted encapsulates everything that we nowadays discuss under the labels of 'panentheism' and 'panpsychism'.

There is no doubt that Douglas Hedley is the leading author on the *imagination* today. Both in the range of its topics and in the depth of its argument, his trilogy[4] is quite easily on a par with the oeuvre of a Hans Urs von Balthasar (with the author's knowledge of the details of modern German intellectual history in particular being nothing short of awe-inspiring). While Aquinas only plays a marginal role in the trilogy, there is a short sentence in the first volume of the trilogy which may be read as a programmatic outline of an intellectual dynamic that leads us straight into the very centre of Aquinas's philosophical thought: 'Psychologically or morally, the imagination is a necessary route to reality.'[5] To my mind, the adverbs could actually be omitted altogether. The exciting topic confronting us is the way imaginings may lead us to reality or, in other words, how fictions may be true.

2 Introduction

Karl Rahner's influence upon twentieth-century Catholic theology surpasses everyone else's. He took up his work in a twofold role, namely as a philosopher of religion and, at the same time, as an author of spiritual texts which he himself viewed not as by-products of his academic career, but as entirely on a par with his academic publications. It is highly revealing that towards the end of his life Karl Rahner actually expressed the wish that 'the prayers scattered throughout his works be collected and put together into a kind of dogmatic of prayer'.[6] The dimension of religious philosophy was all the more prominent at the start of his intellectual career. While his 1936 theological thesis entitled *E latere Christi: An Enquiry into the Typological Meaning of Jn. 19:34*[7] failed to make any lasting impression, the opposite is true of his philosophical thesis *Spirit in the World: On the Metaphysics of Finite Knowledge in Thomas Aquinas*, which was turned down by his Freiburg supervisor Martin Honecker.[8] Completed in 1936, this book was published by Rahner in 1939 regardless, causing quite a stir. The reasons for its rejection as a thesis are, for one thing, connected to the then situation at the Department of Philosophy in Freiburg. For another, however, it was a major factor that this work on Thomas already evidenced Rahner's later lifelong commitment to the early modern notion of the subject. In an introduction to *Spirit in World*, which he later attached to the original work, he writes:

> Not as though it were a question here of the author's own view, as though consciously or unconsciously he wanted to read his own opinions into Thomas.

But he does not think that the danger of this is greater for him than for anyone else, because for him Thomas is not a master who forbids his students to disagree with him. However, the direction of the *questions* which are posed to Thomas are given in advance by a *systematic* concern of the author, especially when these questions are trying to drive the finished propositions in Thomas back to their objective problematic.

Such an objective concern, which the author here explicitly acknowledges, is (or certainly should be) conditioned by the problematic of *today*'s philosophy. If in this sense the reader gets the impression that an interpretation of St. Thomas is at work here which has its origin in modern philosophy, the author does not consider that such a criticism points to a defect, but rather to a merit of the book. And this because he would not know of any other reason for which he could be occupied with Thomas than for the sake of those questions which stimulate *his* philosophy and that of his time.[9]

Karl Lehmann has made a strong case for viewing at least the theologian Rahner's *Spirit in the Word* as propounding a completely independent philosophical approach, which cannot be reduced to the reception of its Thomistic, Kantian or Heideggerian aspects.[10] If this is true, and I think it is indeed, then his second major work is not very likely to be uninfluenced by this approach, even though Rahner himself remarked once that his philosophy had been wholly subservient to his theology since this second book.[11] However, the one thing does not rule out the other. Obviously, this second work is the most interesting one from the vantage point of religious philosophy. Its title reads: *Hearer of the Word: Laying the Foundation for a Philosophy of Religion*,[12] published in 1941.

3 To be all ears

In *Hearer of the Word*, Rahner, to put it in a nutshell, seeks to spell out the essential and aprioric inclination of man towards a possible revelation. His endeavour is not entirely new, however. Maurice Blondel (1861–1949) had undertaken the very same task several decades previously. His thesis *L'Action* of 1893 is devoted to it, and so is his *Lettre sur apologétique* of 1896. It is Blondel's overriding concern that revelation must be a necessary aspect of man's being, while also being entirely indisposable or, in theological parlance, given to man entirely freely:

> If Christianity were only about some conviction or action randomly added to our nature and our reason; if we were able to realize ourselves to the full without this addition; and if it were possible for us to exempt ourselves freely and without punishment from the importunity of this superhuman gift, then there would be no comprehensible communication whatsoever between these two levels the one of which would, from the perspective of reason, continue to exist as if it did not exist at all. Not to ascend would not mean to fall. To forego the honour of a higher vocation

would mean to remain at a median level, to which man can rise by his own power. One could not raise any problem whatsoever for philosophy in the face of revelation. However, once this revelation reaches us in ourselves, as it were, pursuing us into our innermost being; once it views a neutral or negative attitude towards it as a genuine act of apostasy and as a kind of culpable enmity; once the poverty of our finite being is capable of such a sin that eternity must pay for it, then there will be an encounter. The difficulty will have been expressed and the problem will have been raised. For if it is true that the demands of revelation are well-grounded, we cannot any longer say that we still are with ourselves. And of this defect, of this incapability and of this demand there must be a trace in a human being solely qua human being or an echo even in the most autonomous of philosophies.[13]

Blondel's thrust, however impressive, came to naught, arousing suspicion on the part of the church instead. Only decades later, which is not to the credit of the Catholic tradition at all, did Karl Rahner start from scraps again. A true appreciation of Rahner's merit, however, is hampered in a complex way by the process of the revision of the second editions both of *Spirit in the World* and *Hearer of the Word* which Johann Baptist Metz conducted on his behalf.[14] Hence, a reappraisal of Rahner's early work has been called for and rightly so.[15] It is to be done with regard to *Hearer of the Word* on the following pages. Before that, however, we need to explain against which background Rahner adopted his transcendental approach.

One must be wary of summarily dismissing 'neo-scholasticism'. The term designates the attempt at a renewal of scholasticism in the nineteenth and twentieth centuries. Such a philosophy, which was based primarily, but not exclusively, upon St Thomas Aquinas, was deemed an urgently needed bulwark against idealism and materialism from a Catholic perspective. However, one of the problems that it faced was in how far the teachings attributed to Aquinas had actually been held by him. In fact, this project amounted to an intensified version of the officially decreed disregard for the whole of early modern thought since Descartes. Among the few who broke free of this ghettoization was Joseph Maréchal. He engaged in a dialogue with Kant to enquire into the possibility of a metaphysics after Kant, while also making use of other authors for the sake of a transformation of Kant, including Johann Gottlieb Fichte. This attempt at a reconciliation between tradition and the early modern notion of the subject appealed deeply to Rahner and exerted decisive influence upon him.

Moreover, there is another source of Rahner's approach besides his taking up a philosophical challenge which he viewed as essential. This second source is Ignatian spirituality or, to be more precise, the experience of the religious exercises, as first conceived by Ignatius of Loyola (1491–1556). In moving biographical struggles, Ignatius furnished the individual with a way by which she was able to find God's will for herself or, in other words, by which she was led to the discovery of her own God immediacy. Conceptually, the theological reflection upon this spiritual process must to a certain degree address both the individual person as a person and her ability to find the truth, thus sharing with early modern philosophy its fundamental questions. In a fictitious 'Speech of Ignatius of Loyola to a Modern-Day Jesuit' written by the later Rahner, this fact is pointed out succinctly. The text says that it is a key part of Ignatian spirituality, as well as a point of contact with Luther and Descartes, to reckon with the possibility of the experience of divine immediacy.[16] It is on the basis of these two sources, viewed by him as inextricably intertwined, that Rahner puts forth his theology as a mystagogy, that is, an introduction to that experience. The project itself is based upon what may be called an original explication of the early modern notion of the subject, effected, however, in an appropriation in which the concept is redefined in the recourse to classical metaphysics.

The point of departure[17] is the question of being. Every human being enquires about the ultimate whence and whither of all beings and, at the same time, about being as such, thereby inevitably being engaged in metaphysics. The 'inevitably' is not meant rhetorically, as those who either fail to ask the question or expressly reject it have likewise adopted a stance on the question of being. They are indifferent to beings as beings and to being as such. However, that upon which the answer to the question, once it has been posed, hinges cannot itself be called into question again. Hence, only the question itself can be claimed as the starting point for an answer to the general question of being and as the means to the end of an indubitable certainty. As the possibility of enquiring into being is peculiar to the being called man, the metaphysical question of being is also the question of the nature of that very being who is able to raise this question in the first place: 'Hence human metaphysics is also always and necessarily an analytic study of human being. We may be assured, therefore, that we are not looking away from ourselves when, at first, we seem to be concerned only with the most general principles of metaphysics.'[18] It is in this connection of the metaphysics of being and the analytic of man that the turn to early modern philosophy gradually becomes apparent. According to Rahner, the question as the starting point of the question about being implies three things:

- That it enquires about all being as such
- That there must be an enquiry about it
- That this enquiry must be conducted in such a way that we must distinguish between being and beings

However, the fact that the question, from the outset, aims at the whole of being implies a first provisional general knowledge about it, since there could not be an enquiry about something entirely unknown. This, in turn, means that the very fact of the metaphysical enquiry about being implies the assumption that being as such is knowable. In the act of knowing, being and knowledge do not come together as two completely unrelated entities. Instead, they constitute an original unity evidenced in the essential tendency of each being towards being as a potential object of knowledge. The inextinguishable origin of this unity, for Rahner, is the necessary correlation of being and knowledge. Consequently, Rahner deems a being that is unknowable per se a contradiction in terms. Hence it follows:

(4) Therefore being and knowing are related to each other because originally, in their ground, they are the same reality. This does not imply anything less than that being as such, to the extent that it is being, is knowing; it is knowing in original

unity with being, hence it is a knowing of the being who the knower is. Being and knowing constitute an original unity, that is: to the nature of being belongs [and now follows the salient point; K.M.] a relation of knowing with regard to itself. And the other way round: the knowing that belongs to the essential constitution of being is the self-presence of being. The original meaning of knowing is self-possession, and being possesses itself to the extent that it is being.[19]

In this way, Rahner has progressed from a classical metaphysical starting point to *the* core concept of modernity. Interestingly enough, he had already expressed this more clearly in the first edition of his *Spirit in the World* than in *Hearer of the Word* where he says: 'Knowing is the being-present-to-self of being',[20] which is the innermost core of transcendental philosophy. Rahner frequently speaks of being as 'self-presence' or 'self-reflection'. One could also say that being is essentially self-consciousness, although the early Rahner made only sparse use of this concept.

Using the concept of 'self-presence', however, Rahner makes a certain kind of being, that is, knowledge, the original form of being instead of only providing an analysis of either knowledge or one finite being among others, which again raises an alarming problem. The starting point of the whole concept is the question of being which man must pose by necessity. And yet, man must ask this question because, for one thing, he both already knows about being and is being himself. For another, he is also not-being at the same time. Otherwise he would not have to enquire about being at all. As a consequence, man does not possess perfect 'self-presence'. Hence, if there are beings who enquire about being, there must be various degrees of self-presence. Only to the extent that it has being can a being have self-presence and vice versa. Obviously, this amounts to the classic notion of analogy, to which Rahner refers at this point for two reasons. Firstly, the concept of analogy allows him to create a scale between the ontologically primary self-presence and the other kinds of being, including material beings. Secondly, on the basis of this thought, he can attribute a privileged rank to man. Man is a being that is both spiritual and material in nature. He is the only material being in which the ontic structure of self-presence is given a complete articulation, as opposed, significantly, to 'self-presence' per se (in which case man, as we have said, would not have to enquire about being at all).

True to his turn to early modern thought, Rahner also enquires about the condition of the possibility of finite self-presence. Man, he points out, experiences his subjectivity when judging and acting towards worldly things as 'being in himself' vis-à-vis those opposite himself. A closer analysis of the act of judgement reveals the condition of the possibility of being in oneself to be the process of abstraction. When I distinguish myself from a thing, it is by my subsuming it under general concepts. What abstraction does becomes apparent in the experience that the quiddity or 'whatness' of a sensual thing, because of its sensuality, is encountered as something finite. If it were not for our abstraction, it would, therefore, be defined by its 'in-finity'. And if this is true indeed, then the act of knowing an individual thing cannot but always be beyond it. If there is to be no infinite regress, no individual thing of the same kind can be the goal of this 'beyond', from which Rahner concludes:

> This 'beyond' can only be the absolute range of all knowable objects as such. [...] Human consciousness grasps its single objects in a *Vorgriff* that reaches for the absolute range of all its possible objects. That is why in every single act of knowledge it always already reaches beyond the individual objects. Thus it does not grasp the latter merely in its unrelated dull 'thisness', but in its limitation and its relation to the totality of all possible objects. While it knows the individual object and in order to know it, consciousness must always already be beyond it. The *Vorgriff* is the condition of the possibility of the universal concept, of abstraction. The latter in its turn makes possible the objectivation of the sense datum and so human knowing self-subsistence.[21]

It is in keeping with this line of arguing that, according to Rahner, this *Vorgriff*, as the condition of all knowledge and action, implies the recognition of an absolute being or an absolute self-presence, that is, God, since everything whatsoever that is within the range of the *Vorgriff* is objectively possible. Only an absolute being fills this range entirely. It, thus, corresponds to the *Vorgriff* by its very essence. However, as an absolute, it must not be understood as a merely possible entity alone, but, as a reality, a line of reasoning that is close to Anselm's ontological argument. In his conception of our knowledge about God, Rahner himself comes very close to traditional proofs of God's existence. However, he views his own argument as a metaphysical-epistemological reformulation, since the notion of a real finite being that requires an infinite being as the condition of its existence is replaced by another: 'The affirmation of the real finiteness of a being demands as condition of its possibility that we affirm the existence of an absolute being. We do this implicitly in the *Vorgriff* toward being as such, since only through it do we know the limitation of the finite being as such a limitation.'[22] For all its structural parallels – the differences strike me as greater than Rahner himself assumes – it is a knowledge of God in the medium of the judgemental act. It is, thus, drawn completely into the perspective of *subjectivity*, whereas the traditional proofs of God's existence are firmly situated in a context of ontological *objectivity*.

Anyway, Rahner believes that his deductive line of reasoning up to this point has established the fundamental possibility of revelation, since revelation is possible only if its addressee possesses a horizon that is adequate for it. Moreover, this horizon must be strictly infinite if it is not to be restricted *a priori* by any contents of revelation. Hence, the transcendence of human knowledge towards the whole of being as such must be the foundation of an 'ontology of the obediential potency for a possible revelation ... [and] an essential part of a Christian philosophy of religion.'[23] 'Obediential potency' is *the* keyword of Rahner's philosophy, which might fittingly be rendered as the 'ability to be all ears'. It is not difficult for Rahner to then proceed to the dimension of word and language, into which the hearing of God's reality is placed. From the outset, Rahner follows Heidegger in using the term 'luminosity'[24] as a synonym for 'self-presence' or 'self-reflection' to express the identity of being and knowledge. However, insofar as being is light, it must be conceived of as determined by the 'logos'. As such, it is a potential object of revelation.[25]

From the vantage point of religious philosophy, however, this raises an entirely new problem. If man is absolute openness to all being, then he has access to all being by himself. Why, then, should there be a possible revelation at all?[26] It is from a highly audacious continuation of his metaphysical-epistemological deduction up to this point that Rahner manages to infer the necessity of revelation. As he goes on to explain, revelation is necessary, because being, despite its luminosity, is also the most hidden thing. The reason for this is twofold. Firstly, God's infinity can only be known as the outer margin of the knowledge of a finite entity, as it were. The *Vorgriff* does not present us with the infinite as itself, but as something that is affirmed in the process of knowledge alongside finite objects. For this very reason, it is concealed from us in its own nature so that a possible revelation can be meaningful. However, the meaning of revelation, in this case, would be due to the factual nature of the human mind only. As this factualness could be different, that is, one with incomparably more width, the necessity of revelation, as it has been established up to this point, would be relative and could, as a consequence, be overcome. In the strict sense of the word, this necessity can be attained only if the hiddenness of the infinite in itself vis-à-vis man can be proved.

Rahner effects this radicalization of his concept by, secondly, referring to the scholastic convergence of *verum* and *bonum*, that is, of knowledge and will. 'Self-presence' necessarily implies an affirmation of oneself, affirming meaning 'assenting' and having the character of a volitional act. Only in the horizon of such a self-affirmation is the question of being posed. By enquiring about being, man affirms his finiteness, and by having to enquiry about being, he affirms it by necessity. Thus, his existence, for all its contingency consequent upon his finiteness, is deemed unconditioned. However, something contingent can become unconditioned only by an act of will: 'The fact that being opens up for human existence is brought about by the will as an inner moment of knowledge itself.'[27] Against the background of the identity of being and knowledge, it follows from the connection of man's self-affirmation and the luminosity of being that human self-affirmation can only be seen as the participation in a freewill making contingent being unconditioned. Otherwise, human existence viewing itself as unconditioned by its very nature, while necessarily affirming itself as contingent, would have to proceed from an impenetrably dark origin, which would contradict the principal openness of being as such. In other words, man is in a volitional relationship with himself to which belongs a knowledge about both his own contingency and the latter's necessity. Hence, he must conceive of himself as founded in a being that not only exists but is a free power at that. However, this also means that the space of possible actions of the infinite towards man is not restricted to the fact of his existence (or his being willed). Apart from the fact of his createdness, man can and must in principle reckon with further initiatives on the part of that free power, which again implies two things. Firstly, man, as is testified by his openness for being as such, faces a God of revelation who acts in history. Only on this condition can one sensibly talk of incommensurable initiatives. And, secondly, if man, thus, seeks to listen for a possible revelation by nature, he necessarily listens to such a revelation, which can come in two shapes,

> namely, the speaking or the silence of God. And we always and naturally hear the word or the silence of the free absolute God. Otherwise we would not be spirit. Our being spirit does not mean a demand that God should speak. But, should God

not speak, the spirit hears God's silence. [. . .] As spirit we stand before the living, free God, the God who speaks or the God who keeps silent[28]

Only now, with the possibility of God's silence established in deductive reasoning, has Rahner, as he claims, ensured that God's possible self-communication is not identical with the insights man may by himself gain into the first causes and final ends of reality. As has been shown, it is by virtue of his recourse to will that he manages to establish this. Notwithstanding, far from being only a strategic operation that is meant to stabilize the starting point of the deduction, this step further bridges the gap between scholasticism and an early modern form of the question of God, as in scholasticism this free deed is nothing but love. In that way, the finite and contingent can be viewed as an expression of God's love. Thus, human self-affirmation, understood as a participation in God's constitution, implies the love of God as its integral part. Hence it follows: '[We] listen for God's word or God's silence to the extent that we open up in free love for this message of the word or of the silence of God.'[29] Thereby, the openness to God is made a problem of man's 'moral self-determination', another early modern term amidst scholastic concepts. The place where this self-determination is realized is already known, namely history. If, as has been shown earlier, only history can be the medium of God's possible initiatives which go beyond the finite spirit's status as a creature, the discovery and the acceptance or rejection of the message conveyed in these initiatives cannot but be historical in nature. History, in Rahner, implies that a possible revelation of God, if it occurs, occurs in the medium of the human word as it is only in the word that, thanks to its capacity for negation, transcendent being can be perceived.[30] Hence, the early Rahner's project of religious philosophy is encapsulated in the following result: 'We are the beings of receptive spirituality, who stand in freedom before the free God of a possible revelation, which, if it comes, happens in our history through the word. We are the ones who, in our history, listen for the word of a free God. Only thus are we what we should be.'[31] Rahner was well aware that there were many unanswered questions in the draft of *Hearer of the Word*, perhaps more than he himself would have been prepared to admit. It would certainly be worthwhile to pursue them further. For our question, I see four key merits:

(a) Rahner connects the topic of religious philosophy with the sphere of subjectivity and reason in the strictest possible way, which is questioned by some every now and then.[32] In terms of philosophy of religion, his achievement is twofold. He provides religion with an existential foundation, while also keeping it at the level of the public discourse, that is, effecting both an enlightenment and a religious individuation. Perhaps, we need to enquire about the philosophical character and contents of that connection once again.
(b) Rahner's theory has transferred the question of God into the interior, linking it with the rational modes of question and judgement. Moreover, he has also given it a critical turn as the knowledge of God is conceived of solely as being affirmed alongside finite things and as being solely won via the latter reality.
(c) On the basis of a transcendental approach, the question of God is also transformed into something practical. Thereby, Rahner has defined the subject's

moral self-determination as the medium of the experience and knowledge of God in such a way that any ostensible moralization of transcendence is eschewed from the start. The moralization is based not on duties and imperatives, but on the love of God which precedes either of them.

(d) Rahner views the obediential potency as a tendency towards a speaking or silent God. In that way, we are prevented from drawing any conclusions about the contents of a possible revelation from our tendency towards it, let alone impose a criterion on historical claims to revelation. Nevertheless, I do not consider Rahner's view of a God who may remain silent a shortcoming with unacceptable effects made necessary only by his conceptual scheme. On the contrary, this notion, in my view, is one of those of Rahner's intuitions which show him to have been well ahead of his time. His conception allows him to engage in a dialogue with a possible post-theistic mindset, which Rahner not only deemed possible but also, in astonishingly far-sighted anticipation, described as early as 1965:

> The God of the beyond of the world is suspected to be a non-verifiable ghost which must be laid aside, since he does not exist there where we experience, achieve and suffer ourselves and where we suffer ourselves in solitude as the only real bottomless abyss. One tries by thought and action to demythologise everything and to destroy taboos in everything until the only thing left is what seems to survive all this: the incomprehensible something which is experienced as the absurd something which one would like to honour by shocked silence, or as the honest and bitter minimum of everyday duty in the service of others, if one is still inclined to act on and talk about an 'ideal' at all.[33]

In an astonishingly concrete fashion, this well-nigh prophetic potential that is evident in Rahner's early philosophical thoughts and that is reflected in theoretical passages like the one cited recurs in his spiritual texts, especially in his prayers. Time and again, these texts bring home to their reader how far our traditional dogmatic and doxological formulas fall short of what they are meant to say when we talk about or to God. They show, moreover, that the relationship between God and the world and between God and man must be defined in a far more complex and intimate fashion than our usual formulas of faith do. Hence, I do not hesitate to attribute to Rahner a deeply panentheistic conceptual framework critical of traditional theism, which is to be found in his writings from his earliest publications to his very last public lecture.

4 Ourselves in God and God in us: Rahnerian panentheism

I have long wondered how one may possibly hope to understand that God's self-communication and the creatures' autonomy increase, rather than decrease, to a proportionate extent without allowing for a monistic dimension to Rahner's hypothesis or, as Rahner himself puts it:

> This self-bestowal of God, in which God bestows himself precisely *as* the absolute transcendent, is the most immanent factor in the creature. The fact that it is

given its own nature to possess, the 'immanence of essence' in this sense, is the prior condition, and at the same time the consequence, of the still more radical immanence of the transcendence of God in the spiritual creature. [. . .] The conceptual models which are constructed on the basis of the difference between 'inner and outer' break down at this point. The orientation towards the self-bestowal of God as most radically different from the creature is the innermost element of all in it, and it is precisely this that makes the immanence of that which is mot external of all to it possible.[34]

The exact meaning may be gauged from literally countless passages in Rahner's texts, especially those in which speaking about God turns into silence towards God, that is, into the genre of prayer. In a very early text which dates from the 1920s and was first published in 2013, the mutual immanence of God and man is adumbrated in the connection of themes from the mystical tradition of Johannes Tauler, which always played a key role in Rahner, and Ignatius, the founder of his order:

> He dwells in the deepest ground of the soul. God. It is to Him that the soul speaks about its longing for eternal life, [. . .] for home. [. . .] It wants Him and Him alone. Everything else being too small and too poor, it has no problem parting with it. If it is entirely poor, naked and stripped of everything, then it can lift its hands to Him and ask Him: come! Then it waits for the day of the Lord, for the day when God who is concealed in the soul will reveal Himself to it, giving Himself entirely to it. Then God will no longer be with the soul in the country of banishment. Instead, the soul will be with Him in eternal life.[35]

The outlined dialectic of 'God in us' and 'ourselves in God', which constitutes the defining characteristic of what is termed 'panentheism' today, is the theological key criterion in the young Rahner's very first book publication, the famous little volume *Encounters with Silence* which counted among his most celebrated writings. Probably written in 1937 and first appearing in print in 1938, the meditations contained in it were meant by the publishing house to make up for a work which it deemed less likely to be successful, namely *Spirit in the World*, which it went on to publish in 1939.[36] This means that *Encounters with Silence* was written at the very same time as *Spirit in the World* and at the same time when Rahner was preparing *Hearer of the Word*, a series of lectures which he wrote in 1937 and published in 1941. The equal value that Rahner, as he himself emphasized, attached to his theoretical-theological and his spiritual writings is confirmed in a remarkable fashion by another great twentieth-century German-speaking theologian, who was to become one of Rahner's fiercest opponents and severest critics (although his critique was only partially justified). In a review, Hans Urs von Balthasar wrote:

> For a full comprehension of *Spirit in the World*, one also has to consider the little book of stylized literary prayers entitled *Encounters with Silence*, which restate the fundamental insight of the theoretical works at the level of religious experience. This insight is that of man standing between God and the world, before the void

and silence of the infinite which discloses itself only in God becoming man and within the Christian context of everyday life in the world *(conversio)* and the mystical turning towards the God beyond the world *(abstractio)*.[37]

In a nutshell, one has to read the texts on religious philosophy and spirituality side by side. If one chooses to do so, one is sure to gain a host of new insights. Throughout *Encounters with Silence*, one comes across passages which both stress the greatest possible union of God and man only to reject every concrete predicate in close kinship with Nicholas of Cusa. Thus, the author exults that '*Your* Life [has] become *my* life through grace',[38] while writing only a few lines later:

> Are there any titles which I needn't give You? And when I have listed them all, what have I said? If I should take my stand on the shore of Your Endlessness and shout into the trackless reaches of Your Being all the words I have ever learned in the poor prison of my little existence, what should I have said? I should never have spoken the last word about You.[39]

No name is adequate for God and we could not talk about him if we were not 'surrounded by Your distant Endlessness',[40] in which alone man may live. About God he says:

> You are all in all, and in everything that You are, You are all things. [. . .] All that is cramped and confined, oppressed and imprisoned in the narrowness of my finite being, becomes in You the one Infinity, which is both Unity and Infinity combined. Each of Your attributes is of itself Your whole immeasurable Being; each carries in its bosom the whole of reality.[41]

And a few lines later he adds:

> Your Infinity, O God, is thus the salvation of our finiteness. And yet I must confess that the longer I think about You, the more anxious I become. Your Awful Being threatens my security, makes me lose all sense of direction. I am filled with fear and trembling because it often seems to me that your Infinity, in which everything is really one and the same, is meant for You alone. [. . .]
> You must make Your infinite word finite, if I am to be spared this feeling of terror at Your Infinity.
> You must adapt Your word to my smallness, so that it can enter into the tiny dwelling of my finiteness – the only dwelling in which I can live – without destroying it. [. . .] If You should speak such an 'abbreviated' word, which would not say everything but only something simple which I could grasp, then I could breathe freely again.[42]

And this 'abbreviated word' refers to no other event than the incarnation as only the Logos become flesh makes God's infinite all-oneness both bearable and intelligible for man. This panentheistic notion of God can remain orthodox only if it is forced through the narrow confines of Christology, as it is in Rahner. It is against this backdrop that even man's own death, willingly accepted, can serve as a way to happiness or at least the first beginnings of a reconciliation with himself:

> Then will begin the great silence, in which no other sound will be heard but You, O Word resounding from eternity to eternity. Then all human words will have grown dumb. Being and knowing, understanding and experience will have become one and the same. [...]
> No more human words, no more concepts, no more pictures will stand between us.[43]

One could quote countless more passages to this effect from *Encounters with Silence*. Rahner's equally celebrated homilies *The Need and the Blessing of Prayer*, originally delivered in bomb-devastated Munich and thereafter printed in many editions from 1949 onwards, provide a sequel. Again, I shall restrict myself to a few significant passages. The very first page states: 'When man is with God in awe and love, then he is praying. Then he doesn't perform everything at once, because it will never be possible for him, the finite, to do that in in this life. But he is at least with him who is everything, and therefore he does something most important and necessary.'[44] Then, there are passages that are downright reminiscent of Spinoza as when he says in a passage entitled 'The Helper-Spirit':

> If we pray, then what we say and what we notice in our so-called I is only like the last echo, coming from an immeasurable distance, of the shouting in which God calls himself, of the exultation in which God himself is blissful about the splendour of his infinity, of the self-assertion with which the unconditional founds itself in itself from eternity to eternity. [...]
> [H]e hears the unspeakable groaning of his own Spirit who intercedes with God for his holy ones. He hears it as *our* groaning, as those sounds that come from the chaotic dissonances of our heart and life and form a hundred-voiced symphony to the praise of the Most High.[45]

And in his *Little Church Year*, another widely read text of 1954, he consoles a man who despairs of God and his faith in the emptiness of his heart:

> Which God is distant from you in this emptiness of your heart? It is not the true and living God, for he is no other than the incomprehensible and nameless One so that He can really be the God of your boundless heart. Only that God has become distant from you who does not exist: a comprehensible God [...], a very venerable – idol. [...] While all that is happening in your heart, do allow despair to apparently take everything away from you [...]. For if you hold on [...], then you will suddenly realize that your grave and prison only tries to withstand the empty finiteness, that its deadly emptiness is only the width of God's affection, that this silence is filled with a word without words, with the One who is above all names und who is all in all. This silence is His silence: He is telling you that He is there.[46]

If Rahner senses in man's despair God's vastness to which the latter need not find ways since God is already there; if he understands the experience of emptiness as an aspect of God's incomprehensible infinity that turns to man, even though this God may appear to his cramped heart to be nothing, because he is both present and everything; and if, finally, I also consider his concomitant explicit critique of idolatry, then I cannot but hear in Rahner's words the whisper of all those others from Lessing via Karl Leonhard Reinhold, William Warburton and Ralph Cudworth to Nicolas of Cusa and even Hermes Trismegistus whose thought is pervaded throughout by that current of mysterious thought encapsulated in the symbol of *hen kai pan*. It is only in passing, moreover, that I should like to point to the presence of this notion in his theology of the symbol and the sacraments, which must suffice here. It is Rahner's key thesis that the sacraments are not to be conceived of as only transient 'individual incursions of God into a secular world, but as "outbursts" (if we can express it in this way) of the innermost, ever present gracious endowment of the World with God himself into history'.[47] Tellingly, Rahner himself called this insight 'something like an application of a Copernican approach to the general conception of the sacraments',[48] which needs no further comment in this place.

Unsurprisingly, this panentheistic mode of thought is also present in the above-mentioned 'Speech of Ignatius of Loyola to a Modern-Day Jesuit',[49] first published in 1978 and called by Rahner himself a 'sum of my theology as a whole and the way I sought to live' or, later, even his 'spiritual testament'.[50] A passage entitled 'Immediate Experience of God'[51] says that Ignatius wanted to tell people something 'that was meant to redeem their freedom into God's freedom'[52] or into a God of 'modeless incomprehensibility'.[53] Rahner then goes on to present an impressive image of the relationship between subjective experience and the religious institution, which is closely connected with his view on the sacraments cited above. As regards the institutional character of the church, he makes use of the metaphor of 'irrigation systems'[54] conducting water to the heart's ground from without. In that, it is certainly significant for the heart's fertility. Besides that, however, 'there are, as it were, deep drillings in the land itself so that amidst that very land the water of the living spirit may spring from such a source, drilled open in this way, towards eternal life. [. . .] [T]he image is misleading. There is no ultimate opposition between one's own source and the 'irrigating system' from without'.[55] And while being beyond speech and comprehension, this God, in his 'modeless incomprehensibility', remains an addressable 'thou'[56] as he has already promised himself to us in the word

> in which the Father has pronounced himself in His fullness and which was in the beginning with God. And because this Word is spirit, it knows itself und it knows itself as the Word of the Father, hearing the Father's self-pronunciation which it is itself. And this Word which has heard everything from the Father has spoken itself into our heart.[57]

Again, the Christological criterion is at the fore with the leitmotifs of *Spirit in the World* and *Hearer of the Word* being clearly alluded to.

In his last speech before his death entitled *Experiences of a Catholic Theologian*,[58] Rahner emphasizes the principle of analogy which postulates the 'revocation of the affirmative conceptual contents of a positive statement',[59] reminding the reader of the fact 'that the theologian is a true theologian only as long as he does not purport to speak clearly and transparently, but is terrified by the analogical floating between "yes" and "no" above the abyss of God's incomprehensibility, experiencing it and bearing witness to it at the same time'.[60] The talk ends in a passage which can only be read or listened to in awe and which, in its own special fashion, outlines the way all creatures return to God and remain encompassed in him:

> When the angels of death have removed all the meaningless garbage which we call our history from the recesses of our spirit (even though the true essence of realized freedom will remain, of course); when all the stars of our ideals with which we had, in our pretension, adorned the heavens of our own existence, have burned up and lost their light; when death has set up an emptiness of terrible silence and when we have in faith and hope accepted this silence as our true being; when our earlier life, however long, seems to be but one little explosion of our freedom at that time, even though it struck us as being extended in slow motion, an explosion in which question turned into answer, possibility into reality, time into eternity and freedom offered to us into freedom realized; and when, amidst this utter terror of unspeakable joy, it turns out that this emptiness of terrible silence which we deem death is in reality filled with the primordial secret that we call God, with his pure light and with his all-taking and all-giving love; and when from this modeless secret the face of Christ, the holy one, emerges, glancing at us; and when this concreteness is the *divine surpassing* of all our true assumptions about the incomprehensibility of the modeless God, then, perhaps, I do not really describe what is coming, but stammer and hint at what one may expect that which is coming to be like, as one already experiences the end of death itself as the beginning of that which will come. 80 years is a long time. However, the lifetime meted out to everybody is that short moment in which that which is to be comes into being.[61]

It is passages like this that confirm Karl Lehmann's view that Rahner's quest for ever more sublime and more adequate ways of speaking of God, in its deep sense of transcendence, reveals a 'scepticism *vis-à-vis* the presently-given and presently-offered which wants to leave the last word to God himself'.[62]

(translated by Christian Hengstermann).

Response by Douglas Hedley

Klaus Müller's limpid discussion of Karl Rahner may seem anomalous in this volume. As he notes, the links between my project and von Balthasar would seem more obvious. Yet Rahner's idea in *Spirit in the World* is entitled 'The possibility of Metaphysics on the Basis of Imagination' and his idea of a *Vorgriff*, or 'pre-apprehension', is a vision of a *religious a priori* closely akin to the imagination trilogy. In *Hearer of the Word* Rahner, following in the footsteps of Blondel, develops this theme of a predisposition to revelation. Müller shows how Ignatian spirituality fed into the thought of Rahner and how his spiritual writings should not be divorced from his more theoretical compositions. There is a longing for the whence and wither of our existence that is ineluctably metaphysical. At the same time, Müller stresses that Rahner eschews any nominal or abstract transcendence. The exploration of subjectivity in Rahner's thought and the dialectic of God in humanity and man's life in God, the *hen kai pan* that links the tradition of Eckhart and Cusa through the Cambridge Platonists to German Idealism, and thereby to the transcendental approach. The extent of my 'panentheism' is an ambiguity in the project that Müller rightly highlights.

Notes

1. Karl Rahner, *Sämtliche Werke*, 32 vols, edited by Karl Lehmann et al. (Solothurn and Düsseldorf: Benziger; Freiburg, Basel and Vienna: Herder, 1995–2018). References will throughout be given to this authoritative edition (abbreviated SW). Whenever possible, existing English translations have been made use of. If no reference is given, the translation is by Christian Hengstermann.
2. Rahner, *Geist in Welt*, SW 2, 285–300. Translation: Rahner, *Spirit in the World*. Foreword by Johannes B. Metz. Translated. by William Dych, S.J. (New York: Continuum, 1994), 385–408.
3. Ibid., 299. Translation: ibid., 406. The sentence in square brackets is not by Rahner himself, but has been added by J. B. Metz in the second edition.
4. Douglas Hedley, *Living Forms of the Imagination* (London and New York: T&T Clark, 2008); *Sacrifice Imagined: Violence, Atonement, and the Sacred* (New York and London: Continuum, 2011); *The Iconic Imagination* (New York and London: Bloomsbury, 2016).
5. Hedley, *Living Forms* (see n. 4), 39.
6. Karl Lehmann, 'Karl Rahner, ein Portrait', in Rahner, SW 1, XII–LXVII, here XXIX.
7. Rahner, *E latere Christi. Der Ursprung der Kirche als zweiter Eva aus der Seite Christi des zweiten Adam. Eine Untersuchung über den typologischen Sinn von Joh 19,34*, in SW 3, 1–84.
8. Rahner, *Geist in Welt*, SW 2, 3–300.
9. Ibid., 14. Translation: Dych, *Spirit in the World*, lii (italics in the original).
10. Cf. Karl Lehmann, 'Philosophisches Denken im Werk Karl Rahners', in *Karl Rahner in Erinnerung*, edited by Albert Raffelt (Düsseldorf: Patmos-Verlag, 1994), 10–27, here 12–16.
11. Cf. Rahner, 'Gnade als Mitte menschlicher Existenz. Ein Gespräch mit und von Karl Rahner aus Anlaß seines 70. Geburtstages', *Herderkorrespondenz* (1974): 79.

12 Rahner, *Hörer des Wortes. Zur Grundlegung einer Religionsphilosophie*, in SW 4, 1–281. Translation: *Hearer of the Word. Laying the Foundation for a Philosophy of Religion.* Translation of the First Edition by Joseph Donceel. Edited with an Introduction by Andrew Tallon (New York: Continuum, 1994).
13 Maurice Blondel, *Oeuvres complètes*, 2 vols (Paris: Presses Universitaires de France, 1997), Vol. II: 1888–1913, 126–7.
14 For more details, see Klaus Müller, *Glauben - Fragen - Denken*, 3 vols., vol 3: *Selbstbeziehung und Gottesfrage* (Münster: Aschendorff Verlag, 2010), 482–6.
15 Hansjürgen Verweyen, 'Glaubensverantwortung heute. Zu den "Anfragen" von Thomas Pröpper', *Theologische Quartalschrift* 174 (1994): 288–303, here 289.
16 Rahner, 'Rede des Ignatius von Loyola an einen Jesuiten von heute', in SW 25, 299–329.
17 On the following, see *Hörer des Wortes*, I, chs 3 and 4 (SW 2, 48–88/Translation: Donceel, *Hearer of the Word*, 23–44).
18 Ibid., 48. Translation: ibid., 27.
19 Ibid., 52. Translation: ibid., 29–30.
20 *Geist in Welt*, SW 2, 62. Translation: Dych, *Spirit in the World*, 69.
21 *Hörer des Wortes*, SW 4, 76–7. Translation: Donceel, *Hearer of the Word*, 47 (slightly modified).
22 Ibid., 83. Translation: ibid, 50.
23 Ibid., 86. Translation: ibid, 54.
24 Chapter 3 (ibid., 50–70/Translation: ibid., 23–34) is entitled 'The Luminosity of Being'.
25 Ibid., 86.
26 Cf. ibid., 88–92. Translation: ibid., 45–7.
27 Ibid., 108. Translation: ibid., 68.
28 Ibid., 114. Translation: ibid., 72–3.
29 Ibid., 136. Translation: ibid., 88.
30 Ibid., 194. Translation: ibid., 106–7.
31 Ibid., 209. Translation: ibid., 142.
32 Cf., for example, Rüdiger Bubner, 'Wie wichtig ist Subjektivität? Über einige Selbstverständlichkeiten und mögliche Mißverständnisse der Gegenwart', *Merkur* 49 (1995): 235–46.
33 'Über die Einheit von Nächsten- und Gottesliebe', in *Schriften zur Theologie* 6/2 (Einsiedeln, Zurich and Cologne: Benziger, 1968), 277–8, here 279 (= SW 12, 76–91, here 77–8). Translation: 'Reflections on the Unity of the Love of Neighbour and the Love of God', in id., *Theological Investigations* 6, translated by Karl-H. and Boniface Kruger (London: Darton, Longman and Todd, 1969), 231–49, here 233 (slightly modified).
34 Rahner, 'Immanente und transzendente Vollendung der Welt', in *Schriften zur Theologie* 8 (Einsiedeln, Zurich and Cologne: Benziger, 1967), 593–609, 601 (= SW 15, 544–556, 550). Translation: Rahner, 'Immanent and Transcendent Consummation of the World', in id., *Theological Investigations* 10, translated by David Bourke (London: Darton, Longman and Todd, 1973), 273–89, here 281.
35 'Innenleben', in SW 1, 351–2, here 351.
36 On that, see Andreas R. Battlog, 'Editionsbericht', in SW 7, IX–XLIV, here XVIII.
37 Hans Urs von Balthasar, Rev. *Geist in Welt*, *Zeitschrift für katholische Theologie* 63 (1939): 371–9, here 378.
38 Rahner, *Worte ins Schweigen*, in: SW 1, 3–38, 4. Translation: *Encounters with Silence*. Translated by James M. Demske, S. J. (South Bend: St. Augustine's Press, 1960), 4.
39 Ibid. Translation: ibid.

40 Ibid., 5. Translation: ibid., 6.
41 Ibid., 8. Translation: ibid., 13.
42 Ibid., 9. Translation: ibid., 14–16.
43 Ibid., 26. Translation: ibid., 32–3.
44 *Von der Not und dem Segen des Gebetes*, in SW 1, 39–116, here 40. Translation: Karl Rahner, *The Need and the Blessing of Prayer*. A Revised Edition of *On Prayer*, translated by Bruce W. Gillette, introduction by Harvey D. Egan (Collegeville: The Liturgical Press), 1.
45 Ibid., 56–7. Translation: ibid., 22–3.
46 Ibid., 148–9.
47 'Zur Theologie des Gottesdienstes', in *Schriften zur Theologie* 14 (Zurich, Einsiedeln and Cologne: Benziger, 1980), 227–37, here 230 (= SW 29, 391–398, here 393). Translation: Rahner, 'On the Theology of Worship', in id., *Theological Investigations* 19, translated by Edward Quinn (London: Darton, Longman and Todd, 1984), 141–9, here 143. On that, cf. also 'Zum Verständnis des Weihnachtsfestes', in *Schriften zur Theologie* 16 (Zurich, Einsiedeln and Cologne: Benziger, 1984), 336–47, here 340–1 (= SW 29, 169–77, here 172). Translation: 'Understanding Christmas', in ibid., 140–8, here 143–4.
48 He did so first in: 'Überlegungen zum personalen Vollzug des sakramentalen Geschehens', in *Schriften zur Theologie* 16, (Zurich, Einsiedeln and Cologne: Benziger, 1972) (= SW 18, 458– 476, 458). Translation: Rahner, 'Considerations on the Active Role of the Person in the Sacramental Event', in id., *Theological Investigations* 14, translated by David Bourke (London: Darton, Longman and Todd, 1976), 161–78, 161.
49 Rahner, 'Rede des Ignatius von Loyola' (see n. 16).
50 See the references in: Battlog, 'Editionsbericht', XLI–XLII.
51 Rahner, 'Rede des Ignatius von Loyola' (see n. 16), 299.
52 Ibid.
53 Ibid., 301. Cf. also ibid., 302.
54 Ibid., 304.
55 Ibid., 303.
56 cf. ibid., 308.
57 Rahner, 'Freunde Gottes. Homilie zu Joh 15, 12–16', in SW 4, 294–5, 294.
58 Rahner, 'Erfahrungen eines katholischen Theologen', in SW 25, 47–57.
59 Ibid., 49.
60 Ibid.
61 Ibid., 57.
62 Lehmann, 'Karl Rahner' (see n. 6), XXXIX.

7

René Girard and Douglas Hedley on violence, sacrifice and imagination

Per Bjørnar Grande

According to René Girard, the main problem among humans is violence. If people could solve the problem of violence, most other problems would also be solved. Mimetic theory localizes the problem in rivalistic desires. Every time imitation turns into severe rivalry between human beings, violence, either physical or psychological, seems to get the upper hand. Before long the rivals will have forgotten what they were rivalling about. They have become doubles, preoccupied mostly with subverting the other. This is the human dilemma which seems absolutely insoluble – despite an ever-increasing focus on the devastating effects of violence.

1 Sacrifice

Sacrifice is the main outcome of man's desire to imitate each other. In the mimetic delirium which arises when a society is afflicted or in crisis, a frenetic activity arises whereby someone has to be found who is responsible for this terrible situation, someone who, by being sacrificed, can restore peace. In other words, sacrifice has to come about in order to prevent a disintegrating society from dissolving into violence.

In the Prologue of *Sacrifice Imagined*, Hedley writes that 'this book does not try to answer the problem of evil, but endeavors to explore some aspects of the inherited topics of suffering, violence, and atonement as sacrifice imagined'.[1] Despite that sacrifice is not Hedley's main endeavour throughout his three books. It is, especially in his second book of the trilogy, a main focus. Thus, I will try to see if *Sacrifice Imagined* may give us a fruitful insight into the violence which threatens every community and modern civilization as such.

Essential concepts in Hedley's trilogy are 'imagination', 'image' and 'sacrifice'. Hedley is eager to use and connect the same primary concepts from *Living Forms of Imagination* (2008) in his two latter books. Sacrifice, for Hedley, is both real and a part of our cultural imagination. The latter means that sacrifice has a capacity for analogy.[2] Even though the reader might feel uncertain about how to understand *imagination* in sacrifice, the discussion on sacrifice as a life-giving phenomenon of existence, gradually, through *Sacrifice Imagined*, becomes more essential and important in order to understand both religion and culture in general.

In *Sacrifice Imagined*, sacrifice is seen as something positive, especially in theological terms and especially when it is connected to atonement. Sacrifice is the core of existence. Either its meaning is violent or it means sacrificing oneself for the benefit of others. A sacrificial understanding of life enables us to delve into the deepest and most profound areas of existence, something which a purely rationalist view on life can neither fathom nor uncover. In *Sacrifice Imagined*, Hedley delves into Greek tragedy, trying to give tragedy and myth a more positive significance than, especially, what is the case in Girard's early interpretation of sacrifice – even seeing sacrifice and conversion as things dependent upon one another. However, there are only minor differences between the late Girard's and Hedley's understandings of sacrifice. Both would wholeheartedly agree with Simone Weil that the false God changes suffering into violence while the true God changes violence into suffering.[3]

Hedley's view that man cannot avoid partaking in the sacrificial is in accordance with Girard – although Girard first and foremost sees sacrifice in the light of violence. Hedley expands the discussion on sacrifice in order to understand both its theological meaning and its contemporary impact on culture. Thus, sacrifice is located both in the modern and in the secular, as well as in shaping history. Hedley seems to expand the territory of sacrifice in order to come to grips with its nature in its totality, that is, both with its negative and positive effects. Sacrifice, in *Sacrifice Imagined* is, at the end of the day, basically seen as something positive and renewing, despite all its violent connotations.

From a historical point of view, one can see that sacrifice was able to protect a group from dissolving. However, sacrifice also contains lynching and bullying, the most despicable acts of modern culture. There is a direct link between cult sacrifice and lynching, making it impossible to understand the word and phenomenon as only regenerating. Hedley's understanding of sacrifice somewhat lacks an ethical overview. The aesthetical gets prominence and seems to lead to a veneration of sacrifice, despite its violence. A Neoplatonic view on culture can, because it contains an anti-mimetic understanding of order, lead to a certain blindness to the violence and chaos in a society, from where there actually is no refuge. If one omits imitation for the sake of a world of ideas, it becomes easier to see sacrifice in society as only positive.

However, the truest and most advanced form of sacrifice is a non-violent response to violence, an act created by a loving and forgiving God. From such a viewpoint, Hedley is right in criticizing Otto for laying too much emphasis on *tremendum* and too little on *fascinans*.[4]

If sacrifice is seen as atonement, it is easier to see its positive function. Hedley's understanding of atonement emphasizes the logical and loveable. With the help of the analytic philosopher Richard Swinburne, Hedley convincingly argues that man's repentance and apology are insufficient 'tools' for atonement, and that 'reparation and repentance can only be offered by man through Christ'.[5] In certain passages of *Sacrifice Imagined*, Hedley turns out to be a Christian Platonist with a rather sombre view of man. It seems that it is partly through the influence of Joseph de Maistre, himself a Christian Platonist, that Hedley attempts to give a profound and unsentimental understanding of the human condition as deeply imbued by original sin. However, I find this less emphasized in *The Iconic Imagination*. In his last book, Hedley understands images somewhat in the sense you find in Platonic and Jungian archetypes. They point to a transcendent reality: the good, the true and the beautiful. Hedley seems to withdraw from the discussion on violence and imagination is seen as caused within a more sheltered realm of ideas. Thus, seen against a background of a community's chaos and conflicts, the Neoplatonic world of ideas seems to me to be a shaky starting point.

2 Hominization

Hedley emphasizes the imaginative as something unique to man. However, this uniqueness, compared to animals, is rather in degree than in kind. The great leap forward is due to the symbolic and imagination. Becoming human means a shift from the biological to the symbolic. It is by imagination that man gradually becomes the dominant species. Despite such a culturally dominated theory, Hedley's anthropology is seen against a Darwinian backdrop: 'We are forged of the same stuff as all other creatures and, as such, share the similitude of the created order with the author of all things.'[6] However, Hedley wishes to counter any Darwinian objections to there being any link between image and imagination. From my reading of *Sacrifice Imagined*, I find it curious that in his later attempts to make sense of the doctrine of the *imago Dei* sacrifice is not considered the fundamental factor. Probably, due to an expansive view of *imago Dei*, Hedley views all life as a part of God's image.

While Girard sees evolution as related to heightened imitation, imagination, in Hedley's work, replaces the mimetic, changing desire into something more orderly and harmonious. In *Sacrifice Imagined*, Hedley emphasizes original sin but does not see it as stemming from rivalry, which makes it less impossible to view human action as idea-directed. While in Hedley's case the shift from animal to human is caused by the growth of the brain (and this makes it possible to create a symbolic world), Girard emphasizes imitation and scapegoating as decisive for hominization and culture-building. Hedley doubts that Girard's theory, however illuminating, provides a universal mechanism for the understanding of the move from hominids to humanity.[7] However, both emphasize the symbolic among early hominids, but Girard's narrative, which initially is in tune with a Darwinian evolution, changes dramatically after the introduction of the scapegoat, after which time the survival of the fittest becomes indirect and symbolic. The scapegoat changes the whole scene, from instinctual killings to survival through sacrifice, and, gradually, through the veneration of the victim. Thus, at a certain time in history the victim becomes the source cementing a group and thereby becomes the saving element in order to preserve the group. In this way, evolution seems to shift from the biological to the cultural. It is after such a time in history that one can talk about the strength of the weakest link. Religion expresses this birth of culture. In order to prevent a community from being destroyed in violence, one establishes a surrogate victim capable of creating peace. In this way religion upholds society. And because the victim is capable of bringing peace, he/she/they is/are often divinized. Sacrificial religion is therefore a force capable of bringing order to a society, an order which is peace-oriented, yet requires violence. In this respect, the community does not worship the killing, but the peace which is a consequence of the killing. One might say that Girard defines religion as the attempt to prevent violence with the help of the surrogate victim.

In 'Mimetic Paradox and the event of Human Origin', Eric Gans seems to indicate a theory in which Girard's original scapegoat scene is mingled with imagination. Gans's theory is initially Girardian as he claims that any kind of origin is connected with mimesis. He sees the intensification of mimesis as a developing and evolutionary force in both animalistic and prehuman life, which, at a certain time in history, sparks off culture and humanizing projects.[8] But Gans seems to part ways with Girard when claiming that language and culture began with the deferral of violence.[9] There is some sort of (probably awkward) gesture which arises, and, in a way, points to a less violent development. While Girard argues that culture has its origin in the actual violence of spontaneous scapegoating, Gans claims that culture started with a deferral of the same violence. The view that culture arises from an existence mired in violence and from some sort of alternative gesture that is different from reciprocal violence seems to support Hedley's thesis of imagination. Blunt, primitive violence suddenly is met by a response which is not reciprocal and produces a different outcome, and, at some later stage in history, regulates culture through the scapegoat mechanism.

3 Myth

If one considers myth in relation to hominization, Hedley sees it as something specifically human which enriches culture in all its diversity. Symbolic violence seems to moderate and change sacrifice into less violent representations. Myth, which also stems from violence, clearly enriches a culture with imagination. Hedley sees myth as a cultural process of transfiguring history, in which all the myths in the world express a sense of participation in the sacred.[10] Girard, on the other hand, with his more critical understanding of myth, claims that all myths originate in collective violence.[11] 'All myths . . . have their roots in real acts of violence against real victims.'[12] According to Girard, myths try, in different ways, to hide violence, often by transforming this same violence. The last thing a writer of myths will admit to is the guilt and wrongdoing of the community's violence. Myths are written from the community's point of view, meaning the sacrificers' point of view. In this respect myths have a legitimizing effect on society. But usually the immolation is transformed into something fantastic and heroic. The victim is very often divinized, which indicates that the community cannot bear its own violence. Myths try to cover up violence. But, at the same time, myths can, when interpreted rationally and from an anti-sacrificial and de-mythologized point of view, be read as texts of victimizing. Myths, in a hidden way, usually refer to some sort of violent origin. It is on the basis of such a suspicious reading that Girard uses mythical texts to uncover hidden layers of meaning. By uncovering the violence in mythical texts, Girard discovers the hiding and editing process in the making of myths. In this way myths can be seen as an attempt to hide reality. Myths both displace and refer to violence in a society. According to Girard, violence is the force which displaces and mythologizes reality. Seen from this perspective, violence is the birth of culture, since expulsion creates difference and division, an inside and an outside, an *us and them*, a society.

This view of myth as both revealing and concealing is solely worked out in order to understand the violent formation of culture. Hedley thus avoids such a reductive view by insisting on imagination, both in myths and in rituals, thereby providing a much broader understanding of how they function. As myths stem from imagination and imagination shapes history, myths are therefore part of a great cultural enhancement. Hedley's inclusive understanding of myth is radically different from Girard's. Girard sees the passion, the killing of God, as revealing the violence of humankind as such, and by doing this demythologizes culture:

> The Spirit is working in history to reveal what Jesus already has revealed, the mechanism of the scapegoat, the genesis of all mythology, the nonexistence of all gods of violence. (. . .) The Paraclete is the universal advocate, the chief defender of all innocent victims, the destroyer of every representation of persecution. He is truly the spirit of truth that dissipates the fog of mythology.[13]

Girard's extreme deconstruction of myth in order to discover true Christianity is very different from Hedley's all-inclusiveness in nature and scope. Girard's anthropology builds on the premises that we want what other people want. Our desires are always caught up in someone else's desires. A culture's rationality and truth are therefore a part of this basis of human interaction, mingled by our desires and therefore far from obvious. Hedley, on the other hand, basically seems to trust different cultural positions worldwide, even though the greatest obstacle against such broadmindedness seems to be history itself.

4 Logos

Imagination is both the central word and theme in Hedley's trilogy. By emphasizing images and imagination, there is an inherent critique of modern 'logocentrism' where not only the spoken word but also the written word reduces the richness of imagination.[14] Hedley's understanding of truth seems to convey that art in its Platonic manifestations is transcendent. His concept of truth is expansive and goes beyond any dogmatic or confessional ramifications. Everything true, good and beautiful points to God. This seems to be in accordance with St Paul, but the thinking around it is less ethical, as in St Paul's case, and more intellectual and aesthetic. Because of his broadminded theology, Hedley wishes to combine (if not unify) the Greek Logos with its Christian counterpart. The emphasis lies both on the Greek *paideia* and rationality and on the Christian understanding of *agapé* – which shows that violence and expulsion is not regarded as the prime problem either in the concept of the Logos or in culture as such. Hedley sees Athens and Jerusalem as more or less organically interconnected. Their worldviews are different, but there is no fundamental ontological difference.[15]

Girard sees both the modern (such as in the case of Heidegger) and the pre-Socratic understanding of the Logos as fundamentally violent, while the Johannine understanding emphasizes the expulsion of the Logos, the violent manner in which Jesus was treated. The Johannine understanding of Christ as the Logos, despite borrowing the concept from Greek philosophy, marks a break with the Greek meaning of the word.[16] Hedley stands in between Girard's emphasis on the non-violent Christian Logos and the violent Logos of Heidegger. The latter, clearly inspired by Nietzsche and Hegel, saw both the Greek and the Christian Logos as violent. The difference, according to Heidegger, therefore, is not manifested as a totally different approach to violence. Heidegger differentiates the Greek and Johannine Logos in a slave-master context where the Greek Logos is conceived by free men and the Johannine Logos is violence visited upon slaves. Girard's attempt to differentiate the two concepts of Logos is partly an attempt to reveal the difference between a sacrificial and a non-sacrificial world view.[17] With hindsight, one might call this fundamental difference a mimetic struggle between a Greek and a Christian world view. The Christian Logos, as the Gospel of John describes it, is perceived through expulsion. The divine Logos was not received by his own: '*He came to his own and his own people received him not*' (Jn. 1.10-11). The Greek Logos, on the other hand, initiates expulsion by its violence. Different approaches to the Logos will necessarily, according to James Williams, bring about a very different attitude when dealing with victims.[18] Clearly, Girard sees the life of Jesus and the Johannine Logos as one and the same.[19] Both were expelled, both represented God and both incarnated love. The Greek Logos, on the other hand, expels the victim.

5 Imagination

Can imagination be the fundamental factor in order to assume a predominant role in civilization or even the factor which shapes history? Despite a wealth of references in Hedley's trilogy, there is a challenge and difficulty in coming to terms with how to understand 'imagination'. Initially, it stands for the opposite of fantasy. It builds on inherited imagery and, instead of ritual slaughter, refers to participation in life.[20] Imagination is not a specific faculty or a module in the brain, but an activity of the mind.[21] In *Living Forms of Imagination*, imagination, according to Hedley/Collingwood, generates knowledge and helps children to function. It unifies experience into a set of stable objects. It evinces freedom beyond sensation, and it converts sensations into ideas.[22] Both image and imagination point to something transcendent. It consists of the good, the true and the beautiful. Its truth is expansive and points beyond any dogmatic or confessional ramifications. Imagination is seen as something intuitive, the *fascinans* which re-enchants the world. Thus, the imagination is not something which one can label as correct or false, it can be seen more as a vision. It points to God.

Not only does imagination originate in God, but art is also seen as transcendent. Against the backdrop of a Platonic ideal of order and harmony, art is seen as something which enables us to grasp the essential.[23] Seeing this in the light of art experiences in the twentieth century and onwards, transcendence not only consists in works of art but also in the artist whose imaginative temperaments and intuitive insights reveal some sort of divine truth.

The experience of art somewhat replaces Christianity, and, both in art and political life, transforms men into gods.[24] When Christianity is no longer seen as the torchbearer of truth among the majority, varied forms of Gnosticism replace the classic ideals of humility, ideals such as love for one's neighbour and concern for victims. The modern artist, romantic in his artistic role, bohemian in lifestyle, dogmatic in his relativism, deeply individualistic, where love of one's neighbour is replaced by the ongoing intensity of metaphysical rivalry, can be seen as a new kind of prophet. In lack of religion, the world of art creates new ideals and idols, which often consist in self-centredness, pride and lack of concern for others. From such a viewpoint, I see no reason to replace religious belief with a belief in art. It will only, in the long run, degrade one's personality. Neither art as such, nor Platonic ideas, I think, are really able to grasp the essence of the confused minds of people in the twenty-first century. Religion, in certain instances, is.

Theology today needs to be related more closely to anthropology. The Kingdom of God and the Christian emphasis on compassion need, by its imitative and non-metaphysical nature, to be located right in the centre of people's daily challenges. Today's anti-mimetic approach, in order to understand both the mind and the artistic expressions, has made Platonism, outside the universities, a limited tool for making sense of modern life. The modern intellectual climate does not favour the world of ideas. A shift towards thought based on imitation, desire and a stronger commitment to historical references should affect clear-sighted Platonists, who, otherwise, may risk ending up in chains, in the same cave designed for others, staring into a fake world.

According to Hedley, Girard's inspiration is not biology but imaginative literature.[25] In this way Hedley and Girard draw on many of the same sources. However, Girard mostly draws on novels from realism, and is critical of literature he sees as being built on 'the Romantic lie'.[26] People wish to live with the illusion of spontaneous desire and believe that they do. It is this illusion concerning one's autonomy which, according to Girard, some novelists have, with great difficulty, been able to reveal. The difference between the romantic novelist and the romanesque or realist novelist is based upon their different approaches to the mediator.[27] The romantic writer will show and propagate the model or mediator's presence, often as a rival. But he will not reveal the mediator's role in mediating his own desire. The romantic writer believes in the autonomy of the characters, and, according to Girard, is himself governed by a desire for autonomy. The romantic lie consists in seeing desire as spontaneous and linear. The realist novelist both presents and reveals the role of the mediator. The mediator is revealed as the decisive factor in the protagonist's desire. The realist novelist is, according to Girard, the most trustworthy explorer of desire, a desire which Girard labels 'desire according to the other'. And by admitting the influence of the Other, one can, through a personal conversion (closely related to apocalypse), attain religious truth.

6 Conclusion

Hedley's trilogy establishes a Christian theism. It is broadminded and it is learned, and its emphasis on imagination is, loosely speaking, an attempt to build a coherent theory of imagination as the main source of our understanding of human nature, culture and religion. Hedley does an excellent job in showing the similarities of myths in different cultures. Since he views human nature as tainted by original sin, Hedley's romanticism is balanced. It consists in praising the beautiful and the uplifting, and it does not act as a tool for any kind of self-glorification. For Hedley all religions seem to be good in the way that they help people to live a life of imagination. Girard begins by locating the prime motivation in imitation, and, gradually, comes to see that Christianity turns myth and sacrifice around by purging them from violence. Art, for Girard, can, in certain instances, reveal the structure of a Christian conversion, but in most cases art is caught up in fake desires. Hedley gives art a certain priority as it mediates the transcendent. My own hesitancy and refusal to see art and artists as conveying the transcendent can, admittedly, be seen as puritan, but it also saves us from turning art and artists into new 'gods'.

From my point of view, Christian theology becomes most useful when it starts with Christology. By that I mean that any notion of God in Christianity starts with reflections on the stories about Jesus. Natural theology originates in our subconscious: our fear and dreams. The subconscious is, in sum, our encounters with others. In this way, when trying to think one's way to God, all our violent experiences play along in the process. It is therefore understandable that most people and most cultures believe in a legalistic and violent god.

Hedley does a marvellous job in revealing the relevance of Platonism in today's theological thinking. Imagination is shown to be something life-giving and capable of reinvigorating our cultural life. However, would not Hedley's argument have been even stronger if Occam's razor had cut deeper into human misery and religious intolerance, and his argument had thus been given greater urgency?

Response by Douglas Hedley

Per Bjørnar Grande reflects upon the significance of the work of René Girard for my *Sacrifice Imagined*. He also considers the possible ramifications that Girard's work might have for other works in the trilogy. The profound achievement of Girard as a seminal thinker needs little emphasis and his interest in anthropology and science as well as literature is exemplary and instructive. Girard addresses the intellectual giants of the nineteenth century with great vigour and develops a remarkable, powerful and unique vision of the origins of human culture. Grande notes that I do not follow Girard's notion of mimetic rivalry, even if I do (unremarkably) accept the general significance of mimesis. Nor do I see mimetic rivalry as the ground of original sin and I do not accept the idea of religion as the bid to hinder savagery through the instrument of the proxy victim, with the stability of society relying upon the scapegoat mechanism and subsequent veneration of the victim.

Grande notes that for Girard sacrifice is essentially negative. Sacrifice has 'to prevent a disintegrating society from dissolving into violence'. My stress upon the symbolism of sacrifice is related to the polyvalence the symbol. Sacrifice can refer to bloody sacrifices such as egregious barbaric practices of human sacrifice, yet it can also refer to delayed gratification, the rather humdrum 'sacrifices' of self that are part of the rational agent.

Grande is correct to note that I have a different model of the mythical. I agree that myths are often violent, sometimes dire: the Titan Cronos castrating his father Uranus with a sickle or Agamemnon executing his daughter Iphigenia are evident instances of brutality. The mythic location of the great vision of Krishna to Arjuna in the *Bhagavad Gita* before the confrontation of the Pandavas and the Kauravas is on the battlefield. Yet I cannot accept Girard's diagnosis of myth as both a concealing of violence and a form of societal justification. In a sense, much hangs upon the conception of violence. Violence is a fact of the natural world, whether in the behaviour of carnivores or the establishment of hierarchies or the securing of a mate against competition. Much play among mammals or sport among humans is a sublimated form of violence. Much that is valuable in cultures is inspired and driven by aggressive instincts. The question is usually to whom is the act violent and why. The eating of meat is an unacceptable form of violence for the vegetarian or the Hindu; the engaging in war for the pacifist; euthanasia for its opponents.

My fundamental disagreement with Girard is over the logos.[28] Here Girard exhibits his deep debts to Nietzsche and Heidegger when he claims that 'Heidegger recognises that the Greek Logos is inseparably linked with violence'.[29] My own work is a return to the logos of the Alexandrians.[30] The blood-stained logos of Origen is still the expression of the mind of God.

Notes

1 Douglas Hedley, *Sacrifice Imagined, Violence, Atonement, and the Sacred* (New York and London: Continuum, 2011), 6.
2 Ibid., 38.

3   Ibid., 171.
4   Ibid., 36.
5   Ibid., 165.
6   Hedley, *The Iconic Imagination* (New York et al.: Bloomsbury Academic, 2016), 35.
7   Cf. ibid., 87.
8   Eric Gans, 'Mimetic Paradox and the Event of Human Origin', *Antropoetics* I/2 (1995) (no page numbers given).
9   Eric Gans, 'The Unique Source of Religion and Morality', *Contagion* 3 (1996): 51–65, here 52.
10 Hedley, *Iconic Imagination* (see n. 6), 206.
11 For a systematic overview of Girard's understanding of myth, see chapter 3 ('What is a Myth?') in *The Scapegoat*, translated by Yvonne Freccero (Baltimore: Johns Hopkins University Press, 1986), 24–44, and chapter 5 ('Mythology') in *I See Satan Fall Like Lightning*, Maryknoll, translated by James G. Williams (New York: Orbis Books, 2001), 62–70.
12 Girard, *Scapegoat* (see n. 11), 25.
13 Ibid., 207.
14 Hedley, *Iconic Imagination* (see n. 6), 4–6.
15 Hedley, *Sacrifice Imagined* (see n. 1), 57–60 and 137–60.
16 See Girard, *Things Hidden since the Foundation of the World*, translated by Stephen Bann and Michael Metteer (London: Athlone Press, 1987), 263–80.
17 Ibid.
18 See James Williams, 'Foreword', in Girard, *Satan* (see n. 11), ix–xxiv.
19 Girard, *Things Hidden* (see n. 16), 270–6.
20 Hedley, *Sacrifice Imagined* (see n. 1), 11.
21 Hedley, *Iconic Imagination* (see n. 6), xii.
22 Hedley, *Living Forms of the Imagination* (London and New York: Continuum, 2008), 42–8. Robin G. Collingwood, *The Principles of Art* (London: Clarendon Press, 1938), 197, 215.
23 See Hedley, *Iconic Imagination* (see n. 6), 82–6.
24 Klaus Heller and Jan Plamper (eds), *Personality Cults in Stalinism* (Göttingen: V&R Unipress, 2004), 19.
25 Hedley, *Sacrifice Imagined* (see n. 1), 84.
26 Girard, *Deceit, Desire and the Novel: Self and Other in Literary Structure*, translated by Yvonne Freccero (Baltimore: The John Hopkins Press, 1965).
27 The difference between romantic and realist literature is not a difference according to epoch. The difference is based on an approach to desire. There is, however, in Girard's work, a preference for novels written in the realist tradition.
28 René Girard, 'The Logos of Heraclitus and the Logos of John', in *Things Hidden since the Foundation of the World,* translated by Stephen Bann and Michael Metteer (London: Athlone Press, 1987), 263–80.
29 Ibid., 265.
30 Hedley, *Sacrifice Imagined*, 137.

8

Perceptions of God

Reflections on William P. Alston's theory of religious experience

Margit Wasmaier-Sailer

1 Functionalizing religious experience for the justification of faith

Contemporary and 20th century philosophical treatments of religious experience are greatly influenced by William James's *The Varieties of Religious Experience* (1902). James (1842–1910) treated religious experience in observational terms, documenting cases in which individuals report an encounter with an unseen supernatural or spiritual reality. While James treated these experiences as ostensible cognitive apprehensions with evidential significance, his conclusions about the nature of this 'spiritual reality' remained unsettled in his published work. Fluctuating between personal theism (in which God is encountered as a person) and what he called *pluralistic pantheism* (in which God turns out to be a 'higher self'), James seemed more convinced of a negative thesis: religious experiences provide some reason to believe there is more to reality than is disclosed in contemporary, scientific naturalism. Subsequent philosophical, and to some extent psychological inquiry has often taken shape in either denying James's conclusion and demonstrating that naturalism can fully account for religious experience, or in a defence of the cognitive value of such ostensible experiences that can, in principle, vindicate a non-naturalist, religious world view.[1]

The *Oxford Companion to Consciousness* very accurately describes the poles between which contemporary theories of religious experience oscillate with these theories deriving their contours from the tension between naturalism and theism. While naturalistic theories reduce religious experiences to psychological, sociological or physiological factors,[2] theistic theories argue that such experiences actually point to a divine reality. Opposition to naturalism is indeed what unites the various theories in the theistic camp. Whether God is understood as a person according to classical theism, whether as nature according to pantheism or whether as an all-oneness according to a panentheism seems to be of secondary importance. Even William James focused on the phenomenology of religious experience and not on the metaphysical question of the nature of the God encountered in these experiences. James was content with asserting a 'wider world of meanings'.[3] The struggle with naturalism that can already be seen in James's theory is all the stronger in the theories that succeeded it. This is particularly true, though, when it comes to the theories of religious experience that emerged in analytical philosophy of religion in the second half of the twentieth century: naturalism seems to be not only its opponent but almost its only interlocutor. This fixation on naturalism has led representatives of the analytical philosophy of religion to fall under the spell of scientific patterns of thought, despite their clear opposition to naturalism. If everything points to the fact that religious experience is in no way inferior to its sensory counterpart in terms of cognitive content, then sensory experience has long been implicitly recognized as a yardstick of experience.[4]

Through this struggle for recognition, analytical philosophy of religion has forgotten to regard religious experiences in terms of their own internal dynamics. It seems to be interested in experiences of God only insofar as they serve to justify religious beliefs. What such justification addresses is the scientific world and perhaps also the scientific *alter ego* of the philosopher of religion. However, if experiences of God are no longer considered for their own sake, then what is lost sight of is actually the very thing that distinguishes these experiences. Thus, the *proprium* of religious experience is often not even recognizable any longer in the theories under discussion. Douglas Hedley's theory of religious imagination is a promising attempt to get the nature of religious experience back on track. The confrontation with naturalism is always present in his writings, too, but his roots in the Platonic tradition allow him nonetheless to put up some opposition to naturalism.

I want to strengthen my thesis – that analytical philosophy of religion loses the very phenomenon that it is trying to protect with such epistemological vigour – through the example of William P. Alston's theory of religious experience. His approach shows particularly well how the object itself that is in question visibly evaporates through the epistemic safeguarding of religious experience and its functionalization for justifications of faith. I do not wish to diminish Alston's merit in epistemology here. Rather, I would merely like to draw attention to the fact that religious experience in the context of a philosophy of religion that focuses one-sidedly on justifying faith is in danger of being reduced to the status of a mere substitute.[5] This requires that we first outline Alston's theory of mystical experience and then determine the process of evaporation according to three points in order finally to put forward Hedley's theory as a possible alternative.

2 An outline of William P. Alston's theory of religious experience

In *Perceiving God: The Epistemology of Religious Experience*,[6] Alston presents an argumentatively adept epistemological theory of religious experience. That this epistemological theory is dedicated to the justification of religious belief is unmistakable from the very first line:

> The central thesis of this book is that experiential awareness of God, or as I shall be saying, the *perception* of God, makes an important contribution to the grounds of religious belief. More specifically, a person can become justified in holding certain kinds of beliefs about God by virtue of perceiving God as being or doing so-and-so. The kinds of beliefs that can be so justified I shall call 'M-beliefs' ('M' for *manifestation*). M-beliefs are beliefs to the effect that God is doing something currently vis-à-vis the subject – comforting, strengthening, guiding, communicating a message, sustaining the subject in being – or to the effect that God has some (allegedly) perceivable property – goodness, power, lovingness. The intuitive idea is that by virtue of my being aware of God as sustaining me in being I can justifiably believe that God *is* sustaining me in being.[7]

Alston is here concerned with the epistemological status of personal experiences of God: he argues for the recognition of such experiences as a genuine source of religious beliefs. For Alston, if someone becomes aware of the presence of God, then that person has every reason to believe that God actually is present. Behind this epistemological thesis is the defence against sceptical objections to the reality content of religious beliefs. For Alston, the presumption of innocence must apply to beliefs that the believer obtains from his or her personal experiences of God. The burden of proof, therefore, lies not with the person who has a religious experience, but, instead, with the person who denies the reality of this experience.

Drawing on the reports that many mystics provide of their experiences, Alston reconstructs religious experiences as perceptions of God. Alston deliberately focuses on a particular type of such experiences: he is concerned with experiences that he describes as direct perceptions. For Alston, direct perceptions of God are to be distinguished from mystical experiences of oneness on the one hand and from indirect perceptions of God on the other. While in experiences of oneness, Alston argues, a person's own state of awareness can no longer be distinguished from the awareness of God's presence, in direct perceptions of God the subject is still aware of his or her own state of awareness. In the first case, God reveals himself to the subject directly, whereas in the second case, he reveals himself to the subject by means of the subject's state of awareness. On the other hand, Alston urges us to distinguish between direct and indirect perceptions: while God presents himself exclusively by means of a person's own state of awareness in the former, he presents himself by means of an object of perception in the latter. For Alston, an indirect perception is when a person experiences God in the beauties of nature, when a person hears God's voice in the words of the Bible, in sermons or in the demands of his or her own conscience, when a person becomes aware of the providence of God in the events of his or her own life or when a person perceives God's activity in the history of salvation.[8]

Alston's focus on experiences in which the subject becomes aware of God's presence in a direct manner already signals the operation of empiricist criteria in Alston's theory. These experiences can in fact be best described according to the model of sensory perceptions and sensory perception is, as we know, the measure of all knowledge in empiricism:

> I will suggest and defend a 'perceptual model' for the experiences under consideration. That is, I shall argue that if we think of perception in the most general way, in which it is paradigmatically exemplified by but not confined to sense perception, putative awareness of God exhibits this generic character. Thus it is properly termed (putative) perception of God. Any such argument will have to employ some particular account of sense perception, and this is a notoriously controversial topic.[9]

Alston builds his perceptual model in the following way: he first distils from the empiricist concept of perception a purely formal concept of perception and then applies it to the experiences of God in question. Drawing on the 'Theory of Appearing', a perceptual theory of common sense put forward by George D. Hicks,[10] Harold A. Prichard[11] and Winston H. F. Barnes[12] in the first half of the twentieth century, Alston defines perception as follows: 'For S to perceive X is simply for X to appear to S as so-and-so. That is all there is to it.'[13] Since this concept of perception is completely abstracted from the phenomenal content of experience, Alston can apply the concept without further modifications to non-sensory experiences. The theory of appearing provides Alston with a concept of perception that on the one hand corresponds to common sense and on the other is not limited to sensory perceptions. It allows him to identify mystical and sensory perceptions as two types of the same genus.[14] Parallelizing mystical and sensory perception, Alston does not forget to point to the differences between the two types of perception: while in our waking state we cannot escape sensory perception, he points out, mystical perception is usually a very rare phenomenon. While our sensory perception, and especially our visual perception, is active, detailed and highly informative, an experience of God, he argues, is dark, sparse and obscure. While the capacity for sensory perception is shared by every human being, mystical perception is by no means universal.[15] Despite these differences, Alston argues, experiences of God of this type can nonetheless be categorized as perceptions: 'despite these differences I want to claim a generic identity of structure.'[16]

Reconstructing mystical perceptions according to the model of sensory perception leads us to imagine God like an object in the outside world. Alston is aware of this danger – one identified by among others Paul Tillich[17] – and adopts an explicit position:

> Using Tillich's terminology, I am thinking of God as an *object* of perception only in the 'logical' sense. A term like 'object' may have connotations that are inappropriate in this context, but these connotations do not constitute any part of its meaning. In thinking of God as an 'object' of experience, I am not suggesting that God is simply 'one being alongside others' (He is quite a special being), much less that He is a lifeless, inanimate *thing* that passively allows Himself to be scrutinized. On the contrary, He is a supreme personal being with Whom we are in personal interaction and Who is eminently active in our lives. Nor does speaking of God as an object of experience (or even as an 'item' in the phenomenal field) imply that

He is there *alongside* others. [...] That may or may not be the case. He could be an object of experience in the basic sense in question even if He is the only thing of which we are aware when we are aware of Him. In short, to say that God is the *object* of some experience implies no more than that some people sometimes experience God, are experientially aware of Him, that sometimes God presents Himself to our experience.[18]

For Alston, if we speak of God as an object of perception, then we are saying neither that he is just one being among many nor that he is a being that exists *alongside* other beings. Even less are we reducing him to an inanimate object that can be investigated and explored. Rather, for Alston, God is a supreme personal being with whom we have personal contact, a being that itself exercises a large influence on our lives. Alston makes clear that, in describing God as an object of experience, he simply wishes to point out that some people occasionally experience God, that God presents himself to them in these experiences. He uses the notion of object in a logical sense, a move that is above suspicion even for Tillich: 'In the logical sense everything about which a predication is made is, by this very fact, an object. The theologian cannot escape making God an object in the logical sense of the word.'[19] If Alston speaks of God as an object of perception, then this is not to be understood as if he saw no other linguistic option, but ultimately considers this means of expression to be totally inappropriate. By talking of God as a perceptual object, Alston is explicitly taking on ontological commitments: 'My talk of God as an object of experience does definitely presuppose that God exists as an objective reality, indeed that He is maximally real.'[20] This very conception of God as an identifiable object of perception shows that Alston's notion of mystical perception is strongly influenced by the paradigm of sensory perception.

That Alston proposes a model of perception for the religious experiences that he investigates is, on the one hand, due to the fact that the reports provided by many mystics suggest that we should understand experiences of God as non-sensory perceptions.[21] On the other hand, though, this model corresponds to Alston's metaphysical realism, that is, the view that reality is the measure of our knowledge, and not that our knowledge is the measure of reality.[22] That perception gives us direct access to reality distinguishes it, in Alston's view, from other forms of knowledge. With the sources of mystics in mind, Alston characterizes their experiences as follows:

The awareness is *experiential* in the way it contrasts with thinking about God, calling up mental images, entertaining propositions, reasoning, engaging in overt or covert conversation, remembering. Our sources take it that something, namely, God, has been *presented* or *given* to their consciousness, in generically the same way as that in which objects in the environment are (apparently) *presented* to one's consciousness in sense perception. The most fundamental fact about sense perception, at least as far as its intrinsic character is concerned, is the way in which seeing my house differs from thinking about it, remembering it, forming mental images of it, reasoning about it, and so on. It is the difference between *presence* (to consciousness) and absence. If I stand before my house with my eyes shut and then open them, I am suddenly *presented* with the object itself; it occupies part of my visual field; it appears to me as blue and steep roofed. People who report being experientially aware of God take this to contrast with thinking about God in just the same way.[23]

According to Alston, perceiving something is something different from thinking, forming images, balancing propositions, reasoning, engaging in conversations and remembering. The specificity of perception, for Alston, lies in its direct contact to experienced reality. It is this direct contact that is best reflected in the perceptual model. Alston can invoke Francis de Sales, who sees in the awareness of God's presence what distinguishes an experience of God:

> 'Now it fares in like manner with the soul who is in rest and quiet before God: for she sucks in a manner insensibly the delights of *His presence*, without any discourse. [. . .] She sees her spouse *present* with so sweet a view that reasonings would be to her unprofitable and superfluous. [. . .] Nor does the soul in this repose stand in need of the *memory*, for she has her lover *present*. Nor has she need of the imagination, for why should we represent in an exterior or interior image Him whose *presence* we are possessed of?'[24]

Alston differentiates perceptions not only from thoughts, memories and ideas but also from feelings. Feelings, for Alston, may be experiences, but they are purely subjective experiences without objective reference.[25] While feelings may well be the medium of religious experiences,[26] he argues, they have absolutely no cognitive content themselves. For Alston, a theory that identifies religious experiences as emotional experiences therefore has no persuasive force epistemologically:

> The treatment of 'religious experience' as essentially consisting of 'feelings' or other affective states is very common. Thus in Schleiermacher, the fountainhead of concentration on religious experience in the study of religion, we find the basic experiential element of religion treated as a 'feeling of absolute dependence'. Rudolf Otto and William James also concentrate on feelings. It must be confessed that in all these cases the theorists also characterize religious experience as cognitive of objective realities in ways that seem incompatible with the classification as *affective*. I doubt very much that any consistent account of religious experience can be found in the works of any of these people. Nevertheless, it remains true that their concentration on affect has frequently been taken out of context and as such has powerfully influenced succeeding generations.[27]

Having so far examined the classification of religious experiences as non-sensory perceptions, I would now like to indicate briefly how Alston's reconstruction of religious experiences fits into his project of building a religious epistemology. Starting from the observation that sensory perception enjoys great confidence as a source of knowledge, while mystical perceptions are often denied any cognitive value, Alston evaluates philosophical attempts to designate sensory perception as a reliable source of knowledge against sceptical objections. Alston concludes that any argument for the reliability of sensory perception is circular.[28] What is true for sensory perception, he points out, is true for all other sources of our knowledge, for memory, for introspection, for deductive or inductive reasoning: any attempt to designate a form of knowledge as reliable already avails itself of this form of knowledge.[29] This stems from the fact that, with regard to our practices of building beliefs – Alston calls them 'doxastic practices'[30] – we can adopt no external position that allows us to assess its reliability in an objective manner.[31]

Nevertheless, for Alston, we have every reason to trust our doxastic practices, and this precisely because they are deeply embedded in our lives.[32] After his sceptical assessment of theoretical attempts to designate our doxastic practices as reliable, Alston resorts to a pragmatic response: 'what alternative is there to employing the practices we find ourselves using, to which we find ourselves firmly committed, and which we could abandon or replace only with extreme difficulty if at all?'[33] But, for Alston, if we recognize that in a practical sense it is rational to follow the doxastic practices deeply rooted in the psyche and in society, then we are committing ourselves with this recognition through pragmatic implication to the assumption that it is rational to consider these practices as also being reliable sources of knowledge.[34] According to Alston, there is now in Christianity a well-established practice of forming religious beliefs from mystical perceptions – Alston refers to this as 'Christian mystical perceptual doxastic practice'[35] or 'CMP'.[36] Why should it not be rational to follow such a practice?[37] It is along these lines that Alston, therefore, defends Christian mystical doxastic practice from the fifth chapter of *Perceiving God*:

> My main thesis in this chapter, and indeed in the whole book, is that CMP is rationally engaged in since it is a socially established doxastic practice that is not demonstrably unreliable or otherwise disqualified for rational acceptance. If CMP is, indeed, a socially established doxastic practice, it follows from the position defended in Chapter 4 that it is prima facie worthy of rational participation. And this means that it is prima facie rational to regard it as reliable, sufficiently reliable to be a source of prima facie justification for the beliefs it engenders. And if, furthermore, it is not discredited by being shown to be unreliable or deficient in some other way that will cancel its prima facie rationality, then we may conclude that it is unqualifiedly rational to regard it as sufficiently reliable to use in belief formation.[38]

To defend Christian mystical practice, Alston uses an argument of parity: the same is to be treated the same. If there is an established practice in Christianity of moving from experiences of God to religious beliefs, he argues, then there is no reason to classify this practice in an epistemically different manner to other doxastic practices. However, since there is a long tradition in Christianity of building beliefs and theories on the basis of religious experience, this tradition should not be denied its rational recognition. Alston is initially concerned only with prima facie recognition. For him, Christian mystical practice can, like any other well-established practice, lay claim to *unlimited* recognition only when it demonstrates a high degree of internal and external consistency, and is confirmed by its output to a significant extent.[39] This distinction returns again at the level of individual beliefs: according to Alston, from an experience can always emerge only a prima facie justification. For a belief derived from an experience to be justified fully, it should not be refuted by assumptions of the understanding of reality at work in the respective doxastic practice.[40]

3 The price of building a theory on the basis of opposition to naturalism

I share Alston's sympathy for Christian mysticism, and I also share his plea for a rational recognition of this practice. I also believe that his epistemology enables him to circumnavigate various cliffs with great skill. But I question whether he does justice to the phenomenon of religious experience. It is his opposition to naturalism that shapes how he builds his theory. On the one hand, he considers religious experience only insofar as it is open to question by the naturalist; and, on the other, he uses scientistic strategies of argumentation to defend it epistemologically. For Alston, naturalism, with its empiricist criterion of reality, is both counterfoil and yardstick at once. In his effort to ensure the cognitive value of religious experience, Alston loses sight of the phenomenon as such. That this also affects the sustainability of his religious epistemology should be noted here only in passing.

That ensuring the cognitive content of religious experience is bought at the expense of a narrow vision of the phenomenon in Alston's work can be seen first of all in its one-sided localization in the perceptive faculty. By interpreting religious experiences as non-sensory perceptions, Alston can ensure them a place alongside sensory perceptions and therefore allow them to share in their claim to reality. By doing so, however, he loses sight of the holistic character of these experiences. Religious experiences usually lay claim to the whole person. If we believe the reports provided by mystics, then an experience of God involves all the powers of the person – the senses, the will, the intellect, the emotions, the imagination, the memory. Although not all the capacities of the person need be affected to the same extent, to describe religious experiences simply as perceptions does seem to reduce them enormously. That does not mean that perceptions play no role in the experience of God. It means rather that perceptions are at best part of a much broader spiritual dynamics that penetrate the deepest layers of the human being.

Second, Alston's underdetermination of religious experience caused by his epistemological interest can be seen in the lack of context that he provides for the experiences that he outlines. Alston isolates from his underlying sources the moment in which the believer becomes aware of the presence of God. A more accurate description of the essential moments of this experience is missing. Now I would not deny that the becoming aware of the presence of God can be the highest or actual moment of an experience of God. But, contrary to Alston, I do want to point out that experiences of God cannot be reduced to this moment. Mystics agree that the human being has to traverse a path in order to reach God: the soul has to become like God. Alston ignores this development of the soul completely. But what justifies his focus on the moment of encountering God? Should we not see the progress of the soul as also being a stage in the experience of God?

Third, that Alston's theory is deeply indebted to an empiricist way of thinking is shown in his focus on the so-called direct perceptions of God. On account of this focus, he gambles away the opportunity not only to integrate experiences of oneness and the so-called indirect perceptions into his theory but also to question experiences of God in their very essence. But this is massively at the expense of a substantial determination of what actually distinguishes an experience of God in the first place. If Alston is barely able to make plausible his classification of religious experiences according to the types mentioned, then he is even less able to make plausible how the transcendent God can present himself to the believer in a direct manner. Mediation between natural and supernatural reality is missing from Alston's approach – but why should it be provided where the reality of God can be deduced directly through our non-sensory perception?

4   Douglas Hedley's theory of religious imagination as an alternative?

We have seen that Alston's theory is deficient with regard to the phenomenon of religious experience. First, through its one-sided focus on perception, it does not do justice to the holistic character of religious experiences. Second, it disregards the internal mental conditions of religious experiences. Third, the theory cannot explain how the transcendent God can present himself within the world. I would like to conclude by evaluating the extent to which Douglas Hedley's theory of religious imagination can clear these hurdles. Like Alston, Hedley is also concerned with the question of how the human being can become aware of the Divine reality. Like Alston, he also emphasizes the importance of religious experience for every theology: 'Any serious theology must be able to provide examples of the experience of God.'[41] Nevertheless, his approach differs fundamentally from Alston's attempt to explain the experiential dimension of Christian belief philosophically:

> Rather than appeal to the great tradition of inferential proofs of divine existence, or even the claim of distinguished philosophers and theologians that the Divine can be experienced directly, the present work reflects upon those indirect apprehensions of transcendent reality: the forms of imagination. This means the irreducible creativity of human beings that distinguishes them in kind from the rest of the animal kingdom. Through the 'inner eye' of imagination, finite beings can apprehend eternal and immutable Forms.[42]

For Hedley, it is the inner eye of imagination that enables us to apprehend transcendent reality. In contrast to Alston, Hedley believes that we can always only apprehend the divine reality indirectly – namely, through the general forms of imagination. Hedley follows Samuel Taylor Coleridge's thesis that an idea in the highest sense of the word can always only be mediated by a symbol.[43] However, for Coleridge, the symbol is 'characterized [...] above all by a transcendence of the Eternal through and in the Temporal. It always partakes of the reality which it renders intelligible; and while it enunciates the whole, abides itself as a living part in that unity, of which it is the representative.'[44] According to Hedley, the knowledge that we can attain about God by using our imagination is always symbolic. But, for Hedley, the symbol is more than just an image: it shares the reality that it represents.[45] For him, God can therefore be experienced through the power of imagination to transcend the visible to attain the invisible:

> The experience of God is neither to be construed in terms of a quasi-objective presence nor a purely figurative fiction. Imaginative apprehension of the Divine is pre-eminently the awareness of that reality which is pressing and proximate for the soul and yet hard to grasp or articulate in the categories appropriate for the physical domain. For human beings the tension between the material and the spiritual, between inward and outward worlds, is resolved in the imaginative vision of their underlying unity.[46]

Imaginative visions are, therefore, in a sense the medium of religious experience. The divine reality is opened to us through the symbolic; we can perceive it through the symbolic. If, like Hedley, we understand the entire cosmos as a theophany, then the cosmos is a single symbol of the reality of God.[47] To perceive God, 'we have to see through this physical image as in a glass darkly'.[48] Like the mystical tradition, Hedley assumes that the soul must first be enabled to perceive the divine reality. The soul must be reborn in the Holy Spirit to be able to reach God:

> Because the proper perception of the world as sacred requires the soul as well as the senses, the soul must be purified so that it can receive the light of Divine wisdom. [...] It is the imagination reborn that can perceive the sacred: in Christian terms the rebirth of the soul through the Holy Spirit. Sacrifice reveals the Divine nature.[49]

Even this brief sketch indicates that Hedley can solve the above problems much more convincingly than Alston. This applies particularly to the third point, the mediation of inner-worldly and divine reality. In Hedley's theory, this mediation is performed by the symbol as representative and as a medium of the divine. In contrast to Alston, and this brings me to the second point, Hedley does not succumb to the risk of reducing religious experiences to the moment in which the subject becomes aware of God's presence. Hedley assumes that the soul has to undergo a process of purification in order to perceive the transcendent reality. He describes this process using the category of the sacrifice.

Now I come to the first point. If we ask whether Hedley's theory can describe experiences of God as a holistic process, I would answer in the negative against the background of one interpretation, but in the affirmative against the background of a different interpretation. If we consider imagination as one faculty among others, then the reproach levelled at Alston's theory can be levelled at Hedley's theory as well: religious experience can then be seen no longer as an event involving the whole human being. In the case of Hedley's theory, religious experience seems to play only at the level of imaginations; in the case of Alston's theory, only at the level of perceptions. However, if we regard the imagination as a mental force of a higher order, as a capacity for transcendence that gives all mental capacities access to the divine,[50] then this maintains reference to the human as a whole.

Response by Douglas Hedley

The discussion of religious experience in Rahner is complemented by the rich and subtle discussion of William Alston's theory of religious experience in Margit Wasmeier-Sailer. The debts and obligations to Coleridge, William James and Otto in all three volumes of the trilogy are manifest. The analysis of religious experiences as non-sensory 'perceptions' of God, that is, as direct encounters with the Deity furnishes particular problems, which are trenchantly analysed by Wasmeier-Sailer. The formidable epistemological powers of Alston and his speculative audacity provide an oddly truncated account of a spiritual tradition that he wishes to defend. I agree that *perception* is the wrong model for mystical experience for the basically Platonic reason that the *itinerarium mentis in Deum* is a process of ascent and transformation. Yet I also criticize the radical apophaticism of my erstwhile colleague Denys Turner and his *The Darkness of God*. If Alston offends by assimilating the 'mystical' vision to perceptual experience, Turner's God becomes radically inaccessible. Both of these extreme positions seem to me implausible for the viability of theology as a subject. The stress upon imaginative apprehension is precisely intended either as an alternative to a deity of untenable immediacy or as the most remote of inferences. Schelling writes of the vision Divine:

> From time to time, every physical and moral whole needs, for its preservation, the reduction to its innermost beginning. Human beings keep rejuvenating themselves and become newly blissful through the feeling of the unity of their being. It is in precisely this that especially those seeking knowledge continually summon up fresh power. Not only poets, but also philosophers, have their ecstasies.[51]

Notes

1 Charles Taliaferro, 'Religious Experience', in *The Oxford Companion to Consciousness*, edited by Tim Bayne, Axel Cleeremans and Patrick Wilken (Oxford: Oxford University Press, 2009), 562-3.
2 Cf. ibid., 562.
3 William James, *The Varieties of Religious Experience: A Study in Human Nature* (London: Longman Green, 1915), 428.
4 In addition to naturalism, analytical theories of religious experience also deal especially with the plurality of religions. See Friedo Ricken, 'Introduction', in *Religiöse Erfahrung. Ein interdisziplinärer Klärungsversuch*, ed. Friedo Ricken (Stuttgart: Kohlhammer, 2004), 9-14, 9.
5 Since Alvin Plantinga, Nicholas Wolterstorff, Richard Swinburne and William L. Craig follow a similar line of reasoning to William P. Alston's, the problems described apply to their theories as well.
6 William P. Alston, *Perceiving God: The Epistemology of Religious Experience* (Ithaca and London: Cornell University Press, 1991).
7 Ibid., 1.
8 See ibid., 20-8.

9. Ibid., 9.
10. George D. Hicks, *Critical Realism: Studies in the Philosophy of Mind and Nature* (London: Macmillan, 1938).
11. Harold A. Prichard, *Kant's Theory of Knowledge* (Oxford: Oxford Clarendon Press, 1909).
12. Winston F. H. Barnes, 'The Myth of Sense Data', *Proceedings of the Aristotelian Society* 45 (1945): 89–118. Alston refers to Hicks, Prichard and Barnes in 'Back to the Theory of Appearing', *Philosophical Perspectives* 13 (1999): 181–203 n. 1.
13. Alston, *Perceiving God* (see n. 6), 55.
14. See ibid., 54–9.
15. See ibid., 36.
16. Ibid.
17. See ibid., 30–1, where Alston refers to Paul Tillich, *Systematic Theology*, 3 vols., vol. 1: *Reason and Revelation. Being and God* (London: Lisbet & Co., 1953), 191–2.
18. Alston, *Perceiving God* (see n. 6), 31.
19. Tillich, *Systematic Theology* (see n. 17), 191–2.
20. Alston, *Perceiving God* (see n. 6), 31.
21. See ibid., 12–14.
22. Cf. ibid., 4: 'In the present intellectual climate it would be well to make it explicit that this discussion is conducted from a full-bloodedly realist perspective, according to which in religion as elsewhere we mean what we assert to be true of realities that are what they are regardless of what we or other human beings believe of them, and regardless of the "conceptual scheme" we apply to them (except, of course, when what we are talking about is our thought, belief, or concepts). I take this to be a fundamental feature of human thought and talk. Thus, in epistemically evaluating the practice of forming M-beliefs I am interested in whether that practice yields beliefs that are (often) true in this robustly realist sense – not, or not just, in whether it yields beliefs that conform to the rules of the relevant language-game, or beliefs that carry out some useful social function. [. . .] what I am interested in determining, so far as in me lies, is whether the practice succeeds in accurately depicting a reality that is what it is however we think of it.'
23. Ibid., 14–15.
24. Franz von Sales, *Treatise on the Love of God*, book VI, ch. ix, quoted in: Anton Poulain, *The Graces of Interior Prayer*, translated by Leonora Yorke Smith and Jean Vincent Bainvel (London: Routledge and Kegan Paul Ltd., 1950), 75–6.
25. See Alston, *Perceiving God* (see n. 6), 37.
26. See ibid., 50–1.
27. Ibid., 16.
28. See ibid., 102–45, esp. 102–3.
29. See ibid., 146.
30. See ibid., 153–65.
31. See ibid., 150.
32. See ibid., 168–70.
33. Ibid., 150.
34. See ibid., 178–80.
35. Ibid., 184.
36. Ibid.
37. See ibid., 184–5.
38. Ibid., 194.

39 See ibid., 184–5.
40 See ibid., 72, 159.
41 Douglas Hedley, *Sacrifice Imagined: Violence, Atonement, and the Sacred* (London and New York: Continuum, 2011), 22. Cf. also the author's own comprehensive critique of Alston's theory of *Perceiving God* ibid., 94–106.
42 Hedley, *Living Forms of the Imagination* (London and New York: T&T Clark, 2008), 1.
43 See Hedley, *Sacrifice Imagined* (see n. 41), 48. Hedley refers to Samuel Taylor Coleridge, *Biographia Literaria; or, Biographical Sketches of My Literary Life and Opinions*, 2 vols, edited by James Engell and Walter Jackson Bate (Princeton: Princeton University Press, 1984), II, 80.
44 Coleridge, *Lay Sermons*, edited by Reginald J. White (London: Princeton University Press, 1972), 28.
45 See Hedley, *Living Forms* (see n. 42), 5.
46 Ibid., 37.
47 See Hedley, *Sacrifice Imagined* (see n. 41), 59. 'The uncreated and the created realms are not strict opposites but are correlated: they form a dialectical unity in which the Divine is bodied forth in the finite realm. The world is a theophany in Schelling's sense of the world as the *Gegenbild* or counterimage: the icon of the Divine. In creating the world, God makes himself in another mode: the created order is a symbol of the Divine. Thus an image is not simply an index of Divine transcendence, but includes and reveals it.'
48 Hedley, *Living Forms* (see n. 42), 106.
49 Hedley, *Sacrifice Imagined* (see n. 41), 60.
50 Some statements that Hedley makes go in this direction: see Hedley, *Sacrifice Imagined* (see n. 41), 38–40.
51 Friedrich W. J. Schelling, *The Ages of the World*, translated by Jason N. Wirth (New York: State University of New York Press, 2000), XXXVIII.

From Cambridge to Calcutta

The presence of Indian thought in Douglas Hedley's Christian Platonism

Daniel Soars

> *The uncreated and the created realms are not strict opposites but are correlated: they form a dialectical unity in which the Divine is bodied forth in the finite realm. . . . Thus the cosmos is the Divine sacrifice: the metamorphosis of God's identity in difference.*[1]

It might not seem obvious why there needs to be an essay on Indian thought in a collection like this one. References to Hindu iconography and Indian philosophy are scattered throughout Douglas Hedley's three-volume opus on the religious imagination but, apart from a few extended sections on resonant parallels between East and West, such references are generally brief and seemingly ornamental to his core argument. Oriental allusions might simply occupy a place in Hedley's mental library and indicate nothing of particular note beyond the impressive erudition that marks his systematic philosophical theology as a whole. Indeed, casting an eye down the indices of his trilogy, one is struck by the almost bewildering panoply of themes and thinkers: from Aztec sacrifice to Palaeolithic cave paintings, from Beethoven to Joyce, it is perhaps hardly surprising to find that Krishna and Sankara also appear in such a rich and wide-ranging vision of the human and divine.

1 Why India?

I wish to show, however, that Indian thought is more than merely peripheral to Hedley's central concerns and motivations, and that, in fact, this interest has emerged organically out of themes which form the warp and weft of his sacramental conception of reality. While it would be overstating the case to suggest that Indic materials explicitly form a key plank of Hedley's system, I will argue that they are present in spirit, if not in letter, throughout his work, and are particularly evident in the sorts of figures and themes to which he is drawn. As such, we would do Hedley a disservice if we mistook his interest in India (which becomes more obvious as the trilogy goes on) simply as that of a Renaissance polymath, let alone as that of an Orientalist dilettante. After all, Hedley is part of a venerable group of Indologists who have been invited to deliver the prestigious 'Teape' Lectures which were instituted in honour of one of his forebears in the Faculty of Divinity at Cambridge – Brooke Foss Westcott (1825–1901).[2] Named after Westcott's student, William Marshall Teape (1882–1944), the lectures have been exploring the relationship between Christian and Hindu thought since their inception in 1955.[3] Indeed, Hedley draws liberally on such a wide range of intellectual and artistic resources, East and West, in order to develop his concept of the religious imagination – from philosophy and theology to music and poetry – that Westcott, who dreamed of a new Alexandria on the banks of the Yamuna, would surely have seen him as a kindred spirit.

While I would, then, want to reject any accusation that what follows is an idiosyncratic eisegesis of Hedley's texts, some degree of creative extrapolation from his core concerns is needed to make sense of the otherwise relatively unsystematic nature of his references to Indian thought. As such, I would like to suggest that we picture Hedley's system of religious philosophy as a triangular interconnection of two major influences which have given rise over time to his interest in India at the apex. The 'base' of his religious philosophy is formed from a combination of (Neo)-Platonism and Christian mysticism, on the one hand, and the twin movements of Romanticism and Idealism (especially German and British), on the other. For ease of argument, then, we can picture 'Platonic Mysticism' and 'Romantic Idealism' as the two interrelated poles which prop up Hedley's imaginative argument against naturalistic materialism.[4] Explaining the role played by these two points will give us the conceptual foundation of Hedley's vision, and will, therefore, be the first part of my exegesis. I will then argue that an interest in Indian thought is an organic outgrowth from these starting points and its place in his work can be understood as a natural coming together of the twin themes which form the base of his system. In other words, I want to show not only why Hedley is particularly drawn to Platonic mysticism, Romantic Idealism and India but also how the latter interest is related to the first two, and indeed how all three are interconnected.[5]

In order to strengthen the case for interrelatedness, I will highlight three concepts and three individuals that might helpfully be pictured as the 'lines of force' which run between the points of our triangle, appearing, as they do, as leitmotifs in Hedley's work. Given their ubiquity, I will not seek to dislodge these themes and figures from their contexts in Hedley's broader narratives, since that would risk losing a sense of how they fit into his overall vision. Rather than treating them each separately, then, I will indicate how these themes and individuals find their place within the whole. The three conceptual vertices of our triangle, which run between (Neo)-Platonism-Christian mysticism, Romantic Idealism and India are the concepts of Being, participation and Divine Ideas; conversion and subjectivity; and immanence and transcendence. I will suggest that all three conceptual tropes naturally (I do not say 'necessarily') lead to an interest in Indian thought. We will also see how the points of our thematic triangle – namely, (Neo)-Platonism/Christian mysticism, Romanticism/Idealism and India –

come together in the lives and works of three key figures who all, to greater or lesser extents, shared Hedley's interconnected interests: William Jones (1746–94), Samuel Taylor Coleridge (1772–1834) and Rudolf Otto (1869–1937). It is no coincidence that Hedley finds himself drawn to these individuals and that their thought looms large in his intellectual hinterland.

Finally, having sketched out our heuristic triangle, with the points which form the key thematic influences in Hedley's religious philosophy (Platonism/Christian mysticism, Romanticism/Idealism and India), the conceptual lines which connect them (Divine Ideas/participation, conversion/subjectivity and transcendence-and-immanence) and three figures whom Hedley favours as his cross-generational conversation partners (Jones, Coleridge and Otto), I want to suggest that these thematic influences, linking concepts and personalities can all be seen to coalesce in Hedley's interpretation of a pregnant biblical passage to which he returns again and again: the 'I AM WHO I AM' of Exod. 3.14. We might picture his reading of the divine name revealed to Moses as the centre of our triangle where, as it were, Israel, Greece and India come together.

2 From (Neo)-Platonism to Christian mysticism

Hedley's interest in the influence of Greek philosophical thought on Christian theology is evident throughout his work, not least in his earliest published monograph on Samuel Taylor Coleridge – a figure whom he sees as belonging to a 'Christian Platonic tradition stretching from John Scotus Eriugena (815–877) to Hegel (1770–1831)'.[6] Here, Hedley makes clear that the Platonism he has in mind 'is not that of Plato's dialogues, or the "unwritten doctrines" of the Academy, but the allegorising metaphysics of Middle and Neoplatonism which, indeed, formed such a crucial component of Christian theology, and the stream of "Christian Platonism" which was so potent in the early modern period in Florence and Cambridge'.[7] The broader argument for the use of Greek thought as a conceptual vehicle for expressing Christian beliefs – particularly Platonic concepts as developed and structured by key pagan figures in the early centuries of the Christian era, like Plotinus (204–70), Porphyry (232–305), Iamblichus (245–326) and Proclus (412–85) – has been made persuasively elsewhere,[8] so it is not my intention to enter into this conversation here, but simply to note that 'the allegorising metaphysics of Middle and Neoplatonism' is the primary conceptual lens through which Hedley views Christian theology, not least in the Renaissance Florentine (e.g. Marsilio Ficino and Pico della Mirandola)[9] and seventeenth-century Cambridge (e.g. Ralph Cudworth and Henry More) figures to whom he alludes.[10] It is this Neoplatonic lens which draws Hedley towards the 'allegorising metaphysics' of subjectivity/conversion, immanence/transcendence and, especially, the doctrines of Divine Ideas and participation.

Given its fullest early treatment by Augustine in the forty-sixth of his *Eighty-Three Different Questions*,[11] and taken up as a significant theme by Thomas Aquinas,[12] the concept of the Platonic ideas existing in the mind of God as exemplar causes of the sensible world provides, for Hedley, a theologically defensible metaphysics of 'connection' or even *continuity* between divine and human reality.[13] The primary motivation for his recourse to the doctrine is to avoid a naturalistic bifurcation of reality into two hermetically sealed compartments of divine and mundane, and to argue, rather, for the role of the religious imagination in perceiving the spiritual *in* the material – not least, in nature and in the rich imagery and symbolism provided by music, art and poetry. Indeed, it is not difficult to see how this sacramental conception of the world inevitably draws Hedley towards (and is, no doubt, shaped by) precisely the sort of Romanticism we find in figures like Coleridge, for it is surely this ontological continuity between divine and human that allows his fellow Lake poet, Wordsworth,[14] to feel

> A presence that disturbs me with the joy
> Of elevated thoughts; a sense sublime
> Of something far more deeply interfused,
> Whose dwelling is the light of setting suns,
> And the round ocean and the living air,
> And the blue sky, and in the mind of man:
> A motion and a spirit, that impels
> All thinking things, all objects of all thought,
> And rolls through all things.[15]

Such an imaginative vision is possible because it is precisely by *participating* in these eternal and immutable Ideas that created realities exist at all, and so the whole cosmos comes to be seen as theophanic. These related doctrines (of Divine Ideas and participation) have important implications for Hedley's understanding both of God and of world, and of the human creature in particular.

When it comes to God, Hedley sees the doctrine of Divine Ideas as the best philosophical means of avoiding a dualistic separation between Creator and creation – a separation which ends up leading to domesticated conceptions of transcendence as spatial distance and an emphasis on the divine *will*, as opposed to the divine nature, as the 'connection' between God and world. In contrast, the 'allegorical metaphysics' of Divine Ideas 'implies a real connection, however mysterious, between God's essence and the created world, the necessary and the contingent. This, in turn, is tied to the rejection of an arbitrary deity. . . . The tenet of Divine ideas forms a way of insisting upon God as goodness itself, the culmination of being, rather than a continent and wilful being.'[16] While the origins of the concept are clearly Platonic, Hedley does not want to suggest – any more than did Augustine or Aquinas – that the realm of Ideas is some sort of inferior hypostasis or intermediate emanation between the divine source and the physical world, but simply *is* the mind of God.[17] This, indeed, is one of the key differences between a strict Neoplatonic henology, which will countenance no hint of multiplicity in the One, and the Christian assimilation of Neoplatonism in figures like Victorinus and Augustine, which can allow for an element of difference within the divine unity (not least, of course, as this relates to the Christian understanding of God as triune).[18] 'It is the fusion of supreme principle with the intellect and the vision of the supreme principle as consubstantial with the intelligible paradigm of the sensible world which provides the metaphysical foundations for a Platonic Christian.'[19] We will return presently to Hedley's conception of God, but it is important to note how this 'vision of the supreme principle as consubstantial with the intelligible paradigm of the sensible world' ('however mysterious the connection') also has consequences for how we see the world and our relation to the divine.

Ontological continuity between transcendent cause and particular effects is the (Neoplatonic) metaphysical architecture Hedley requires to underpin his vision of the physical cosmos as mirror of the Divine,[20] but it is by holding the doctrine of Divine Ideas together with the doctrine of participation that he is able to rebut potential misrepresentations of his system as pantheistic.[21] Far from arguing for any kind of numerical or qualitative identity between God and world, Hedley's point is that creatures exist by sharing finitely in the infinite fullness of divine Being, which is, therefore, both immanent in and yet transcendent to the created order. Indeed, the doctrines of Divine Ideas and participation entail more than just an intellectual model of an immanent God and a sacramental cosmos; they are, for Hedley, a clear 'summons to conversion',[22] in that they invite us to realize the active presence of God within: 'Since the ideas were placed within the divine mind in the second century AD, Platonists identified the idea with God's creative intellect, and saw philosophy as the journey or ascent of the finite mind towards the absolute intellect; part of a struggle to become "like God".'[23] As he points out, it is for this reason that many Neoplatonic texts take the form of meditative treatises, designed to lead the reader out of the cave into the divine light, and why Coleridge is so fond of appealing to the Delphic oracle, 'Know Thyself!'.[24] Turning within in order to discover God becomes the quintessential task of the Neoplatonic philosopher and it is this conception of philosophy – as a spiritual exercise of contemplative introspection – which makes it so attractive not only for the sorts of intellective metaphysical reasons we have been discussing (i.e. Divine Ideas and participated being) but also for the imaginative–experiential goal of realizing our union with the divine (i.e. conversion/subjectivity). This is why Hedley can say: 'The central idea [viz. philosophy as the journey or ascent of the finite mind towards the absolute intellect; part of a struggle to become "like God"] is Platonist, or, to employ a dangerous but pertinent term, "mystical".'[25]

Hedley does not need to spell out exactly why the term 'mystical' might be both 'dangerous' and 'pertinent', or precisely why he seems to be using it as a tentative synonym for 'Platonist', for the implications of this pregnant sentence to be clear. Surely, the term 'mystical' is 'dangerous' because of the way it tends to be used, at least in conventional discourse, to connote a broad and imprecise range of loosely related ideas, which make it prone to ambiguity and misunderstanding. Indeed, it was only in the early modern period that 'mysticism' started to be used as a noun to denote a specific conceptual or experiential category of Christian spirituality. Nevertheless, it is 'pertinent' to Hedley's argument because *mystikos* (as an adjective) was present from the beginnings of the Christian tradition as an epithet used to refer to what is 'hidden'. This could be, for example, the 'mystical' meaning of the sacraments – what is 'hidden' within or beneath the material elements of bread, wine and water – or, most often, the 'hidden' meaning of scripture.[26] The idea of a 'mystical theology' *tout court* was not coined as a term until Dionysius's fifth-century treatise by the same name, and, in the Pseudo-Areopagite's insistence that the theologic (i.e. manner of speaking about God) he is espousing is as much a spiritual *practice* as it is an intellectual exercise,[27] we can start to see how, over centuries, a term originally used to denote the 'real' or 'deeper' meaning of divine self-revelation in texts also came to signify something closer to what Hedley has in mind – namely, to a 'mystical' experience of union with God. In other words, in the (Neo)-Platonic understanding of philosophy as an ascent of the finite mind towards the absolute intellect, coming closer to the 'hidden' meaning of the sensible world does not involve merely rational thought, but a wholehearted attempt to draw closer to the God who is simultaneously revealed and hidden there.

That the word 'mystical' did come to acquire connotations of union with ultimate reality, and that it did so in the Christian tradition at least partly via the mediating thought of Pseudo-Dionysius (*c*. late fifth to early sixth century CE) is not a coincidence, but precisely one of the reasons why Hedley can suggest a connection between the 'Platonist' conception of philosophy as ascent towards God and this 'dangerous but pertinent term'. It is why, alongside Plato, Plotinus and Proclus, Hedley is so manifestly drawn to 'mystical' figures in the Christian tradition who have been influenced by the 'allegorising metaphysics of Middle and Neoplatonism'. From Augustine to Aquinas, from Eckhart to Boehme, Hedley sees kindred spirits in these 'philosophical mystics'[28] and their deep sense of the presence of a God who is *interior intimo meo*. This is not to claim that every individual whom the Christian tradition would tend to recognize as a 'mystic' has also been a Neoplatonist[29] (at least not self-consciously) or that the metaphysical-experiential notion of 'union' with the divine must necessarily always be parsed in terms of Neoplatonic philosophy, but simply to suggest that for many Christian mystics in the early and medieval periods, their vision of the physical world and the forms of religious experience they cultivated were deeply influenced by Platonic themes and insights.[30] If Hedley's focus on the Neoplatonic doctrines of Divine Ideas and participation draws him towards mysticism, and 'Neoplatonic mysticism' helps to explain his focus on subjectivity and the *gnōthi seauton* of the Delphic oracle, the case is starting to build for seeing this conceptual matrix as one densely connected 'angle' of the triangle which is his systematic vision of religious philosophy. This matrix shapes his sacramental conception of the world, his spiritual anthropology and his understanding of God. In short, it is a core building-block of his 'Platonic' or 'mystical' monotheism,[31] which stands in opposition both to a materialistic atheism which would seek to explain consciousness in purely naturalistic terms and to a 'monarchical theism' which would stress such a gulf between God and world that the latter can reveal little to nothing of the former.

It was in order to revive the idea of divine immanence in the world that, according to Hedley, the founder of the Romantic movement in England – Samuel Taylor Coleridge – turned to the philosophical tradition of German Idealism and thus became in his own right the first of the nineteenth-century British Idealists.[32] Just as Hedley belongs, like Coleridge, to the 'Christian Platonic' tradition, his vision of the religious imagination is also deeply Idealist and Romantic.

3 From (Neo)-Platonism and Christian mysticism to Idealism and Romanticism

Not unlike 'mysticism', the terms 'Idealism' and 'Romanticism' can be notoriously polyvalent and imprecise. By 'Idealism', Hedley simply means a philosophical position which would deny that reality at its most profound can be accounted for purely in terms of material objects, and which affirms, rather, the ontological priority of mind, consciousness, spirit or personality 'behind' the physical world.[33] In this sense, he is surely correct to assert that '[m]any theists are idealists in that they claim the dependency or derivation of the material realm upon or from the spiritual.'[34] Clearly, this position does not have to entail the subjectivism of a Bishop Berkeley (for Hedley, it certainly does not), nor, Hedley is at pains to stress, should it be confused with pantheism – that is, that 'God-is-all' in a sense which equates God with the world. Again, this is where the doctrine of participation is so helpful: while a philosopher like Spinoza thought that God's infinity had to entail pantheism since there can be only one Absolute and, therefore, no beings could exist 'outside' God (which is why 'God' and 'world' become coterminous – *deus sive natura*), a Neoplatonic mystic like Plotinus or Augustine will affirm the ontological priority of spirit but explain the multiplicity of the physical world in terms of a 'sharing in' this one, unified reality: 'For the Christian Platonic tradition, the one true being is God and all other beings participate in this supreme being. As finite beings are limited, they are only partially real. God is the only entirely adequate object of intellection.'[35] Indeed, the sort of Idealism Hedley chiefly has in mind is that found in German universities like Jena and Munich in the late eighteenth and early nineteenth centuries, which was, in part, a response to the pantheism of Spinoza a generation earlier. This was an Idealism already deeply imbued with Christian theology (Hegel and Schelling both originally trained as theologians) and which drew upon what Hedley calls the 'intellectualist strand' of Neoplatonism.[36] By this, he means the emphasis on the possibility of a return to the One through direct, intuitive knowledge. By drawing on the early Neoplatonism of Plotinus and Augustine, rather than the increasingly apophatic theology found in later figures like Proclus and Pseudo-Dionysius, German Idealism moved in the opposite conceptual direction – rejecting the starkly apophatic epistemology of Kant, who had denied any possibility of knowledge beyond the phenomenal, and towards an emphasis on the Absolute as radical subjectivity.[37]

In other words, knowledge of the ultimate source was, according to the post-Kantian German idealist tradition, possible precisely through self-knowledge.[38] Hedley sees this idea of absolute being as subjectivity as the key philosophical development of German Idealism,[39] one which had its roots in the so-called *Pantheismusstreit* of 1783 when F. H. Jacobi revealed Lessing's alleged pantheism. By 1795, Schelling was able to claim that '[t]he I contains all Being, all reality',[40] which is why Hedley helpfully suggests that Schelling's philosophy can be described as 'objective idealism [because reason is thought of as an objective structure rather than as the capacity of finite beings for thinking] of absolute subjectivity' (because the 'I' contains all being).[41] It is this 'objective idealism of absolute subjectivity', which we have already found present in certain forms of Neoplatonism, that has such an influence (via Schelling and German Idealism) on Coleridge and, as is evident to any reader of his *Imagination* trilogy, on Hedley.[42] Many of the complex ways in which this mystical Neoplatonic Idealism shape Hedley's vision of God, the world and the individual subject can be seen in the following summative analysis he makes of the same set of interrelated issues in the work of Coleridge, his Romantic muse:

> The Idealist move (which influenced Coleridge) was the attempt to preserve both the idea of the infinity and of the personality of God by combining the Spinozistic (ultimately Neoplatonic) idea of 'hen kai pan' or all-unity with the concept of absolute *subjectivity*. Whereas Spinoza saw God as the absolute object, Schelling (and Hegel) wanted to see God as the absolute subject: as the great I AM. On this model the world is not 'outside God' but participates in God. Hence the younger Schelling employs the concept of 'intellectual intuition' for knowledge of the absolute in order to suggest a knowledge which is not a knowledge of an object but which is rather participation in the absolute subjectivity.[43]

Here we can see how many of the themes which we have discussed so far come together. If Neoplatonic mysticism and its metaphysics of Divine Ideas and participated being form one point of the conceptual triangle which represents Hedley's religious philosophy, the base of his system is completed by a form of Idealism which draws on and develops the insight so central to thinkers from Socrates to Plotinus, from Augustine to Eckhart – that to know God, we need only turn inward. It is for this reason that Hedley suggests that 'the highest forms of religion are those where the Godhead is perceived and encountered as absolute subjectivity: I AM THAT I AM'.[44]

We will return to this daring characterization of the divine in our sections on Indian thought and Exodus, but firstly we need to complete the basic building blocks of Hedley's system by turning to the influence of Romanticism – seen most obviously in the unifying focus in his trilogy on the concept of the religious imagination. Hedley's rejection of scientific materialism and his willingness to utilize the resources of art, music and poetry in his philosophical theology make him an enthusiastic inheritor of the cultural and intellectual movement which flourished in Europe during the first half of the nineteenth century as a response to perceived threats from an Enlightenment and Industrial modernity. The 'Romanticism' of Hedley's 'Romantic Idealism' is most apparent in his argument for the centrality of a supra-rational religious imagination as a cross-cultural means of apprehending the divine:

> The Romantic extolling of Imagination was often the rearguard action of those who lamented the loss of a vital cosmos reflecting the Divine creative energy; the sigh of those who insisted upon viewing art as the perception of the infinite in the finite, or as Coleridge says so memorably, 'a repetition in the finite mind of the eternal act of creation in the infinite I Am'.[45]

Hedley's objection is not to rational natural theology, but to the sort of intellectualism which ignores the role of emotions in the human encounter with God in and beyond the physical world, which is why aesthetic experiences (especially of the 'sublime') take such prominence in his trilogy. We have already seen how many of Hedley's conceptual and thematic influences draw him to the figure of S. T. Coleridge, but the nature of his interest in Rudolf Otto, the German scholar of comparative religion, is also illuminative.

Otto is discussed in various places in the trilogy,[46] but Hedley's most detailed treatment of this 'great sage of Marburg' comes in a recent article written to mark the centenary of the publication of his seminal work *Das Heilige* (1917).[47] Hedley (perhaps unfashionably) argues that Otto's *Das Heilige* is one of the great theological works of the last century and warrants renewed attention for its continuing philosophical and theological relevance.[48] We need only look to its subtitle to see why it has been such an influence on Hedley: *Über das Irrationale in der Idee des Göttlichen und sein Verhältnis zum Rationalen*[49] – Otto's exploration of the numinous is no more a denigration of the place of reason in theology than is Hedley's conception of the religious imagination. The case Otto and Hedley both want to make is for the importance of the *supra*-rational dimension of our encounter with the sacred and its relation to the rational. Both appeal to a human religious experience that goes not only beyond reason but also beyond any specific social and cultural contexts, which is why Hedley credits Otto with seeing that 'the sacred' is more appropriate as a category in philosophical theology than 'theism'.[50]

The shared roots of their conception of the sacred as the *mysterium tremendum et fascinans* run deep and bring us to the end of our exploration of the 'base' of Hedley's religious philosophy, formed, as we have seen, from a combination of (Neo)-Platonic mysticism and Romantic Idealism. Otto, like Hedley, sees the Platonic tradition, in particular, as maintaining a sense of the limits of rationality within Christian theology and of serving as a powerful reminder of the supra-rational aspect of the Holy, which can only be accessed via imagination and feeling (love, above all) and indicated by means of art and myth.[51] This is why Hedley suggests that 'Otto is perhaps best thought of as the inheritor of the German Romantic tradition, including Goethe and Schleiermacher. He does not wish to deny the importance of the Enlightenment but he wishes to criticise its narrow focus.'[52] He then goes on a few lines later to propose that '[u]ltimately, Otto is perhaps best seen within the German Christian mystical tradition of Meister Eckhart and his followers.'[53] Like Otto, Hedley is also deeply rooted in the Platonic tradition, an inheritor of German (and English) Romantic Idealism, and perhaps best understood within the Anglo-Celtic and German Christian mystical traditions of Eriugena, Eckhart and others. It is within this context that Hedley's interest in Indian thought makes sense, and can be seen as a natural outgrowth of his fundamental influences. Indeed, where Hedley speculates that 'it not accident that Otto exhibited a rare and sophisticated awareness of the mystical traditions of the Indian subcontinent and the Far East',[54] I would venture to say that Hedley's interest is no accident either. In order to substantiate this, we will have to look back through the strata of Hedley's conceptual influences in reverse chronological order – to see how his Romantic Idealism is perhaps the proximate cause of his turning towards Indian philosophy, but that the more profound resonances are with his deep roots in (Neo)-Platonism.

4 Platonic Idealism on Indian soil

There is little explicit mention of Indian thought in the first volume of Hedley's trilogy (*Living Forms*, 2008), but by the time of *Sacrifice Imagined* (2011), there is a short section on William Jones and the following fascinating aside on 'Brahmanic theology' found in one of Jones's letters:[55] 'The doctrine is that of Parmenides and Plato, whom our Berkley [*sic*] follows, and I am strongly inclined to consider their philosophy as the only means of removing the difficulties which attend the common opinions concerning the Material world.'[56] The 'Brahmanic theology' to which Jones refers is the systematic tradition of interpreting the Upanishads, known as Vedanta: 'a tradition of textual exegesis and commentary, as well as philosophical reflection, which has been of immense importance in Brahmanical Hindu religious thought and practice, becoming the central ideology of the Hindu Renaissance in the nineteenth and early twentieth centuries.'[57] In other words, Jones is comparing Vedantic teachings with those found in Parmenides and Plato and suggesting that there is something of fundamental philosophical importance in the Greek and Indic traditions which may be 'the only means of removing the difficulties which attend the common opinions concerning the material world'. His allusion to Berkeley would imply that the means he has in mind – and which he claims to find in similar form in India and in Greece – is some kind of philosophical idealism. The question of how far any of the different Vedantic schools which developed in India during the second millennium of the Common Era – each offering distinctive accounts of the metaphysical world view found in the Upanishads[58] – neatly map on to what a Western philosopher is likely to understand by 'idealism' is a complex one, not least given the conceptual diversity of the term even within Western traditions.[59] With this proviso in mind, however, it is true to say that the 'Brahmanic theology' Jones would have encountered certainly is 'idealist' in Hedley's minimal sense of claiming 'the dependency or derivation of the material realm upon or from the spiritual'.[60]

The dominant school of Vedanta (in the sense that it became the archetype against which doctrinal opponents would, explicitly or implicitly, set their own arguments) became the non-dual or '*advaita*' (literally, 'not-two') form as found in its most celebrated exponent, Sankara (*c*. 788–820 CE).[61] Typically taken to be a reading of scripture which holds that there is, transcendentally speaking, only *one* changeless ground of being (*Brahman*) and that the manifold world of experience is, from an ultimate perspective, merely an 'appearance' of this simple and undivided reality, Advaita Vedanta is usually seen as a form of monistic idealism.[62] In the period after Jones, during the 'Hindu Renaissance' which emerged in Calcutta (the imperial capital until 1911) in the nineteenth and twentieth centuries, 'neo-Hindu' figures like Brahmabandhab Upadhyay (1861–1907), Swami Vivekananda (1863–1902) and Sarvepalli Radhakrishnan (1888–1975) sought to counter Christian missionary polemic against a 'polytheistic' and 'idolatrous' popular Hinduism by promoting *Advaita* Vedanta as the intellectual and spiritual heart of 'true' Hinduism.[63] Part of the effect of this was to arouse a sense of affinity in nineteenth-century European idealist philosophers for a system based on a metaphysical oneness grounded in the fundamentally spiritual nature of reality. German thinkers, especially, 'were greatly attracted to the Upanishadic teaching (as they understood it) that the world as we know it through our ordinary senses is not the "real" world, but only appearance, even an illusion (*māyā*), and that the goal of life was the realisation of the self – *ātman* – through its identification with the absolute – *brahman*'.[64] In other words, the ontological monism ostensibly at the heart of the Upanishads resonated with the post-Kantian idealist tendencies of certain nineteenth-century European thinkers.[65]

This philosophical interest in Vedanta as a form of Idealism was reinforced in Germany and England by an artistic and literary attraction to an idyllic Orient which seemed to be the very antithesis of cold Enlightenment Europe. India, in particular, became a focal point of the German and English Romantic movements, which were central to what Raymond Schwab has famously identified as Europe's 'Oriental Renaissance'.[66] Motivated by what they perceived to be Europe's own problems, and disillusioned with prevailing European modes of thought (i.e. Judeo-Christian 'dogmatic' theology, on the one hand, and the anti-religious materialism of the Enlightenment on the other), many Romantics wanted to see India as the source of pristine wisdom and the fount of civilization. As Schwab points out, the metaphysical speculations and ostensibly 'mystical' inclinations of Indian thought were obviously at odds with the Enlightenment project, but it was precisely these aspects which were so appealing for the Romantics, whose desire for *renewal* (i.e. for spiritual wholeness; for a rejection of urban industrialism; for a valorization of rusticity; for oneness with nature; for a reunification of religion, philosophy and art) acted as the conceptual and experiential filters through which they would view India: 'Mirroring the philosophical preoccupations of the time, Indian thought became selectively identified in the minds of European intellectuals with the monistic and idealist philosophy of the *Vedānta*, an attitude which inevitably gave rise to the myth of the exalted spirituality of India by contrast with the materialist West'.[67] There is much evidence of the appeal of this idea of deep metaphysical unity in the works of J. G. Herder (1744–1803)[68] and Goethe (1749–1832) and in the *Naturphilosophie* of F. W. J. Schelling (1775–1854).[69] While they saw the Vedas as pointing to the primitive, unfragmented and uncorrupted unity of the human race, it was chiefly to the Upanishads that these and later German thinkers turned to discover Eastern wisdom at its most profound. In part, at least, they found what they wanted to, as '[t]he appeal of the Upanishads to Goethe, Herder, and to the great philosophers of the Romantic period, lay in what was perceived as that scripture's monistic idealism'.[70] An idealized India appealed to the Romantic imagination and the metaphysical system at the heart of the Upanishads resonated with the post-Kantian tendencies of certain German idealist philosophers.[71] Often via these German conduits, Oriental imagery and Indian philosophy came to influence the Romantic movement in England and (though less explicitly) British idealist philosophers as well. In turn, some later understandings of Vedanta, developed in locations such as Calcutta and Madras, were influenced by this series of 'German-Indian-English' feedback loops of interpretative readings. Especially after the introduction by the British of Western philosophical curricula in India, modern Vedantins like Radhakrishnan would read Sankara's doctrines through a comparative engagement with British Idealists such as T. H. Green, E. Caird and F. H. Bradley, who had themselves creatively appropriated certain aspects of German Idealism.[72]

Indeed, it was largely thanks to pioneering British Indologists like Jones (as well as missionary journals and travelogues) that European access to Indian thought was made possible at all.[73] Owing to the founding by Hastings and Jones, in 1784, of the Asiatic Society of Bengal, ground-breaking translations of Indic texts barely known until then in the West started to appear: Charles Wilkins produced the first English translation of the *Bhagavadgītā* in 1785, and Jones's 1789 translation of Kālidāsa's *Śakuntalā* would go on to influence Goethe's *Faust*. Indeed, Jones's writings on India and translations of key texts were widely disseminated in Europe, and his influence on seminal thinkers of the age extended via personal friendships with figures as varied as Benjamin Franklin and Joseph Priestley. He was also a poet in his own right, and the interest in India of later English Romantic poets like Shelley, Byron and, especially, Coleridge can, in part, be attributed to their knowledge of Jones's work.[74]

The argument for seeing Hedley as an inheritor of this Anglo-German tradition of admiration for and creative appropriation of Indian thought is surely a persuasive one. Like Coleridge, Hedley is attracted both to German Idealist philosophy and to the Romantic sense for the importance of what lies beyond or outside the grasp of reason alone, and, like Schelling and Schlegel, he is drawn to echoes of this Romantic Idealism in the 'Brahmanic theology' encountered by Jones. To be sure, his reading of Vedanta leans far more towards Plato than it leans towards Schopenhauer (or, indeed, Berkeley) – what appeals to Hedley is the strong conviction in the Upanishads that the material realm 'derives from or is dependent on' the spiritual, not that the two are metaphysically identical.[75] As we have seen in Hedley's focus on the doctrines of Divine Ideas and participation, his is a vision of ontological *continuity* between the One and the many, not of pantheistic identity, and this is precisely what he claims to find in Vedanta: 'Such a monotheism posits an ultimate transcendent source of all being- the principle of all but which is different from all (and hence distinct from any monism of strict identity). While emphasising difference or separation like the Abrahamic theist, the Indian theist nevertheless flinches from making the division into rupture.' Ultimately, it is probably not Hedley's interest in Idealism and Romanticism which *led* him to Indian thought, so much as a set of deeply held philosophical and religious convictions which, at various stages in his intellectual and spiritual journey, have found their natural home in certain places – whether the idealist Romantic poetry of Coleridge, the mystical sense of the sacred in Otto, or Jones's enthusiasm for the Sanskritic philosophical traditions of India. The roots of these core philosophical and religious convictions are deeply embedded, in Hedley's case, in Platonism, and it is, I would suggest, the echoes of ancient Greek thought in India which can provide the fullest explanation for Hedley's 'Orientalism'.[76] For a commentary on the thought-provoking comparison between 'Brahmanic theology' and 'Parmenides and Plato' drawn by Jones, and for Hedley's fullest direct treatment of Indian thought, we have to look to the eighth chapter – on 'Mythology and Theogony' – of his final volume, *Iconic Imagination* (2016). Here, Hedley suggests that what he calls 'speculative theology' emerged in Greece and India at around the same time (*c.* sixth century BCE) and he claims, like Jones, that the same 'ultimate concern' of the Hellenic tradition stretching back to Parmenides and Plato can also be found in the Upanishads.[77] The aspect of this 'ultimate concern' upon which Hedley focuses is a conception of the Absolute as supreme Being, or the *sat-cit-ananda* of the Upanishads.[78] Simmering beneath the surface of these comparisons made by Jones and Hedley is a long-standing question of the possible relation between some forms of Greek and Indian idealistic monisms – specifically, between (Neo)-Platonism and (Advaita) Vedanta.

There are two distinct issues at stake here: an empirical one of historical cross-fertilization between the two traditions and a hermeneutical philosophical one of structural and conceptual analogies which may or may not result from actual instances of historical encounter.[79] We cannot know from Hedley's trilogy where he stands on the historical question, but given his sympathy for Otto's appeal to a human religious sense that goes beyond social and cultural contexts, the likelihood is that he would side with R. T. Ciapola and J. R. Mayer in seeing parallels between Neoplatonism and Vedanta as pointing towards a 'perennial philosophy'.[80] In other words, such parallel insights which transcend history and culture may well have been reached independently because they result not from actual historical interaction, but from a preconceptual human sense of the 'sacred'. The most interesting question for our purposes is the one of precisely *which* philosophical and conceptual themes have drawn scholars to ask in the first place about possible Eastern influences in Neoplatonism – for it is these themes which we would expect to find in Hedley's work if there really is a connection between his Hellenism and his interest in Indian thought.

The most detailed full-length study of the issue of philosophical convergence specifically between Neoplatonism and Advaita Vedanta provides strong support for our hypothesis that there is indeed a profound connection between the two systems in Hedley's work.[81] Notwithstanding important and significant differences between the two traditions, J. F. Staal argues that there are deep conceptual resonances to be found in certain doctrines – not least, in the focus in both systems on the Absolute as unlimited Being and on union through self-knowledge.[82] While it might be objected that the Absolute in Plotinus's *Neo*platonism is 'beyond being',[83] Staal sees no contradiction between this and Sankara's affirmation that Brahman is *sat*, for both intend the same thing – that the Absolute is beyond qualified and intelligible being. Both Plotinus and Sankara, moreover, would agree, Staal insists, that the physical world is *a-dvaita* with the Absolute: 'Nothing is separated, which originates from the One, but nothing is identical with it either.'[84] This is precisely the kind of mystical idealism (in which the material derives from and is dependent on the spiritual) that we find in Hedley's work. Indeed, in a famous comparative essay on the concept of 'spirit' in Neoplatonism and Vedanta (i.e. *cit* and *noûs*),[85] P. Hacker argues for the vital importance to any religious philosophy of

> the Platonic concept of Idea, which Neoplatonism has incorporated into *noûs*, thus preparing the way for classical Christian cosmology. If theistic metaphysics is to survive, if the doctrine of God is not to degenerate into an ideology ancillary to anthropology, it is indispensable that we should uphold this heritage of Platonism and Neoplatonism. In monistic Vedāntism, monism, with its corollary, illusionism, made it indeed hard to explain the origin of the perishable world from the Absolute; all the more notable is the fact that even in this system there emerges an adumbration of Platonic Ideas.[86]

As we have seen, Hedley too sees the doctrine of Divine Ideas as the lifeblood of his theistic metaphysics, necessary precisely to avoid 'the doctrine of God degenerating into an ideology ancillary to anthropology'. If similar conceptions of the Absolute and its relation to the physical world can be found in Neoplatonism and Vedanta – conceptions which seem conducive to the sacramental view of the world we find in Hedley's trilogy, as well as his understanding of a non-contrastive dialectic between immanence and transcendence – then it is also true to say that the implications of this non-dualism between the One and the many are similar in both ancient systems and central to Hedley's vision: that is, that we find God/Brahman by 'turning inward':

> Leave the thus-ness of saying: 'I am thus', and you become the all; for also previously you were the all. . . . But in as far as you were something different and extra beyond the all, you became, though it is due to a surplus, less: for this surplus is not due to being (nothing could be added to it), but to non-being. You have become 'somebody' because of non-being: you are the universal entity, when you abandon this non-being.[87]

This vision of ontological continuity between my 'I' and the divine 'I AM' leads us to the end of our exploration of the presence of Indian thought in Douglas Hedley's philosophical theology. Having begun in Greece, and travelled to India, we will finish our journey in Israel because it is here that, in a sense, all the angles and vertices of our conceptual triangle come together. In the divine name revealed to Moses in Exodus, we find not only a leitmotif of Hedley's work but also the sacred ground on which key aspects of his philosophy of the religious imagination coalesce.

5 I AM THAT I AM

From his early work on Coleridge and throughout the *Imagination* trilogy, Hedley follows the lead of his academic mentor, Werner Beierwaltes, in exploring the question of 'God-Being' in Christian Platonism – specifically, as this onto-theological trope is manifested in the long and varied interpretation history of a single scriptural verse and its hidden, or 'mystical' meaning.[88] Hedley returns again and again to the enigmatic divine name revealed to Moses on Mount Horeb (Exod. 3.14, 'I am he who is' / *'ehyeh 'asher 'ehyeh*)[89] in order to show that the readings of the particular figures he chooses (especially Augustine, Aquinas and Eckhart) are both *Platonist* and *Christian*.

In *Living Forms*, Hedley focuses on Augustine's reading and, in particular, on the idea that God as the great 'I AM' is *true* Being. Just as previous figures like Philo and the church fathers had seen in this pivotal verse a confirmation of God's eternal, simple and unchanging nature, so Augustine follows these Platonic themes in his interpretation and emphasizes the relative 'non-being' of creatures apart from their participation in God.[90] In a remarkable passage in the *Confessions*, the then bishop recounts his discovery of God's nature as Being itself by means of a 'conversion' or turning inward of his gaze:

> By the Platonic books I was admonished to return into myself. With you as my guide I entered into my innermost citadel. . . . When I first came to know you, you raised me up to make me see that what I saw is Being, and that I who saw am not yet Being . . . and I found myself far from you 'in the region of dissimilarity' and heard as it were your voice from on high: 'I am the food of the fully grown; grow and you will feed on me. And you will not change me into you like the food your flesh eats, but you will be changed into me.' . . . And you cried from far away: 'Now, I am who I am.' (Exod. 3.14)[91]

It was thanks to these 'Platonic books' that Augustine was able to leave behind his Manichean dualism and gradually 'seek for immaterial truth'[92] and find God as Spirit, as He who 'truly is'. Augustine's subsequent commentaries on Exod. 3.14 confirming God as 'Being' itself helped to establish 'He who is' as 'the main divine name in the Latin West'.[93] The stage had been set for Augustine by the Platonism of figures like Plotinus,[94] Porphyry and Marius Victorinus,[95] but his reading is also distinctively *Christian*, as we can see in the Eucharistic 'feeding' imagery he uses[96] and parallels he draws between the *Ego sum qui sum* of Mount Horeb and the 'I am' sayings in John's Gospel.[97] While the 'Platonists' books' had shown him the vision of 'what truly is',[98] they could not take him there. This 'way' he came to find in the Christian scriptures and, in particular, in the mediatory figure of Christ.[99]

In *Iconic Imagination*, Hedley turns to Aquinas and, in particular, Eckhart. While Augustine focuses on the connotations of Exod. 3.14 in terms of divine eternity and immutability, Aquinas's emphasis rests on God as the pure activity of Being – the 'I am' by which all creatures are sustained and in which they reside. In his focus on God as the 'self-subsistent act of existence',[100] through which all things 'are', Aquinas turns to Neoplatonic concepts in order to explain the sui generis nature of the causation involved in creation – that is, the very *causing-to-be* of creatures.[101] The implications are that:

> As the cause of all creatures outside of whom nothing would exist, one cannot take up a position 'outside' of the relationship between cause and effect, Creator and creature. Rather, the human intellect can know anything about God only by *participation* in God's wisdom itself. We must 'enter into' God's wisdom or Word in order to understand it, just as we must 'enter into' the light in order to see the light.[102]

Eckhart takes this notion of ontological continuity between creature and Creator to its metaphysical extreme. In the 'AM', Eckhart sees the identity of existence and essence in the divine Being – the sui generis equivalence which is precisely what allows God to be both immanent in and transcendent to all created beings, both distinct and indistinct at the same time. This is not for Eckhart, any more than it is for Hedley, a pantheistic continuum. The relation between creature and Creator is neither one of simple identity nor of straightforward difference. In his Latin sermon on grace, it is possible to hear an echo of Exod. 3.14 when Eckhart says that it is 'by God's grace [that] I am what I am' (his rendering of 1 Cor. 15.10)[103] – the pure being (*istichkeit*) in which we are enjoined to participate through grace in Christ and apart from which we are 'pure nothing'.[104] The more 'indistinct' we can become through material and spiritual detachment, the more we come to realize our non-difference from Being as such: 'When my "is" and "God's is", my "I am" and God's "I am" are one and the same "I am Who am", then there is one being, one knowing, and one working that is 'greatly fruitful' like grace.'[105] As Hedley points out, the distinctively (Neo)-Platonic aspect of the interpretations of Exod. 3.14 we find in Augustine, Aquinas and Eckhart builds on Aristotle's conception of God as 'thought thinking itself' and 'is intensified by the Christian reception of the Neoplatonic idea of the νοῦς as the identity of being and thought'.[106] The implications of this identity are precisely the sorts of implications we have seen in Hedley's religious philosophy – namely, creaturely being as a participation in divine Being; God as subject, not object; knowledge through introspection; and a sacramental vision of reality mediated not only through reason but also through the imagination. It is not difficult to see why Idealists and Romantics seized upon this verse and various patristic and medieval philosophical interpretations of it.[107] Given the key influences on Hedley's religious philosophy already outlined, we would have expected to find these themes central to his vision in Christian thinkers whose indebtedness to (Neo)-Platonism is well attested, but it is revealing that this verse (Exod. 3.14) is also one which Vedantins commonly point to in support of an *advaitic* understanding of the Christian doctrine of God and world.[108]

The connections between Neoplatonism and Vedanta which have drawn figures from both of these thought-worlds to the same verse are the parallels which, I have argued, help to explain the presence of Indian thought in Douglas Hedley's religious philosophy – not merely as erudite ornamentation, but as a fertile meeting point of many of Hedley's most deeply rooted motivations and convictions. The resonant echoes he finds in Vedantic philosophy and Hindu iconography of his own moorings in Neoplatonism and Christian mysticism, on the one hand, and German Idealism and English Romanticism, on the other, are ones he has become more consciously aware of (as suggested by the increasing references to India from *Coleridge* in 2000 to *Iconic Imagination* in 2016), but the echoes have been there all along. In his most recent article, Hedley agrees with Otto that these convergences between East and West are the result of 'an astonishing conformity in the deepest impulses of human spiritual experience, which – because it is almost entirely independent of race, clime and age – points to an ultimate inward hidden similarity of the human spirit'.[109] Indeed, in his examination of the parallels between Sankara and Eckhart, Otto draws specifically on the Rhinelander's interpretation of Exod. 3.14 in order to substantiate his case that these two mystics, separated by time and geography, are working with 'an almost identical metaphysic'.[110] It is a metaphysic of continuity between the One and the many which can be found in Christian Neoplatonism and Hindu Vedanta, and which has been central to the philosophical and cultural movements of Idealism and Romanticism. It is also a metaphysic which is present, if perhaps underemphasized, in certain dimensions of the Christian traditions – as we have seen in Augustine, Aquinas and Eckhart. Indeed, it is why Bede Griffiths is able to say, in a near echo of the citation from Hedley with which we began this chapter, that

> The created world is a 'reflection' of the uncreated archetypal world. Like an image in a mirror, it has only a relative existence. Its existence is constituted by this relation to God. It is in this sense that we can say with the Hindu school of Advaita, that God and the world are 'not two' (*advaita*).[111]

Hedley's work, when looked at through the conceptual lenses we have been utilizing, points towards a tantalizing fusion of Platonic Christian mysticism and Vedantic idealism. Indeed, his wide-ranging religious philosophy suggests not that 'East is East, and West is West, and never the twain shall meet', in the too-often-quoted sentiment of that iconic Anglo-Indian, Rudyard Kipling, but, in fact, as Kipling wrote in the following couplet, that 'there is neither East nor West, Border, nor Breed, nor Birth, [w]hen two strong men stand face to face, though they come from the ends of the earth'.[112] Hedley offers us a rich and challenging vision of the human and divine unhindered by such physical and conceptual borders.

Response by Douglas Hedley

Christian theology was often conducted in the twentieth century in splendid isolation. This is no longer sustainable in the 'global village' of the digital age. Comparative religion is an important aspect of contemporary theology in the West, and rightly so. The interest in Indology in the trilogy is part of the tradition of Ancient Theology. There is an interest in 'religion' and a human *a priori* and in common tenets shared by great religions that goes back to the church fathers of Alexandria, Nicholas of Cusa, Ficino, the Cambridge Platonists, Sir William Jones and Friedrich Creuzer. Some of the pivotal figures of the study of religion in the twentieth century, such as Rudolf Otto, Mircea Eliade, Henry Corbin and Ananda Coomaraswamy, were Platonists and inheritors of the *prisca theologia*.

Soars is quite correct to see the project as emerging out of Alexandrian Platonism, through an Idealistic and Romantic prism. Sir William Jones, S. T. Coleridge and Rudolf Otto are formative influences upon the theophanic view of the created realm as a 'dark glass' of the Divine: *nam et creatura in deo est subsistens, et deus in creatura mirabili et ineffabili modo creatur, se ipum manifestans, invisibilis visibilem se faciens*.[113]

I would be wary of designating this as 'perennialism' in any strict sense. I would rather see it as the extension of the principle of the 'continuity of esteem' and the Alexandrian principle of the spermatic Logos.

Notes

1. Douglas Hedley, *Sacrifice Imagined: Violence, Atonement, and the Sacred* (New York and London: Continuum, 2011), 59.
2. Hedley was the appointed Teape lecturer in 2006 and spoke in Delhi, Bangalore and Calcutta on the theme of 'The One and the Many' in Indian and Western philosophy. I will not be drawing on these lectures in this chapter for two reasons: firstly, I wish to keep the focus on Hedley's published work – especially on his 'Imagination' trilogy – to which this collection is primarily devoted; secondly, and more importantly, because he explored in the lectures themes and ideas which only came to fuller fruition in the trilogy and whose significance to his broader philosophical-theological outlook is, therefore, best understood in the context of this later work.
3. Westcott was the regius professor of Divinity at Cambridge, bishop of Durham and one of the founders of the (Anglican) Cambridge Mission to India (now known as the Cambridge-Delhi Christian Partnership) in 1877. In 1881, the Mission led to the establishment of what would become one of Delhi University's most prestigious institutions – St Stephen's College. Hedley discusses Westcott in the final book of his trilogy, *The Iconic Imagination* (New York and London: Bloomsbury, 2016), 188–9. I will refer to this simply as *Iconic Imagination* from here on.
4. It is not my intention to conflate Platonism and mysticism, on the one hand, or Romanticism and Idealism, on the other. In Hedley's work, however, we will see that each 'pair' is closely related, which is why I have suggested grouping them together in our heuristic triangle.

5 These are obviously all complex and open-ended themes in their own right. Lest I be accused of painting in brushstrokes which are unforgivably broad, I should point out from the start that my focus (as with the linking themes and figures I come on to discuss) is on their place within Hedley's work.
6 Douglas Hedley, *Coleridge, Philosophy and Religion* (Cambridge: Cambridge University Press, 2000), 6–7. Elsewhere, it is clear that Hedley sees this tradition going much farther back than Eriugena, to the early church fathers.
7 Ibid.
8 See, for example, Dominic J. O'Meara (ed.), *Neoplatonism and Christian Thought* (Albany: State University of New York Press, 1982).
9 Ficino (1433–99) led the fifteenth-century Platonic Academy in Florence, which aimed at reviving Neoplatonism through the translation into Latin of the works of Plato, Plotinus and other Neoplatonic figures. Pico della Mirandola (1463–94) was one of the members of the Academy and founded the tradition of Christian kabbalah.
10 Both members of a group of theologians who would later become known as the 'Cambridge Platonists', Cudworth (1617–88) was Regius Professor of Hebrew and Master of Clare Hall (now Clare) and then Christ's College, where More (1614–87) was also a fellow.
11 Augustine, *De diversis quaestionibus LXXXIII*, q. 46.2
12 For studies of the doctrine in Thomas, see John F. Wippel, *Thomas Aquinas on the Divine Ideas* (Toronto: Pontifical Institute of Mediaeval Studies, 1993), Vivian Boland, *Ideas in God According to Saint Thomas Aquinas* (New York: E. J. Brill, 1996), and Gregory T. Doolan, *Aquinas on the Divine Ideas as Exemplar Causes* (Washington, DC: The Catholic University of America Press, 2014).
13 The doctrine appears throughout Hedley's trilogy, but see, in particular, *Iconic Imagination*, 126.
14 *Coleridge, Philosophy and Religion*, 2.
15 William Wordsworth, *Lines Composed a Few Miles above Tintern Abbey*, On Revisiting the Banks of the Wye during a Tour. 13 July 1798.
16 *Iconic Imagination*, 142.
17 *Coleridge, Philosophy and Religion*, 59–65.
18 Ibid., 64.
19 Ibid., 65.
20 *Iconic Imagination*, 139. Despite the popularity of this kind of imagery, I think that a better metaphor is to see creation as a window – since it is not so much that we see in the world 'reflections' of the divine (as in a mirror), as that, with our imaginative faculties, we can see the divine always and everywhere already present *in* and *through* the created order.
21 Ibid., 139–40.
22 Ibid., 148.
23 *Coleridge, Philosophy and Religion*, 8.
24 Ibid., 9.
25 Ibid.
26 In a related etymological and semantic field, Hedley notes the closeness of the English terms 'sacred' and 'mystery', since the Latin *sacer* (which also gives us 'sacrament') is the root of both (obviously in the case of 'sacred' but less obviously in the case of 'mystery', where *sacer* was used to translate the Greek *mysterion*). 'Sacrifice' is, therefore, a 'making holy, sacred' or perhaps even a 'making mysterious' (*sacra facere*). See *Sacrifice Imagined*, 11 and 26.

27 Cf. Pseudo-Dionysius, *Mystical Theology*, 997B-1000A: 'with your understanding laid aside . . .strive upward as much as you can toward union with him who is beyond all being and knowledge. By an undivided and absolute abandonment of yourself and everything, shedding all and freed from all, you will be uplifted to the ray of the divine shadow which is above everything that is.'
28 A phrase he uses of Coleridge by which he means 'exactly this temper of mind in Plotinus that veers between a strongly contemplative rationalism and an emphasis upon that which resists conceptual analysis: will; life; experience; God' (*Coleridge, Philosophy and Religion*, 11).
29 Obviously, not every Neoplatonist was a Christian.
30 A far more detailed case is put in Andrew Louth, *The Origins of the Christian Mystical Tradition: From Plato to Denys*, 2nd edn (Oxford and New York: Oxford University Press, 2007).
31 In *Living Forms of the Imagination* (London and New York: Continuum, 2008), 89, he describes the Platonic monotheism transmitted to Augustine and Eckhart as '[t]hat form of monotheism [which] was a *via media* between the unrelenting transcendence of the God of Aristotle and the materialism and pantheism of the Stoics'. In a similar way, he uses the phrase 'mystical theism' to mean a form of theism that has been 'nourished by Neoplatonism' (*Iconic Imagination*, 138). For a detailed exploration of this concept, see John Peter Kenney, *Mystical Monotheism: A Study in Ancient Platonic Theology* (Eugene: Wipf and Stock, 2010).
32 *Coleridge, Philosophy and Religion*, 10. While British Idealism did more than just accept the doctrines of Kant, Fichte, Hegel et al. wholesale, the movement was deeply indebted to and influenced by aspects of German culture and philosophy. For more on this, see W. J. Mander, *British Idealism: A History* (Oxford: Oxford University Press, 2011), esp. Ch. 2: 'Beginnings and Influences'.
33 Ibid., 23.
34 Ibid.
35 *Living Forms*, 101. It is for this same reason that 'Plotinus's monism does not mean the extinction of individuality but the realization of the true self – which is "the One in us"' (cf. *Enneads* V.7, I.1.7, III.8.9), quoted in *Living Forms*, 92–3.
36 *Coleridge, Philosophy and Religion*, 11–16.
37 Ibid., 65.
38 Ibid., 59.
39 Ibid., 66.
40 Schelling, *Ausgewählte Schriften*, vol. I: 1794–1800, 76, cited by Hedley in *Coleridge, Philosophy and Religion*, 68.
41 Ibid.
42 For a recent study of the concept of God as both unitary and personal ground of Selfhood, see Cia Van Woezik, *God – Beyond Me: From the I's Absolute Ground in Hölderlin and Schelling to a Contemporary Model of a Personal God* (Leiden: Brill, 2010).
43 Ibid., 70.
44 *Sacrifice Imagined*, 37.
45 Ibid., 58.
46 See especially *Sacrifice Imagined*, 26–37.
47 Douglas Hedley, 'Affective Attunement and the Experience of the Numinous: Reflections on Rudolf Otto's *Das Heilige*', *International Journal of the Study of the Christian Church* 17 (2017): 33–45 (the 'great sage of Marburg' designation is Hedley's, ibid., 42). He takes the title of his article from Otto's phrase '*numinose*

Gemüts-gestimmtheit' which Hedley renders as 'affective attunement by the experience of the numinous'.
48 Ibid.
49 *An Inquiry into the Non-Rational Factor in the Idea of the Divine and its Relation to the Rational.*
50 Cf. ibid., 39: 'Otto's attempts to convey or evoke the pre-linguistic experience of the holy that he proposes as a generic and transcultural feature of humanity is also what made his work unfashionable against reductionist accounts of religion such as those of Marx, Mauss, or Durkheim. '
51 Ibid., 34, and *Sacrifice Imagined*, 29.
52 'Affective Attunement' (see n. 47), 34.
53 Ibid.
54 Ibid.
55 Along with Charles Wilkins (1749–1836) and Henry Thomas Colebrooke (1765–1837), William Jones (1746–94) is widely recognized as one of the most important Orientalists of the Company era in India. Supported by the then governor-general, Warren Hastings (1732–1818), the pioneering work of these civil servant scholars opened up Indology as an academic discipline for future generations. For more on this period, see David Kopf, *British Orientalism and the Bengal Renaissance: The Dynamics of Indian Modernization 1773–1835* (Berkeley and Los Angeles: University of California Press, 1969).
56 *Sacrifice Imagined*, 183. The citation comes from William Jones in Garland H. Cannon (ed.), *The Letters of Sir William Jones* (Oxford: Clarendon Press, 1970), 669–70, and is taken by Hedley from Urs App, 'William Jones's Ancient Theology', in *Sino-Platonic Papers 191* (Philadelphia: University of Pennsylvania, 2009), 18.
57 Martin Ganeri, *Indian Thought and Western Theism: The Vedānta of Rāmānuja* (London and New York: Routledge, 2015), 4.
58 For a comprehensive overview of these different interpretations of the Upanishadic revelation, see Eric J. Lott, *Vedantic Approaches to God* (London: Macmillan, 1980).
59 To follow up this question of how far different Indian philosophical systems can be considered 'idealist', and what precisely this might mean, see Uma Pandey, *Śankara: A Realist Philosopher* (Jalandhar: Kautilya Prakashan, 2015), 26–44.
60 *Coleridge, Philosophy and Religion*, 23.
61 Hedley discusses Sankara and his later opponent, Ramanuja, in *Iconic Imagination*, 194–5.
62 For a survey of different interpretations of Advaita Vedanta (from realist to idealist), see Bradley Malkovsky, *The Role of Divine Grace in the Soteriology of Sankaracarya* (Leiden: Brill, 2001), 46–50.
63 Hedley discusses these figures and their role in the nineteenth-century 'Bengal Renaissance' in *Iconic Imagination*, 189–191. For more detailed analyses of how and why Advaita Vedanta came to be the focus of the Hindu Renaissance, as well as of nineteenth- to early twentieth-century European receptions of Indian philosophical thought, see Wilhelm Halbfass, *India and Europe: An Essay in Understanding* (Albany: State University of New York Press, 1988), and Richard King, *Orientalism and Religion: Post-Colonial Theory, India and 'The Mystic East'* (London and New York: Routledge, 1999).
64 J. J. Clarke, *Oriental Enlightenment: The Encounter between Asian and Western Thought* (London: Routledge, 1997), 61.
65 Perhaps the most obvious example of a European idealist philosopher who was drawn to the Upanishads was Arthur Schopenhauer (1788–1860). See, for example,

the preface to his magnum opus, *The World as Will and Representation* (1818). Hegel also wrote at length on Indian thought, especially in his *Lectures on the Philosophy of History* (1837) where he drew on the work of Colebrooke, Jones and James Mill. He also studied and responded to W. von Humboldt's essays on the *Bhagavadgītā* – see his review, *On the Episode of the Mahabharata Known by the Name Bhagavad Gita by Wilhelm von Humboldt*, edited and translated by H. Herring (New Delhi: Indian Council of Philosophical Research), reproduced in Aakash Singh Rathore and Rimina Mohapatra, *Hegel's India: A Reinterpretation, with Texts* (Oxford: Oxford University Press, 2017), 87–140.

66 Raymond Schwab, *The Oriental Renaissance: Europe's Rediscovery of India and the East, 1680–1880* (New York and Guildford: Columbia University Press), 198. One of the leading German Romantics influenced by Indian thought was F. Schlegel (1772–1829).

67 Schwab, *The Oriental Renaissance*, 56. This predilection for Vedanta has dominated Western academic engagement with Hinduism until relatively recently.

68 Herder is usually thought of as a forerunner of the Romantic movement, rather than belonging to it proper. For more on the influence of Indian material in Herder, see Clarke, *Oriental Enlightenment* (see n. 64), 61–3; Halbfass, *India and Europe*, 69, and Herder's own *Auch eine Philosophie der Geschichte zur Bildung der Menschheit* (1774).

69 Cf., for example, Schelling's concepts of 'absolute identity', the illusory nature of the finite world, pantheism, the 'world-soul' as well as his interest in Indian mythology.

70 Clarke, *Oriental Enlightenment* (see n. 64), 63.

71 For a detailed examination of these cross-cultural currents, see Joanne Miyang Cho, Eric Kurlander and Douglas T. McGetchin (eds), *Transcultural Encounters between Germany and India: Kindred Spirits in the 19th and 20th Centuries* (London and New York: Routledge, 2014).

72 See Ankur Barua, 'The Absolute of Advaita and the Spirit of Hegel: Situating Vedānta on the Horizons of British Idealisms', *Journal of the Indian Council for Philosophical Research*, Springer, 2016.

73 For an explanation of where German Romanticism was getting its images of India from, see A Leslie Willson, *A Mythical Image: The Ideal of India in German Romanticism* (Durham: Duke University Press, 1964).

74 For more on Jones and these wider connections, see Clarke, *Oriental Enlightenment* (see n. 64), 58–9. For a fascinating overview of Coleridge's engagement with the East, see David Vallins, Kaz Oishi and Seamus Perry (eds), *Coleridge, Romanticism and the Orient: Cultural Negotiations* (London and New York: Bloomsbury Academic, 2013), esp. the essays by D. Coleman, 'Coleridge and William Hodges' *Travels in India* (1793)', A. Warren, 'Coleridge, Philosophy, Orient', D. Vallins, 'Immanence and Transcendence in Coleridge's Orient', and N. Tal Harries, '"The One Life Within Us and Abroad": Coleridge and Hinduism'.

75 Metaphysical identity is perhaps the more traditional reading of Advaita Vedanta. Again, see Malkovsky, *The Role of Divine Grace in the Soteriology of Sankaracarya* (n.62) on this.

76 John H. Muirhead puts this argument forward in respect of British Idealism in his *Platonic Tradition in Anglo-Saxon Philosophy* (London: George Allen & Unwin LTD; New York: The Macmillan Company, 1931), 13–16 – that is, that British Idealism owed as much to an indigenous revival of Platonism, as it did to German Kantian and post-Kantian philosophy.

77 *Iconic Imagination*, 184.

78 Ibid., 185.
79 The first issue has tended to centre on the question of whether the similarities between elements of Neoplatonism as found in Plotinus and aspects of Indian thought are merely the result of coincidental osmosis or evidence of more direct influence. This historical debate captured the imagination of certain scholars in the twentieth century. Some, like the French philosopher Emile Bréhier, advocated a strong 'Oriental hypothesis', while others, like A. H. Armstrong and John Rist, pointed to significant divergences between Plotinus's Hellenistic theism and Upanishadic monism. For an overview of the scholarship on this question, see Albert M. Wolters, 'A Survey of Modern Scholarly Opinion on Plotinus and Indian Thought', in *Neoplatonism and Indian Thought*, edited by R. Baine Harris (Virginia: State University of New York Press, 1981), 293–309. On Plotinus's failed attempt to get to India, see Paulos Gregorios, *Neoplatonism and Indian Philosophy* (Albany: State University of New York Press, 2002), 13–17.
80 See R. T. Ciapola, 'Bréhier and Rist on Plotinus', and John R. A. Mayer, 'Plotinus and Sri Aurobindo', in Gregorios, *Neoplatonism and Indian Philosophy*, 71–9 and 164–72.
81 J. F. Staal, *Advaita and Neoplatonism: A Critical Study in Comparative Philosophy* (Madras: University of Madras, 1961).
82 M. Just sees Plotinus's focus on subjectivity and mystical union, in contrast to a more typically 'Hellenic' emphasis on rationality, clarity and objectivity as *the* reason to suppose that Plotinus might have had 'Eastern' influences. See Michael Just, 'Neoplatonism and Paramadvaita', *Comparative Philosophy* 4 (2013): 1–28, here 3.
83 *Ennead* V 5,6, from ἐπέκεινα τῆς οὐσίας in *Republic* 509b.
84 *Ennead* V 3,12.
85 Paul Hacker, 'Cit and Nous, or the Concept of Spirit in Vedantism and Neoplatonism', in *Philology and Confrontation: Paul Hacker on Traditional and Modern Vedānta*, edited by Wilhelm Halbfass (Albany: State University of New York Press, 1995), 211–26. It should be noted that Hacker sees the three hypostases of One – noûs – soul as subordinative in Plotinus, whereas the *sat-cit-ananda* of Vedanta are identical designations of the one reality.
86 Hacker, 'Cit and Nous, or the Concept of Spirit in Vedantism and Neoplatonism', 225.
87 *Ennead* VI 5,12.
88 See W. Beierwaltes, *Platonismus und Idealismus* (Frankfurt am Main: Vittorio Klostermann, 1972).
89 New Jerusalem Bible translation. Clearly, this verse raises all sorts of philological, exegetical and theological questions, which I do not pretend to solve in this chapter.
90 Hedley discusses, in particular, Augustine's commentary on Psalm 38: 'Anyone who takes the road away from him who truly *is* necessarily goes toward non-being' (Augustine, *Expositions of the Psalms*, Exp. Ps. 38, §225, translated by M. Boulding (New York: New York City Press, 2000), vol. 2, 193) quoted in *Living Forms*, 202.
91 *Conf.* VII. x (16).
92 *Conf.* VII. xx (26).
93 Emilie Zum Brunn, *St. Augustine: Being and Nothingness* (New York: Paragon House, 1988), vii.
94 Plotinus's influence can be seen overtly in the passage from Augustine's *Confessions* quoted above – not least in the idea of 're-turning inward' (cf. *Ennead* V 1,1) and the physical world being a 'region of dissimilarity' from the One (cf. *Ennead* I 8,13, from Plato, *Statesman* 273d).

95 *Conf.* VIII. ii (3).
96 For more on Augustine's (and Aquinas's) Christological interpretations of Exod. 3.14, see Janet Soskice, 'Aquinas and Augustine on Creation and God as "Eternal Being"', *New Blackfriars* 95 (2014): 190–207, here 203.
97 See, for example, *In Iohannis evangelium* 2, 2. For more on the correspondences Augustine draws between Exod. 3.14 and Gospel passages like Rom. 1.20, cf. Zum Brunn, *Being and Nothingness* (see n. 93), 110–11.
98 *Conf.* VII. xx (26).
99 Ibid., VII. xx (27).
100 *ST* I.4.2.
101 Hedley discusses the influence on Aquinas and Eckhart of the Neoplatonic *Liber de Causis* in *Iconic Imagination*, 137.
102 Robert J. Dobie, 'Thomas Aquinas and Meister Eckhart on Exodus 3:14: Exegesis or Eisegesis?', *Medieval Mystical Theology* 24 (2015): 124–36, here 126.
103 Eckhart, Sermon XXV, n.257, in *Meister Eckhart, Teacher and Preacher*, edited by Bernard McGinn (New York: Paulist Press, 1986), 218.
104 Eckhart, *In agro dominico* art.26: *Omnes creaturae sunt unum purum nihil: non dico, quod sint quid modicum vel aliquid, sed quod sint unum purum nihil.*
105 Dobie, 'Thomas Aquinas and Meister Eckhart' (see n. 102), 134–5 (cf. Sermon 83, Colledge and McGinn, trans., *Meister Eckhart: The Essential Sermons, Commentaries, Treatises and Defense* (London: S.P.C.K., 1981)).
106 *Coleridge, Philosophy and Religion*, 76.
107 Hedley looks at how the verse is interpreted, for example, by Berkeley, Cudworth, Donne and Coleridge, and discusses in some detail the central role it plays in Schelling's speculative theology – see ibid., 75–87 (this section is, in fact, Hedley's most detailed treatment of the verse).
108 The well-known twentieth-century Advaitin, Ramana Maharshi (1879–1950), claimed that the whole of Vedanta is contained in two biblical passages: 'Be still and know that I am God' (Ps. 46.10) and 'I am that I am' (Exod. 3.14) – cf. *Talks with Ramana Maharshi*, Tiruvannamalai: Sri Ramanasramam, 1984, 307, quoted in J. Glenn Friesen, *Abhishiktananda (Henri Le Saux): Christian Nondualism and Hindu Advaita* (Calgary: Aevum Books, 2015), 35.
109 Rudolf Otto, *Mysticism East and West: A Comparative Analysis of the Nature of Mysticism* (London: Macmillan and Co., 1932), v., discussed by Hedley in 'Affective Attunement' (see n. 47), 39.
110 Otto, *Mysticism East and West*, 4–10.
111 Bede Griffiths, *The Marriage of East and West: A Sequel to The Golden String* (London: Fount, 1982), 85, cited by Hedley in *Iconic Imagination*, 198. Griffiths (1906–73) was a Benedictine monk, who, in 1968, took over the Saccidananda ashram in Tamil Nadu from Henri Le Saux.
112 Rudyard Kipling, 'The Ballad of East and West', The Works of Rudyard Kipling, edited by R. T. Jones (Hertfordshire: Wordsworth Editions Limited, 1994), 245.
113 Eriugena, *Periphyseon* III, 678c. 'For both creation (*creatura*), by subsisting, is in God; and God, by manifesting Himself, in a marvellous and ineffable manner creates Himself in creation, the invisible making Himself visible.'

10

Imagination and religion

Some Shakespearian reflections

Douglas Hedley

The trilogy was not conceived as an exhaustive 'history of ideas'. The history of the term 'imagination' in the West was a part of my brief, but it was not my objective.[1] Nor was it a definitional exercise to examine the concept of 'imagination'. Certainly, we were not committed to a faculty psychology, whereby the mind is a gathering of distinct faculties, each entrusted with distinct mental functions. There is a distinct range of mental activities where the mind does not perceive, and yet nevertheless one encounters phenomena, for example, dreams, daydreams and fantasies. 'If one wants to talk about anything religious, some kind of relation has to be established with the invisible.'[2] Religion and art employ the stuff of imagination to convey a world or worlds other than some quotidian *res extensa*. The philosophical paradox that I explore throughout the trilogy is that we need imagination to escape fantasy. This is linked to the most ancient challenge of the (Hellenic–Western) philosophical tradition: Know Thyself.

One might distinguish for a moment the aesthetic imagination from the moral and the epistemological. Let us consider the moral imagination as the capacity to envisage the world from the perspective of other agents and their interests. The epistemological imagination allows us to form hypotheses about the world that are underdetermined by the data. Newton's theory of gravity and Einstein's of relativity are complex theories or conjectures about the world that cannot be simply inferred from experience, even if such theories are corroborated by evidence. The aesthetic imagination is rather distinct from the moral or epistemological. It can furnish a world that is neither true nor false. The great artist facilitates the operation of the imagination in an audience. Consider what Coleridge aptly names the 'suspension of disbelief'. When we are in the theatre, we can imagine 'the cloud-capped towers' and 'gorgeous towers' (*The Tempest* 4.1.152). Shakespeare dwells upon the phenomenon of imagination and the mysterious capacity of the mind to suspend disbelief. He often does this in a humorous manner as when the mechanicals explain to their aristocratic audience that there is no need to fear the lion since the lion is, in fact, Snug the joiner (*A Midsummer Night's Dream* 3.1.861). We might be tempted to distinguish between the problem-solving or 'instructive' dimension of the imagination and the transcendent.³ Perhaps it is the latter that propels us to escapism and fantasy. The former, by contrast, is a healthy tool to cope with the 'hic et nunc'.

There are two reasons why that account does not work. One is psychological and the other is political. If the human subject is in Freud's celebrated terms 'nicht einmal Herr ... im eigenen Hause', 'not master in its own house' but subject to pressures and forces of which it is barely or inchoately aware, those often dark landscapes of the human psyche, then the role of the imagination in its more venturesome aspects should not be undervalued. Perhaps the mythopoetic figure of King Lear is a particularly potent instrument for perceiving the perils of vanity or some of the agonies of parenthood that remain otherwise submerged or ignored. The outlandish-primordial mythic Britain of King Lear is a world which contains certain assumptions about family relations. It is not just about age, frailty or violence. It presupposes assumptions and tenets about the closest human bonds and their betrayal. Its exploration of vanity and self-deception requires the notion of the father. But this has to be *understood* for the tragedy to work.⁴ There is a cognitive component to the play, and this is the root of its aboriginal power, the very whence of its alchemy.

The second reason is political. One of the greatest European poets, the great silver age Russian poet Mandelstam perished in a Gulag for comparing Stalin's moustache to cockroaches: the poetic depiction of the sadism of the dictator is all the more effective for its imaginative extravagance. He gives voice to a horror that millions suffered through his imaginative powers. The poets are the lamp bearers. They give testimony and bear witness.

The rich imaginative life of the Greeks cannot be divorced from their political innovations. And poetry was never more important than in some of the cruel and repressive regimes of the last century. But in the trilogy, I am employing a transcendent, and one might say playful, imagination. Human subjectivity is, upon reflection, mysterious to itself and self-knowledge is arduous and oblique. In art we are presented with characters as unified and luminous, whereas our own experience of the world and ourselves is often opaque. The vanity of King Lear is transparent in Shakespeare's play. Such images as Lear are constructed unities of a kind that one cannot encounter directly in experience.

A lack of self-knowledge is, however, ethically perilous. In *Living Forms of the Imagination*, I explore the idea that the *proper* functioning of imagination is key to a healthy psyche and ethics. The self that cannot imaginatively engage with other centres of consciousness is much diminished; it is literally 'autistic' or narcissistic. A properly ethical agent must be able to imagine the needs and concerns of others. By analogy, if imagination is requisite for the proper functioning at this psychological and ethical level, why not at the religious?

My predecessor in the Cambridge Divinity Faculty, Don Cupitt, could be seen as making very similar claims in his non-realist philosophy of religion. Religion can be seen as a way of living as if there were metaphysical substances or beings such as God or the soul or the Son of God, but these are imaginative constructions with no metaphysical basis. More recently, the secular anthropologist Yuval Noah Harari in his *Sapiens: A Brief History of Humankind* (London: Harper, 2014) has made remarkably similar claims, albeit with very different aims. He argues that after the cognitive revolution of around 70,000 BC mankind is able to cooperate particularly effectively through the working of a collective imaginary, especially after the agricultural revolution in 12,000 BC and the Scientific Revolution of the sixteenth and seventeenth centuries in Europe. These constructions of the human imagination such as gods, money, nations and legal institutions, or more recently social welfare and human rights, have been a key to human success. I concur that the imagination is key to the distinctive capacities of humanity; I take issue with the claim that this capacity should be thought of as a motor of useful fictions. The weakness of Harari's account is due to the absence of a theological dimension. The German philosopher Schelling notes:

> Allein die göttliche Imagination, welche die Urache der Spezification der Weltwesen ist, ist nicht die menschliche, daß sie ihren Schöpfungen bloß idealistische Wirklichkeit ertheilt. Die Repräsentationen der Gottheit können nur selbständige Wesen sein; denn was ist das Beschränkende unsrer Vorstellungen als eben daß wir Unselbständiges sehen? Gott schaut die Dinge an sich an. An sich ist nur das Ewige, auf sich selbst Beruhende, Wille, Freiheit.[5]

The work has a central theological element. It is not that the phenomena of the world provide a basis for inferring to a first cause. It is rather that religion provides a way of seeing the facts of the world. C. S. Lewis draws an analogy between Christianity and the sun in this respect: you see the world through it.[6] Such an imaginary is not irrational. And it can provide support for science that some of its naturalistic competitors do not. Theism furnishes some account of why human beings have an instinct for discovering truths, whereas if the cause of our beliefs is oblivious to truths, it is not clear, for example, why natural selection should exhibit any preference for truth over falsehood.

The trilogy is an exploration of a particular vision of the religious imagination, inspired by and drawing from S. T. Coleridge and the Cambridge Platonists. I take the influence of the Cambridge Platonists upon Coleridge and Wordsworth as an instance of the way in which aesthetics and religion need to be viewed in conjunction. Henry More observes in his *Enchiridion Ethicum*:

> And it is the most perfect state of Life, to love good things, and to hate the bad, at least; to bear them with indignation, whenever they are obtruded on us. For this gives testimony, that the inferior part of the soul submits, and is overawed by the superior; and that the whole man is as it were in the firy [sic] Chariot of his Affections, *Elias*-like, carried up towards God and Heaven.[7]

Like Henry More, I used the same emblem of the chariot as an image of the transforming power of the imagination.

Platonism has a special relationship to the aesthetic. If Platonism is primarily concerned with the sovereignty of the Good, its expression is frequently perceived as beauty. The influence of Platonism has often been felt most powerfully outside the university and outside 'philosophy' in the narrow sense. In particular, Plato's dialogues, especially *Symposium* and *Phaedrus*, and Plotinus's seminal theory of art have exerted an enormous impact upon Western art, poetry and aesthetics. Dante presents himself in the *Purgatorio* 9 as Ganymede, the boy seized by Zeus in the shape of an eagle to Mount Olympus as a cupbearer to the gods. This is an image for Dante, as later for Landino, of the contemplation of the Divine Being. In the dedication to his father of *The Philosophical Poems* (1647) More recalls his father reading *The Faerie Queene* of Spenser, 'a Poem as richly fraught with divine Morality as Phansy'.[8]

Plato deployed myths philosophically, and myth is an imaginative form. Griffiths notes of Plato's myths: 'The Myth is the reflection in the human imagination of these archetypal ideas, these cosmic principles and powers, which were known in the ancient world as the gods or angels.'[9] The 'ideas' of Plato were subsequently fused with the angelic powers of Hellenic church fathers, Iranian-Arabic thought, the schoolmen and the Renaissance. Shakespeare is an inheritor of such Neoplatonic lore. Shakespeare's religion is a contentious issue. Nor is he often thought of as a *poeta doctus*, especially since Milton's arresting picture of Shakespeare 'warbling his native woodnotes wild'.[10] Yet Shakespeare, like his creation Prospero, is a bookish man. The fashion for a sceptical Shakespeare (e.g. parallels with Montaigne and the early modern sceptical tradition), reinforced by post-structuralist scepticism, tends to occlude the deeply religious and realist aspects of the plays. I think that Shakespeare is talking about facts through his dramatis personae. He draws upon Renaissance ideas of the artist:

> The poet's eye, in a fine frenzy rolling,
> Doth glance from heaven to earth, from earth to heaven;
> And as imagination bodies forth
> The forms of things unknown, the poet's pen
> Turns them to shapes, and gives to airy nothing
> A local habitation and a name. (*A Midsummer Night's Dream* 5.1.12–17)

Shakespeare draws upon the theory of Platonic beauty in Ficino as we find it in the Elizabethan form of Sir Philip Sidney's *Defence of Poetry* 1579 or Edmund Spenser's *Faerie Queene* of 1590. An obvious instance of the legacy of Platonic love is in Berowne's words to his friends in *Love's Labour Lost*:

> From women's eyes this doctrine I derive:
> They sparkle still the right Promethean fire;
> They are the books, the arts, the academes,
> That show, contain, and nourish all the world. (*Love's Labour's Lost* 4.3.344–347)

Erotic love becomes, as in the *Phaedrus* or *Symposium*, a vehicle of religious transport.[11]

Shakespeare's work was a retelling of stories/myths in his plays. Even the historical or quasi-historical plays have mythic dimensions and structures. Shakespeare presents true fictions: imaginative depictions of humanity poised between good and evil, sin and salvation.

> Lovers and madmen have such seething brains,
> Such shaping fantasies, that apprehend

> More than cool reason ever comprehends.
> The lunatic, the lover, and the poet
> Are of imagination all compact. (*A Midsummer Night's Dream* 5.1.4–8)

Shakespeare, I think, was – however ironically – claiming that the imaginative force of a great poet, in making ideas sensuous, supplies more 'than cool reason ever comprehends'. We might say today that the poet can offer a narrative vision of human experience that eludes the natural sciences *toto caelo*.

Hamlet is a good example of a quasi-historical work that deals with perennial themes, and especially the sacred and desecration. Consider the passage where Claudius tries to pray after murdering his brother:

> My words fly up, my thoughts remain below.
> Words without thoughts never to heaven go. (*Hamlet* 3.3.97–98)

The new King of Denmark, Claudius, has just told Rosencrantz and Guildenstern to take the troublesome Hamlet to England. Polonius says that he will hide and observe Hamlet with his mother. Claudius kneels to pray: not out of remorse and for forgiveness (he has killed his brother), but for divine aid. Hamlet sees him at prayer and refrains from killing him. Claudius, unaware of Hamlet, rises and expresses his recognition that his own prayer is worthless. Shakespeare's *Hamlet* is full of the sacred and desecration. Hamlet is outraged by the desecration wrought by his wicked and cunning uncle.

Can we still understand this side of Shakespeare? Max Weber raised the issue of the disenchantment of the modern world (*Entzauberung*), the inexorable loss of the sacred, the eclipse of ritual and cosmic order. Is the realm of the sacred a world 'well lost', an archaic and atavistic burden upon modern civilization? There is a widespread hostility to science that is lamentable and irrationalist. Much, if not all, of this hostility is fuelled by religious fundamentalism, ignorance and superstition. Donne's lament that the 'new philosophy calls all in doubt' and as a result ''Tis all in pieces, all coherence gone',[12] is shared by many sophisticated critics of modern society like Alasdair MacIntyre. Henry More, like Coleridge later, was not hostile to empirical science. On the contrary, he openly uses Bacon's criticism of the *eidola* of the cave in his polemic with the wild fancies of the enthusiasts. The strictly empirical methods of science, however, have their limits. For example, beauty and art are widely considered to be not merely life-enhancing but consoling and healing. Evolutionary psychologists have reductive explanations. One reads that landscape painting is reminiscent of human prehistory in the African savannah, etc. Yet the explanatory range of biological concepts like natural selection and random mutation seems unduly taxed in the aesthetic just as much as in the ethical. The reason for this lies in the capacity of beauty in art and nature to convey a sense of the sacred.

What is the Holy? Rudolf Otto (1869–1937) provides a seminal (and unfairly maligned) theory of religion as grounded in the human experience of the mystery of the divine presence that is 'numinous'. It is the numinous (modelled on 'ominous'). This is the experience of *mysterium tremendum et fascinans*. The Holy is both terrifying (*tremendum*) and attractive (*fascinans*). *Homo sacer* precedes *homo faber* and enhanced material well-being or technology can never supplant the need for the sacred. One can see that in the arts. In *The Iconic Imagination*, we considered those ancient cave paintings such as those of Chauvet in France. In *Sacrifice Imagined*, we explored the roots of tragic drama in the sacrificial festival of Dionysus.

What does the experience of the sacred described so eloquently by Otto tell us? It says that we cannot reduce religion to social structures (Durkheim) or psychological needs (Freud). The human need for the sacred persists, and it requires mediation through poets, priests and prophets. Bede Griffiths observes: 'The language of myth and poetry, of the concrete imagination, engages the senses, the feelings, the affections and the will as well as the reason, and so leads to the transformation of the whole man.'[13]

One advantage of the language of the holy is that it allows for a consideration of non-theistic religion. While the emphasis in the trilogy is upon the Western Christian tradition, I have tried to consider other perspectives, especially Hinduism. Many of the leading theorists of imagination in the twentieth century were scholars of Islam, Hinduism or Buddhism. Ananda Kentish Coomaraswamy, Mircea Eliade, Henry Corbin constitute striking examples of this phenomenon.[14]

Secularization as the historical process by which religion is replaced by secular institutions and values (Marx, Durkheim) has been acutely problematized by Charles Taylor in his enormous work *A Secular Age*, where he critiques 'the subtraction thesis' – and his own sophisticated account calls this the modern 'cosmic imaginary'.[15] The crisis of modernity is in part a narrowing of the perspective. Since the seventeenth century, there has been an increasing reliance upon the literal truth conditions of utterances. For the highly specific and abstract concerns of the natural sciences, this is usually appropriate (although even here at the quantum scale this seems to break down with wave-particle duality). The polyvalence of the symbolic and the poetic is more attuned to the ambiguities of human experience than the rigidly scientific. The great enhancement of effective technological control has been associated with increasing disenchantment and a diminished sense of affective involvement with the world. Yet living with ambiguity and polyvalence is arduous. The longing for unambiguous certainties is intelligible and reinforced in our highly technocratic societies.[16]

One of the most baneful illusions of recent human history has been the idea that science and technology can provide a form of salvation. This apparently optimistic view of human nature has in fact produced some of the cruellest forms of persecution from eugenics to the mass deportations and savage cultural revolutions of ideologues since the French and Russian Revolutions. This illusion has been less cruel in our own cultural world, but I think it is the source of one major challenge to the humanities. Those great texts that spoke to our longings and anxieties in this *region of unlikeness* (*regio dissimilitudinis* of *Confessions* 7,10, 16) seem out of place in the utopian world of technology and sovereign rights, best practice and institutional transparency.

In *Macbeth*, the eponymous Scottish thane says to Lady Macbeth:

But wherefore could not I pronounce 'Amen'?
I had most need of blessing, and 'Amen'
Stuck in my throat. (*Macbeth* 2.2.30–32)

Macbeth cannot say 'Amen', the Hebrew word that the Christian says as an affirmation or a response to a blessing. Macbeth cannot say the word 'amen' after murdering Duncan. He cannot pray. And there is a perverse reflection of Christ at the crucifixion. Macbeth is forsaken like Christ. Yet unlike Christ, Macbeth is not innocent: he is stunned by guilt. Lady Macbeth says to him:

> Get some water,
> and wash this filthy witness from your hand. (*Macbeth* 2.2.46–47)

There may well be reference to Pilate washing his hands of his guilt. Ironically, it is Lady Macbeth who is haunted by images of blood. When sleepwalking, she is trying to rub away a spot of blood.

Shakespeare is fascinated by the difference between regret and remorse. I might *regret* going to the cinema rather than the opera, but I will not feel remorse about it. Macbeth is speaking of *guilt,* not shame, *remorse*, not regret. I feel remorse about an injury done to a person. Words such as punishment, sin and guilt are out of favour in the contemporary world; they can seem crude and lacking in psychological sophistication, perhaps even cruel and atavistic. Is this merely the introjection of social mores, reinforced by the traumatic lessons and punishment of early childhood? And is this not morbid or pathological? Perhaps not. As human beings, even if we have not committed egregious crimes like Macbeth, we know and experience guilt. It is the psychopath or the narcissist who seems guilt free, but the healthy psyche is troubled. It is an acute consciousness of the Holy that leads St Paul to say: 'Who will deliver me from this body of death?' (Rom. 7.24). Do we not have in *Macbeth* a vision of someone who cannot say 'amen' to life? Macbeth has chosen separation from God. Consider the words of approach to communion in the solemn beauties of Cranmer's prayer book in the prayer of Humble Access: 'We do not presume to come to this thy Table, O merciful Lord, trusting in our own righteousness, but in thy manifold and great mercies.'[17] Joseph Pieper, in his illuminating little book called *Death and Immortality*, considers and defends the ancient view of death as a punishment for sin, that is, the conscious turning from God. This may seem archaic-mythic, but Pieper notes that punishment, properly understood, is a correction, a remedy and a making good. Death so construed is much more gladdening than in its secular versions. The English word 'end' can mean both cessation and fulfilment. Unlike the existentialist resoluteness about the inevitability of death which masks a view of the cosmos as grim absurdity (Heidegger) and quasi-heroic-fatalistic resolute 'being toward death', the Christian view is the witness to the commitment to ultimate goodness as the ground of being. And to speak of the belief in that ultimate and transcendent good means that death is not just an end as termination but end as telos and goal, to find communion with the source of our aspiration and longing. Lear says to Cordelia:

> Upon such sacrifices . . . .
> The gods themselves throw incense. (*King Lear* 5.3.20–21)

Lear has struck many as a post-Christendom play set in a pre-Christian era. Yet it is clearly about good and evil. The themes of foolishness and wisdom are clearly

Christian. Lear is an image of vanity, taken in by the flattery of Goneril and Regan and misusing his power and wealth.

The Fool says to Lear: 'Thou had'st little wit in thy bald crown when thou gavest thine golden one away' (1.4.155-156). The dead Cordelia has sometimes been likened to an inverted pieta. She says: 'O dear father, / It is thy business I go about' (4.4.2), recalling Christ's remarks to his parents in the Temple: 'Wist ye not that I must be about my Father's business?' (Lk. 2.49). Or when a man says to Lear: 'Thou hast one daughter who redeems nature from the general curse which twain have brought her to' (4.6.2).

There may be classical associations. A father losing his daughter has obvious parallels in Greek tragedy. Aeschylus's *Oresteia* is a paradigm: Agamemnon has upset the goddess Artemis and the goddess insists that he must sacrifice his daughter for his ships to sail to Troy. Upon his return from Troy, Agamemnon is killed by Clytemnestra, who is in turn killed by her son Orestes. This paradigmatic circle of violence becomes for centuries the model of tragic drama, and the reflection upon revenge and justice in its wake.

In *Sacrifice Imagined*, I considered the oddness of the phenomenon of 'sacrifice'. Sacrifice is a feature common to the great religious cultures and yet it is puzzling. Its wastefulness is bewildering given that human evolution is largely a battle with scarcity. For us creatures of scarcity, why the waste? After all, the object of sacrifice is usually precious. The Christian image of sacrifice is one of dreadful pain and suffering. The shocking cruelty of the cross in the ancient world was meant to shock and deter hardened and cynical criminals as well as resolute and reckless patriots. It also expresses the demonic dimension of the psyche. There is a sickness of the soul which is not mere dysfunction but perversion. Joseph de Maistre (1753-1821) was an influence at this stage of the work. No philosophy that ignores the violence and cruelty in the world 'saves the phenomena'. I initially encountered Maistre through an essay by Isaiah Berlin and was repulsed by the plausible account of the proto-fascist Savoyard. Yet Isaiah Berlin had a blind spot with regard to religion, and when I came to read and study the works of Maistre, I discovered a dimension ignored by the Oxford savant's portrait, that of Maistre's Origenism and his link to the Cambridge Platonists. Maistre is a profoundly interesting figure within the Platonic tradition. He took Cudworth's *True Intellectual System of the Universe* over the Alps when the French Revolutionary Army descended upon Chambery in Savoy. It seemed to me that there is phenomenological truth in Maistre's unflinching depiction of relentless cruelty and violence. Bede Griffiths notes that 'in every great religious tradition, it has been recognised that to reach the final truth one must pass through death. It is the meaning behind Aeneas's descent into the underworld in Virgil, and of Dante's descent into hell in the *Divine Comedy*. It is, of course, the meaning of the Christian baptism.'[18]

In *Sacrifice Imagined*, I considered René Girard's scapegoat theory, especially in his seminal work *Violence and the Sacred* (1972). For Girard, sacrifice should be understood as a process of scapegoating. The 'scapegoat mechanism' is the basis of all ancient religions. If Girard is correct about the violent potential of mimetic rivalry, this imitative rivalry surges and will explode unless the rivals can agree to direct their violence upon a scapegoat. The diversion of violence towards the victim-scapegoat secures peace and the scapegoat attains holy status. We find this in all cultures, and it was finally exposed by Christianity.[19] Jesus is the scapegoat who recognized the nature of his death and forgave the perpetrators. On Girard's view, Christianity is the ultimate antidote to sacrifice understood as scapegoating. It unveiled the scapegoating mechanism by insisting upon the innocence of the victim.

There are various problems with Girard's theory. Firstly, on imitation. Imitation for Girard is largely negative. Mimetic rivalry fuels violence in society. But Christianity stresses a form of imitation that is positive, beneficial and productive: the imitation of Christ. Only in an Evelyn Waugh novel satirizing Anglo-Catholic foibles in an Oxonian biretta belt can one imagine this being a competitive activity in the Girardian sense. The profound sense of the imitation of Christ is grounded upon the doctrine of sanctification as the pith and kernel of our faith. Sonship is imparted, not merely imputed. The deeper meaning of St Paul's doctrine of sonship in the new creation wrought by the death and resurrection of our Lord is grounded in the doctrine of the imitation of Christ. Secondly, Christ is more properly seen as the *Christus consummator*. He is the crowning and culmination of sacrifice rather than the ultimate repudiation of sacrifice. If the lives of Christians are meant to be 'living sacrifices' (Rom. 12.1), it is because they reflect the great sacrifice of our high priest Christ that redeems and fulfils the sacrificial practices of the ancient Hebrews. Note the etymology *sacra-facere*, 'making holy'. We referred to Otto's subtle explication of the primordial sense of the holy. There is a profoundly human longing for the Holy: it is not a need for psychotherapy, for mutual reassurance, the aesthetics of ancient language and ritual or disquiet about the social ills of the contemporary world. These may all be explanatory factors in the pilgrimage. But to encounter the transcendent sacred in broken profane lives is to confront this renewing transformative power in the beauty of holiness. We come to encounter the Holy as Christ, victim and priest.

The English word 'Imagination' has the word 'image' in it, and its Christological connotations are buried in the etymology of the world. The claim of the Christian church, from the evangelists to the Councils, is that Christ has revealed the divine nature. Christ is the εἰκών or image of God (2 Cor. 4.4, Col. 1.15). Here Christ is no contingent likeness, but is an essential derivation. The genius of Stoic and Platonic philosophy was fused with the prophetic insight of the ancient Hebrews into the personal and transcendent dignity of the Godhead in the great doctrine of the Logos. St Paul tells us that this Logos is the 'εἰκών of the Invisible God' (Col. 1.15): 'Through him are all things' (cf. Rom. 11.36) and he is 'all and in all' (Col. 3.11). Christ is the 'life-giving Spirit' (1 Cor. 15.45) and it is the vocation of Christians to transform themselves into his image (cf. 2 Cor. 3.18). Thomas Traherne is drawing upon this when he writes:

> O give me Grace to see thy face, and be
> A constant Mirror of Eternitie
> Let my pure soul, transformed to a thought,
> Attend upon thy Throne and as it ought
> Spend all its time feeding on thy love,
> And never from thy sacred Presence move.[20]

This is not the perversion of pristine Rabbinic Judaism with convoluted Greek metaphysics. The upshot is intensely practical and theologically challenging. When faced with the harrowing problem of evil and suffering in the world, many theologians retreat into the language of analogy. We cannot properly worship a Being who is not univocally good. John Stuart Mill was right to say: 'I will call no being good who is not what I mean by good when I apply the word to my fellow creatures.'[21]

The world cannot be moral mayhem. Yet the 'ought' of the ethical is suspended in this world between failure and success. Christians are encouraged to believe in the process of the gradual transformation of the world, the slow impact of the leaven, while repudiating any false optimism or repression of hard realities. The manifest evils in the world point to deep-seated intuitions of goodness (otherwise they would be experienced as brute facts).

The Divinity is revealed in the affront and scandal of the cross. In the exquisite performance of the *Passion of St John*, one hears those opening words:

Zeig uns durch deine Passion,
daß du, der wahre Gottessohn,
zu aller Zeit,
auch in der größten Niedrigkeit,
verherrlicht worden bist.[22]

Not shame but glory attends the death of Jesus: the Divine suffering and abasement on the cross is not merely seen as an isolated aspect or incident within the economy of redemption, but the revelation of the divine love overcoming evil. Meeting evil with goodness is to accept suffering: 'Surely he hath borne our griefs and carried our sorrows' (Is. 53.4). Divine self-sacrifice and suffering is part of the good news. The duchess of York says to her son: 'Bloody thou art, bloody will be thy end' (*Richard III* 4.4.195).

There is little reference to the historical Jesus; indeed, why is the Jesus of history important? We might consider an analogy with a figure from one of Shakespeare's great dramas. There is a long tradition of scepticism about the historical accuracy of Shakespeare's depiction of Richard III, attributing the bulk of this image of the rank tyrant to the imagination of the great Bard. Of course, on such a view Shakespeare was evidently a propagandist of the Tudors: that is precisely why (on this view) he would present Richard III as a man deformed both spiritually and physically. Quite recently, an enthusiast for the dead king tried to find his grave. It was, quite remarkably, discovered someway from the Battle of Bosworth where Richard fell in 1485 in what is now a car park in Leicester (and was a Grey Friars Church). With carbon dating and DNA it was discovered to be the remains of the 32-year-old monarch. To the astonishment of the archaeologist (and disappointment of the Richard III society), the bones revealed not only the expected battle wounds but the curved spine. The poet was correct: not quite a hunchback but very close. The imaginative construction of the king was not fanciful. This is relevant for the problem of the historical Jesus.

Bloody thou art, bloody will be thy end.
Shame serves thy life and doth thy death attend. (*Richard III* 4.4.195–196)

Tellingly, it is Richard's mother who says this to him, the woman who bore him into the world. The force of Shakespeare's narrative lies in its depiction of evil. Even though he is writing much later after the event than our evangelists about Christ, there are historical truths there. Yes, in a way, the death of Richard is a perverse reversal of Christ's. He dies in the midst of the will to power. Like Macbeth, who uses the same imagery of blood:

> For mine own good,
> All causes shall give way: I am in blood
> Stepp'd in so far that, should I wade no more,
> Returning were as tedious as go o'er. (*Macbeth* 3.4.134–137)

Shakespeare presents Richard as consummate evil, violence engendering its own demise through wicked designs, bloody to its own end, just as the evangelists present Jesus as goodness embracing and overcoming evil through great personal cost. Yet neither is Richard's death nor that of Jesus *merely* poetic or imaginative:

> Now I want
> Spirits to enforce, Art to enchant;
> And my ending is despair,
> Unless I be relieved by prayer,
> Which pierces so, that it assaults
> Mercy itself, and frees all faults. (*The Tempest*, Epilogue 13–18)

Here is Prospero at the very end of *The Tempest*, a play about revenge and forgiveness. It is about a bookish man who has been outmanoeuvred by wily and scheming relatives, but who gets the last word. Prospero has been controlling the Island, but he is now returning to his home. Prospero has been using magic to produce good and reconciling effects. Now this great Renaissance magus is appealing to God.

Prospero has been injured since his kingdom has been wrested from him by Antonio, his own brother, together with Alonso, King of Naples. This play is not only about the punishment for this usurpation but also about forgiveness and reconciliation. Forgiveness, like sacrifice, constitutes a real problem. We are used to thinking of forgiveness in positive terms. Yet who has the right to forgive? And when? What about justice? Here we get into the thorny question of punishment. Many think of retributive justice as merely atavistic and claim that the only purpose of punishment can be deterrence or rehabilitation. We need to understand the profound link between punishment and justice which the great philosophers from Plato to Hegel insist upon. Hegel, for example, says that the breaker of a law is as a rational being possessing free will honoured by appropriate and just punishment. Punishment is the 'restoration of freedom'.[23] Forgiveness cannot be condoning or a lazy collusion with sin:

> But I say to unto you which hear, love your enemies, do good to them which hate you. Bless them that curse you, and pray for them which despiseth you. . . . For if ye love them which love you, what thank have ye? For sinners also do even the

same. But love your enemies, and do good, and lend, hoping for nothing again. (Lk. 6.27-35)

We have a reflection of this command in Prospero's

> the rarer action is
> In virtue than in vengeance. They being penitent,
> The sole drift of my purpose doth extend
> Not a frown further. (*The Tempest* 5.1.28–31)

Here Prospero is claiming that it is better to forgive than to hate one's enemies. The play is about redemption and the restoration of order and harmony. Too often it is claimed that Prospero does not fully forgive, but that is to overlook the subtlety of the Bard. Shakespeare, no less than Plato or Hegel, has a deep sense of cosmic and spiritual justice.

Is not talk of sacrifice the crude and violent language of a bygone age? We discussed briefly the theory of Girard and I offered two reasons why we might reject Girard's account. The kingdom of God is necessarily a social structure, but the reverence for the individual is immensely important. Christianity forbids the idea that lives can or should be sacrificed for instrumental reasons. Even Kant's view of a person as an end in itself comes out of this Christian perspective and tradition. Pagan Greek ethics is characterized by 'tough love'; and we find little patience for Christian sympathy. If one compares Clement or Origen with their pagan contemporaries, there is a much deeper emphasis upon compassion. Origen presents us with the wonderful image of the blood-stained logos. He has a much keener sense of human vulnerability than Plotinus or even Seneca, who can say that only weak eyes weep in sympathy. Still others might say, is this not the violence that religion engenders? Christ is both the great high priest and the victim. The image of the lamb is very central in the Book of Revelation as a revelation of Jesus Christ. The lamb in Revelation is both redeemer and judge. The lamb is not a witless scapegoat. Our divine model is, as Plato prophesied in the *Republic*, one who did right and suffered injustice until he was crucified.[24] As C. S. Lewis says, 'only a Man who . . . served in our sad regiment as a volunteer . . . could perform this perfect dying.'[25]

In the context of *Christus consummator*, we should remember that ancient sacrifices were not just killings but feasts. Christianity recognizes the fact of evil. But it also encourages a sense of joy. Yet it is a joy that confronted, rather than ignored or repressed the facts of evil or suffering. The sacrifice is a feast on the work of Christ in which we participate. And contemplating Christ's heavenly priestly work and knowing our forgiveness, this should free us to earthly service. Knowing that we are loved, Christians are freed from hate and resentment and exhorted to live in joy and charity. Why do we contemplate a story of first-century Palestine repeated, this remote ancient history? Even the most beautiful worship can mask complacency and idolatry. The recondite English poet Geoffrey Hill writes of the Crucified Lord bound to the 'judas-kiss of our devotion, bowed beneath the gold'.[26] This is the blindness to the one for whom the heavens have opened. Sight can be an idol; yet vision can also unite us to the object of our aspirations.

The schoolmen spoke of the *status viatoris* or the pilgrim status of mankind: we are properly understood as in a process of transition. *Viator* means 'wanderer' or 'pilgrim'. For the Neoplatonists and their medieval and Renaissance offspring, humanity dwells in two orders: the holy and the eternal and the profane and historical, and it is on account of this tension that mankind is dissatisfied with the merely profane and historical order. Humanity's restlessness and anxiety emerges out of this fact, and this has been explored by all the great spiritual writers. In the Epistle to the Heb. 11.8-10, 15-16, Abraham is seeking a new dwelling place. The poetry of the Psalms is suffused with this longing for transcendence.

There is an experience of the Divine – of an invisible but known world, and there is a cloud of witnesses: prophets, poets and priests. As William Law says, we have a 'key to the treasures which heaven has to bestow on us'.[27] The Holy shows that the world is not primarily an arena of power conflicts or a realm to be exploited for human benefits, but a Temple of the Divine, a forecourt of the sacred. In this ambiguous and perplexing world, we encounter the divine presence. Rudolf Otto was a great scholar of the mystics in East and West, especially Meister Eckhart. Eckhart held to the existence of a soul centre, a spark from the heavenly altar.

Of course, there is the anxiety that this communion is just fantasy: a worst projection of some disturbing part of the psyche or at best an ethical idealization. John Damascene says that prayer is the 'elevation of the mind and the heart to God'.[28] The goal of prayer is union with God. We are considering the ascent of the mind to the supreme reality, the 'soul's citizenship of the eternal world'. Augustine in the *Confessions* says that 'he entered the secret chamber of my soul, and beheld the immutable light soul, transcending his intelligence'.[29] Different from any earthly illumination, it is superior to him: it is his creative source.

Contemporary philosophers of religion talk about divine hiddenness. But are we hiding from God? The great mystics insist that it is not God who hides his countenance. We must recognize that it is we who are in exile and it is we who must knit our centre to that centre that is everywhere and whose circumference is nowhere. It is what we all possess but few use.

Contemplation properly precedes praxis. One has to contemplate one's own real self before one can act appropriately in the world. The pursuit of goodness is an exploration of the *foro interno*, a journey within as it were, rather than measuring outward data, predicting actions or modelling patterns of behaviour. I think that when Kant writes of the good will as the *sole good* without qualification, his is – like Eckhart's before him – a version of the true self doctrine, a rendering of the Delphic Oracle's 'Know Thyself'! With Prussian scrupulosity, Kant seems to assume that we will readily recognize the difference between inclination and duty, between some instrumental or prudential good and that which is absolutely and purely good. The task is, in fact, much harder. In the words of the General Confession for Morning Prayer in *Book of Common Prayer* in the Church of England: '*We have left undone those things* which *we ought to have done*; And we have *done* those things which we ought not to have *done*; And there is no health in us.'[30]

In ethics, however, it does not suffice to distinguish between instrumental goods and what is bad but we need to account for good and evil. Again, Kant reveals his colours in his avowal of 'radical evil'. For a metaphysician like Spinoza, everything that exists is rational and necessary. For the great theistic tradition of the West, good and evil are constitutive elements of reality and ethics hinges upon the recognition of the 'facts' of good and evil. The God of Spinoza's *Ethics* is not a moral being. And Spinoza is opposed to Western morality in his refusal to recognize evil. For all the differences in the metaphysical apparatus and content, Spinoza's *Ethics* is as radical as Hume's ethics of approbation and disapproval. Spinoza's God is not a lawmaker or a judge, Spinoza's substance is beyond 'good and evil', and even more radical in his anti-moralism (look at what he says about pity, sadness and remorse). Indeed, our habitual and inchoate sense of good and evil is, for the great rationalist philosopher, the product of our all too human 'inadequate ideas'. One might compare this with Hume's functional account of value. Good and evil emerge from attributions of praise and blame. Somewhat ironically, these tough-minded philosophers have limited conceptual resources to deal with the egregious fact of evil. Both philosophers wrest an exiguous fare from the 'immanent frame' in their forlorn attempt to give an account of human behaviour on the same plane as inanimate objects, machines or animals. Perhaps we have to move outside the 'immanent frame' to account for the spiritual capacity of rational free beings to counter evil with goodness, to forge beauty in art and to engage in disinterested intellectual inquiry. Both Spinoza and Hume lacked the categories to provide a satisfying rationale for human ethical and the aesthetical endeavours. For both, ethics is essentially about relative and proximate ends, for example, the increase of pleasure and the diminishing of pain. Good and bad only make sense in terms of a causal relation to specific ends. Hume and Spinoza seem highly pertinent for an age inclined to view values as neural constructs, and the Good as mere *flatus vocis*. Behind Hume and Spinoza we find the bête noir of the Cambridge Platonists: Thomas Hobbes. It is in the genius of Hobbes that the seeds of game theory and evolutionary psychology lie.

Through the surpassing glass of Shakespeare's vision we encounter images of life in the shadows of a being who is identical with absolute goodness; the bard imparts an imaginative vision of the beauty of that goodness, a realm within which agents have a vocation to try to realize something of that supreme goodness and to avoid the evil that is essentially ruinous and divisive. *King Lear* is supposed to be the most pagan and tragic of Shakespeare's works:

Restoration hang
Thy medicine on my lips. (*King Lear* 4.7.26–27)

Lear is mad and the doctor is trying to help him with music, and Cordelia kisses Lear. There is no bitterness or gratification in her father's self-wrought misery, remarkable given Lear's cruel treatment of his daughter. What are signs of restoration and reconciliation in the play? Lear initially fails to recognize his own folly: 'I am a man more sinned against than sinning' (*King Lear* 3.2.56). Lear still views himself as a victim at this stage. There is a real amendment, conversion more accurately, in his joy when reunited with his daughter, notwithstanding the fact that he is a prisoner. In *King Lear*, Shakespeare presents the capacity to love as a window into a deeper reality, the truths that the myopic interests and proximate obsessions of the bustling busybody me, embodied in Lear's cantankerous vanity and blindness, cannot see. The capacity to love is a sign of health. 'He prayeth best who loveth best,' says Coleridge's Mariner.[31] If we are fortunate, we see this best in home and friendship. Friendship and love as depicted in *King Lear* between Father and daughter are portals into the appreciation of what Charles Williams calls 'co-inherence', linked to Williams's conviction that it is a distinctive human vocation to bear each other's burdens. The Christian journey is not a 'flight of the one to the One', to quote the theology of great Platonic Alexandrian pagan Plotinus. Yet there is a wonderful passage in Plotinus:

> All is transparent: no shadow there obstructs the view; all spirits see each other and penetrate each other to the depths. Light is recognized by light. Every spirit comprehends in itself the whole world of spirits, and beholds it in its entirety in every spirit. All things there are everywhere; everything is all, and all is each, and infinite is the glory.[32]

Consider how in estrangement and sadness one feels 'singular' and at odds with those we love. We feel alienated and remote from the interpenetration that Plotinus describes in his inspired depiction of transcendence, his great model of a manifold and rich unity in the divine Intellect, an interpenetration and communion that Christianity envisages as the Heavenly Jerusalem. A sanctified imagination is a means to communion.

Earlier in this chapter I wrote of the *status viatoris*, but if we are pilgrims and if we live as a community, we are called to share joy and also to bear each other's burdens. Charles Williams uses the Trinitarian language of co-inherence. Sometimes he speaks of 'exchange', sometimes 'substitution', sometimes 'Romantic love'. The basis of the theology of Williams lies in the Christian mystical tradition and the interpretation of Gal 2.20: 'Not I but Christ in me.' It is a doctrine of the true self, from the surface 'I' to the depths of our being and that joy in Christ that can withstand the sorrows and sadness of the world. There is an exchange between the poor, sinful and sorry self and the new being in Christ that Paul preaches. Yet this metaphysical and psychological new being is social not atomic: the idea of the body of Christ (1 Corinthians 12). The city is deliberately a central image of this exchange for the Londoner Williams.

There is a further metaphysical dimension here. There is a co-inherence of flesh and spirit. Flesh and spirit are not opposites but mutually linked through the *via affirmativa*. The positive way of affirming images of the Divine rather than merely denying them. That is why, by the way, the real Gnostics are indifferent to those sins of the flesh that are degrading and desecrating within the Christian tradition. This mutuality of flesh and spirit is the basis of both the symbol and the sacrament. In the sacrament, nature becomes a vehicle of the spiritual and the foundation for real joy, transformation and healing.

St Paul says: 'Therefore if any one is in Christ, he is a new creation. The old has passed away; behold all things have become new' (2 Cor. 5.17). The Cambridge Platonists liked to insist that virtue is a power rather than a habit. Habit has a role, but is subordinate to power. Henry More means that it requires freedom and the ability to recognize the good and to act through love. He speaks of the 'boniform faculty', that part of us (almost godlike in More) that is able to relish goodness.[33] The cross and resurrection of Christ working in us, our participating in his life, can be a source of great transformative power and energy. This is Christianity at its most simple, re-creation into the image of Christ and participating in his life through the spirit:

> Then I saw a new heaven and a new earth; for the first heaven and the first earth had passed away. . . . And I saw the holy city, the New Jerusalem, coming down . . . and I heard a great voice from the throne saying: Behold, the dwelling of God is with men . . . he will wipe away every tear from their eyes and death shall be no more, for the former things have passed away . . . Behold, I make all things new. (Rev. 21.1-5)

Shakespeare presents in his dramas worlds of destruction and renewal. The Temple is the place of the sacred, devoted to the holy, the isthmus of the finite and the infinite. The Temple is where one encounters the holy and the drama of renewal. The sense of the numinous described by Otto is most evident in the dread of Good Friday, the scandal, awe and terror of divine suffering. The Temple curtain, the reminder of sins, is torn. The author of the Epistle to the Hebrews presents the Temple as pointing to the great high priest Jesus, where the sacrifices and offerings in the earthly Temple are types and images of the heavenly counterpart (cf. Heb. 8.5). At his baptism, the heavens open. At his crucifixion the curtain is rent asunder and we can see God in him. Just as the transfiguration becomes the revelation of Christ, where the disciples can contemplate Christ in his heavenly glory. In words of the Prayerbook of the Church of England, at the point of the liturgical drama of the *sanctus*:

> Therefore with angels and archangels,
> and with all the company of heaven,
> we proclaim your great and glorious name,
> for ever praising you and saying
> Holy, Holy Holy.

Those approaching the altar – as it were – enter the heavens to encounter and participate in the life of the great high priest.

Contemplation antecedes praxis. The awareness of the arbitrary destructive potential of the human psyche and the redemptive possibilities of creative work and love are aspects of the religious significance of the ethical. The etymology of the notion of contemplation is linked to the word 'Temple'. Contemplation might be thought of as going into the Temple, perhaps inspired and uplifted by the drama of a fine liturgy, voices and exquisite music. Music has a special role in opening the human heart and sustaining the spirit to imagine the invisible. We encounter beauty, truth and goodness that we perceive in the world enigmatically. But here in the Temple the veil of familiarity is lifted. Faith is not, as the cultured despisers of Christianity have sneered throughout the centuries, the believing of impossible propositions; it is fidelity to our own being renewed and reborn in the power of transcendent divine Love.

Notes

1. Murray W. Bundy, *The Theory of Imagination in Classical and Mediaeval Thought* (Urbana: University of Illinois, 1927); Eva T. H. Brann, *The World of the Imagination: Sum and Substance* (Savage, MD: Rowman & Littlefield, 1991). There is a vast literature. Cf. the useful collection of essays edited by Amy Kind, *The Routledge Handbook of the Philosophy of the Imagination* (London: Routledge, 2016).
2. Roberto Calasso, *Ardor* (Harmondsworth: Penguin, 2015), 336.
3. Amy Kind and Peter Kung (eds), *Knowledge Through Imagination* (Oxford: Oxford University Press, 2016), 2.
4. Robin G. Collingwood, *The Principles of Art* (Oxford: Clarendon Press, 1938), 294–5.
5. Friedrich W. J. Schelling, *Untersuchungen über das Wesen der menschlichen Freiheit und der damit zusammenhängenden Gegenstände* (Reutlingen: Enßlin 1834), 20–1. Translation: F. W. J. Schelling, *Philosophical Inquiries into the Nature of Human Freedom*. Translation by James Gutmann (LaSalle: Open Court, 1936), 20: 'However, divine imagination, which is the cause of the differentiation of the world's beings, is unlike human imagination and never gives to its creations a merely ideal reality. The products of divine imagination must be independent beings, for wherein does the limitation of our imagination consist than precisely in our seeing things as dependent? God beholds all things in themselves. Only the Eternal exists in itself, as Self-secured, Will, Freedom.'
6. Cf. 'Is Theology Poetry?', in *The Weight of Glory*, edited with an introduction by W. Cooper (New York: HarperCollins, 1980), 116–41, 140: 'I believe in Christianity as I believe that the sun has risen: not only because I see it, but because by it I see everything else.'
7. *Enchiridion Ethicum. The English Translation of 1690: An Account of Virtue*, translated by Edward Southwell (London, 1690), 40.
8. *A Platonick Song of the Soul*, ed. with an Introductory Study by Alexander Jacob (Lewisburg: Bucknell University Press; London: Associated University Presses, 1998), 139.
9. Bede Griffiths, *The Marriage of East and West* (London: HarperCollins), 46, 69.
10. 'L'Allegro', l. 134, in *The English Poems of John Milton*, introduction and notes by Laurence Lerner (London: Wordsworth Editions Limited, 2004), 24–7, 27.
11. The key Renaissance text is Ficino's *De amore* of 1484.
12. John Donne, 'An Anatomy of the World: The First Anniversary', ll, 205, 214, in *The Major Works,* edited by John Carey (Oxford: Oxford University Press, 2008), 463.
13. Griffiths, *Marriage of East and West* (see n. 9), 103.
14. Morny Joy, 'Images: Images and Imagination', in *The Encyclopaedia of Religion*, edited by Mircea Eliade, 16 vols (New York: Macmillan; London: Collier Macmillan, 1987), vol. VII, 104–9.
15. Charles Taylor, *A Secular Age* (Cambridge, MA and London: The Belknap Press of Harvard University Press, 2007), 322–51.
16. See Iain McGilchrist, *The Master and His Emissary* (New Haven: Yale University Press, 2009).
17. Charles Hefling and Cyntia Shattuck (eds), *The Oxford Guide to the Book of Common Prayer: A World Wide Survey* (Oxford and New York: Oxford University Press, 2006), 25.
18. Griffiths, *Marriage of East and West* (see n. 9), 65–6.

19 René Girard, *Things Hidden Since the Foundation of the World*, translated by Stephen Bann and Michael Metteer (London: Athlone Press, 1978).
20 Thomas Traherne, 'Thoughts IV', ll, 95–100. For the full poem, see *Selected Poems and Prose*, edited by Alan Bradford (London: Penguin Books, 1991), 73.
21 John Stuart Mill, 'An Examination of Sir William Hamilton's Philosophy, and of the Principal Philosophical Questions Discussed in His Writings', in *Collected Works* 9, edited by John M. Robson (Toronto: University of Toronto Press; London: Routledge & Keegan Paul, 1979), 103.
22 Johann Sebastian Bach, Johannespassion I,1. Translation: 'Show us, through Your passion, / That You, the true Son of God, / Through all time, / Even in the greatest humiliation, / Have become transfigured!' (Text and translation: http://www.bach-cantatas.com/Texts/BWV245-Eng3.htm (last accessed on 10 July 2018)).
23 Josef Pieper, *Death and Immortality*, translated by Richard and Clara Winston (South Bend: St. Augustine's Press, 2000), 72.
24 Plato, *Republic*, II, 360–1; cf. Clement of Alexandria, *Stromata*, V, 12.
25 C. S. Lewis, *Miracles: A Preliminary Study* (New York: Simon & Schuster, 1996), 172.
26 Geoffrey Hill, 'Lachrimae Antiquae Novae', l, 4, in G. Hill, *Broken Hierarchies: Poems from 1952–2012*, edited by Kenneth Haynes (Oxford: Oxford Univesity Press, 2015), 124.
27 William Law, *The Spirit of Prayer; Or the Soul Rising Out of the Vanity of Time into the Riches of Eternity*, 3rd edn (London: Innys ad Richardson, 1816), 5.
28 John Damascene, *De fide orthodoxa*, 24.
29 Augustine, *Confessions*, VII 10,16: *intravi et vidi qualicumque oculo animae meae supra eundem oculum animae meae, supramentem meam, lucem incommutabilem . . . ita erat supra mentem meam.*
30 Hefling and Shattuck, *Oxford Guide to the Book of Common Prayer* (see n. 17), 140.
31 Samuel T. Coleridge, 'The Rime of the Ancient Mariner', l, 614, in *The Major Works, including Biographia Literaria*, edited with an Introduction and Notes by H. J. Jackson (Oxford: Oxford University Press, 2000), 48–68, 68.
32 Enn. V 8,4.
33 Cf. Henry More in his *Enchiridion Ethicum/Account of Virtue* (see n. 7), 6, 156–7.

Index of names

Abraham 68, 197, 222
Aeschylus 14, 36, 217
Alighieri, Dante 11, 213, 217
Alston, William P. 58, 173–85
Ammonius Saccas 9
Anaximander 7
Anselm of Canterbury 64, 151
Aquinas, Thomas 9, 51, 145–6, 148, 188–9, 191, 199–201, 204, 209
Aristotle 3, 6–7, 9, 30, 40, 48, 115, 122–3, 126, 140, 184, 201, 205
Armstrong, Arthur H. 126, 208
Augustine 10, 22–3, 46, 48, 51, 64–6, 68–70, 188–93, 199–201, 204–5, 208–9, 222, 227
Ayers, Michael 14

Bacon, Francis 214
Balthasar, Hans Urs von 74–5, 88, 90, 91, 146, 155, 160–1
Barnes, Winston H. F. 176, 184
Barth, Karl 12, 51
Baxter, Richard 8
Beaumont, Joseph 6–7
Beethoven, Ludwig van 186
Beierwaltes, Werner 55, 61, 67, 69, 124, 140–1, 199, 208
Berkeley, George 3–4, 14, 19–20, 56, 141, 192, 195, 197, 209
Berlin, Isaiah 217
Blackburn, Simon 22
Blondel, Maurice 145, 147–8, 160, 161
Bloom, Harold 16
Boehme, Jacob 7, 118, 191
Boethius 3, 48
Bonaventure 74, 88–9
Bradley, Arthur C. 57
Bradley, Francis H. 10, 196
Bramhall, John 22
Bréhier, Emile 208
Bruno, Giordano 117

Buber, Martin 51
Bulgakov, Mikhail 40
Burke, Edmund 34–5
Burkert, Walter 34–5
Burnet, Gilbert 8
Byron, Lord 197

Caird, Edward 196
Caird, John 51
Calvin, John 39, 65
Caterus, Johannes 96
Cecilia 44
Chalmers, David 18
Charles I 94
Ciapola, R. T. 198, 208
Clement of Alexandria 61, 75–6, 90, 221, 227
Coakley, Sarah 74, 88–9
Colebrooke, Henry Th. 206
Coleridge, Samuel Taylor 3–4, 7–8, 11, 13, 15–18, 20–25, 27, 47–8, 55–60, 62, 65–8, 70, 99, 127–42, 181, 183, 185, 188–91, 193–5, 197, 199, 201, 203–12, 214, 224, 227
Coleridge, Sarah 140
Collingwood, Robin G. 57, 168, 172, 226
Coomaraswamy, Ananda K. 203, 205
Copernicus, Nicolaus 158
Corbin, Henry 203, 215
Cornford, Francis M. 10, 16
Craig, William L. 183
Cranmer, Thomas 216
Creuzer, Georg, F. 25, 55, 59, 69, 203
Cudworth, Ralph 4–12, 9, 14–17, 22, 30, 37–8, 44, 47, 49, 57, 63, 65–7, 94–6, 100–1, 105–9, 111–26, 158, 188, 204, 209
Cupitt, Don 211
Cusa, Nicholas of 4, 48, 67, 117, 139, 156, 158, 160, 203

Darwin, Charles 13, 29, 165
Dawkins, Richard 36
Descartes, René 12, 31, 94–126, 148–9
Dietrich von Freiberg 51
Dillon, John 74, 77, 84–5, 88–90
Dionysius the Areopagite 102, 191–2, 205
Donne, John 209, 214, 226
Dostoevsky, Fedor M. 12, 33
Durkheim, Émile 206, 215

Eckhart, Meister 4, 24, 51, 63, 69, 118, 160, 191, 193–4, 199–201, 205, 209
Einstein, Albert 28, 60, 210
Eliade, Mircea 203, 215, 226
Epicurus 7
Eriugena, John Scotus 4, 48, 61, 69, 188, 194, 204, 209
Euripides 36
Ezekiel 26–7, 43

Farrer, Austin 43, 51, 57, 64, 70
Fichte, Johann G. 140, 148, 205
Ficino, Marsilio 4, 8, 188, 203, 204, 213, 226
Findlay, John N. 10, 16
Flasch, Kurt 66
Francis de Sales 178
Franklin, Benjamin 197
Freud, Sigmund 13, 25, 211, 215

Galilei, Galileo 8, 38
Gandhi, Mahatma 12
Gans, Eric 166, 172
Gaspers, Jan Baptist 7
Gassendi, Pierre 95
Gavrilyuk, Paul 74, 88–9
Gibbon, Edward 3, 14
Girard, René 9, 34–5, 163–72, 217–18, 221, 227
Goethe, Johann W. von 99, 194, 196–7
Green, Thomas Hill 5–6, 10, 196
Griffiths, Bede 201, 209, 213, 215, 217, 226

Hacker, Paul 198, 208
Hallywell, Henry 6, 14, 124
Harari, Yuval N. 211–12
Hastings, Warren 197, 206

Hauck, John 79–80, 91
Hebblethwaite, Brian 12, 57
Hegel, Georg Wilhelm Friedrich 4, 14, 38, 57, 138, 168, 188, 192–3, 205, 207, 220–1
Heidegger, Martin 13, 55, 59, 147, 151, 168, 171, 216
Herder, Johann G. 196, 207
Hermes Trismegistus 158
Hick, John 12
Hicks, George D. 176, 184
Hobbes, Thomas 7–9, 13, 19–20, 22, 38, 56, 95, 112, 117, 124, 223
Hölderlin, Friedrich 138, 205
Honecker, Martin 146
Humboldt, Wilhelm von 207
Hume, David 3–4, 22, 32, 46, 52, 66, 68, 121, 223
Hunt, John 8, 15

Iamblichus 188
Ignatius of Loyola 148, 155, 158, 161–2
Isaac 68
Isaiah 34, 75, 91

Jacobi, Friedrich H. 192
James, William 23, 58, 63, 173–4, 178, 183
Jansenius, Cornelsen 65
Jerome 91
Jesus Christ 75, 81, 83, 100, 109, 167–8, 170, 218–21, 225
John Damascene 222
John of Patmos 26–7, 43–8, 52, 65, 68, 99, 168, 200, 219
John the Baptist 37
Jonas, Hans 31, 56, 61
Jones, William 188, 195–8, 203, 206–7, 209
Joyce, James 186
Jung, Carl G. 25, 59, 165

Kant, Immanuel 7, 15, 19, 30–2, 35–7, 41, 43, 46, 56, 61–3, 121–2, 126, 141, 147–8, 192, 196, 205, 207, 221–2
Kekulé, August 28
Kenney, John P. 205
Kierkegaard, Soren 12, 68

Kipling, Rudyard   202, 209
Krämer, Hans J.   67
Krishna   171, 186, 195–6

Landino, Cristoforo   213
Law, William   222, 227
Lehmann, Karl   147, 159–61
Leibniz, Gottfried Wilhelm   3, 28, 41, 124
Lessing, Gotthold E.   158, 192
Levitin, Dimitri   5–6, 8, 14, 119
Lewis, Clive S.   55, 212, 221, 227
Lewis, Marilyn A.   14
Locke, John   3–4, 14, 117, 126, 141
Louth, Andrew   82, 92, 205
Luther, Martin   65, 149

MacIntyre, Alasdair   214
Mackinnon, Donald   15, 40, 64
Mackintosh, James   7
Maharshi, Ramana   209
Maistre, Joseph de   34, 41–2, 46, 64–5, 164, 217
Mandelstam, Ossip M.   211
Maréchal, Joseph   148
Marx, Karl   13, 206, 215
Maurice, Frederick D.   8, 15
Mauss, Marcel   206
Mayer, John R.   198
McGinn, Colin   17–18, 209
McInroy, Mark J.   74, 77, 88–90
Mendeléev, Dmitri   28
Metz, Johann B.   148, 160
Mill, James   207
Mill, John Stuart   219, 227
Milton, John   213, 226–7
Montaigne, Michel de   213
More, Henry   5–9, 12, 14–15, 17, 22, 38, 43, 49–50, 55, 57, 65, 68, 95, 98, 100–5, 107–10, 112, 114–18, 120–6, 204, 212–14, 224, 227
Moses   59, 110, 126, 188, 199
Muirhead, John H.   5, 14, 207
Murdoch, Iris   15

Newton, Isaac   3, 11, 210
Nietzsche, Friedrich   13–14, 55, 59, 168, 171
Norris, John   100, 122, 125

Occam, William of   170
Origen   4, 9, 15, 22, 37, 41–2, 45–6, 49, 57, 61, 64–6, 69, 73–94, 99, 118–19, 121–2, 124, 126, 171, 217, 221
Otto, Rudolf   11, 24, 34, 55, 58–9, 106, 164, 178, 183, 188, 194, 197–8, 201, 203, 205–6, 209, 214–15, 218, 222, 225
Parker, Samuel   6
Parmenides   26, 95, 197
Pascal, Blaise   12
Paul   22, 35, 52, 59, 75, 83, 100, 107, 167, 216–18, 224
Philo the Jew   29, 87, 110, 199
Pico della Mirandola   204
Pieper, Joseph   216, 227
Pilate, Pontius   216
Plantinga, Alvin   183
Plato   3–4, 6–8, 10, 14–16, 31–2, 36, 54, 60–1, 63, 73, 86–7, 91–3, 115, 122, 142, 191, 195, 197, 204–5, 208, 213, 220–1, 227
Plotinus   4, 8–10, 18, 25, 30, 32, 37, 46, 49, 58–9, 62, 66–70, 73–4, 76, 83–8, 91–3, 99–100, 102, 121, 131, 188, 191–3, 198, 200, 204–5, 208, 212, 221, 224
Plutarch   99
Porphyry   188
Prichard, Harold A.   176, 184
Priestley, Joseph   197
Proclus   4, 188, 191–2
Pröpper, Thomas   161
Proust, Marcel   23, 58
Ps.-Longinus   35
Pythagoras   44, 100, 122

Radhakrishnan, Sarvepalli   195–6
Rahner, Karl   145–62
Ramanuja   206
Raphael   44, 65
Reid, Thomas   3
Reinhold, Karl L.   158
Rist, John   208
Rust, George   6, 46, 66, 98, 107, 111, 124–5

Sankara   186, 195, 198, 201, 206
Sartre, Jean-Paul   55, 61

Saux, Henri Le   209
Schelling, Friedrich Wilhelm Joseph   7, 25, 52, 59, 70, 128, 133, 137–41, 183, 185, 192–3, 196–7, 205, 207, 209, 212, 226
Schiller, Friedrich   11, 37
Schlegel, Friedrich   197, 207
Schleiermacher, Friedrich D. E.   178, 194
Schopenhauer, Arthur   36, 62, 197, 206
Schwab, Raymond   207
Scruton, Roger   61
Shaftesbury, Anthony Ashley Cooper   3
   Earl of   3, 139
Shakespeare, William   20, 22, 31–2, 37, 45, 50, 52, 57, 63, 66, 69–70, 93, 210–27
Shelley, Percy B.   138, 197
Sidney, Philip   213
Simeon the New Theologian   74
Smith, John   7–9, 15, 17, 22, 57, 73, 98–100, 108, 120–1, 125
Socrates   7, 10, 30, 62, 168, 193
Solomon   79
Spenser, Edmund   213
Spinoza, Baruch de   7, 9, 13, 15, 38, 40, 46–9, 51–2, 64, 67–8, 70, 133, 157, 192–3, 223
Staal, J. F.   198, 208
Stalin, Joseph   211
Stenzel, Julius   10
Stewart, Dugald   7
Strato of Lampsacus   7
Swinburne, Richard   164, 183

Taliaferro, Charles   14, 64, 118–20, 183
Tauler, Johannes   155

Taylor, Alfred E.   10, 15–16
Taylor, Charles   215, 226
Teape, William M.   187, 203
Thorndike, Herbert   6
Tillich, Paul   38, 63, 176–7, 184
Tolkien, John R. R.   55
Traherne, Thomas   39, 63, 218, 227
Tulloch, John   119
Turner, Denys   58, 183

Upadhyay, Brahmabandhab   195

Vaughan, Thomas   122
Verweyen, Hansjürgen   161
Vico, Giambattista   25, 52
Victorinus, Marius   189, 200
Virgil   217
Vivekananda, Swami   195

Warburton, William   158
Waugh, Evelyn   218
Weber, Max   214
Weil, Simone   164
Westcott, Brooke F.   187, 203
White, Robert   7
Wilkins, Charles   197
William of Auxerre   74, 89
Williams, James   168, 172
Williams, Rowan   15
Wittgenstein, Ludwig   58
Wolterstorff, Nicholas   183
Wordsworth, William   17, 21, 138, 142, 189, 204, 212, 226

Xenophanes   14

www.ingramcontent.com/pod-product-compliance
Lightning Source LLC
Chambersburg PA
CBHW072149290426
44111CB00012B/2014